THE RUSSIAN ROOTS OF NAZISM

White Émigrés and the Making of National Socialism, 1917–1945

This groundbreaking book examines the overlooked topic of the influence of anti-Bolshevik, anti-Semitic Russian exiles on Nazism. White émigrés contributed politically, financially, militarily, and ideologically to National Socialism. This work refutes the notion that Nazism developed as a peculiarly German phenomenon. National Socialism arose primarily from the cooperation between *völkisch* (nationalist/racist) Germans and vengeful White émigrés.

From 1920 to 1923, Adolf Hitler collaborated with a conspiratorial far right German-White émigré organization, Aufbau (Reconstruction). Aufbau allied with Nazis to overthrow the German government and Bolshevik rule through terrorism and military/paramilitary schemes. This organization's warnings of the monstrous "Jewish Bolshevik" peril helped to inspire Hitler to launch an invasion of the Soviet Union and to initiate the mass murder of European Jews. This book uses extensive archival materials from Germany and Russia, including recently declassified documents, and it will prove invaluable reading for anyone interested in the international roots of National Socialism.

MICHAEL KELLOGG is an independent researcher and a past recipient of the prestigious Fulbright-Hays Doctoral Dissertation Research Abroad Grant.

NEW STUDIES IN EUROPEAN HISTORY

Edited by

PETER BALDWIN, University of California, Los Angeles
CHRISTOPHER CLARE, University of Cambridge
JAMES B. COLLINS, Georgetown University
MÍA RODRÍGUEZ-SALGADO, London School of Economics
and Political Science
LYNDAL ROPER, University of Oxford

The aim of this series in early modern and modern European history is to publish outstanding works of research, addressed to important themes across a wide geographical range, from southern and central Europe, to Scandinavia and Russia, and from the time of the Renaissance to the Second World War. As it develops the series will comprise focused works of wide contextual range and intellectual ambition.

For a full list of titles published in the series, please see the end of the book.

THE RUSSIAN ROOTS
OF NAZISM

White Émigrés and the Making of National Socialism,
1917–1945

MICHAEL KELLOGG

CAMBRIDGE
UNIVERSITY PRESS

PUBLISHED BY THE PRESS SYNDICATE OF THE UNIVERSITY OF CAMBRIDGE
The Pitt Building, Trumpington Street, Cambridge, United Kingdom

CAMBRIDGE UNIVERSITY PRESS
The Edinburgh Building, Cambridge, CB2 2RU, UK
40 West 20th Street, New York, NY 10011–4211, USA
477 Williamstown Road, Port Melbourne, VIC 3207, Australia
Ruiz de Alarcón 13, 28014 Madrid, Spain
Dock House, The Waterfront, Cape Town 8001, South Africa

http://www.cambridge.org

First published 2005

Printed in the United Kingdom at the University Press, Cambridge

Typeface Adobe Garamond 11/12.5 pt.   *System* LATEX 2$_\varepsilon$ [TB]

A catalogue record for this book is available from the British Library

Library of Congress Cataloguing in Publication data
Kellogg, Michael, 1972–
The Russian roots of Nazism : white émigrés and the making of National Socialism,
1917–1945 / by Michael Kellogg.
p.   cm. – (New studies in European history)
Includes bibliographical references and index.
ISBN 0 521 84512 2 (alk. paper)
1. Russians–Germany–Political activity.   2. Aufbau (Organization).   3. Anti-communist
movements–Germany.   4. Antisemitism–Soviet Union–History–20th century.
5. Antisemitism–Germany–History–20th century.   6. Nationalsozialistische Deutsche
Arbeiter-Partei.   I. Title.   II. Series.
DD78.R87K45   2004
320.53′094309041 – dc22   2004051101

ISBN 0 521 84512 2 hardback

I dedicate this work to my father, who found the courage to accept himself as he is.

Contents

Acknowledgments

I offer thanks first and foremost to the members of my Ph.D. Committee at the University of California, Los Angeles: Professors Saul Friedländer, David Sabean, Ivan Berend, and Rogers Brubaker, who have given me excellent advice over the years. Professor Peter Baldwin of UCLA granted me valuable advice and support. Professor Arch Getty of UCLA helped me to gain an overview of important archival materials in Moscow. Others associated with UCLA who aided me in writing this book include Julie Jenkins, who gave me editing advice, Barbara Bernstein and Kathleen Addison, who took care of administrative matters for me while I was abroad, and Julia Wallace, who helped me to revise my text.

Many non-Americans gave me valuable assistance in carrying out this project. German academics who considerably aided my research include Michael Hagemeister and Karl Schlögel of Europe University-Viadrina in Frankfurt/Oder, Heinrich Winkler of Humboldt University in Berlin, Hermann Beyer-Thoma of the East European Institute in Munich, and Dr. Johannes Baur of Munich. In Moscow, Vasily Tsvetkov of Moscow State Pedagogical University alerted me to important archival materials, and Natasha Petina and Ludmilla Novikova helped me to translate difficult Russian texts. Joanna Grynczuk of Berlin translated Polish intelligence files for me. Dominika Plümpe of Berlin gave me helpful insights into my work. The Welsh journalist and historian Michael Joseph offered me a valuable critique.

I received generous funding that enabled me to carry out extensive research in Germany and Russia from the Fulbright-Hays Doctoral Dissertation Research Abroad Program, the Deutscher Akademischer Austauschdienst (DAAD), the International Studies Abroad Program (ISOP), the Center for German and European Studies at the University of California, Berkeley, and the Center for European and Russian Studies at the University of California, Los Angeles.

Finally, I thank my father John and my mother Carolyn for their editing advice and emotional support.

Abbreviations

ARCHIVES

BAB	Bundesarchiv (Federal Archives in Berlin).
BAK	Bundesarchiv Koblenz (Federal Archives in Koblenz).
BA/MF	Bundesarchiv, Militärarchiv Freiburg (Federal Archives, Military Archives in Freiburg).
BHSAM	Bayerisches Hauptstaatsarchiv München (Bavarian State Archives in Munich).
BHSAM/AK	Bayerisches Hauptstaatsarchiv München, Abteilung Kriegsarchiv (Bavarian State Archives in Munich, Military Archives Department).
BSAM	Bayerisches Staatsarchiv München (Bavarian Regional Archives in Munich).
GARF	Gosudarstvennyi arkhiv Rossiiskoi Federatsii (State Archives of the Russian Federation, Moscow).
GSAPKB	Geheimes Staatsarchiv Preussischer Kulturbesitz (Secret State Archives of Prussian Cultural Property, Berlin).
IZG	Institut für Zeitgeschichte (Institute for Modern History, Munich).
PAAA	Politisches Archiv des Auswärtigen Amtes (Political Archives of the Foreign Office, Berlin).
RGASPI	Rossiiskii gosudarstvennyi arkhiv sotsialno-politicheskoi istorii (Russian State Archives of Socio-Political History, Moscow).
RGVA	Rossiiskii gosudarstvennyi voennyi arkhiv (Russian State Military Archives, Moscow).

RGVA (TsKhIDK)   Former Tsentr khraneniia istoriko-dokumentalnych
                 kollektsii (Center for the Preservation of
                 Historical-Documentary Collections, now part of
                 RGVA, Moscow).

GERMAN AGENCIES

AA	Auswärtiges Amt (Foreign Office).
AGM	Amtsgericht München (Munich District Court).
A9N	Amt für den 9. November (Office for November 9th).
APA	Aussenpolitisches Amt (Foreign Policy Office, specifically for the National Socialist Party).
APA/AO	Aussenpolitisches Amt, Abteilung Osten (Foreign Policy Office, Eastern Department).
BSMÄ	Bayerisches Staatsministerium des Äussern (Bavarian Foreign Ministry).
BSMI	Bayerisches Staatsministerium des Innern (Bavarian Interior Ministry).
DDVL	Deutsche Diplomatische Vertretung für Lettland (German Diplomatic Representation for Latvia).
DGBel	Deutsche Gesandtschaft in Belgrad (German Legation in Belgrade).
DGBer	Deutsche Gesandtschaft in Bern (German Legation in Bern).
DGBud	Deutsche Gesandtschaft in Budapest (German Legation in Budapest).
DGR	Deutsche Gesandtschaft in Riga (German Legation in Riga).
FA/AFK	Fremdenamt, Abteilung für Fremdenkontrolle (Alien Office, Department for Alien Supervision).
FZO	Flüchtlingszentrale Ost (Refugee Head Office East).
HGE/Ia	Heeresgruppe Eichhorn, Ia (Army Group Eichhorn, Ia).
HSKPA	Hauptstelle Kulturpolitisches Archiv (Main Office of the Politico-Cultural Archives).
JM	Justizministerium (Department of Justice).
KR	Kanzlei Rosenberg (Rosenberg Chancellery).
LGMI	Landgericht München I (Munich District Court I).

LGPO	Landesgrenzpolizei Ost (National Border Police East).
LGPOP	Landesgrenzpolizei Ostpreussen (National Border Police East Prussia).
MR	Ministerialrat ([Bavarian] Assistant Head of Government Department).
NSDAPHA	NSDAP Hauptarchiv (NSDAP Main Archives).
OHLHGE	Oberste Heeresleitung Heeresgruppe Eichhorn (Army High Command Army Group Eichhorn).
OKO	Oberkommando Ost (Army High Command East).
PBH/AII	Polizeibehörde Hamburg, Abteilung II (Hamburg Police Authorities, Department II).
PDB	Polizeidirektion Bremen (Bremen Police Headquarters).
PDM	Polizeidirektion München (Munich Police Headquarters).
PKAH	Privatkanzlei Adolf Hitler (Adolf Hitler Private Office).
PP/AIA	Polizeipräsidium, Abteilung IA (Police Headquarters, Department IA).
PPS	Polizeipräsidium Stuttgart (Stuttgart Police Headquarters).
PVE	Polizeiverwaltung Elberfeld (Elberfeld Police Administration).
RA/ZSS	Reichsarchiv, Zweigstelle Spandau (State Archives, Spandau Branch).
RK	Reichskanzlei (State Chancellery).
RKÜöO	Reichskommissar für die Überwachung der öffentlichen Ordnung (State Commissioner for the Supervision of Public Order).
RMbO	Reichsministerium für die besetzten Ostgebiete (State Ministry for the Occupied Eastern Territories).
RMI	Reichsministerium des Innern (State Ministry of the Interior).
RP	Regierungs-Präsident ([Bavarian] Chairman of the Regional Council).
RSHA	Reichssicherheitshauptamt (State Security Main Office).

RuSHA-SS/VP	Rasse und Siedlungshauptamt-SS, Verwaltung Prag (SS Race and Settlement Main Office, Prague Administration).
RWM	Reichswehrministerium (Army Ministry).
SALM	Staatsanwalt bei dem Landgerichte München (Prosecuting Attorney at the Munich District Court).
SAM	Staatsanwaltschaften München (Munich Prosecuting Attorneys' Office).
SAUV	Sitzung des Ausschusses zur Untersuchung der Vorgänge vom 1. Mai 1923 und der gegen Reichs- und Landesverfassung gerichteten Bestrebungen vom 26. September bis 9. November 1923 (Sitting of the Committee for the Investigation of the Events of May 1, 1923 and of the Efforts from September 26 up to November 9, 1923 that Were Directed Against the National/State Constitution).
SKöO	Staatskommissar für öffentliche Ordnung (State Commissioner for Public Order).

FRENCH AGENCIES

DB	Deuxième Bureau (Second Section, primary intelligence agency).
ÉMG	État-Major Général (General Staff Headquarters).
ÉMMF	État-Major du Maréchal Foch (Staff Headquarters of Marshall Foch).
IIA	International Information Agency, Paris.
MAÉ	Ministère des Affaires Étrangères (Ministry of Foreign Affairs).
MG	Ministère de la Guerre (Ministry of War).
MMFH	Mission Militaire Française en Hongrie (French Military Mission in Hungary).
MMFP	Mission Militaire Française en Pologne (French Military Mission in Poland).
MMFT	Mission Militaire Française en Tchécoslovaquie (French Military Mission in Czechoslovakia).
QB/SO	Quatrième Bureau, Section d'Orient (Fourth Section, Eastern Department).

SG	Sûreté Générale (General Security).
SN	Sûreté Nationale (National Security).
VNCCP	Ville de Nancy Commissariat Central de Police (Nancy Central Police Station).

RUSSIAN AGENCIES

ATsVO	Administretivnyi Tsentr vnepartinnogo obedineniia (Administrative Center of the Non-Party Association, a Russian émigré organization in Prague).
KI	Komintern (Communist International, Comintern).
OKL	O. K. London (military organization).
ROVS	Russkii Obshii-voinskii soiuz (Russian Universal Military Union).

POLISH AGENCY

SGOD	Sztab Główny Oddział drugi (Main Headquarters Second Section, primary intelligence agency).

Introduction

In the aftermath of the Russian Revolution of October 1917, anti-Bolshevik exiles from the former Russian Empire, known as "White émigrés," contributed extensively to the making of German National Socialism. This book examines the formative political, financial, military, and ideological influences that White émigrés exerted on Adolf Hitler's National Socialist movement. This study of White émigré contributions to Hitlerism demonstrates that National Socialism did not develop merely as a peculiarly German phenomenon. National Socialism arose in the early post-World War I period (1918–1923) from an international radical right milieu in which embittered *völkisch* (nationalist/racist) Germans collaborated with vengeful White émigrés in an anti-Entente (Britain and France), anti-Weimar Republic, anti-Bolshevik, and anti-Semitic struggle.

From 1920 to 1923, Hitler allied himself with a conspiratorial *völkisch* German/White émigré association headquartered in Munich, Aufbau: Wirtschafts-politische Vereinigung für den Osten (Reconstruction: Economic-Political Organization for the East), hereafter Aufbau. This secretive union sought to combat international Jewry and to overthrow both the German Weimar Republic and the Soviet Union in league with National Socialists. Aufbau contributed considerable sums of money to Hitler's National Socialist movement. Moreover, early National Socialist ideology combined *völkisch* notions of Germanic racial and spiritual superiority with the apocalyptic White émigré Aufbau conspiracy theory in which Jews, who operated as a seamless web of conniving finance capitalists and murderous Bolsheviks, threatened to conquer the world and then to send it to perdition. Aufbau left a powerful anti-Bolshevik and anti-Semitic legacy to National Socialism after 1923 as well.

Prominent White émigré Aufbau members who influenced Hitler's political and military strategies as well as his anti-Bolshevik and anti-Semitic *Weltanschauung* (world-view) included First Lieutenant Max von

Scheubner-Richter, General Vladimir Biskupskii, Colonel Ivan Poltavets-Ostranitsa, Lieutenant Piotr Shabelskii-Bork, Colonel Fedor Vinberg, and Alfred Rosenberg. Scheubner-Richter *de facto* led Aufbau until he was shot fatally while marching with Hitler and General Erich von Ludendorff during the disastrous Hitler/Ludendorff Putsch of November 1923. Hitler subsequently asserted that Scheubner-Richter alone of the "martyrs" of the failed undertaking had proved irreplaceable.[1]

General Biskupskii acted as Scheubner-Richter's invaluable partner at the head of Aufbau, and he later directed the White émigré community in the Third Reich.[2] Poltavets-Ostranitsa led Aufbau's Ukrainian section, and he sought to establish a National Socialist Ukraine.[3] Shabelskii-Bork transferred *The Protocols of the Elders of Zion,* an inflammatory forgery that influenced National Socialists and other anti-Semites around the world, from the Ukraine to Berlin for publication in German shortly after World War I.[4] Vinberg held detailed ideological discussions with Hitler, and he convinced the Führer that the Soviet Union represented a "Jewish dictatorship."[5]

Rosenberg has been largely overlooked in the historical literature despite his crucial contributions to National Socialism.[6] The White émigré served as the leading National Socialist philosopher after Hitler himself. He collaborated with Dietrich Eckart, Hitler's early mentor, in the newspaper *Auf gut deutsch: Wochenschrift für Ordnung und Recht* (*In Plain German: Weekly for Law and Order*). He *de facto* took over the editorship of the National Socialist periodical the *Völkischer Beobachter* (*Völkisch Observer*) from the ailing Eckart in 1923. He conceived a dire threat to the racially and spiritually superior Germans from a worldwide Jewish capitalist-Bolshevik conspiracy. He led the National Socialist Party during Hitler's imprisonment following the Hitler/Ludendorff Putsch.[7] Finally, he directed Germany's rule over formerly Soviet areas in World War II, and he participated in the atrocities

[1] Georg Franz-Willing, *Ursprung der Hitlerbewegung 1919–1922* (Preussisch Oldendorf: K. W. Schütz KG, 1974), 198.

[2] DB reports from November 11, 1922 and May 22, 1936, RGVA (TsKhIDK), *fond* 7, *opis* 1, *delo* 386, reel 2, 157; *opis* 4, *delo* 168, reel 1, 1.

[3] "Ukraine und Nationalsozialismus," *Wirtschafts-politische Aufbau-Korrespondenz über Ostfragen und ihre Bedeutung für Deutschland,* May 17, 1923, 4.

[4] Gestapo report from April 13, 1935, RGVA (TsKhIDK), *fond* 501, *opis* 3, *delo* 496a, 208.

[5] Adolf Hitler, notes for a speech on November 2, 1922, *Sämtliche Aufzeichnungen 1905–1924,* eds. Eberhard Jäckel and Axel Kuhn (Stuttgart: Deutsche Verlags-Anstalt, 1980), 716.

[6] Johannes Baur, *Die russische Kolonie in München, 1900–1945: Deutsch–russische Beziehungen im 20. Jahrhundert* (Wiesbaden: Harrassowitz Verlag, 1998), 271.

[7] Max Hildebert Boehm, "Baltische Einflüsse auf die Anfänge des Nationalsozialismus," *Jahrbuch des baltischen Deutschtums,* 1967, 63.

of the Final Solution through his post as Reichsminister für die besetzten Ostgebiete (State Minister for the Occupied Eastern Territories).[8]

The overall cohesion of this book is aided by the fortunate circumstance that a surprisingly stable core group of White émigré adventurers repeatedly conspired with *völkisch* German colleagues, including National Socialists, in various anti-Bolshevik and anti-Weimar Republic schemes from 1918 to 1923. Moreover, with the notable exceptions of Scheubner-Richter, who was killed in 1923, and Vinberg, who moved to Paris the same year, this central group of Aufbau White émigrés, including Biskupskii, Poltavets-Ostranitsa, Shabelskii-Bork, Rosenberg, and others who will be introduced below, went on to serve the National Socialist cause after Hitler came to power in Germany in January 1933.

Failure represents a recurrent theme in this work. Far right movements in the Russian Empire and Imperial Germany attained only a small fraction of the political influence that they desired and which has subsequently been attributed to them. The principal White émigré figures in this book's primary period of consideration, 1917 to 1923, proved three-time losers. They fell short in various anti-Bolshevik undertakings in the course of the Russian Civil War. They regrouped in East-Elbian Germany only to undergo a severe setback when the far right Kapp Putsch collapsed in March 1920. They reorganized once again in Bavaria only to suffer near-catastrophic defeat and even death in the Hitler/Ludendorff Putsch of November 1923. White émigré fortunes did improve considerably after Hitler's ascension to power. With the utter military defeat of the Third Reich in World War II, however, White émigré aspirations of toppling the Soviet Union in league with National Socialist Germany disappeared.

Using the word "Russian" in conjunction with the exiles from the collapsed Russian Empire who most shaped National Socialism's genesis and development proves problematic given the extreme complexity of multi-ethnic Imperial Russia.[9] Many of these refugees from the East came from Baltic German or Ukrainian ethnic backgrounds, but they had belonged to the Russian Empire politically. Numerous Baltic German and Ukrainian expatriates had resented the Imperial Russian state. I refer to right-wing exiles from the former Russian Empire who opposed the "Red" Bolsheviks, or Majority Social Democrats, as "White émigrés." This term is employed in Russian academic circles. Former subjects of Imperial Russia who fought

---

[8] Karlheinz Rüdiger, "Reichsminister für die besetzten Ostgebiete Alfred Rosenberg," KR, BAB, [November 1941], NS 8, number 8, 2.

[9] Geoffrey Hosking, *Russia: People and Empire 1552–1917* (Cambridge: Harvard University Press, 1997), xix, xx.

the Bolsheviks became known as "Whites" since Bolshevik leaders insulted their foes by calling them this in the early part of the Russian Civil War. The Bolsheviks wished to associate their enemies with the reactionary Bourbon Dynasty that had ruled France after Emperor Napoleon Bonaparte's defeat and exile in 1815.[10]

The significance of substantial White émigré influences on Hitler's *Weltanschauung* has become more apparent since Brigitte Hamann convincingly argued in her 1996 work, *Hitlers Wien: Lehrjahre eines Diktators* (*Hitler's Vienna: Apprentice Years of a Dictator*), that Hitler was not yet antiSemitic during his "hunger years" in Vienna from 1908 to 1913. He even defended the Jews in intense political arguments with those who denounced them.[11] Hamann's book refutes the earlier historical consensus which had contended that Hitler developed an acutely anti-Semitic world-view during his time in Vienna.[12]

Further indications of the relatively late development of Hitler's far right political ideas exist. Hitler's correspondence and private writings from World War I (1914–1918) lack anti-Semitic passages.[13] Hitler's comrades during World War I did not detect anti-Semitic views among his beliefs.[14] Moreover, according to Aide-de-Camp Hans Mend, Hitler's immediate commanding officer on the Western Front in World War I, Hitler occasionally praised Jews, and he exhibited socialist leanings. He often held "rabble-rousing speeches" in which he called himself a representative of the "class-conscious proletariat."[15] Hitler only began to crystallize his virulent anti-Bolshevik, anti-Semitic *Weltanschauung* in Munich in late 1919 in the context of intercultural collaboration between alienated *völkisch* Germans and radical White émigrés.

Debate on modern German history has dealt with an idea that gained momentum in the 1960s, namely that of a pernicious German *Sonderweg* (special path). According to the *Sonderweg* theory, bourgeois Germans brought about a historical deviation through their weakness that ultimately

---

[10] Brian Crozier, *The Rise and Fall of the Soviet Empire* (Rocklin, CA: Prima Publishing, 1999), 19.

[11] Brigitte Hamann, *Hitlers Wien: Lehrjahre eines Diktators* (Munich: Piper, 1996), 239–241, 499, 500.

[12] See, for instance, Alan Bullock's *Hitler: A Study in Tyranny* (New York: Harper and Row, 1962), 36, and Joachim C. Fest's *Hitler*, trans. Richard and Clara Winston (New York: Harcourt Brace Jovanovich, 1974), 42.

[13] Hitler, *Sämtliche Aufzeichnungen*, 60–84, 1,256, 1,257.

[14] Ian Kershaw, *Hitler 1889–1936: Hubris* (London: Penguin Press, 1998), 64.

[15] Hans Mend, "Protokoll aufgenommen am 22. Dezember 1939 mit Hans Mend, Reitlehrer und Verwalter auf Schloss Eltzholz Berg bei Starnberg a/See, ehemals Ulan im kgl. bayer. x. Ulanenregiment zugeteilt als Ordonnanzreiter im Oktober 1914 dem Inf. Rgt. 'List.' Seit Juni 1916 befördert zum Offizier-Srellvertreter und zugeteilt dem 4. bayer. Feldartillerieregiment, Munitionskolonne 143 (Tankabwehr). Bei der Truppe bekannt als der 'Schimmelreiter,'" BHSAM/AK, *Handschriftensammlung*, number 3231, 2, 5.

led to the Third Reich and its crimes.[16] The German historian Ernst Nolte attacked the *Sonderweg* thesis in his 1987 work, *Der europäische Bürgerkrieg 1917–1945: Nationalsozialismus und Bolschewismus* (*The European Civil War 1917–1945: National Socialism and Bolshevism*). He maintained that National Socialism fundamentally represented a reaction against Bolshevism.[17]

In the *Historikerstreit* (Historians' Debate) in the second half of the 1980s, most scholars rejected Nolte's ideas of causation.[18] The majority of the historians involved in the *Historikerstreit* affirmed the horrific singularity of National Socialism in general and the Holocaust in particular.[19] In the 1990s, the American scholar Daniel Goldhagen sparked a second *Historikerstreit* by reintroducing an extreme version of the *Sonderweg* theory in his book *Hitler's Willing Executioners: Ordinary Germans and the Holocaust.*[20] He placed allegedly unparalleled "eliminationist" German anti-Semitism at the center of his historical schema.[21] German academics in particular attacked Goldhagen's ideas as dangerously simplistic.[22]

The positions of Goldhagen and Nolte represent opposing views of German and foreign influences on National Socialism. In *Hitler's Willing Executioners*, Goldhagen argues for the peculiarly German nature of National Socialism and the Holocaust. He emphasizes what he terms the "eliminationist mind-set" of "German antisemitism" to the exclusion of virtually all other factors. He asserts that it is "not essential to discuss German antisemitism comparatively." He nevertheless concludes, "No other European country came close" to equaling Germany's anti-Semitism. "The unmatched volume and the vitriolic and murderous substance of German antisemitic literature of the nineteenth and twentieth centuries alone indicate that German antisemitism was *sui generis.*"[23] Goldhagen thus avoids a sufficient comparative analysis in his treatment of supposedly unequaled German anti-Semitism.

---

[16] Charles Maier, *The Unmasterable Past: History, Holocaust, and German National Identity* (Cambridge: Harvard University Press, 1988), 102, 104.

[17] Ernst Nolte, *Der europäische Bürgerkrieg 1917–1945: Nationalsozialismus und Bolschewismus* (Frankfurt am Main: Propyläen Verlag, 1987), 15.

[18] Peter Baldwin, *Reworking the Past: Hitler, the Holocaust, and the Historians' Debate* (Boston: Beacon Press, 1990), 9.

[19] Maier, *The Unmasterable Past*, 53.

[20] Ullrich Volker, "Hitlers willige Mordgesellen: Ein Buch provoziert einen neuen Historikerstreit: Waren die Deutschen doch alle schuldig?" *Ein Volk von Mördern? Die Dokumentation zur Goldhagen-Kontroverse um die Rolle der Deutschen im Holocaust*, ed. Julius Schoeps (Hamburg: Hoffmann und Campe, 1996), 89.

[21] Daniel Goldhagen, *Hitler's Willing Executioners: Ordinary Germans and the Holocaust* (New York: Alfred A. Knopf, 1996), 393.

[22] Joseph Joffe, "Goldhagen in Germany," *The New York Review of Books*, November 28, 1996, 18.

[23] Goldhagen, *Hitler's Willing Executioners*, 6, 9, 25, 419.

Nolte, on the other hand, stresses the crucial influence of the Bolshevik seizure and consolidation of power in Russia on the National Socialist movement. He is known for arguing that scholars must "historicize" the Final Solution by comparing it with other mass slaughters, most notably those committed under Soviet rule.[24] In *The European Civil War 1917–1945*, Nolte argues that resistance to Bolshevism formed National Socialism's "most fundamental point." He downplays the importance of German anti-Semitism in the genesis and development of National Socialism. He argues that National Socialism's essence existed "neither in criminal tendencies nor in anti-Semitic obsessions." Rather, the "fear and hate-filled relation to Communism was in fact the moving center of Hitler's feelings and of Hitler's ideology." Nolte further stresses: "Bolshevism was both nightmare and example for National Socialism."

In the conclusion of his work, Nolte provocatively asserts that by holding the Jews responsible for the menace of Bolshevism, Hitler and *Reichsführer SS* (State Leader SS) Heinrich Himmler "carried the original Bolshevik concept of destruction to a new dimension." Nolte further maintains: "The Gulag Archipelago is more original than Auschwitz and . . . a causal nexus exists between them."[25] Nolte's views contain merit in that National Socialists fiercely resisted Bolshevism at the same time that it awed them. Nolte's arguments, however, can lead one to consider National Socialism's Final Solution as a mere reaction to foreign developments.

While I tend more towards Nolte's views than those of Goldhagen, I defend a middle position between Goldhagen's German-specific explanation of National Socialism's murderous development and Nolte's Bolshevik-centered analysis of National Socialism's crimes. National Socialism had both German and Russian roots. The National Socialist movement developed primarily as a synthesis of radical right German and Russian movements and ideas. National Socialism arose out of a radical right post-World War I Munich milieu of vengeful *völkisch* Germans and rancorous White émigrés. Several of the latter despised Bolshevism and yet admired the determination of its leaders as well as its practices of subversion followed by strict centralization, thorough militarization, and the ruthless elimination of political enemies.

I stress Aufbau's pivotal role in guiding National Socialists and White émigrés in a joint anti-Entente, anti-Weimar Republic, anti-Bolshevik, and anti-Semitic struggle. While National Socialism developed largely in

---

[24] Maier, *The Unmasterable Past*, 66, 67.
[25] Nolte, *Der europäische Bürgerkrieg*, 15, 16, 21, 22, 545, 548.

the framework of the *völkisch* movement, White émigré Aufbau members significantly influenced Hitler's political, military, and ideological views. Aufbau shaped early National Socialist strategies for combating both the Weimar Republic and the Soviet Union. The conspiratorial organization under Scheubner-Richter, who served as Hitler's close counselor and foreign policy advisor, sought to form an international alliance headed by nationalist and even National Socialist Germans and Russians (actually Russians, Ukrainians, and Baltic peoples) against the Entente, the Weimar Republic, and "Jewish Bolshevism." Aufbau goaded a doomed putsch against the Weimar Republic under Hitler and Ludendorff. Finally, Aufbau warned the early National Socialist movement that "Jewish Bolshevism" posed an apocalyptic danger that threatened to engulf Germany, Europe, and even the entire world.

This book improves a weakness in historical inquiry, as previous works on White émigré influences on National Socialism remain few and far between. In his groundbreaking 1939 book, *L'Apocalypse de notre temps: Les dessous de la propagande allemande d'après des documents inédits* (*The Apocalypse of Our Times: The Hidden Side of German Propaganda According to Unpublished Documents*), Henri Rollin stressed that "Hitlerism" represented a form of "anti-Soviet counter-revolution" which employed the "myth of a mysterious Jewish-Masonic-Bolshevik plot." Rollin investigated the National Socialist belief, which was taken primarily from White émigré views, that a vast Jewish-Masonic conspiracy had provoked World War I, toppled the Russian, German, and Austro-Hungarian Empires, and unleashed Bolshevism after undermining the existing order through the insidious spread of liberal ideas. German forces promptly destroyed Rollin's work in 1940 after they occupied France, and the book has remained in obscurity ever since.[26]

Almost thirty years passed before Walter Laqueur noted the lack of historical research on White émigré contributions to National Socialism in his book *Russia and Germany: A Century of Conflict*. Laqueur remarked: "In the search for the origins of German National Socialism some highly abstruse and improbable influences have been prominently featured, but the more tangible and substantial impact of refugees from Russia has usually been overlooked." Laqueur argued that historians of the National Socialist movement had generally been neither interested in White émigré influences nor qualified to analyze them, while the post-Hitler/Ludendorff Putsch development of National Socialism overshadowed earlier National

---

[26] Henri Rollin, *L'Apocalypse de notre temps: Les dessous de la propagande allemande d'après des documents inédits* (Paris: Gallimard, 1939), 9, 11, 168.

Socialist–White émigré collaboration. Laqueur's book performed a valuable service by drawing attention to National Socialist–White émigré interaction. Laqueur's work nonetheless offered a relatively superficial overview of White émigré contributions to National Socialism, largely because of the research constraints of the Cold War period.[27]

Since the 1960s, a few historians have addressed National Socialist–White émigré collaboration, including Norman Cohn in his work *Warrant for Genocide: The Myth of the Jewish World-Conspiracy and the "Protocols of the Elders of Zion,"* Robert Williams in his book *Culture in Exile: Russian Émigrés in Germany, 1881–1941,* and the editor Karl Schlögel in his anthology *Russische Emigration in Deutschland 1918 bis 1941: Leben im europäischen Bürgerkrieg* (*The Russian Émigré Community in Germany 1918 to 1941: Life in the European Civil War*). Cohn's work examines the fabrication and dissemination of the notorious anti-Semitic forgery *The Protocols of the Elders of Zion* from Russia to Germany, where they influenced National Socialists.[28] A German expert on the *Protocols,* Michael Hagemeister, has recently challenged Cohn's conclusion that the Imperial Russian Okhrana (Secret Police) in Paris fabricated the *Protocols.*[29] We will return to this theme in Chapter Two.

The books of Williams and Schlögel serve as valuable reference works on White émigré matters in general, but they do not focus on White émigré influences on National Socialism. Williams does briefly address White émigré contributions to National Socialism. He notes: "With the Third Reich came the new anti-Semitic virulence of the Nazis nurtured by the extreme right wing Russians and Balts who had discovered Hitler in Munich in the early 1920s." William's book does not, however, examine the alliance between National Socialists and many White émigrés in detail.[30] Schlögel's work serves as a useful reference book on White émigrés, but it treats White émigré influences on National Socialism as an ancillary topic.[31]

Among Russian historians, only Rafael Ganelin has examined the ideological contributions of White émigrés to National Socialism substantially.

[27] Walter Laqueur, *Russia and Germany: A Century of Conflict* (London: Weidenfeld and Nicolson, 1965), 53.

[28] Norman Cohn, *Warrant for Genocide: The Myth of the Jewish World-Conspiracy and the "Protocols of the Elders of Zion"* (Chico, CA: Scholars Press, 1981), 61, 62.

[29] Michael Hagemeister, "Der Mythos der 'Protokolle der Weisen von Zion,'" *Verschwörungstheorien: Anthropologische Konstanten – historische Varianten,* eds. Ute Caumanns and Matthias Niendorf (Osnabrück: Fibre Verlag, 2001), 99.

[30] Robert Williams, *Culture in Exile: Russian Émigrés in Germany, 1881–1941* (Ithaca: Cornell University Press, 1972), 371.

[31] *Russische Emigration in Deutschland 1918 bis 1941: Leben im europäischen Bürgerkrieg,* ed. Karl Schlögel (Berlin: Akademie, 1995).

He has noted that many right-wing exiles from the former Russian Empire believed that Jewish finance capitalism had supported the Bolshevik Revolution. This view became part of National Socialist ideology. Ganelin did not undertake large amounts of primary research. His most important essay, "Russian Black Hundreds and German National Socialism," relies primarily upon secondary Western publications.[32]

A relatively detailed work examining White émigré influences on National Socialism only appeared in 1998 with the publication of Johannes Baur's *Die russische Kolonie in München 1900–1945: Deutsch–russische Beziehungen im 20. Jahrhundert* (*The Russian Colony in Munich 1900–1945: German–Russian Relations in the Twentieth Century*). Baur asserts that White émigrés influenced Hitler's conception of the Bolshevik Revolution. Moreover, the "anti-Semitic prophets of the emigration" helped to form National Socialist ideology by combining extreme anti-Bolshevism with anti-Semitism. These White émigrés exhibited the "intention to destroy entire segments of the population and peoples." Baur nonetheless minimizes the extent of the "interaction between the Munich segment of the Russian monarchical right with the National Socialists." He maintains that the cooperation between these two groups was limited to a short period of time, with ideological and political differences extant from the beginning.[33]

Ideological and power-political divergences certainly existed between early National Socialists and Bavarian-based White émigrés. Members of both sides sought to use the other for their own purposes. Nonetheless, despite inevitable divergences as found in any cross-cultural collaboration, many National Socialists and White émigrés possessed substantial common ground. They launched a joint struggle against what they regarded as nefarious international Jews who manipulated both predatory finance capitalism in the West and bloody Bolshevism in the East. Four Aufbau members from the same Riga fraternity in Imperial Russia in particular bridged the gap between National Socialists and White émigrés, as they belonged to both groups: Scheubner-Richter, Arno Schickedanz, Otto von Kursell, and Rosenberg.

Given the expanded research opportunities of the post-Cold War epoch, historians need to emphasize Russian influences on National Socialism more. Archival materials housed in Moscow that have only recently become available to historians in particular necessitate a reevaluation of White

---

[32] Rafael Ganelin, "Rossiiskoe chernosotenstvo i germanskii natsional-sotsializm," *Natsionalnaia pravaia prezhde i teper, Istoriko-sotsiologicheskie ocherki, chast 1: Rossiia i russkoe zarubezhe* (Saint Petersburg: Institut Sotsiologii rossiiskoi akademii nauk, 1992), 130.

[33] Baur, *Die russische Kolonie in München*, 279, 316.

émigré contributions to National Socialism. During the summer of 1945, Soviet occupying forces in German Lower Silesia discovered vast German archives as well as great amounts of documents that the Germans had seized from occupied countries, most notably France and Poland. The entire archival collection was transported to Moscow, where it was stored in secrecy from the public and even from workers in other Soviet archives.[34] While Soviet authorities returned some of these records to East Germany during the Cold War, most of the seized archival collection remained under wraps in Moscow.

Russian authorities only admitted to possessing files looted from Germany and declassified them in 1991 after the Soviet Union had collapsed. Historians were allowed to investigate the huge archival collection at the Center for the Preservation of Historical-Documentary Collections, which had become part of the Russian State Military Archives by the time I examined materials there in 1999–2001.[35] I was temporarily denied access to the former Center in March 2001, likely as part of the chilled American–Russian relations that arose after the February 2001 arrest of the FBI operative Robert Hanssen as a double agent for both the Soviets and the Russians.[36]

In its heyday, the former Center contained large amounts of files dealing with National Socialist–White émigré collaboration, including reports from Hitler's Geheime Staatspolizei (Secret State Police, commonly known as the Gestapo) and the Reichskommissar für die Überwachung der öffentlichen Ordnung (State Commissioner for the Supervision of Public Order), the secret intelligence office of the Weimar Republic that reported on political developments and observed foreigners in Germany.[37] Regrettably, many State Commissioner files, most likely including one devoted specifically to Aufbau, have long been housed at the Sluzhba vneshnoi razvetki (Foreign Intelligence Service), where historians are not allowed to examine them. As a further hindrance, Russian authorities "temporarily" transferred the remaining State Commissioner documents there during the

---

[34] Götz Aly and Susanne Heim, *Das Zentrale Staatsarchiv in Moskau ("Sonderarchiv")* (Düsseldorf: Hans-Böckler-Stiftung, 1992), 7; Patricia Kennedy Grimsted, "Displaced Archives and the Restitution Problems on the Eastern Front in the Aftermath of the Second World War," *Contemporary European History*, vol. 6, March 1997, 60.

[35] Grimsted, *Archives of Russia Five Years After: "Purveyors of Sensations" or "Shadows Cast to the Past"?* (Amsterdam: International Institute of Social History, 1997), 65; Grimsted, "Displaced Archives," 45.

[36] Adrian Havill, *The Spy Who Stayed out in the Cold: The Secret Life of FBI Double Agent Robert Hanssen* (New York: St. Martin's Press, 2001), 7, 216–219.

[37] *Quellen zur Geschichte der UdSSR und der deutsch–sowjetischen Beziehungen 1917–1945* (Potsdam: Zentrales Staatsarchiv, 1984), 106.

summer of 2001, fortunately after I had examined them thoroughly. I believe that I am the last Western scholar to investigate these valuable materials.

The former Center still houses important personal papers that I examined. For instance, the former Center possesses the extensive private collection of Ludwig Müller von Hausen. This *völkisch* publicist received *The Protocols of the Elders of Zion* from Shabelskii-Bork in 1919. He had the *Protocols* translated into German, and then he published them with commentary, thereby disseminating them to National Socialists and other anti-Semites.[38] The former Center also holds the unpublished diary of Walther Nicolai, the head of German Army Intelligence during World War I who subsequently provided anti-Bolshevik intelligence to Aufbau and the National Socialist Party.[39]

The former Center also contains valuable documents of French and Polish provenance that I analyzed. In particular, the institution possesses copies of French intelligence files from the Sûreté Générale (General Security) and its successor organization beginning in 1934, the Direction Générale de la Sûreté Nationale (General Department of National Security). The former Center also holds copies of military intelligence reports from the Deuxième Bureau (Second Section). Moreover, the former Center houses Polish Sztab Główny Oddzial drugi (Main Headquarters Second Section) intelligence reports on White émigré activities. The Narodnyi komissariat vnutrennikh del (People's Commissariat for Internal Affairs, NKVD) began collecting these files in September 1939 after the Soviet Union invaded eastern Poland.[40]

This book is arranged thematically and chronologically. Chapter One provides background on National Socialism's genesis primarily as a synthesis of German and Russian radical right movements and ideologies by examining the development of the far right in the German and Russian Empires. Imperial German and Russian radical rightists, who considered themselves to possess spiritual and even racial superiority, developed elaborate anti-Western, anti-socialist, and anti-Semitic views. The redemptive aspect of *völkisch* German thought associated with the philosopher Arthur Schopenhauer, the composer Richard Wagner, and the author Houston Stewart Chamberlain stressed that Germans needed to oppose materialistic

---

[38] Gestapo report from April 13, 1935, RGVA (TsKhIDK), *fond* 501, *opis* 3, *delo* 496a, 208.
[39] Walther Nicolai's commentary on his letter to Erich von Ludendorff from April 19, 1922, *Tagebuch* (Diary), RGVA (TsKhIDK), *fond* 1414, *opis* 1, *delo* 20, 174.
[40] Grimsted, *Trophies of War and Empire: The Archival Heritage of Ukraine, World War II, and the International Politics of Restitution* (Cambridge: Harvard University Press, 2001), 289, 296, 302.

Jews and to deny the will to live, thereby attaining salvation. Drawing inspiration from the mystically inclined authors Fedor Dostoevskii and Vladimir Solovev, Imperial Russian far rightists propagated Orthodox Christian superiority and warned that an apocalyptic battle loomed between Russia at the head of all Slavs and conspiratorial international Jewry, where Russians would assume the role of Christ, and Jews would take the part of the Antichrist.

Despite their development of detailed religiously inspired anti-Western, anti-socialist, and anti-Semitic beliefs, far rightists in the German and Russian Empires failed politically in the period leading up to the Bolshevik Revolution of 1917. The *völkisch* German right could not gain a mass following, nor could it replace the Kaiser with a military dictatorship under General Ludendorff in 1917. In Imperial Russia, the far right "Black Hundred" movement, of which the *Soiuz russkago naroda* (Union of the Russian People) formed the most important part, gained some initial popular successes in the aftermath of the Revolution of 1905. The Black Hundred movement soon split into factions, however, that could not thwart the Tsar's abdication and the Bolshevik seizure of power in 1917. The combined German-White/White émigré far right only began to thrive after the Bolsheviks had come to power and Germany had lost World War I. *Völkisch* Germans and Whites/White émigrés primarily blamed these catastrophes on the Jews.

Chapter Two is divided into two parts. The first section focuses on the Ukraine in 1918 as the theater of the first large-scale anti-Bolshevik German–White military collaboration. The German–White anti-Bolshevik interaction in and just outside the Ukraine established a precedent for further cooperation between rightist Germans and Whites/White émigrés both in Germany and abroad, notably as conducted in the Baltic region the following year. Many White officers who served in the Ukraine under German occupation went on to join Aufbau and to foster the National Socialist cause, including General Biskupskii, Colonel Vinberg, Colonel Poltavets-Ostranitsa, Lieutenant Sergei Taboritskii, and Lieutenant Shabelskii-Bork.

The second segment of Chapter Two deals with the Ukraine's role as a transfer zone for White ideology to postwar *völkisch* German circles in general and to Hitler in particular. During the winter of 1918/1919, German military personnel evacuated thousands of White officers from the Ukraine. One of them, Shabelskii-Bork, carried *The Protocols of the Elders of Zion* with him to Berlin. Once there, he gave the fabrication to the *völkisch* publicist Hausen for translation and publication in German. The *Protocols'* warnings of an insidious Jewish plot to achieve world domination through both insatiable finance capitalism and revolutionary turmoil greatly affected *völkisch* Germans and White émigrés, including Hitler's mentors Eckart and Rosenberg. They in turn influenced Hitler's anti-Semitic views. Hitler used the *Protocols* as a blueprint of Jewish schemes to conquer the world, notably through the use of starvation as a means to subjugate nationalist majorities.

Chapter Three focuses on nationalist German–White/White émigré collaboration in the Baltic region and in Germany in 1919–1920. The first part of the chapter analyzes the anti-Bolshevik campaign of a combined German Freikorps (volunteer corps) and White Russian army in the Latvian Intervention of 1919. After allowing and even fostering the creation of Freikorps in the Baltic region, the Entente and the largely socialist German government ordered these units to end their anti-Bolshevik operation in tandem with White formations in Latvia. The early director of the Latvian Intervention, General Count Rüdiger von der Goltz, complied with the demands of the Entente and the Weimar Republic, but thousands of Germans defied their orders by remaining in Latvia along with their White comrades. The Western Volunteer Army, as the combined German/White force in Latvia was called, came under the command of Colonel Pavel Bermondt-Avalov, who had served in the Ukraine under German occupation in 1918. After some early successes, Bermondt-Avalov's army suffered defeat. While the Latvian Intervention failed militarily, it fostered a strong sense of German/White solidarity.

In addition to serving as a German/White anti-Bolshevik crusade abroad, the Latvian Intervention complemented international far right efforts to overthrow the Weimar Republic. Nationalist Germans grouped around Wolfgang Kapp and Ludendorff hoped for support for their intended putsch from rightist German and White members of Bermondt-Avalov's Western Volunteer Army after they had triumphed over Bolshevism in Latvia and Russia. After the defeat of Bermondt-Avalov's forces, Kapp and Ludendorff used demobilized Germans and White émigrés from the Latvian Intervention to undermine the Weimar Republic. National revolutionary undertakings climaxed with the abortive Kapp Putsch of March 1920, which Ludendorff, Scheubner-Richter, Biskupskii, Vinberg, Shabelskii-Bork, Taboritskii, and even Hitler and Eckart supported. While the Kapp Putsch failed in Berlin, it succeeded in Munich, and it set the stage for increased cooperation between *völkisch* Germans, including National Socialists, and White émigrés there.

Chapters Four through Seven examine Aufbau's rise and fall in Munich from 1920 to 1923. Aufbau gained its initial impetus from the cooperation between former *völkisch* German and White émigré Kapp Putsch conspirators located in Bavaria and General Piotr Vrangel's Southern Russian Armed Forces, which were based on the Crimean Peninsula in the Ukraine. Scheubner-Richter led a dangerous mission to the Crimea to specify the terms of mutual support between his right-wing German and White émigré backers in Bavaria and Vrangel's regime. The Red Army soon overran the Crimean Peninsula and sent Vrangel and his soldiers fleeing, but Scheubner-Richter nonetheless turned Aufbau into the dynamic focal point of *völkisch* German–White émigré collaboration.

Aufbau linked important *völkisch* Germans, most notably Hitler and General Ludendorff, whom Scheubner-Richter introduced to each other in the framework of Aufbau, with prominent White émigrés. Important White émigré members of Aufbau included First Secretary Scheubner-Richter himself, Vice President Biskupskii, Deputy Director Schickedanz, Ukrainian faction leader Poltavets-Ostranitsa, Vinberg, Shabelskii-Bork, Taboritskii, Rosenberg, and Rosenberg's collaborator in Eckart's newspaper *In Plain German*, Kursell. In addition to serving in Aufbau, Scheubner-Richter, Schickedanz, Kursell, and Rosenberg played active roles in the National Socialist Party. Aufbau's second secretary, the German Max Amann, also served as the National Socialist Party secretary.

After it consolidated itself into a powerful conspiratorial force in the first half of 1921 under Scheubner-Richter's *de facto* leadership, Aufbau tried and failed to unite all White émigrés behind Grand Prince Kirill Romanov in league with National Socialists. Aufbau hoped to lead all White émigrés in Europe in an anti-Bolshevik crusade that would replace Soviet rule with nationalist Russian, Ukrainian, and Baltic states. Instead of unifying all White émigrés, Aufbau engaged in bitter internecine struggle with the Supreme Monarchical Council under the former Union of the Russian People faction leader Nikolai Markov II. The Council supported Grand Prince Nikolai Nikolaevich Romanov, who had close ties to the French government, for Tsar. Markov II's Council sought to reestablish Imperial Russia in its former borders with French military assistance. Aufbau detested the Council's pro-French undertakings to such a degree that it entertained a hazardous tactical alliance with the Red Army.

To further complementary right-wing German and Russian interests, Hitler assisted the pro-Kirill Aufbau in its struggle with Markov II's Supreme Monarchical Council. For its support, Kirill granted Hitler's National Socialist Party considerable subsidies in the context of the "German–Russian national cause." While Aufbau could not unite all White émigrés in Germany (and beyond) behind Kirill and in harness with National Socialists, the Aufbau ideologues Scheubner-Richter, Vinberg, and Rosenberg called for "Germany–Russia above everything." They succeeded in convincing Hitler of the need for a nationalist German–Russian alliance against the Entente, the Weimar Republic, the Soviet Union, and international Jewry.

In addition to urging German–Russian collaboration, Aufbau engaged in terrorism. Biskupskii placed a contract for the assassination of Aleksandr Kerenskii, the former head of the 1917 Provisional Government in Russia. Two Aufbau colleagues, Shabelskii-Bork and Taboritskii, accidentally shot the prominent Constitutional Democrat Vladimir Nabokov in their attempt to murder the Russian Constitutional Democratic leader Pavel Miliukov. The Aufbau co-conspirators Biskupskii, Ludendorff, and his advisor Colonel Karl Bauer (at the least) colluded in the assassination of Weimar Germany's Foreign Minister, Walther Rathenau. In this undertaking, the Aufbau associates conspired with Organization C, a radical right union based in Munich under the important Kapp Putsch participant Captain Hermann Ehrhardt. This association carried out terrorist acts, planned military campaigns against the Weimar Republic and the Soviet Union, and upheld close relations with Hitler's National Socialists.

As well as engaging in terrorism, Aufbau coordinated joint National Socialist–White émigré efforts to topple the Soviet Union through the use of military force. Aufbau's goals vis-à-vis the Soviet Union became those of the National Socialist Party, as Scheubner-Richter rose to become Hitler's leading foreign policy advisor and one of his closest consultants in general. Aufbau's foreign policy called for weakening the Bolshevik regime through internal revolt and then overthrowing it with interventionary forces. Aufbau then planned to establish National Socialist successor states in the Ukraine, in the Baltic region, and in the Great Russian heartland. Hitler, who had not yet developed his concept that Germany needed to acquire *Lebensraum* (living space) in the East, approved of Aufbau's plans for reconstituting the Soviet Union. He especially wished to foster an independent National Socialist Ukraine under Poltavets-Ostranitsa.

In addition to scheming to overthrow the Soviet Union in league with National Socialists, Aufbau played a pivotal role in coordinating Hitler's preparations for a putsch aganst the Weimar Republic. Aufbau helped the National Socialist Party to build a substantial war chest for its intended coup by contributing funds from Aufbau members or allies such as Kirill as well as by channeling funds from Henry Ford, the wealthy American industrialist and politician. Scheubner-Richter played a leading role in the increasingly belligerent Kampfbund (Combat League), a paramilitary organization under Hitler and General Ludendorff. In preparing for a putsch against the Weimar Republic, Scheubner-Richter drew from the perceived Bolshevik example, where a few determined men had shaped world history through subversion followed by strict centralization and militarization. Scheubner-Richter brought Hitler and Ludendorff together at the head of the Combat League for a determined show of force in the Hitler/Ludendorff Putsch of November 1923. He paid for this doomed undertaking with his life.

Chapter Eight analyzes Aufbau's early ideological contributions to National Socialism. Hitler, who only began to develop intense anti-Bolshevik and anti-Semitic beliefs in late 1919 in the context of *völkisch* German–White émigré interaction, learned a great deal from his early mentor Eckart and three Aufbau members: Scheubner-Richter, Vinberg, and Rosenberg. These ideological comrades served as the "four writers of the apocalypse." They influenced National Socialist ideology by adding White émigré conspiratorial-apocalyptic anti-Semitism to existing *völkisch-*redemptive notions of Germanic spiritual and racial superiority.

In the vein of Dostoevskii, the four writers of the apocalypse argued that a sinister worldwide Jewish conspiracy manipulated the twin evils of rapacious finance capitalism and bloodthirsty Bolshevism. They excoriated what they regarded as "Jewish Bolshevism." The ideological quartet warned that "Jewish Bolshevism" had killed many millions of Russians in general, and, in a more sinister manner, had exterminated Russia's nationalist intelligentsia. They emphasized that "Jewish Bolsheviks" threatened to annihilate the German nationalist intelligentsia and to slaughter many millions of other Germans in their bloody quest to achieve tyrannical world rule. While Bolshevism horrified him, Rosenberg nonetheless learned from what he perceived as its brutal method of eliminating political enemies. The four writers of the apocalypse radicalized the early National Socialist Party by warning that the "Jewish Bolshevik" peril threatened to pass from world conquest to world destruction.

This work concentrates on the genesis of National Socialism from 1917 to 1923, but Chapter Nine analyzes Aufbau's political, financial, military, and ideological legacy to National Socialism after 1923. Scheubner-Richter's tragic death at Hitler's side during the Hitler/Ludendorff Putsch served as a model of heroic sacrifice for the National Socialist cause. Biskupskii in particular continued to channel funds to the National Socialist Party after 1923. Rosenberg, Schickedanz, and Biskupskii held high posts in the Third Reich. Hitler and Rosenberg continued to use Ukrainian separatists under Poltavets-Ostranitsa to undermine the Soviet Union. Hitler's insistence on winning the Ukraine for Germany in the vein of Aufbau during World War II led him to divert powerful formations of the German Army southwards away from Moscow in 1941, with disastrous military results.

After subsiding somewhat during the National Socialist seizure and consolidation of power, Hitler's virulent anti-Bolshevism and anti-Semitism, which he had largely derived from Aufbau thought, found pronounced expression in the later years of the Third Reich. Hitler's intense anti-Bolshevism, which Aufbau had shaped, largely led him to launch a risky invasion of the Soviet Union in 1941. Fundamental Aufbau-inspired National Socialist ideas on the pernicious nature of Jewish world conspirators continued to evolve after 1923, and they helped to motivate the National Socialist attempt to annihilate European Jewry in the Final Solution. As the State Minister for the Occupied Eastern Territories, Rosenberg aided Hitler in his dual crusades against Bolshevism and Jewry, which the Führer often combined into a single struggle against "Jewish Bolshevism."

Popular notions notwithstanding, National Socialism did not arise as a mere continuation of peculiarly German radical right-wing politics. This book seeks to foster understanding of National Socialism and its attendant atrocities primarily as the result of cross-cultural interaction between groups defeated in World War I and the Bolshevik Revolution: alienated *völkisch* Germans and rancorous White émigrés. Many anti-Bolshevik and anti-Semitic White émigrés contributed extensively to the rise and development of National Socialism in Germany. They affected aggressive National Socialist political and military strategies, provided Hitler with extensive funding, influenced National Socialist ideology by warning apocalyptically of impending "Jewish Bolshevik" destruction, and helped to spur the Final Solution.

CHAPTER I

The far right in the German and Russian Empires

National Socialism with its intensely anti-Bolshevik and anti-Semitic ideology arose primarily as a synthesis of radical right German and Russian movements and ideas. This chapter illuminates the background of National Socialism's genesis by examining the development of the far right in Imperial Germany and the Russian Empire up to the Bolshevik Revolution of 1917. During a dynamic period of increasing industrialization and democratization in the late nineteenth and early twentieth centuries, Imperial German and Russian radical rightists feared for their elevated societal positions, and they developed intensely anti-Western, anti-socialist, and anti-Semitic views. These beliefs later found prominent expression in Hitler's National Socialist movement, which fought against what it perceived to be an insidious international Jewish alliance between ravenous finance capitalism and murderous Bolshevism.

Völkisch German ideology increasingly represented Jews as racial parasites, but it also regarded the Jewish essence metaphysically as the manifestation of shallow materialism. In the spirit of the "denial of the will to live," a concept that the German philosopher Arthur Schopenhauer championed, *völkisch* theorists such as the composer Richard Wagner and the author Houston Stewart Chamberlain sought German religious redemption. This German struggle against the perceived worldly Jewish nature primarily took place on the spiritual plane and not on the political stage. While *völkisch* ideologues in Imperial Germany developed a substantial ideology based on hopes for German inner redemption as racially and spiritually superior beings, they could not achieve anything approaching the modest political success of Imperial Russian far rightists in the years leading up to the Russian Revolution of 1917.

In the Russian Empire, "conservative revolutionaries," to borrow a phrase from one of their leading members, the author Fedor Dostoevskii, demonstrated more vitality than their right-wing German counterparts. They used religiously inspired notions of Orthodox Christian superiority and the apocalyptic battle for Russia's salvation from scheming Jews in a moderately successful political struggle against perceived materialistic, westernizing, and socialist Jewish elements. At the height of their powers immediately following the 1905 Revolution, Imperial Russian far rightists, most notably members of the Soiuz russkago naroda (Union of the Russian People), disseminated their anti-Western, anti-socialist, and anti-Semitic message to the broad masses far more effectively than pre-World War I *völkisch* Germans ever did.

Ultimately, far right alignments in Imperial Germany and the Russian Empire failed to develop into powerful societal forces. *Völkisch* German political activities culminated in "national opposition" efforts to replace Kaiser Wilhelm Hohenzollern II, seen as a weak leader, with a military dictatorship under the *völkisch* General Erich von Ludendorff in 1917. These endeavors miscarried. After a brief period of moderate success, Imperial Russian radical rightists faded into relative political insignificance. While they sought to uphold the autocratic prerogatives of Tsar Nikolai Romanov II, they could not thwart either the Tsar's abdication or the Bolshevik seizure of power in October 1917. German and Russian far right movements only came into vogue after the outbreak of the Russian Revolution and the defeat of Imperial Germany in World War I. *Völkisch* Germans, including National Socialists, and White émigrés blamed both of these catastrophes primarily on sinister international Jewish conspirators.

THE *VÖLKISCH* RIGHT IN IMPERIAL GERMANY

In order to understand the rise of *völkisch* ideology in Germany, one must examine the political development of the German state. The German Empire became a political entity only in 1871, and even then it failed to include millions of ethnic Germans. Late and incomplete German unification spurred a substantial *völkisch* ideology in the course of the nineteenth and early twentieth centuries that Hitler ultimately drew upon. The adjective "*völkisch*" derives from the word "*Volk*" (people). Proponents of *völkisch* thought believed the German people to be an autonomous agent above the state largely because of its transcendental essence.[1] *Völkisch* ideas developed from German Romanticism, which opposed parliamentarianism, Westernism, and the Jewish spirit. *Völkisch* theorists rejected the modern, liberal, and capitalist world they associated with soulless Western

---

[1] Max Hildebert Boehm, *Das eigenständige Volk in der Krise der Gegenwart* (Vienna: Wilhelm Braumüller, 1971), 1.

Zivilisation (civilization) in favor of an organic and spiritual *Gemeinschaft* (community). *Völkisch* ideologues equated Jews with an essentially pernicious materialism.[2]

The historian Saul Friedländer has termed one current of *völkisch* ideology "redemptive anti-Semitism." This spiritual aspect of the *völkisch* movement conceived the "sacredness of Aryan blood" and fused this belief "with a decidedly religious vision, that of the need for a German (or Aryan) Christianity."[3] The transcendental ideas of the German philosopher Schopenhauer helped to crystallize the redemptive features of *völkisch* thought. In his 1844 *magnum opus, The World as Will and Idea*, Schopenhauer expressed a concept that developed into an important component of later *völkisch* beliefs, namely that the denial of the will to live led to salvation.

In *The World as Will and Idea*, Schopenhauer argued that most people strove to affirm their "will to live" with "sufficient success to keep them from despair, and sufficient failure to keep them from ennui and its consequences." The enlightened few, however, realized: "Existence is certainly to be regarded as an erring, to return from which is salvation." He found this belief to play a central role in Christianity. He maintained, "The doctrine of original sin (assertion of the will) and of salvation (denial of the will) is the great truth which constitutes the essence of Christianity." Thus true Christians had to deny their worldly desires in order to achieve spiritual purity.

Schopenhauer did not explicitly attribute the ability to deny the will to live to Germans or Aryans, but he did argue that Jews lacked this capacity. He stressed, "Christianity belongs to the ancient, true, and sublime faith of mankind, which is opposed to the false, shallow, and injurious optimism which exhibits itself in . . . Judaism." He further asserted that the Old Testament was "foreign to true Christianity; for in the New Testament the world is always spoken of as something to which one does not belong, which one does not love, nay, whose lord is the devil."[4] Schopenhauer upheld Christian idealism as the opposite of Jewish materialism.

As cited by Dietrich Eckart, Hitler's early *völkisch* mentor, Schopenhauer elaborated on Judaism's overwhelmingly materialistic nature in his work

[2] Peter Pulzer, *The Rise of Political Anti-Semitism in Germany & Austria* (Cambridge: Harvard University Press, 1988), 31; George Mosse, *The Crisis of German Ideology: Intellectual Origins of the Third Reich* (New York: Howard Fertig, 1964), 4–7.

[3] Saul Friedländer, *Nazi Germany and the Jews: Volume I: The Years of Persecution, 1933–1939* (New York: HarperCollins, 1997), 86, 87.

[4] Arthur Schopenhauer, *The World as Will and Idea*, vols. I and III, trans. R. B. Haldane and J. Kemp (London: Kegan Paul, Trench, Trübner and Co., 1909), vol. I, 422, 524; vol. III, 423, 447.

Parerga. He asserted, "The true Jewish religion . . . is the crudest of all religions, since it is the only one that has absolutely no doctrine of immortality, nor even any trace of it." He also maintained: "Judaism . . . is a religion without any metaphysical tendency." This argument corresponded with his claim that what passed for the Jewish religion merely represented a "war-cry in the subjugation of foreign peoples."[5] According to Schopenhauer, Jews focused on shallow worldly gain and could not negate the will to live in order to achieve salvation.

In constructing his *Weltanschauung* of Germanic redemption through self-negation, the German composer Richard Wagner borrowed extensively from Schopenhauer's philosophy of achieving salvation by repudiating the will to live. Wagner read Schopenhauer's *The World as Will and Idea* four times in 1854 and 1855. He enthused of the philosopher: "His cardinal idea, the ultimate negation of the will to live, is terribly solemn but uniquely redeeming. It was not new to me, of course, and cannot be entertained at all by anyone in whom it does not already reside."[6] Wagner ultimately claimed that the only path to "true hope" meant establishing "the Schopenhauerian philosophy as the basis of all further intellectual and moral culture."[7]

Wagner expressed anti-Semitic views in his schema of attaining salvation by negating the will to live. He ended his notorious essay, "Judaism in Music," which he originally wrote in 1850 and revised in 1869, by urging "the Jew" to attain redemption along with the German, for which he would have "to cease being a Jew." Wagner named a Jewish author, Ludwig Börne, who had achieved this transformation after realizing that the Jews could only find salvation with their "redemption into true men." Wagner stressed, "Börne of all people teaches us as well that this redemption . . . costs sweat, affliction, anxieties, and an abundance of pain and suffering." He then exhorted the Jews:

Take part in this regenerative work of redemption through self-destruction, and then we will be united and undifferentiated! But consider that only one thing can be your redemption from the curse that weighs heavily upon you: the redemption of Ahasuerus: downfall![8]

---

[5] Quoted from Dietrich Eckart, "Das Judentum in und ausser uns: Grundsätzliche Betrachtungen von Dietrich Eckart: I," *Auf gut deutsch: Wochenschrift für Ordnung und Recht*, January 10, 1919, 12; quoted from Eckart, "Das ist der Jude! Laienpredigt über Juden- und Christentum von Dietrich Eckart," *Auf gut deutsch*, [August/September], 1920, 55; quoted from Eckart, "Der Baccalaureus," *Auf gut deutsch*, October 23, 1919, 7.

[6] Cited from Martin Gregor-Dellin, *Richard Wagner: His Life, His Work, His Century* (New York: Harcourt Brace Jovanovich, 1983), 257.

[7] Richard Wagner, "Was nützt diese Erkenntniss?" *Gesammelte Schriften und Dichtungen*, vol. X (Leipzig: C. F. W. Siegel, 1907), 257.

[8] Wagner, "Das Judenthum in der Musik," *Gesammelte Schriften und Dichtungen*, vol. V, 85.

In this passage, Wagner referred to the myth of Ahasuerus, or the Wandering Jew, a cobbler who, according to seventeenth-century legend, had mocked Jesus and had thereby brought a curse upon himself to live until the second coming of Christ. Only then would he be granted the release of death.[9] Wagner called upon the Jews to join the Germans in effecting regenerative redemption through self-negation. By admonishing them that only their downfall would redeem them, however, he seems to have thought that this in itself would daunt them. For Wagner, the Jews remained too attached to their own worldly interests to renounce their materialism, and thus they would by and large remain beyond the bounds of redemption.

Wagner's *magnum opus*, the four-part opera cycle based on Teutonic mythology and legend, *Der Ring des Nibelungen* (*The Ring of the Nibelung*), powerfully expresses the alleged Germanic capacity to negate the will to live heroically as compared to the Jewish drive for earthly power. Wagner wrote of his work, "Here everything is tragic through and through, and the will that wanted to shape a world according to its plan can in the end attain nothing more satisfying than to break itself through a dignified downfall."[10] In the *Ring*, Wotan, the chief god, seeks to transcend "divine splendor's boasting ignominy." He exclaims: "I renounce my work. I only want one thing more: the end, the end!"[11]

In his quest for a "dignified downfall," Wotan arranges for his daughter, the Valkyrie Brünnhilde, to work a "world-redeeming deed." She carries out this mission by riding into the funeral pyre of her dead lover, Wotan's heroic grandson Siegfried, while wearing the ring of the Nibelung, which grants earthly power. Brünnhilde's heroic self-negation purifies the ring of its dread curse and allows Wotan to destroy Valhalla, his splendid castle in the sky, with its assembled gods and heroes.[12] After this conflagration, a purified new world arises from out of the old order's destruction.[13]

Wagner's *Ring* portrays heroic Germanic self-abnegation in contrast to the Jewish lust for earthly power. The Germanic deities Wotan and Brünnhilde destroy themselves to redeem the world. The fiendish Alberich, on the other hand, who crafts the accursed ring in the first place, and his son Hagen, who dastardly stabs Siegfried in the back, remain slaves to their material desires. They exhibit no redemptive spiritual tendencies.

---

[9] "Wandering Jew," *The Jewish Encyclopedia*, 1916, 462.

[10] Wagner, "Über Staat und Religion," *Gesammelte Schriften und Dichtungen*, vol. VIII, 220.

[11] Wagner, *Die Walküre*, Act Two, Scene Two, *Gesammelte Schriften und Dichtungen*, vol. III, 111.

[12] Wagner, *Siegfried*, Act Three, Scene One, *Gesammelte Schriften und Dichtungen*, vol. III, 222; Wagner, *Götterdämmerung*, Act Three, Scene Three, *Gesammelte Schriften und Dichtungen*, vol. 3, 311–313.

[13] William O. Cord, *The Teutonic Mythology of Richard Wagner's "The Ring of the Nibelungen"* (Queenston, Ont.: Edwin Mellen Press, 1991), 84.

Hagen meets his doom in an ignominious manner. He leaps to his death in a final grab for the ring "as if insane."[14] Wagner intended Alberich and Hagen to represent what he regarded as the worldly and corrupting Jewish essence. Alberich symbolized the menace of purebred Jews and his son Hagen embodied the threat inherent in the bastardized offspring of Germans and Jews.[15]

In his later prose writings and in his final opera, *Parsifal*, Wagner advocated a "true religion" for Germans as opposed to Jews in which compassion arose from suffering.[16] He drew heavily upon Schopenhauerian thought in advocating this "true religion" based on the "annulment of the will" that could effect a "great regeneration." He stressed that Jews were incapable of attaining this "true religion." He even asserted that Jesus had not been a Jew.[17] In formulating his ideas, Wagner borrowed from the racist notions of the French author Count Arthur de Gobineau, who had released his *Essai sur l'inégalité des races humaines* (*Essay on the Inequality of the Human Races*) in 1855.[18] Gobineau conceived an "Aryan ruling race."[19] Wagner, for his part, argued that the "so-called white race" manifested the "ability of deliberate suffering to an exceptional degree."[20] "The Jew," on the other hand, possessed

no religion whatsoever, but rather only a belief in certain promises of his God that by no means extends to an atemporal life beyond . . . , but solely to precisely this present life on earth, on which power over everything alive and lifeless . . . remains promised to his tribe.[21]

Wagner thus upheld a strict racist divide between idealistic Germans and materialistic Jews. Subsequent *völkisch* theorists drew upon this dichotomy.

Wagner tended to avoid concrete proposals for combating the Jewish menace, though he did address this topic on at least two occasions. He wrote in a revised version of "Judaism in Music" in 1869 that he was "unable to decide" whether the "downfall of our culture can be arrested by a violent

[14] Wagner, *Das Rheingold*, Scene Four, *Gesammelte Schriften und Dichtungen*, vol. III, 59; Wagner, *Götterdämmerung*, Act Three, Scene Three, *Gesammelte Schriften und Dichtungen*, vol. III, 311–313.
[15] Marc A. Weiner, *Richard Wagner and the Anti-Semitic Imagination* (Lincoln, NE: University of Nebraska Press, 1995), 310, 311.
[16] Friedländer, "Hitler und Wagner," *Richard Wagner im Dritten Reich: Ein Schloss Elmau-Symposium*, eds. Friedländer and Jörn Rüsen (Munich: Verlag C. H. Beck, 2000), 172.
[17] Wagner, "Religion und Kunst," *Gesammelte Schriften und Dichtungen*, vol. X, 232, 243, 245.
[18] Ivan Hannaford, *Race: The History of an Idea in the West* (Washington, DC: The Woodrow Wilson Center Press, 1996), 264.
[19] Michael Burleigh and Wolfgang Wippermann, *The Racial State: Germany 1933–1945* (Cambridge: Cambridge University Press, 1991), 28.
[20] Wagner, "Heldenthum und Christenthum," *Gesammelte Schriften und Dichtungen*, vol. X, 281.
[21] Wagner, "Erkenne dich selbst," *Gesammelte Schriften und Dichtungen*, vol. X, 271.

ejection of the destructive foreign element," meaning the Jews.[22] In his 1881 essay, "Know Thyself," he prophesied that when the "demon of suffering humanity" no longer had a place to lurk among the Germans, "there will also no longer be – any Jew." He then asserted that the "current movement that has only just become conceivable among us again could make this great solution possible for us Germans sooner than for every other nation as soon as we carry out that 'know thyself' into the innermost core of our existence."[23] While imprecise in his language, Wagner clearly displayed a menacing attitude towards Jews.

After Wagner's death in 1883, the *völkisch* ideologue Houston Stewart Chamberlain disseminated Wagnerian ideas to a large audience. Chamberlain was a born Englishman who married Wagner's daughter Eva and moved into Wagner's former villa *Wahnfried* in Bayreuth, Bavaria.[24] Chamberlain asserted in 1883: "I must confess I doubt whether humanity ever produced a greater, perhaps as great a genius as Richard Wagner."[25] His first book dealt with Wagner, the "great German *Meister*." In his work *Richard Wagner*, Chamberlain summarized many of Wagner's somewhat abstruse views. He asserted that Wagner had traced the fundamental causes of human decadence to the "deterioration of the blood" and to the "demoralizing influence of the Jews." He summed up Wagner's doctrine of regeneration as the belief, "Out of the inner negation of the world the affirmation of redemption will be born."[26]

With his major work, *Foundations of the Nineteenth Century*, which was first published in 1899 and went through twenty-four German editions by 1938, Chamberlain wished to establish himself as a great *völkisch* thinker in his own right.[27] He clearly owed a great debt to Wagnerian thought, however. In *Foundations*, Chamberlain continued in the vein of Wagner's racist dichotomy between idealistic Germans and materialistic Jews. With regard to the "Teutons," he asserted: "A race so profoundly and inwardly religious is unknown to history." The Jewish people, on the other hand, remained "quite stunted in its religious growth."

---

[22] Wagner, "Appendix to 'Judaism in Music,'" *Richard Wagner's Prose Works*, vol. III, trans. William Ashton Ellis (London: Routledge and Kegan Paul Ltd., 1894), 121.

[23] Wagner, "Erkenne dich selbst," 274.

[24] Geoffrey G. Field, *Evangelist of Race: The Germanic Vision of Houston Stewart Chamberlain* (New York: Columbia University Press, 1981), 15, 347–349.

[25] Winfried Schüler, *Der Bayreuther Kreis von seiner Entstehung bis zum Ausgang der Wilhelminischen Ära* (Münster: Verlag Aschendorff, 1971), 74, 113.

[26] Houston Stewart Chamberlain, *Richard Wagner*, trans. G. Ainslie Hight (Philadelphia: J. B. Lippincott Co., 1900), 171, 182, 387.

[27] Field, *Evangelist of Race*, 225; Schüler, *Der Bayreuther Kreis*, 117.

In Chamberlain's view, the profound Germanic religious nature as opposed to the Jewish lack of deep spiritual feeling also manifested itself when one compared German and Jewish heroes. Chamberlain argued that the "Germanic" character possessed the notion of "victory in downfall (in other words, the true heroism centered in the inner motive, not in the outward distress)." This self-negating aspect as well as "loyalty" distinguished "a Siegfried, a Tristan, a Parzival" from a "Semitic Samson whose heroism lies in his hair." Chamberlain thus argued that while Jewish heroes perhaps defied death, they did not transcend it as Germanic ones did.

Chamberlain used Schopenhauerian philosophy in maintaining a spiritual gulf between Germanics and Jews. He praised the "unworldly, speculative, ideal tendency of mind" that had "received monumental expression in the nineteenth century in Schopenhauer's doctrine of the negation of the will to live." He noted: "The will is here in a way directed inwardly. This is quite different in the case of the Jew. His will at all times took an outward direction; it was the unconditional will to live." Chamberlain further argued that in opposition to the "Aryan negation of the will," the Jews displayed the "enormous predominance of will." He asserted, "For while the Indian taught the negation of the will, and Christ its 'conversion,' religion is for the Semite the idolization of his will, its most glowing, immoderate and fanatical assertion."

Chamberlain used ominous language when he described the battle between Germanics and Jews. He emphasized: "To this day these two powers – Jews and Teutonic races – stand, wherever the recent spread of the Chaos has not blurred their features, now as friendly, now as hostile, but always as alien forces face to face." He warned, "No arguing about 'humanity' can alter the fact that this means a struggle. Where the struggle is not waged with cannon balls, it goes on silently in the heart of society. . . . But this struggle, silent though it be, is above all others a struggle for life and death."[28] Chamberlain, the leading *völkisch* theorist around the turn of the nineteenth and twentieth centuries, thus believed that an unbridgeable chasm divided will-denying Germans from will-affirming Jews.

While German far rightists who drew inspiration from the ideas of Chamberlain, Schopenhauer, and Wagner possessed a coherent *völkisch* ideology that asserted German racial and spiritual superiority over the materialistic Jews through the German ability to negate the will to live, the Imperial German *völkisch* right could not establish a politically successful

---

[28] Chamberlain, *Foundations of the Nineteenth Century*, vols. I and II, trans. John Lees (New York: Howard Fertig, 1968), vol. I, 213, 214, 226, 246, 256, 257, 419, 507, 578; vol. II, 43, 259.

movement. After the founding of the German Empire in 1871, Chancellor Otto von Bismarck focused on a "domestic preventive war" against what he perceived as dangerous internal enemies: not Jews, but Catholics, in what became known as the *Kulturkampf* (Culture Struggle).[29] The modest acme of anti-Semitic *völkisch* political success in Imperial Germany arrived in the early 1890s. In 1892, the Conservative Party adopted the Tivoli Program, which asserted: "We combat the widely obtruding and decomposing Jewish influence on our popular life." Ardent anti-Semitic parties won 2.9 percent of the parliamentary vote in 1893. After this slight victory, however, German political parties specifically devoted to anti-Semitism declined to insignificance.[30]

The most noteworthy twentieth-century Imperial German *völkisch* manifestation began when Heinrich Class gave the then little-known Alldeutscher Verband (Pan-German League) with approximately 14,000 members a pronounced anti-Semitic character when he became chairman in February 1908.[31] Class had familiarized himself with the racist ideas of Count Arthur de Gobineau and Houston Stewart Chamberlain. He honored both thinkers as "great men." As the leader of the Pan-German League, he required the regional branches of the organization to acquaint themselves with Gobineau's work on the inequality of the races and to hold discussion sessions on it.[32] In 1909, Class released a work influenced by Chamberlain that he intended to serve as a popular history, *Deutsche Geschichte* (*German History*). He treated what he deemed the heroic struggles of Germanic peoples and also warned of the "Jewish peril."[33] He ultimately received personal praise from Chamberlain himself for his book.[34]

While the "Jewish question" had remained relatively dormant in German politics from 1894 on, it flared up again after the so-called "Jewish elections" of 1912, when the Social Democratic vote rose from 53 to 110 seats in the Reichstag, the German parliament.[35] In response to the elections, Class wrote an anti-Semitic book, *Wenn ich der Kaiser wär'* (*If I Were the Kaiser*), in March and April 1912 under the pseudonym Daniel Frymann.[36] He

[29] David Blackbourn, *Marpingen: Apparitions of the Virgin Mary in a Nineteenth-Century German Village* (New York: Vintage Books, 1993), 85, 86.

[30] Pulzer, *The Rise of Political Anti-Semitism in Germany & Austria*, 112, 114, 119.

[31] Protocol from a meeting of the Alldeutscher Verband leadership on March 2, 1918, BAB, 8048, number 117, 6; Heinrich Class, *Wider den Strom: Vom Werden und Wachsen der nationalen Opposition im alten Reich*, vol. 1 (Leipzig: Koehler, 1932), 33, 88, 128.

[32] Class, *Wider den Strom*, vol. I, 87, 88, 131.

[33] Einhart [Class], *Deutsche Geschichte*, second edn. (Leipzig: Dietrich'schen Verlagsbuchhandlung, 1909), v, 290.

[34] Class, *Wider den Strom*, vol. II, BAK, *Kleine Erwerbung* 499, 331.

[35] Friedländer, *Nazi Germany and the Jews*, 75.

[36] Class, *Wider den Strom*, vol. I, 233.

noted: "Today the entire people is dissatisfied with the way it is governed." After remarking that the Kaiser had expressed admiration of Chamberlain and had expedited the printing of thousands of copies of *Foundations of the Nineteenth Century*, Class asked, "Has the Kaiser read and understood the book? How is it then possible that directly afterwards he became a patron of the Jews . . . ?" Class further called for the rebirth of "German idealism," and he asserted, "The Jews are the upholders and teachers of the materialism that reigns today."

In his *Kaiser* work, Class proposed drastically curtailing Jewish rights. He advocated halting all future Jewish immigration into Germany, expelling all Jews who had not become German citizens, and subjecting remaining Jews in Germany to alien status. All those who had belonged to the Hebraic religion in January 1871 along with the descendents of such people, even if only from one parent, were to be classified as Jews. Jews would be forbidden to serve as civil servants, officers, enlisted men, lawyers, teachers, and theater directors, and they would possess neither the right to vote nor to own land. They would only be allowed to write for "Jewish" newspapers, and they would have to pay twice as many taxes as German citizens. Class concluded his work with the appeal that the National Socialists subsequently stressed: "Germany to the Germans!"[37] Class' *Kaiser* book went through five editions of 5,000 copies each before World War I. Class later lamented, however, that while his work had found many readers and was generally considered "interesting," Germany's political elite had disregarded his anti-Semitic warnings and proposals.[38]

Class' *Kaiser* book was not the only manifestation of increased anti-Semitic activity in Germany in 1912. In February of that year, Ludwig Müller von Hausen, a fervent admirer of Schopenhauer, founded the Verband gegen Überhebung des Judentumes (Association against the Presumption of Jewry) in Berlin.[39] The association's statutes asserted that the organization sought "to waken racial pride, to boost *völkisch* consciousness, and to work against any Jewish presumption." Only Germans of "Aryan descent" could serve as regular members, while certain foreigners could become extraordinary ones.[40]

Hausen sought to gain Class' favor. He soon established that the latter had written the *Kaiser* book that he esteemed, and he joined Class'

[37] Daniel Frymann [Class], *Wenn ich der Kaiser wär' – Politische Wahrheiten und Notwendigkeiten*, fifth edn. (Leipzig: Dietrich'schen Verlagsbuchhandlung, 1914), 3, 32, 35, 74–76, 132, 135.

[38] Class, *Wider den Strom*, vol. I, 236; vol. II, 373, 374.

[39] Letter from Ludwig Müller von Hausen to Maria Groener from June 25, 1920, RGVA (TsKhIDK), *fond* 577, *opis* 1, *delo* 221, 54.

[40] Statutes of the Verband gegen Überhebung des Judentumes, RGVA (TsKhIDK), *fond* 577, *opis* 1, *delo* 6, 1, 4.

Pan-German League. Hausen sought to impress Class with the influence of his Association against the Presumption of Jewry. Hausen wrote Class that while his organization possessed only a few hundred members, they included large landowners, important industrialists, high-ranking governmental officials, and leading officers.[41] Incidentally, the future National Socialist Party secretary, Martin Bormann, joined Hausen's Association in July 1920.[42]

Class and Hausen established a personal relationship that thrived for a while but then deteriorated. They met for the first time in September 1913 in Berlin and then met again in October and November of that year. Class gave Hausen 1,500 marks to support the work of the Association against the Presumption of Jewry, followed by another 1,000 marks later on.[43] Class and Hausen later had a serious falling out, however, in one of the many examples of Class' pronounced weakness at maintaining amicable relations with other important *völkisch* leaders, ultimately including Hitler.[44] Hausen developed derogatory views of Class. He claimed in 1922, "I have never had a high opinion of Class, holding him to be a conceited, cowardly person of very mediocre education."[45]

Despite the efforts of Class and Hausen to alert the Germans to the supposed Jewish peril, anti-Semitism remained much less extreme in Imperial Germany than in France, the Austro-Hungarian Empire, and Imperial Russia on the Eve of World War I.[46] Neither Class' Pan-German League nor Hausen's Association against the Presumption of Jewry gained mass followings. Moreover, after modest successes in the late nineteenth century, the fortunes of German parties specifically devoted to anti-Semitism declined in the prewar period.[47] German *völkisch*-redemptive anti-Semitism did not flourish until after the catastrophic outcome of World War I.

During World War I, Kaiser Wilhelm Hohenzollern II managed to weather national opposition intrigues from the right. The Kaiser surmounted rightist opposition stemming primarily from Heinrich

---

[41] Letters from Hausen to Class from November 11 and December 11, 1912; Hausen's 1912 membership card for the Alldeutscher Verband, Ortsgruppe Berlin, RGVA (TsKhIDK), *fond* 577, *opis* 1, *delo* 218, 3, 5, 218.

[42] Martin Bormann's Verband gegen Überhebung des Judentumes membership card number 1086 from July 7, 1920, RGVA (TsKhIDK), *fond* 577, *opis* 1, *delo* 27, 24.

[43] Letters from Hausen to Class from October 8, 1913 and December 21, 1916; letters from Class to Hausen from October 10 and November 4, 1913, RGVA (TsKhIDK), *fond* 577, *opis* 1, *delo* 218, 17, 19, 22, 86.

[44] Class, essay fragment, 1936, BAK, *Kleine Erwerbung* 499, 12.

[45] Letter from Hausen to K. Duncker from April 21, 1922, RGVA (TsKhIDK), *fond* 577, *opis* 1, *delo* 213, 8.

[46] Friedländer, *Nazi Germany and the Jews*, 81.

[47] Pulzer, *The Rise of Political Anti-Semitism in Germany & Austria*, 119, 292.

Class' Pan-German League and the Deutsche Vaterlandspartei (German Fatherland Party) under Wolfgang Kapp, the Generallandschaftsdirektor (General Countryside Director) of East Prussia.[48] In late August 1917, Kapp invited his close comrade General Count Rüdiger von der Goltz to collaborate in the official formation of the German Fatherland Party.[49] Kapp served as the chairman of the German Fatherland Party, and Goltz acted as the second chairman of the East Prussian branch of the organization.[50] Goltz went on to coordinate an anti-Bolshevik intervention of German/White Russian forces in Latvia in 1919 with Kapp's backing. The German Fatherland Party collected nationalist forces into a powerful behind-the-scenes force. The organization secretly planned to place Admiral Alfred von Tirpitz at the head of a nationalist German government as a "strong man" with Kapp as his advisor.[51]

The *völkisch* leaders Kapp and Class cooperated with one another in their national opposition undertakings. Kapp valued the right-wing activities of Class' Pan-German League. In order to gain support for his own conspiratorial alliance, Kapp asked Class to serve on the German Fatherland Party's Advisory Committee. Class agreed. By this time, membership in Class' Pan-German League had reached 37,000. The *völkisch* theorist Houston Stewart Chamberlain, who had been granted German citizenship in August 1916, played a leading role in the association.[52] Kapp, Class, and Chamberlain collaborated on the editorial staff of a *völkisch* newspaper in 1917: *Deutschlands Erneuerung: Monatsschrift für das deutsche Volk* (*Germany's Renewal: Monthly for the German People*). This publication provided a theoretical underpinning for the German Fatherland Party's bid for power.[53]

In addition to receiving assistance for his nationalist schemes from Class and Chamberlain, Kapp obtained the support of Ludwig Müller von Hausen, the leader of the Association against the Presumption of Jewry, in 1917. Hausen had curtailed his political activities during the first half of World War I before becoming more politically active again in the war's later years. Despite his advanced age, he had served as an artillery captain on both the Eastern and Western Fronts. He had received the Iron Cross,

---

[48] Elisabeth Schwarze, "Einleitung," *Nachlass Wolfgang Kapp* (Berlin: GSAPKB, 1997), VI.

[49] Letter from Wolfgang Kapp to Rüdiger von der Goltz from August 28, 1917, GSAPKB, *Repositur* 92, number 455, 3.

[50] Foundational Protocol of the Deutsche Vaterlandspartei on September 3, 1917, GSAPKB, *Repositur* 92, number 460, 4.

[51] Schwarze, "Einleitung," VII.

[52] Class, *Wider den Strom*, vol. II, 66, 209, 214; protocols of the Alldeutscher Verband meeting in Berlin on June 29 and 30, 1918, RGVA (TsKhIDK), *fond* 577, *opis* 1, *delo* 844, 110.

[53] Erich Kühn, "Werbung für Mitarbeit" (Munich: J. F. Lehmanns Verlag, June 1916), GSAPKB, *Repositur* 92, number 792, 12, 35.

First Class, for his efforts. He had corresponded with General Erich von Ludendorff, the chief of the Army General Staff. In fact, he had served the general in an advisory capacity. In 1917, Hausen worked to increase the membership of Kapp's German Fatherland Party.[54]

Hausen's *völkisch* colleague General Ludendorff played an important role in right-wing intrigues against the Kaiser. Ludendorff was Germany's most valuable military strategist as well as a leading *völkisch* activist who later allied himself closely with Hitler. He supported Kapp's German Fatherland Party. He regarded the organization as a means of strengthening the German will to win the war.[55] He also followed the activities of Class' Pan-German League with great interest. He admired the association's determination to fight on until final victory. Class visited Ludendorff at Army Headquarters in October 1917 with the backing of both his Pan-German League and Kapp's German Fatherland Party. Working in the vein of what he termed "national opposition," Class tried to convince the influential general to seize dictatorial powers.

Class stressed that the Kaiser had long since lost the trust of the people, whereas the Army High Command enjoyed widespread popular support. Ludendorff should therefore inaugurate a military dictatorship to see the German people through to victory. Ludendorff replied that this plan was not realistic, since he was fully occupied with directing military affairs and could not run the country politically as well. Class and Kapp's collaboration deteriorated in the face of this setback. Frictions developed between them. Kapp jettisoned the Advisory Committee of the German Fatherland Party in which Class played a prominent role at the end of 1917.[56] The Kaiser was spared removal in a putsch from the right and instead fled to the Netherlands under the pressure of revolution from the left in November 1918.

RUSSIAN CONSERVATIVE REVOLUTIONARIES UP TO THE BOLSHEVIK REVOLUTION

In a manner similar to anti-Semitic *völkisch* German theorists who argued that the Germans possessed the heroic capability to achieve redemption by

---

[54] Letter from Hausen to Kapp from October 17, 1917, RGVA (TsKhIDK), *fond* 577, *opis* 1, *delo* 219, 2; letter from Hausen to the RA/ZSS from March 23, 1923, RGVA (TsKhIDK), *fond* 577, *opis* 1, *delo* 2, 2–4; Hausen's note on a letter from E. Rumpler Luftfahrzeugbau from August 25, 1914, RGVA (TsKhIDK), *fond* 577, *opis* 1, *delo* 1, 2.

[55] Walther Nicolai, *Tagebuch* (Diary), August 17, 1917, RGVA (TsKhIDK), *fond* 1414, *opis* 1, *delo* 15, 12.

[56] Class, *Wider den Strom*, vol. I, 22; vol. II, 226, 233, 234, 237.

denying the will to live, Imperial Russian conservative revolutionaries used concepts of superior Russian or Slavic spirituality to further their anti-Western, anti-socialist, and anti-Semitic arguments. Russian far rightists also propagated apocalyptic notions of Europe's imminent demise largely through the agency of the Jews. Many conservative revolutionaries associated the Jews with the Antichrist, the foe of Jesus who is written of in the biblical Book of Revelation.

While they failed to reshape Imperial Russian society according to their desires, Imperial Russian far rightists nonetheless managed to transcend mere theoretical musings to achieve a concrete political dimension superior to that of their German counterparts. Russian conservative revolutionaries better implemented their ideas in the political sphere than politically weak *völkisch* leaders in Germany. Imperial Russian revolutionary nationalists urged the Russian Empire to lead the entire Slavic world in launching a determined political action to escape allegedly decadent Europe's imminent demise.

The author and journalist Fedor Dostoevskii crystallized conservative revolutionary ideology in Imperial Russia much like Wagner shaped *völkisch* views in Germany. Like Wagner, Dostoevskii failed at socialist revolutionary undertakings in his youth. He was even sentenced to death before receiving a last-minute reprieve. He subsequently refocused his energies into joining those whom he termed "revolutionaries . . . out of conservatism."[57] Dostoevskii's intellectual development resembled that of one of his greatest literary creations, Rodion Raskolnikov, the protagonist of *Crime and Punishment*. Raskolnikov commits a brutal double homicide in pursuit of utopian revolutionary ideals before ultimately embracing Orthodox Christianity with its emphasis on the redemptive powers of suffering.

While he is best known for his psychologically insightful novels, Dostoevskii expressed his ideological views most clearly in his *Diary of a Writer*, which he published in 1873, 1876, 1877, 1880, and January 1881 immediately before his death.[58] As we will see in Chapter Eight, this work greatly influenced White émigré views. Dostoevskii supported the altar and the throne in *Diary of a Writer*. He argued that the Russians possessed "two awful strengths," namely their "spiritual indivisibility" and their "closest unity with the monarch." He placed the "idea of the Russian people"

---

[57] Fedor Dostoevskii, *Dnevnik pisatelia, Polnoe sobranie sochinenii F. M. Dostoevskago*, vol. X (Saint Petersburg: A. F. Marks, 1895), 221.
[58] Dostoevskii, *Tagebuch eines Schriftstellers*, trans. E. K. Rahsin (Munich: Piper, 1992), 641.

squarely within Orthodox Christianity.[59] Here he clearly demonstrated the conservative aspect of his conservative revolutionary outlook.

Dostoevskii described himself as a member of the particularly fervent wing of Slavophilism that believed: "Our great Russia, at the head of the united Slavs, will speak its own new, wholesome, and as yet unheard of word . . . to the entire world." His Slavophile beliefs contained strong apocalyptic overtones. Writing in January 1877, he stressed that the time had arrived for something "eternal, millenary." He heralded the approach of a final confrontation between the "Catholic idea," meant in political as well as religious terms, its opponent Protestantism, an "only negative" belief, and "the third world idea, the Slavic idea, an idea coming into being." He noted that the resolution of these great world-views could not be submitted to "petty, Judaizing, third-rate considerations." He remained vague on what the "Slavic idea" represented in this passage. In an earlier section of *Diary of a Writer*, however, he wrote of "our world purpose" to become the "servants of all, for universal reconciliation" to bring about the "final unification of humanity."[60]

Dostoevskii exhibited pronounced anti-Semitic beliefs, which he expressed most clearly in Chapter Two of the March 1877 section of *Diary of a Writer*, "The Jewish Question." He blamed the Jews for perennially form-ing a "*status in statu*" (state within the state). He accused them of exhibiting "estrangement and alienation." He blamed them for believing, "Only one true people exists on the earth, the Jewish one, and . . . although there are others, it is nevertheless necessary to regard them as non-existent." He lamented that Jews controlled the stock market, capital, credit, and interna-tional politics. He warned of them: "Their kingdom is approaching, their entire kingdom! The triumph of ideas is coming before which feelings of philanthropy, thirst for the truth, Christian feelings, national and even folk pride of the European peoples will flag" in the face of "materialism, the blind, lustful craving for personal material security."

While Dostoevskii attributed a salvational role to the Russian people at the head of the united Slavs, he apocalyptically foretold Europe's imminent demise, largely because of Jewish machinations. Writing in August 1877, he stressed that "Europe" faced a "general, common, and terrible fall." He prophesied: "All these parliamentarisms, all currently prevailing civil theories, all accumulated riches, banks, sciences, Jews, all of these will

---

[59] Dostoevskii, *Dnevnik pisatelia*, vol. X, 440; vol. XI, 8.
[60] Dostoevskii, *Dnevnik pisatelia*, vol. X, 225, 226; vol. XI, 5, 6, 8, 240, 241.

tumble down in an instant without leaving a trace, except perhaps the Jews, who even then will not be at a loss to profit from the situation." He claimed that this collapse stood "'near, in the doorway,'" referring to Revelation 3:20, a passage of the last book of the Bible that foretells the destruction of the sinful world in great upheaval and chaos, after which the Kingdom of God will appear on earth.[61]

In the vein of Dostoevskii, many Imperial Russian far rightists around the turn of the nineteenth and twentieth centuries believed that the Kingdom of God would only come after the destruction of Western civilization.[62] Most notably, the author Vladimir Solovev treated this theme in 1900 by releasing "A Short Tale of the Anti-Christ" as part of his *Three Conversations*. He dealt with the "man of the future," the Anti-Christ, in order "to reveal in advance the deceptive mask behind which the abyss of evil is hiding." In Solovev's tale, the Anti-Christ gains power with the help of Freemasons and the Comité permanent universel (Standing Universal Committee). This conspiratorial organization could easily be interpreted in an anti-Semitic manner as the Alliance israélite universelle (Universal Jewish Alliance).[63]

Solovev's Anti-Christ story deeply impressed Sergei Nilus, who became famous for disseminating the infamous anti-Semitic forgery *The Protocols of the Elders of Zion*. Nilus regarded Solovev's story as a prophetic warning, and he related it to contemporary political conditions in the Russian Empire.[64] He rejected modern Western civilization and regarded Jews and Freemasons as the forerunners of the Anti-Christ.[65] He anticipated the Anti-Christ's imminent arrival and the destruction of Western civilization, after which the Kingdom of God would appear.[66] The Imperial Russian radical right in general tended to view the Orthodox Christian struggle against Jewry and Freemasonry as the final battle between Christ and Anti-Christ along the

---

[61] Dostoevskii, *Dnevnik pisatelia*, vol. XI, 94, 98, 114, 495.

[62] Otto-Ernst Schüddekopf, *Linke Leute von rechts: Die nationalrevolutionären Minderheiten und der Kommunismus in der Weimarer Republik* (Stuttgart: W. Kohlhammer Verlag, 1960), 33.

[63] Michael Hagemeister, "Vladimir Solov'ëv: Reconciler and Polemicist," *Eastern Christian Studies 2: Selected Papers of the International Vladimir Solov'ëv Conference held at the University of Nijmegen, the Netherlands, in September 1998* (Leuven: Peeters, 2000), 287, 289, 290.

[64] S. A. Stepanov, *Chernaia Sotnia v Rossii 1905–1914* (Moscow: Izdatelstvo Vsesoiuznogo zaochnogo politekhnicheskogo instituta, 1992), 28; Hagemeister, "Vladimir Solov'ëv," 288.

[65] Hagemeister, "Die 'Protokolle der Weisen von Zion' und der Basler Zionistenkongress von 1897," *Der Traum von Israel: Die Ursprünge des modernen Zionismus*, ed. Heiko Haumann (Weinheim: Beltz Athenäum Verlag, 1998), 257.

[66] James Webb, *The Occult Establishment* (La Salle, IL: Open Court, 1976), 260; Schüddekopf, *Linke Leute von rechts*, 33.

lines of the last book of the Bible, Revelation.[67] Apocalyptic anti-Semitism formed an integral component of the Imperial Russian far right.

On a more practical level, Imperial Russian far rightists drew material for their anti-Semitic arguments from the societal segregation of the Russian Empire's 5,215,800 Jews (as of 1897) from Gentiles.[68] Whereas large numbers of Jews in Germany desired to assimilate into German society, Russian Jews as a whole maintained their own distinct culture, religion, and literary language. Largely because of restrictive laws, as of the 1880s, only 0.7 percent of Russian Jews worked in agriculture, while 38.7 percent participated in commerce.[69] Jews often faced harsh conditions in the Russian Empire. Large-scale anti-Semitic pogroms erupted in 1871, and the Imperial Russian government expelled many Jews in 1881.[70]

Jews, who composed approximately 4 percent of the population in the Russian Empire overall but 12 percent in the Pale of Settlement where they were concentrated, participated disproportionately in revolutionary activities. In some areas of the Pale of Settlement during the period from 1901 to 1904, the proportion of political prisoners who were Jewish reached nearly $\frac{2}{3}$. The figure was 48.2 percent in the Kiev region, and in the Odessa district the ratio of Jewish political prisoners reached 55 percent. From 1892 to 1902, Jews made up 23.4 percent of the members of the Social Democrats. At the time of the 1905 Revolution, Jews constituted 18.9 percent of the membership of the Bolsheviks, the "majority" faction of the Social Democrats.[71]

Concerned with the rising number of Jewish (and Gentile) revolutionaries in Imperial Russia, a group of writers and publicists under the leadership of Prince D. P. Golitsyn founded the Russkoe Sobranie (Russian Assembly) in January 1901. Other leaders of the right-wing organization included Vladimir Purishkevich, an official in the Interior Ministry, and Prince Mikhail Volkonskii, an author. The Russian Assembly warned of the "danger" of the "cosmopolitanism of the upper levels of our society," and it sought to uphold "Orthodoxy, autocracy, and national character." The association's statutes urged members to conduct the "study of the phenomenon of Russian and Slavic folk life in its present and past" with the

[67] D. I. Raskin, "Ideologiia russkogo pravogo radikalizma v kontse XIX nachale XX vv," *Natsionalnaia pravaia prezhde i teper, Istoriko-sotsiologicheskie ocherki, chast 1: Rossiia i russkoe zarubezhe* (Saint Petersburg: Institut Sotsiologii rossiiskoi akademii nauk, 1992), 39.

[68] Stepanov, *Chernaia Sotnia v Rossii 1905–1914*, 23.

[69] Mosse, *German Jews Beyond Judaism* (Bloomington: Indiana University Press, 1985), 6; Stepanov, *Chernaia Sotnia v Rossii*, 25, 26.

[70] Hannaford, *Race*, 318.

[71] Stepanov, *Chernaia Sotnia v Rossii*, 23, 27.

special task of "safeguarding . . . the purity and correctness of Russian speech." The Russian Assembly thus cast itself as a defender of imperiled Russian values.

The Russian Assembly distinctly represented upper-class interests. The great majority of the organization's members came from the nobility, and the association received the explicit support of Tsar Nikolai Romanov II. The Russian Assembly adopted a rather exclusivist membership policy. The Assembly had approximately 120 members at first, though the number of members increased significantly thereafter. The outbreak of the 1905 Revolution soon demonstrated the need for greater mass support of right-wing endeavors.

In October 1905, in the midst of socialist revolutionary upheaval, members of the Russian Assembly gathered like-minded conservative reformers in Saint Petersburg to form a new right-wing organization. The small assembly elected Aleksandr Dubrovin, a Saint Petersburg physician and a leading figure in the Russian Assembly, to lead the new organization, the Soiuz russkago naroda (Union of the Russian People). Dubrovin possessed a strong will and a coarse personality. His associate Purishkevich, the second man in the Union who also played a leading role in the Russian Assembly, exhibited a far more refined demeanor. He came from a noble landed family, had graduated with honors from the Historical-Philological Department of Novorossiisk University, and possessed formidable speaking abilities.[72]

Early anti-Semitic Union ideology drew from the Slavophile legacy in the vein of Dostoevskii to protest against the increasing westernization of Russian society, and it also exhibited racist tendencies. The Union opposed liberal bourgeois sentiments and idealized the old order that had existed up until the time of the westernizer Tsar Peter the Great, who had ruled Imperial Russia from 1689 to 1725.[73] The goals of the Union resembled those of its parent organization the Russian Assembly. The Union statutes stressed that the organization worked for the "preservation of Orthodoxy, absolute Russian autocracy, and national character." The Union statutes further demonstrated racist thinking similar to that of *völkisch* German thought. The statutes stipulated that only "born Russian people" could join the Union, with "Great Russians," "Belorussians," and "Little Russians" (Ukrainians) all considered "Russians." Jews, on the other hand, could not enter the Union "even in the case that they adopt Christianity."[74]

---

[72] Stepanov, *Chernaia Sotnia v Rossii*, 32, 33, 90, 91, 110; *Spisok chlenov Russkogo Sobraniia s prilozheniem istoricheskogo ocherky sobraniia* (Saint Petersburg: Tip. Spb. Gradonachalstva, 1906), 1, 21, 27, 55.
[73] Raskin, "Ideologiia russkogo pravogo radikalizma," 5.
[74] "Ustav Obschestva pod nazvaniem 'Soiuz Russkago Naroda,'" GARF, *fond* 116, *opis* 1, *delo* 6, 14–17.

The Union established conservative revolutionary squads popularly known as "Black Hundreds." These fearsome groups gave their name to the Russian far right from 1905 to 1917. Black Hundreds carried out anti-revolutionary pogroms in October 1905 in which they killed a total of 1,622 people, 711 of whom were Jews. The pogroms of October 1905 proved the worst manifestation of Black Hundred violence.[75]

Despite the Union's use of illegal Black Hundred squads to terrorize and assassinate Jewish and socialist opponents, Imperial authorities supported the Union. Piotr Rachkovskii, the head of the Okhrana (Tsarist Secret Police) abroad, supported the Union's activities.[76] He even acted as Union leader Dubrovin's advisor.[77] Representatives of the Union received even greater official recognition when they met with Tsar Nikolai Romanov II in December 1905. The Tsar assured them: "I am counting on you."[78]

Mikhail Kommissarov, a prominent member of the Saint Petersburg Okhrana, provided the Union with additional support. Kommissarov proved a most colorful adventurer who underwent many permutations in his career of intrigue and deceit. He ultimately helped to establish Aufbau, the Munich-based *völkisch* German/White émigré organization that greatly influenced the National Socialist movement, in 1920 as a double agent before he openly joined the Soviet cause. After the outbreak of socialist revolution in the Russian Empire in 1905, he established a clandestine printing press in the basement of Okhrana headquarters. He used this press to print anti-Semitic leaflets calling for pogroms. He lost his position because of his unauthorized dissemination of pogrom literature, but his writings galvanized Black Hundred violence against Jews and socialist revolutionaries.[79]

At the time of elections for the first Duma (Parliament) in 1906, intense anti-Semitism and fear of popular unrest marked Union ideology. An early Union campaign poster urged voters to elect the

best Russian people. . . . in order that the Orthodox faith is not trampled upon in Russia, in order that Russia is for the Russians, in order that non-Russians, Jews and Jewified traitor-plotters do not seize power and enslave the Russian people,

---

[75] Stepanov, *Chernaia Sotnia v Rossii*, 57, 142.

[76] Abraham Ascher, *The Revolution of 1905: Russia in Disarray* (Stanford: Stanford University Press, 1988), 238–242.

[77] Rafael Ganelin, "Chernosotennye organizatsii, politicheskaia politsiia i gosudarstvennaia vlast v tsarskoi Rossii," *Natsionalnaia pravaia*, 78.

[78] Vladimir Purishkevich, "Izbiratelnaia programma Soiuza Russkago Naroda, Russkomu Narodu," *Russkoe Znamia*, September 19, 1906, 2.

[79] RKÜöO report from January 29, 1923, RGVA (TsKhIDK), *fond* 772, *opis* 3, *delo* 539, 33; LGPO report to the RKÜöO from August 8, 1921, RGVA (TsKhIDK), *fond* 772, *opis* 3, *delo* 539, 17.

and in order that the volition of the autocratic Tsar does not become lower than the decisions of various parties in the State Duma and does not become distorted by careless and mercenary bureaucrats.[80]

Virulent anti-Semitism found a central place in the Union election platform that Purishkevich, a prominent Union member and an official in the Interior Ministry, drew up in 1906. Purishkevich dedicated the longest section of the text to the "Jewish question," the "fateful question for all civilized peoples alike." The document accused the Jews of manifesting "unbelievable misanthropy" and "irreconcilable hatred of Russia and everything Russian." The election platform further claimed that the "revolutionary movement in Russia" represented "business almost exclusively in the hands of Jews."

The Imperial Russian government already greatly limited Jews' rights, forbidding them from governmental service, for instance, and severely restricting where they could live. Purishkevich went further. In his election platform, he called for all Jews residing within Imperial Russian borders to be "deemed foreigners immediately, but without the rights and privileges granted to all other foreigners." This would mean that Jews could not serve in the armed forces or in the civil service, would be subject to even stricter residency regulations, would be forbidden to attend institutions of learning with Gentiles, and would be excluded from several professions, notably those in the fields of medicine and the press. Russian trade and industry were to be taken from the hands of "foreigners and Jews."[81] Purishkevich's anti-Semitic election platform helped him to become elected to the Duma as a representative from Bessarabia.[82] He went on to serve in the second, third, and fourth Dumas.[83]

Black Hundred parties including the Union of the Russian People received 6.1 percent of the vote in the first Duma elections of 1906. These electoral results proved considerably more impressive than those of any comparable *völkisch* groupings in Germany, but they were much less than anticipated. Black Hundred organizations achieved their best electoral results in the Pale of Settlement where the Jewish population was the greatest. They faired more poorly in the Great Russian heartland. Nonetheless, the Union in particular influenced the Imperial Russian government beyond what its modest electoral standing suggested.

---

[80] "Obedinennyi russkii narod," GARF, *fond* 116, *opis* 1, *delo* 1, 14.
[81] Purishkevich, "Izbiratelnaia programma Soiuza Russkago Naroda," 2, 3.
[82] MG report to the QB/SO from January 12, 1919, RGVA (TsKhIDK), *fond* 198, *opis* 17, *delo* 484, reel 1, 24.
[83] Ganelin, "Chernosotennye organizatsii," 87.

The Union of the Russian People grew rapidly. It soon overshadowed all other more elitist Black Hundred organizations such as its parent organization, the Russian Assembly, and the Monarchical Party. The Union appealed to a wide population base since members of the intelligentsia played the leading roles in the organization. Of the forty-seven members of the Union's Head Council, only fifteen belonged to the nobility. The Union also included substantial contingents of farmers and workers. The Union established local divisions in every major Imperial Russian city and in the countryside as well. It comprised over 900 branches throughout Imperial Russia by April 1907. Membership in the Union peaked in the first half of 1908 at over 100,000 of the approximately 400,000 members of all Black Hundred organizations.[84]

The Union propagated its anti-Semitic far right views through its newspaper, *Russkoe Znamia* (*The Russian Banner*). The Union leader Dubrovin edited the paper. *The Russian Banner* had approximately 14,500 readers, including the Tsar.[85] A July 1907 article, "The 'Peaceful' Conquest of Russia," argued that Zionism was an "illusion." In reality, Imperial Russia's Jews intended to create their own state "in Russia itself." The piece warned that in less than a decade, the country would only appear to be Russian, while "as a matter of fact, the state will be Jewish." Jews would rule as "masters" whereas Russians would serve as the Jews' "labor force," would suppress internal discord, meaning "the remnants of Russian national consciousness," and would protect the borders of the "Jewish state" from foreign enemies.[86]

Largely because of internal strife, the Union of the Russian People failed to spread its warnings of an insidious Jewish conspiracy to the degree it desired. In the fall of 1907, the talented Union leader Purishkevich vehemently criticized Dubrovin's authoritarianism and left the Union. He grouped together others dissatisfied with Dubrovin's leadership and formed the Russkii narodnyi soiuz imeni Mikhaila Arkhangela (Michael the Archangel Russian People's Union). The new organization's March 1908 statutes approved of the Duma, but noted: "In all other respects, the program of the Michael the Archangel Russian People's Union concurs with the program of the Union of the Russian People." With the split of the Union of the Russian People, the Black Hundred movement in the Russian Empire entered a period of decline.

[84] Stepanov, *Chernaia Sotnia v Rossii*, 93, 95, 105, 109, 111, 112, 123, 167; LGPO report to the RKÜöO from November 28, 1921, RGVA (TsKhIDK), *fond* 772, *opis* 1, *delo* 96, 46, 47.

[85] Stepanov, *Chernaia Sotnia v Rossii*, 104, 266.

[86] Andrei Chernyi, "'Mirnoe' zavoevanie Rossii," *Russkoe Znamia*, July 19, 1907, 2.

Black Hundred fortunes only briefly improved beginning in March 1911, when a twelve-year-old boy was butchered in Kiev and the belief spread among the populace that Jews had killed him as part of a ritual. A member of the Union of the Russian People in Kiev wrote an appeal that appeared throughout the city: "Russian People! If you value your children, then kill the Yids! Kill them until there is not even a single Yid in Russia!" In April 1911, Purishkevich and Nikolai Markov II, the influential leader of the Kursk branch of the Union of the Russian People, argued before the Duma that Jews had murdered the boy in Kiev as part of a demonic ritual.[87] An article in a July 1911 edition of the Union newspaper *The Russian Banner* warned, "Our poor dear children, fear and be afraid of your primordial enemy, tormenter and infanticide, accursed of God and man – the Yid!" The article further admonished Russian children to avoid "the Yid" as if he were a "plague-stricken pest."[88]

A front-page article in an August 1913 edition of *The Russian Banner* asserted: "The guilt of the Kiev Jewish Kahal in this matter is established," no matter what verdict the court would pronounce in the ritual murder case (the accused were found not guilty). Moreover, Jewry deserved to be "expelled from Russia to a country where the use of human blood is not considered a crime." The article argued that the Russian government had to adopt severe measures against this "accursed people," the Jews. The piece stressed, "The Yids must be placed artificially in conditions such that they continually die out."[89] The Union thus served as the first European political group seriously to propose physically exterminating Jews.

While the public uproar over the supposed Jewish ritual murder in Kiev aided the far right's cause in Imperial Russia, a new split weakened the Black Hundred movement in 1911. At the All-Russian Congress of the Union of the Russian People in Moscow in November 1911, Markov II challenged Union leader Dubrovin's authority. Other members of the Union's Head Council backed Markov II, and he received the outside support of Purishkevich, who had already left the Union. Dubrovin reacted by dismissing the offending members from the Union's Head Council and reconstituting it with reliable supporters.[90] In August 1912, Dubrovin renamed the organization the Vserossiiskogo Dubrinskogo soiuza russkoga naroda (All-Russian Dubrovin Union of the Russian People) with himself as lifetime leader.

---

[87] Stepanov, *Chernaia Sotnia v Rossii*, 168, 174, 175, 266, 270.
[88] U. Soiuznik, "Russkim detiam," *Russkoe Znamia*, July 7, 1911, 2.
[89] "Istoriia ubiistva Iuschinskago," *Russkoe Znamia*, August 9, 1913, 1.
[90] Aleksandr Dubrovin, "Gorechovskomu Otdelu Soiuza russkago Naroda," March 1912, GARF, *fond* 116, *opis* 1, *delo* 1, 32.

Markov II formed another faction of the Union of the Russian People in November 1912.[91]

Dubrovin struggled to maintain his authority in far right Russian circles. Two close colleagues and friends, Aleksandr Bork, who belonged to the Union's Head Council, and his wife Elsa Shabelskii-Bork, who regularly attended Head Council meetings in an advisory capacity, aided him in his efforts to maintain control of the Union. The couple submitted articles to *The Russian Banner* in accordance with Dubrovin's wishes.[92] The pair also began publishing a newspaper, *Svoboda i poriadok* (*Freedom and Order*), with police money in December 1913.[93] The Tsar himself avidly read this paper.[94]

In his opening editorial from December 1913, Bork struck an apocalyptic tone. He quoted from *Revelation* 3:16 in castigating "superficial servants of Christ's church" who were "neither cold nor hot." He further warned that "dark forces" were leading humanity to "ruin." He called for struggle against "Jewish Freemasonry," which was preparing a "violent . . . anti-Christian revolution" in Imperial Russia along the lines of those that had "already succeeded in so many countries."[95] Bork thus viewed Jewry as an apocalyptic force bent on destruction.

In the Russian Empire on the outbreak of World War I, anti-Semitism was relatively widespread, but the Black Hundred movement remained in a disorganized state. As war with Germany loomed, the predominantly pro-German attitude of the Black Hundred movement exacerbated its political weakness. Union of the Russian People leadership tended quite early towards a pro-German stance, largely because of Imperial Russia's continuing rivalry with Great Britain in Central Asia.[96] In May 1914, the Union faction leader Nikolai Markov II asserted in the Russian Duma that a "small alliance with Germany" was superior to a "great friendship with England."[97] The majority of rightist monarchists in Imperial Russia favored a German–Russian alliance along the lines that Markov II proposed.[98]

[91] Stepanov, *Chernaia Sotnia v Rossii*, 192.
[92] Stepanov, *Chernaia Sotnia v Rossii*, 189; letters from Aleksandr Bork and E. A. Shabelskii-Bork to Dubrovin from September 3, 1903, and in the period from 1905 to 1910, GARF, *fond* 116, *opis* 1, *delo* 807, 1, 2, 14, 18, 34.
[93] Ganelin, "Rossiiskoe chernosotenstvo i germanskii natsional-sotsializm," *Natsionalnaia pravaia*, 142.
[94] Piotr Shabelskii-Bork, "Über Mein Leben," March 1926, GSAPKB, *Repositur* 84a, number 14953, 91.
[95] Bork, editorial, *Svoboda i poriadok*, December 1, 1913, 1.
[96] Hans Rogger and Eugen Weber, *The European Right: A Historical Profile* (Berkeley: University of California Press, 1965), 495.
[97] Stepanov, *Chernaia Sotnia v Rossii*, 322.
[98] LGPO report to the RKÜöO from December 24, 1921, RGVA (TsKhIDK), *fond* 772, *opis* 1, *delo* 96, 56.

The generally positive attitude towards the German Empire in the Black Hundred movement also applied to the Baltic German population of the Russian Empire. While Union of the Russian People ideology generally disapproved of minority nationalities in Imperial Russia, Baltic Germans proved an exception. In fact, Baltic Germans generally enjoyed a favorable reputation in the Russian radical right. Point 17 of the statutes of Purishkevich's Michael the Archangel Russian People's Union expressed "particular trust in the German population of the Empire." This point had to be removed after the outbreak of World War I, but a generally pro-Baltic German attitude remained among members of the Imperial Russian far right.[99]

The activities and views of right-wing Baltic German subjects of the Russian Empire deserve greater attention than they have received because of the key role that some Baltic Germans subsequently played in the National Socialist movement. The Rubonia Fraternity at the Riga Polytechnic Institute (named after the Rubon, the Roman term for the Duna River that flows through Riga) spurred Baltic German pride. The majority of the Rubonia Fraternity members came from upper-class Baltic German families in the Russian Baltic provinces.[100] Four members of the Rubonia Fraternity eventually immigrated to Germany and played important roles in Aufbau and the National Socialist Party: Max von Scheubner-Richter, Otto von Kursell, Arno Schickedanz, and Alfred Rosenberg.

Scheubner-Richter was born Richter in Riga in 1884 to an Imperial German father and a Baltic German mother. He received his double name in the course of a love affair with Mathilde von Scheubner, the noble wife of a prominent member of Riga society. He absconded from Riga to Munich with Mathilde, who was almost thirty years his senior, and married her in 1911. A relative of Richter's wife adopted him and granted him her noble name von Scheubner in 1912, entitling him to the name von Scheubner-Richter.[101]

While he was still known as Richter, Scheubner-Richter became friends with Kursell, who had been born into a noble Estonian Baltic Germany family in Saint Petersburg in 1884.[102] Scheubner-Richter and Kursell had

99 Stepanov, *Chernaia Sotnia v Rossii*, 22, 323.
100 Woldemar Helb, *Album Rubonorum, 1875–1972*, fourth edn. (Neustadt an der Aisch: Verlag Degener & Co., 1972), 7.
101 Helb, *Album Rubonorum*, 148; Karsten Brüggemann, "Max Erwin von Scheubner-Richter (1884–1923) – der 'Führer der Führers'?" *Deutschbalten, Weimarer Republik und Drittes Reich*, ed. Michael Garleff (Köln: Böhlau Verlag, 2001), 124; Boehm, "Baltische Einflüsse auf die Anfänge des Nationalsozialismus," *Jahrbuch des baltischen Deutschtums*, 1967, 59.
102 RKÜöO report from May 7, 1925, RGVA (TsKhIDK), *fond* 772, *opis* 4, *delo* 52, 145.

first met at the Petri High School in Reval, in what became Estonia. The two Baltic Germans began studying together at the Riga Polytechnic Institute as members of the Rubonia Fraternity in 1905. Scheubner-Richter specialized in chemistry and Kursell studied architecture. Kursell valued Scheubner-Richter as a "popular, cheerful comrade" who held a variety of leadership positions in the Rubonia Fraternity.[103] Kursell was himself a charismatic person and, like Scheubner-Richter, a ladies' man.[104]

While he was legally considered a subject of Imperial Germany, Scheubner-Richter spoke fluent Russian from his early Russian school-ing, and he regarded himself as a Baltic German since he had spent his entire youth in the Imperial Russian Baltic ports Riga and Reval and had risked his life for Baltic German interests in 1905. During the Revolution of 1905, nationalist Latvians and Estonians had joined forces with socialist rev-olutionaries to overthrow Baltic German landowners who held the leading societal role in the Baltic provinces. Scheubner-Richter had been shot in the knee while serving in the Baltic German Selbstschutz (Self-Protection) forces that had combated this anti-Baltic German alliance.[105]

The two other Rubonia Fraternity members who went on to play impor-tant roles in Aufbau and the National Socialist movement, Rosenberg and Schickedanz, entered Rubonia in 1910 and studied there together until 1917. Rosenberg had been born in 1893 in Reval to merchant Baltic German parents. His colleague Schickedanz had been born into a Riga merchant family in 1893. Rosenberg majored in architecture and Schickedanz studied chemistry.[106] Rosenberg admired *völkisch* ideology. As a young man, he read Germanic mythology, Schopenhauer, and Houston Stewart Chamberlain. He characterized the last as "the strongest positive influence in my youth." Russian literature also strongly affected him, most notably the works of Dostoevskii.[107] Rosenberg later helped to shape National Socialist ideology by synthesizing *völkisch* German ideas with White émigré views.

Unlike the Rubonia Fraternity members Scheubner-Richter, Kursell, Schickedanz, and Rosenberg, a man of noble Baltic German ancestry who went on to influence the National Socialist movement, Fedor Vinberg,

---

[103] Otto von Kursell, "Dr. Ing. Max Erwin von Scheubner-Richter zum Gedächtnis," ed. Henrik Fischer (Munich, 1969), 1; Helb, *Album Rubonorum*, 141, 148.

[104] Julia Hass (Otto von Kursell's daughter), personal interview, January 21, 2003.

[105] Aleksandr von Lampe, *Dnevnik* (Diary), Berlin, November 21, 1923, GARF, *fond* 5853, *opis* 1, *delo* 13, reel 2, 5860; Kursell, "Dr. Ing. Max Erwin von Scheubner-Richter zum Gedächtnis," 3, 9.

[106] Helb, *Album Rubonorum*, 164, 165.

[107] Robert Cecil, *The Myth of the Master Race: Alfred Rosenberg and Nazi Ideology* (London: B. T. Batsford Ltd., 1972), 12, 14, 17.

regarded himself unequivocally as a Russian.[108] Vinberg grew up in Saint Petersburg as the son of a general who eventually served as a member of the Highest Russian Military Council. He studied at the Classical Gymnasium in Kiev in his youth and subsequently joined the army, reaching the rank of colonel in 1913.

Vinberg attained a high status in Imperial Russia. In 1913, the Tsar named him to serve as his court equerry, meaning that he frequently participated in important ceremonies at the Tsar's court. With the outbreak of World War I, Colonel Vinberg was assigned command of an infantry regiment. He used his connections to receive an audience with Tsaritsa Aleksandra Romanov, with whom he developed an intense personal relationship if not an outright affair. He pleaded to be allowed to serve in a cavalry regiment. The Tsaritsa saw to it that he received a position in the staff headquarters of the Second Russian Army as he desired.[109]

Vinberg participated in the Black Hundred movement. He belonged to Purishkevich's Michael the Archangel Russian People's Union. Purishkevich "especially impressed" Vinberg early on, though they became somewhat alienated from each other as World War I progressed.[110] After the Tsar's abdication during the February Revolution of 1917, Vinberg refused to serve the Provisional Government under Aleksandr Kerenskii. Kerenskii's regime suppressed Black Hundred organizations before any other political groupings. In May 1917, Vinberg launched a counter-revolutionary initiative by founding a secret alliance, Officer's Duty, which included both members of the officer corps and a few hundred men from outside it.[111] Vinberg remained a staunch supporter of the monarchy in the face of revolutionary upheaval.

Counter-revolutionary activities in which Vinberg participated during the period of Kerenskii's Provisional Government culminated in the unsuccessful Kornilov Putsch of August 27–30, 1917 under the leadership of General Lavr Kornilov. Vinberg and members of his conspiratorial Officer's Duty organization took part in this undertaking.[112] Lieutenant Piotr

---

[108] Ganelin, "Rossiiskoe chernosotenstvo i germanskii natsional-sotsializm," 139.

[109] Fedor Vinberg's testimony included in a PDM report to the BSMI from March 30, 1922, BHSAM, BSMI 22, number 71624, fiche 3, 92, 93.

[110] Vinberg, *Der Kreuzesweg Russlands: Teil I: Die Ursachen des Übels*, trans. K. von Jarmersted (Munich: R. Oldenbourg, 1922), 59.

[111] Vinberg's March 30, 1922 testimony, BHSAM, BSMI 22, number 71624, fiche 3, 93; Stepanov, *Chernaia Sotnia v Rossii*, 327.

[112] Vinberg, *Der Kreuzesweg Russlands*, 59; Vinberg's March 30, 1922 testimony, BHSAM, BSMI 22, number 71624, fiche 3, 93; fiche 4, 1; Stepanov, *Chernaia Sotnia v Rossii*, 327.

Shabelskii-Bork, the son of the couple who had published the Union of the Russian People newspaper *Freedom and Order* and a member of both the Union of the Russian People and Purishkevich's Michael the Archangel Russian People's Union, also supported the Kornilov Putsch. Lieutenant Sergei Taboritskii, Shabelskii-Bork's comrade from the Cavalry Regiment of the Caucasian Division, also took part in this counter-revolutionary endeavor.[113] Like Vinberg, both Shabelskii-Bork and Taboritskii went on to serve Aufbau and the National Socialist cause.

In the summer of 1917, Lieutenants Shabelskii-Bork and Taboritskii formed an organization of officers loyal to the Tsar. They traveled to the front at the end of June 1917 to assess which cavalry regiments would best serve for a monarchical coup in the capital Petrograd, as Saint Petersburg was then known. Shabelskii-Bork and Taboritskii planned to assist General Kornilov by using loyal Tsarist cavalry officers to storm the Winter Palace and to arrest Kerenskii's Provisional Government in August 1917, but their preparations were discovered and thwarted beforehand.[114] The failed Kornilov Putsch increased public fears of repressive right wing counter-revolution. The unsuccessful undertaking undermined remaining public confidence in Russian army officers, and it helped to bring Vladimir Lenin's Bolsheviks out of the isolation that they had engendered through their own armed protest in July 1917.[115]

After the Kornilov Putsch collapsed, Colonel Vinberg continued to oppose leftist forces in Russia. He collaborated with Purishkevich, who formed an underground monarchical organization in September 1917 that included many former members of the now dissolved Michael the Archangel Russian People's Union.[116] Vinberg contributed articles to the "non-socialist" newspaper *Narodnyi Tribun* (*The People's Tribune*), which Purishkevich began publishing in September 1917.[117] In an October 1917 essay, "Fighting Value," Vinberg lamented that the "Revolution" had "torn out" the "lofty religious, public, and civil ideals" from the "souls of the soldiers" in Russia.[118] At this time, he was primarily concerned with the dissolution of the Russian Army as a potent fighting force.

[113] Norman Cohn, *Warrant for Genocide: The Myth of the Jewish World-Conspiracy and the "Protocols of the Elders of Zion,"* (Chico, CA: Scholars Press, 1981), 127; JM charge against Shabelskii-Bork and Sergei Taboritskii from May 29, 1922, GSAPKB, *Repositur* 84a, number 14953, 16.

[114] Shabelskii-Bork, "Über Mein Leben," GSAPKB, *Repositur* 84a, number 14953, 99.

[115] Rogger, *Russia in the Age of Modernization and Revolution 1881–1917* (New York: Longman, 1983), 284.

[116] Stepanov, *Chernaia Sotnia v Rossii*, 328.

[117] Purishkevich, editorial, *Narodnyi Tribun: Organ Purishkevicha*, September 5, 1917, 1.

[118] Vinberg, "Voesposobnost," *Narodnyi Tribun*, October 19, 1917, 3.

Vinberg wrote an article for *The People's Tribune* a few days later in which he again lamented the current state of affairs in Russia. In his essay, "Contrasts," he claimed that while the Italian Army was fighting bravely against an overwhelming German force, soldiers of the numerically far superior Russian Army were running "unrestrained" from German troops. Moreover, "Native fields and settlements have been pillaged and destroyed by our own soldiers and peasants." Vinberg used the language of a disappointed lover in expressing his woe: "My poor people! . . . I loved and believed in you so! . . . What *they* have done to you!"[119] The spread of revolution and the dissolution of the army devastated Vinberg.

Vinberg's impotent frustration as expressed in Purishkevich's *The People's Tribune* underscored the inability of the Black Hundred movement to thwart the Bolshevik seizure of power.[120] The Bolsheviks closed *The People's Tribune* after they had overthrown Kerenskii's Provisional Government in October 1917 (according to the Julian calendar then used in Russia).[121] Vinberg was suddenly faced with the rule of what he termed the "Jewish Bolsheviks."[122] The success of the "October Revolution," as the Bolshevik seizure of power became known, forced Black Hundred activities in Russia to become strictly conspiratorial.[123]

After the Bolsheviks came to power, Vinberg's co-conspirator in the Kornilov Putsch, Shabelskii-Bork, retreated to his estate near Petrograd, where he researched the causes of the February and October Revolutions for Purishkevich's underground monarchical organization. Shabelskii-Bork concluded that the Entente (Britain and France) had fomented revolution in Imperial Russia since it had feared the "Russian peril" as much as the German one. He decided that the restoration of the Russian monarchy could not be achieved with Entente aid, but only through the "reestablishment of the traditional friendship between Russia and Germany."[124]

Bolshevik leaders broke up Purishkevich's underground monarchical organization and imprisoned Purishkevich, Vinberg, and Shabelskii-Bork, among others, in December 1917. Bolshevik authorities charged the three comrades with organizing a monarchical conspiracy against the fledgling Soviet regime.[125] At their trial that began in late December, Shabelskii-Bork

[119] Vinberg, "Kontrasty," *Narodnyi Tribun*, October 22, 1917, 2.
[120] Raskin, "Ideologiia russkogo pravogo radikalizma," 12.
[121] *Narodnyi Tribun*, October 24, 1917.
[122] Vinberg's March 30, 1922 testimony, BHSAM, BSMI 22, number 71624, fiche 4, 1.
[123] LGPO report to the RKÜöO from November 28, 1921, RGVA (TsKhIDK), *fond* 772, *opis* 1, *delo* 96, 47.
[124] Shabelskii-Bork, "Über Mein Leben," GSAPKB, *Repositur* 84a, number 14953, 95, 96, 98.
[125] Stepanov, *Chernaia Sotnia v Rossii*, 329.

impressed Vinberg with his fervent monarchism.[126] Vinberg moved Shabelskii-Bork by assuring the tribunal, "My head can roll off of your execution block, but it will never bow to the Revolution."[127] The Bolshevik court convicted and imprisoned Purishkevich, Vinberg, and Shabelskii-Bork.[128] Vinberg and Shabelskii-Bork shared the same prison cell, where Vinberg received the thanks of the similarly incarcerated former Tsar for working on his behalf.[129] Vinberg and Shabelskii-Bork began a close friendship in this cell that later led to the transfer of Black Hundred ideology to the early National Socialist movement, most notably in the form of *The Protocols of the Elders of Zion*.

CONCLUSION

Far rightists in Imperial Germany and the Russian Empire established detailed anti-Western, anti-socialist, and anti-Semitic ideologies in the period leading up to the 1917 Russian Revolution. Largely internally orientated *völkisch* German thought drew on the idealistic views of Arthur Schopenhauer, Richard Wagner, and Houston Stewart Chamberlain. *Völkisch* ideology conceived a pernicious materialistic Jewish essence that the spiritually and racially superior Germans needed to transcend by negating the will to live, thereby redeeming the world. More externally fixated Russian radical right beliefs, which were associated with the Slavophiles in general and the authors Fedor Dostoevskii and Vladimir Solovev in particular, expressed apocalyptic visions of Jewish world conspirators who threatened to ruin Imperial Russia and eventually the world. Russians needed to lead all Slavs to combat this menace in a concrete political struggle. Anti-Semitic National Socialist ideology later arose largely as a synthesis of German *völkisch*-redemptive and Russian conspiratorial-apocalyptic thought.

While the Black Hundred movement in Imperial Russia, of which the Union of the Russian People formed the most important component, managed to disseminate its anti-Semitic ideology to a considerably broader audience than any comparable *völkisch* German alliance, far right movements in both Imperial Russia and the German Empire nonetheless failed to achieve their political aspirations. Russian conservative revolutionaries

---

[126] Vinberg's March 30, 1922 testimony, BHSAM, BSMI 22, number 71624, fiche 4, 1, 3.

[127] Shabelskii-Bork, "Über Mein Leben," GSAPKB, *Repositur* 84a, number 14953, 99, 103.

[128] Stepanov, *Chernaia Sotnia v Rossii*, 329; Vinberg's March 30, 1922 testimony, BHSAM, BSMI 22, number 71624, fiche 4, 1.

[129] Shabelskii-Bork, "Über Mein Leben," GSAPKB, *Repositur* 84a, number 14953, 101, 103.

fiercely defended the Tsar, but after initial moderate successes, the Black Hundred movement's influence declined dramatically. Far rightists could not prevent the Tsar's abdication, nor could they thwart the Bolshevik seizure of power in 1917. The Russian far right only regained a powerful drive and coherence that had been lacking of late after the Bolshevik Revolution. The Bolshevik "Reds" provided an insidious political foe for "Whites" that fit earlier apocalyptic Black Hundred warnings.

No powerful political *völkisch* movement developed in Imperial Germany up to the Bolshevik seizure of power in 1917. Heinrich Class' Pan-German League, Ludwig Müller von Hausen's Association against the Presumption of Jewry, and Wolfgang Kapp's German Fatherland Party all failed to attract mass followings. Numerically slight *völkisch* elements that grouped around Kapp and Class ultimately concluded that a military dictatorship under the *völkisch* General Erich von Ludendorff represented a superior option to the rule of the ineffectual Kaiser. *Völkisch* Germans could not establish such a dictatorship, however.

In any case, although the days of the Kaiser were numbered, German prospects for victory in World War I improved considerably when the Russian Empire collapsed in 1917. German forces advanced deep into former Imperial Russian territory in 1918, most notably into the Ukraine, where right-wing German officers interacted with their monarchical Russian or Ukrainian counterparts on a large scale for the first time. German–White cooperation in the Ukraine set a precedent for further international right-wing alliances after Imperial Germany lost World War I, notably as seen in the Baltic region in 1919. Hitler's National Socialists subsequently drew upon the tradition of German–White collaboration that had been established in the Ukraine.

CHAPTER 2

At the extreme in the Ukraine and in Germany

The term "Ukraine" derives from the meaning "at the extremity," referring to the area's early location at the periphery of the Russian and Polish spheres of influence. During the final stages of World War I and in the immediate postwar period, the semi-autonomous Ukraine served as a seedbed of extremist movements and ideas, as right-wing Germans interacted with anti-Bolshevik Whites on a large scale for the first time. After the Imperial Russian Army collapsed because of military reverses and internal revolution, Imperial German occupying forces in the Ukraine formed a largely clandestine common front with Whites against the fledgling Bolshevik regime to the north.

Although Imperial German efforts to establish a stable Ukrainian satellite state ultimately failed because of German military reverses on the distant Western Front and revolution at home, the alliance between right-wing Germans and Whites in the Ukraine strengthened pro-German sentiments throughout the White movement. The German Ukrainian Intervention established a precedent for further large-scale nationalist German–Russian military collaboration, notably as conducted along the Baltic Sea in Latvia during 1919. The international anti-Bolshevik cooperation that began in the Ukraine ultimately fostered close National Socialist collaboration with White émigrés.

German military personnel retreating from the Ukraine around the turn of the year 1918/1919 took thousands of pro-nationalist German White officers with them, and many other Whites who had participated in anti-Bolshevik operations in or just outside the Ukraine traveled to Germany through other means. Several of these White officers went on to join Aufbau and to serve the National Socialist cause, notably General Vladimir Biskupskii, Colonel Fedor Vinberg, Colonel Ivan Poltavets-Ostranitsa, Colonel Pavel Bermondt-Avalov, Lieutenant Sergei Taboritskii, and Lieutenant Piotr Shabelskii-Bork.

Shabelskii-Bork arrived in Berlin on a German troop train in early 1919 with a fateful copy of the rabble-rousing anti-Semitic forgery *The Protocols of the Elders of Zion*. He gave the *Protocols* to the *völkisch* publicist Ludwig Müller von Hausen for translation and publication in German. After Hausen published the *Protocols*, they greatly affected the *völkisch* German/White émigré milieu from which the National Socialist Party emerged. Hitler's early mentor Dietrich Eckart, who worked closely with the White émigré Alfred Rosenberg, recoiled in horror at the contents of the *Protocols* and most likely made Hitler aware of them. The *Protocols* influenced Hitler's views of an international Jewish conspiracy that manipulated liberal capitalism, fomented revolutionary movements, and used starvation to subdue opponents in order to achieve world domination.

GERMAN–WHITE COOPERATION IN THE UKRAINIAN INTERVENTION

In late 1917, the German General Staff supported Vladimir Lenin and Lev Trotskii's Bolsheviks not because it approved of them ideologically, but in order to weaken the Russian Army. Following the Bolshevik Revolution in October 1917, the German Empire's tactical pro-Bolshevik foreign policy led to extensive negotiations between Imperial German and Soviet representatives in the city of Brest-Litovsk. General Max Hoffmann led the German side of the talks in Brest-Litovsk despite his inner disgust at the Soviet delegation under the People's Commissar for Foreign Affairs Trotskii.[1] Trotskii noted the artificial cordiality with which Hoffmann treated him at the negotiations in Brest-Litovsk.[2]

Generals Hoffman and Erich von Ludendorff, the chief of the Imperial German Army General Staff, wished to keep the strategically and agriculturally valuable Ukraine out of the control of advancing Bolshevik forces. Nonetheless, Bolshevik troops captured Kiev, the Ukrainian capital, in late January 1918. Working-class Jews there warmly welcomed the occupying Bolshevik forces, and many of them enthusiastically collaborated with the Bolsheviks. These acts inflamed anti-Semitic resentments among the local population.[3] In early February 1918, Hoffmann called for German measures to stop the Bolshevik drive southwards. He stressed that the Ukraine

---

[1] MR report to the BSMÄ from January 14, 1918, BHSAM, BSMÄ 33, number 97676, 116.
[2] Leon Trotsky, *My Life: The Rise and Fall of a Dictator* (London: Thornton Butterworth, 1930), 312.
[3] DB report from March 6, 1919, RGVA (TsKhIDK), *fond* 198, *opis* 9, *delo* 4474, reel 1, 48.

represented the "most vital element in Russia." Ludendorff argued that if the Germans did not intercede more forcefully, then the Bolsheviks would "beat the Ukraine to death," thereby rendering it useless to Germany.[4]

The German Army High Command refused to let the Soviets consolidate their power in the Ukraine. While German and Austro-Hungarian troops officially marched into the Ukraine on February 9, 1918 at the request of the marginally independent Ukrainian government, the Rada, historians write of a *de facto* Central Power occupation of the Ukraine.[5] With the advance of German and Austro-Hungarian forces, Bolshevik troops evacuated Kiev at the end of February 1918. Primarily German occupying forces officially took control there at the beginning of March 1918.[6] Generals Ludendorff and Hoffmann saw their wishes to gain the Ukraine for Germany fulfilled.

A leading Ukrainian anti-Bolshevik, General Pavel Skoropadskii, who went on to lead the Ukraine under German occupation, displayed ambivalence towards the German advance into his homeland. He resented outside help in the struggle against Bolshevism, but given his own losing battle against the Red Army as commander of the 34th Corps, he knew that the Ukrainians needed foreign assistance to rid themselves of the Bolsheviks.[7] Skoropadskii was descended from Hetman Ivan Skoropadskii, who had ruled an autonomous Ukraine at the beginning of the eighteenth century. He owned two estates in the Ukraine. When Bolshevik forces had captured Kiev, Skoropadskii had hid in the countryside. Politics had followed him there, as he had ironically lodged with a Jew, who had angered him by asserting that the Bolsheviks would inevitably triumph in the Ukraine, and that this turn of events would help the Jews.

Skoropadskii watched German troops march into Kiev at the end of February 1918 with mixed emotions. On the one hand, he was pleased to be back in the Ukrainian capital. On the other hand, he acutely felt the "disgrace" of the situation in which the Ukrainian spectators of the German advance not only acquiesced to this occupation, but were also "secretly happy" because the Germans had liberated them from the "hated yoke of the Bolsheviks." Skoropadskii estimated that Bolshevik forces had killed at least three thousand officers and tortured countless others during

[4] Protocol of an RK conference on February 5, 1918, BAB, 43, number 2448/4, III, 130.
[5] Wlodzimierz Medrzecki, "Bayerische Truppenteile in der Ukraine im Jahr 1918," *Bayern und Osteuropa: Aus der Geschichte der Beziehungen Bayerns, Frankens und Schwabens mit Russland, der Ukraine, und Weissrussland*, ed. Hermann Beyer-Thoma (Wiesbaden: Harrassowitz Verlag, 2000), 441.
[6] DB report from March 6, 1919, RGVA (TsKhIDK), *fond* 198, *opis* 9, *delo* 4474, reel 1, 47.
[7] Ivan Poltavets-Ostranitsa's 1926 *curriculum vitae*, RKÜöO, RGVA (TsKhIDK), *fond* 772, *opis* 1, *delo* 105b, 9.

their brief rule in Kiev, a time of "pure hell."[8] While he approved of the German defeat of Bolshevism in the Ukraine, he resented having to bow to German authority.

Around the time that German forces marched into the Ukraine to the mixed feelings of Skoropadskii, German military leaders feared and distrusted the new Soviet regime even while German representatives negotiated with it. As of early March 1918, Walther Nicolai, the head of the German Army High Command Intelligence Service who went on to supply intelligence to the National Socialist Party, believed that Bolshevism now represented the true danger to Germany's Eastern security. He regarded Lenin as a threat to emerge as the "Napoleon of this epoch" who would endanger the power of the established elites in Germany and beyond. General Ludendorff agreed with Nicolai.[9]

Despite the reservations that many Imperial German military leaders felt towards negotiating with the Bolsheviks, the Treaty of Brest-Litovsk was concluded between the German Empire and Bolshevik Russia on March 10, 1918. The pact granted Germany control of considerable formerly Russian territories, including the Ukraine, and it allowed the German General Staff to transfer approximately one million soldiers from the Eastern Front to the Western Front.[10] German military authorities began playing a double game. They officially respected the peace between Imperial Germany and the Bolshevik regime, but at the same time they clandestinely fostered anti-Bolshevik operations in the Ukraine.

After establishing themselves in the Ukraine in the course of March 1918, the leaders of Army Group Eichhorn, as the German occupying force in the Ukraine was termed, worked to undermine the existing Ukrainian government, the Rada. Army Group Eichhorn leaders dismissed the Rada as a "debate club" and desired a more reliable pro-German regime.[11] The Rada lacked authority with the masses, and it proved too leftist and too intellectual to win the support of the landowners and to collaborate smoothly with German occupying forces.[12] German occupying authorities desired a government that better represented Ukrainian large landowners and capitalists, who were grateful to the Germans for returning the property that

---

[8] Pavel Skoropadskii, *Erinnerungen von Pavlo Skoropadsky aufgeschrieben in Berlin in der Zeit von Januar bis Mai 1918*, trans. Helene Ott-Skoropadskii (Berlin, 1918), IZG, *Ms* 584, 51, 102, 113, 116.
[9] Walther Nicolai, *Tagebuch* (Diary), March 6, 1918, RGVA (TsKhIDK), *fond* 1414, *opis* 1, *delo* 16, 77.
[10] Letter from Max Hoffmann to his wife from August 15, 1918, BA/MF, *Nachlass* 37, number 2, 231.
[11] Wilhelm Groener report from March 23, 1918, BA/MF, *Nachlass* 46, number 172, 4.
[12] Interrogation of Ambassador Herbert von Dirksen from October 1945, The National Archives, Records of the Department of State, Special Interrogation Mission to Germany, 1945–46, IZG, number 679, roll 1, 411.

the Bolsheviks had appropriated during their brief period of rule in the Ukraine.[13]

Ukrainian Cossacks, the descendents of frontiersmen who had been organized as cavalry units in the Tsarist Army, played an important role in the German scheme to topple the Rada. The ataman, or leader, of the Ukrainian Cossacks who called himself Colonel Ivan Poltavets-Ostranitsa quickly established contact with the German and Austro-Hungarian General Staffs in Kiev.[14] He would later lead a Ukrainian Cossack National Socialist movement in tandem with Hitler. Poltavets-Ostranitsa fit the description of the term "Cossack," which derives from a Turkish word meaning "adventurer." He claimed, without basis, to be descended from a Ukrainian hetman, or ruler, Ostranitsa, on his mother's side.[15] He actually did not come from the nobility. He had changed the spelling of his given name from "Poltavtzev" and added the noble title "Ostranitsa."[16]

Whatever deceptions he employed regarding his ancestry, Poltavets-Ostranitsa had served admirably as a soldier during World War I, and he aroused the interest of German occupying authorities in the Ukraine since he had become a staunch opponent of the Rada. As a cavalry officer in the Imperial Russian Army, he had been wounded twice and had received several decorations for bravery. After Aleksandr Kerenskii had established the Provisional Government in early 1917, Poltavets-Ostranitsa had traveled to Kiev, where he had been elected to serve in the Military Committee of the Rada.[17] He had acted as the leading organizer of anti-Bolshevik forces on the Rada's behalf.[18] He had soon come into conflict with the socialist leadership in the Ukrainian government, however, and had had to leave the body.[19]

Poltavets-Ostranitsa had begun his own bid for power in the Ukraine. According to one source, he had financed his anti-Rada activities by using men loyal to him to plunder and then burn the estate of a Polish countess that they had been hired to protect.[20] Poltavets-Ostranitsa had led a

---

[13] Wilhelm Groener report from March 23, 1918, BA/MF, *Nachlass* 46, number 172, 6.

[14] Poltavets-Ostranitsa's 1926 *curriculum vitae*, RKÜöO, RGVA (TsKhIDK), *fond* 772, *opis* 1, *delo* 105b, 9.

[15] DB report from August 11, 1933, RGVA (TsKhIDK), *fond* 7, *opis* 1, *delo* 954, reel 5, 355.

[16] RKÜöO report from July 26, 1926, RGVA (TsKhIDK), *fond* 772, *opis* 1, *delo* 101, 5.

[17] Poltavets-Ostranitsa's 1926 *curriculum vitae*, RKÜöO, RGVA (TsKhIDK), *fond* 772, *opis* 1, *delo* 105b, 9.

[18] SGOD report from December 22, 1928, RGVA (TsKhIDK), *fond* 308, *opis* 7, *delo* 265, 5.

[19] Poltavets-Ostranitsa's 1926 *curriculum vitae*, RKÜöO, RGVA (TsKhIDK), *fond* 772, *opis* 1, *delo* 105b, 9.

[20] RKÜöO report from July 26, 1926, RGVA (TsKhIDK), *fond* 772, *opis* 1, *delo* 101, 6.

small and yet efficient force that had defeated a punitive expedition from the Rada. The charismatic Cossack leader had established a new Cossack governing body. He had called a Ukrainian National Cossack Assembly for October 1917. He later claimed that 60,000 Cossacks had attended. He had been elected hetman, or leader, but he had refused the title, claiming that he was too young, only twenty-eight. He had recommended General Skoropadskii as honorary hetman.

In the course of March 1918, Army Group Eichhorn authorities decided that Poltavets-Ostranitsa and the Ukrainian Cossacks he represented could be used to overthrow the Rada. German military leaders approved of the Ukrainian National Cossack Organization that Poltavets-Ostranitsa *de facto* led. This association sought to create an independent Ukraine, defeat Bolshevism, and maintain close relations with the German and Austro-Hungarian Empires. Central Power occupational authorities held a large conference at the end of March 1918, and they decided to give Poltavets-Ostranitsa one million marks to overthrow the Rada.[21]

Largely because of Poltavets-Ostranitsa's German-backed intrigues, the days of the unpopular Rada were numbered. Poltavets-Ostranitsa joined forces with the older Skoropadskii to overthrow the Rada. Poltavets-Ostranitsa supported Skoropadskii's Party of the Ukrainian People's Union, which declared that while Jewry opposed the "Ukrainian idea," the Germans would "kill the parasitical tendencies of Jewry with their creative work."[22] Poltavets-Ostranitsa arranged a congress at the end of April 1918 that included Cossacks loyal to him as well as members of Skoropadskii's Party of the Ukrainian People's Union.[23] The assembly chose Poltavets-Ostranitsa to serve as Cossack Chancellor of the Ukraine, and Skoropadskii was declared the Hetman of the Ukraine, thereby nullifying the Rada's rule.[24] German occupying authorities officially adopted a neutral policy in the Ukrainian power struggle, but they secretly helped Poltavets-Ostranitsa and Skoropadskii to overthrow the Rada.[25]

---

[21] Poltavets-Ostranitsa's 1926 *curriculum vitae*, RKÜöO, RGVA (TsKhIDK), *fond* 772, *opis* 1, *delo* 105b, 9; 1926 memorandum on behalf of Poltavets-Ostranitsa; RKÜöO, RGVA (TsKhIDK), *fond* 772, *opis* 1, *delo* 105b, 7.

[22] Proclamation from Skoropadskii from April 20, 1918, BA/MF, *Nachlass* 46, number 172, 57.

[23] 1926 memorandum on behalf of Poltavets-Ostranitsa, RKÜöO, RGVA (TsKhIDK), *fond* 772, *opis* 1, *delo* 105b, 7.

[24] Letter from Poltavets-Ostranitsa to Adolf Hitler from March 25, 1929, PKAH, RGVA (TsKhIDK), *fond* 1355, *opis* 1, *delo* 3, 57; Poltavets-Ostranitsa's 1926 *curriculum vitae*, RKÜöO, RGVA (TsKhIDK), *fond* 772, *opis* 1, *delo* 105b, 9.

[25] Skoropadskii, *Erinnerungen*, 173.

After the successful coup against the Rada, Poltavets-Ostranitsa strength-ened his Ukrainian National Cossack Organization. This league formed the only significant military basis of Skoropadskii's regime besides occu-pying Central Power troops. Poltavets-Ostranitsa submitted a program to Hetman Skoropadskii calling for a close alliance with Germany, the "liber-ation" of the Caucasus region, and the inclusion of the Caucasus in a Black Sea League in which the Ukraine would play the leading role. Poltavets-Ostranitsa's idea of a pro-German Black Sea League later influenced National Socialist Eastern policies. In his drive to create a pro-German Black Sea League, Poltavets-Ostranitsa increasingly experienced problems with his nominal superior, Skoropadskii, who doubted the Central Powers' prospects for victory and increasingly sided with the Entente in a clandestine manner.[26]

In addition to supporting Poltavets-Ostranitsa, German military leaders fostered the creation of White armies in and just outside the Ukraine after initial reservations. Despite generally smooth relations between Army Group Eichhorn and Skoropadskii's Hetmanate, in which Poltavets-Ostranitsa played a leading role, German military leaders initially feared a Ukrainian revolt and therefore did not arm Ukrainian forces. At the end of May 1918, however, German military authorities in the Ukraine agreed to implement a plan that the Rada had drafted to create an army composed of eight corps.[27] The Imperial German Army funded what became known as the Ukrainian Volunteer Army, and the members of this force wore old German officer uniforms. The Ukrainian Volunteer Army contained large numbers of Tsarist officers, including many who had taken refuge in Kiev after fleeing from the Bolsheviks to the north.[28]

In a June 1918 situation report, General Ludendorff expressed strong anti-Bolshevik and pro-White views. He stressed that he utterly distrusted "dishonest" Soviet machinations. He argued: "We cannot expect anything from this Soviet government although it only lives through our mercy. It is a perpetual danger for us." He emphasized that while the German gov-ernment could officially only deal with the Bolshevik regime, it should nonetheless "establish contact with rightist, more monarchical groups in some way and influence them so that the monarchical movement will march

---

[26] Poltavets-Ostranitsa's 1926 *curriculum vitae*, RKÜöO, RGVA (TsKhIDK), *fond* 772, *opis* 1, *delo* 105b, 9.

[27] Skoropadskii, *Erinnerungen*, 222.

[28] DB report from March 6, 1919, RGVA (TsKhIDK), *fond* 198, *opis* 9, *delo* 4474, reel 1, 47; interrogation of Ambassador Herbert von Dirksen from October 1945, The National Archives, IZG, number 679, roll 1, 412.

in full accordance with our wishes when it has established its position."[29] Members of the Ukrainian Volunteer Army gave good grounds for Ludendorff's optimistic expectations of them. They thanked the Germans for saving their property from Bolshevik confiscation and for protecting their lives.[30]

General Vladimir Biskupskii played a prominent role in the Ukrainian Volunteer Army. He was a prince from a noble landed Ukrainian family in the Kharkov region.[31] He had belonged to the far right Union of the Russian People. He later claimed to have collaborated closely with Aleksandr Dubrovin, the leader of the Union, and he proudly asserted that the Union had represented the world's first manifestation of "Fascism/National Socialism."[32] The White general had displayed considerable military competence and bravery. He had graduated with top honors from a military academy and had received several decorations for courage and initiative during World War I. He had belonged to the pro-German faction of the Tsarist Army. After the Russian Empire had collapsed, he had made his way to the Ukraine. Skoropadskii named him the commander of the 1st Cavalry Division of the Ukrainian Volunteer Army in June 1918.[33] Biskupskii went on to cooperate closely with Hitler in the context of Aufbau.

A far right monarchical grouping in the Great Russian heartland to the north of the Ukraine where Biskupskii served Skoropadskii exerted increasing influence over Ukrainian matters. This group helped to create a new military formation, the Southern Army. From Petrograd, Nikolai Markov II, the former leader of a faction of the Union of the Russian People, led the Soiuz vernych (Union of the Faithful). This association sought to restore the Russian monarchy. Markov II directed the Union as a highly conspiratorial organization. The Union had a southern branch that increased its right-wing activities in the Ukraine in the summer of 1918.

In July 1918, the southern branch of the Union of the Faithful formed the Monarchical Bloc in Kiev. The Bloc supported Hetman Skoropadskii and guided his policies towards a Great Russian stance and a firm

---

[29] Letter from Erich von Ludendorff to the Reichskanzler, June 9, 1918, BA/MF, *Nachlass* 46, number 173, 35–37.
[30] OHLHGE report from June 14, 1918, BA/MF, *Nachlass* 46, number 173, 60.
[31] LGPO report to the RKÜöO from July 20, 1921, RGVA (TsKhIDK), *fond* 772, *opis* 3, *delo* 81a, 19, 24.
[32] Translation of Vladimir Biskupskii's September 7, 1939 comments, APA, BAB, NS 43, number 35, 49.
[33] LGPO report to the RKÜöO from July 20, 1921, RGVA (TsKhIDK), *fond* 772, *opis* 3, *delo* 81a, 19, 24, 35; DB report from May 22, 1936, RGVA (TsKhIDK), *fond* 7, *opis* 4, *delo* 168, reel 1, 1.

German–Russian alliance.[34] Fedor Evaldt served as a prominent member of the Bloc.[35] Evaldt went on to join Aufbau in postwar Munich. Other leading members of the Monarchical Bloc included Boris Pelikan, a former member of the far right Russian Assembly, and Konstantin Scheglovitov, a former member of the Union of the Russian People and the son of the former Imperial Russian Minister of Justice.[36] In 1920, both Pelikan and Scheglovitov helped to form Aufbau.

Beginning in July 1918, the Monarchical Bloc collaborated with Army Group Eichhorn, notably through Scheglovitov, to organize the Southern Army under the leadership of Bloc member Count P. Keller.[37] German military authorities could not back the Southern Army openly because of the official German alliance with the Bolshevik regime, but they clandestinely supported the White army by supplying it with weapons, munitions, and money.[38] Right-wing German circles approved of the creation of the Southern Army.[39] This force served as the primary anti-Bolshevik grouping in the southern regions of the former Russian Empire. It based its operations just outside the Ukraine in the city of Voronezh on the Don River. Despite its impressive name, the Southern Army only reached a strength of approximately 16,000 volunteers, of which a disproportionately high 30 percent were officers.[40]

The adventurer who became known as the dashing Caucasian noble Colonel Pavel Bermondt-Avalov first played a leading role in White affairs in the Southern Army under the simple name of Bermondt.[41] Bermondt had belonged to the Black Hundred movement in Imperial Russia.[42] He had reached the rank of lieutenant by the end of 1915. When the Imperial Russian Army had collapsed in 1917, he had commanded a unit in the Ukraine. He

[34] LGPO reports to the RKÜöO from November 28 and December 24, 1921, RGVA (TsKhIDK), *fond* 772, *opis* 1, *delo* 96, 48, 57.

[35] MMFT report to the DB from December 24, 1923, RGVA (TsKhIDK), *fond* 7, *opis* 2, *delo* 2575, reel 2, 134.

[36] *Spisok chlenov Russkogo Sobraniia s prilozheniem istoricheskogo ocherky sobraniia* (Saint Petersburg: Tip. Spb. Gradonachalstva, 1906), 52; RKÜöO report from June 17, 1922, RGVA (TsKhIDK), *fond* 772, *opis* 3, *delo* 539, 21a, 21v.

[37] LGPO report from June 3, 1921, GSAPKB, *Repositur* 77, title 1813, number 2, 7; LGPO report to the RKÜöO from November 28, 1921, RGVA (TsKhIDK), *fond* 772, *opis* 1, *delo* 96, 49.

[38] Telegram from HGE/Ia to OKO from July 1918, BA/MF, *Nachlass* 46, number 173, 115.

[39] Letter from Pavel Bermondt-Avalov to Wolfgang Kapp from November 9, 1919, GSAPKB, *Repositur* 92, number 815, 88.

[40] Bermondt-Avalov, *Im Kampf gegen den Bolschewismus: Erinnerungen von General Fürst Awaloff, Oberbefehlshaber der Deutsch-Russischen Westarmee im Baltikum* (Hamburg: Von J. J. Augustin, 1925), 45.

[41] Letter from Baron von Delingshausen to the RKÜöO from January 18, 1922, RGVA (TsKhIDK), *fond* 772, *opis* 3, *delo* 71, 88.

[42] Letter to the editorial staff of *Volia Rossii* from February 28, 1921, ATsVO, GARF, *fond* 5893, *opis* 1, *delo* 201, 87.

had subsequently joined Skoropadskii and Poltavets-Ostranitsa's White cause. Skoropadskii promoted him to the rank of colonel and named him the leader of the counter-intelligence agency of the nascent Southern Army.[43] Bermondt later became famous under the name Bermondt-Avalov in the 1919 Latvian Intervention, where he commanded a joint German–Russian anti-Bolshevik force.

The Southern Army in which Bermondt made a name for himself was to cooperate with the Cossack General Piotr Krasnov's Vsevelikoe Voisko Donskoe (Great Don Host), which promulgated the vitriolic tract known in English as the *The Protocols of the Elders of Zion*. Like the Southern Army, the Great Don Host received considerable German material support through secret channels.[44] Krasnov expressed his anti-Semitism by permitting Ivan Rodionov, a Ukrainian Cossack who had been active in the Black Hundred movement, to print the *Protocols* in *Chasovoi* (*The Sentinel*), the official newspaper of the Great Don Host.[45]

The *Protocols* ultimately influenced National Socialists and other anti-Semites around the world. It is worth noting that the *Protocols* had not been widely distributed in pre-Revolutionary Russian society, even in far right circles. They only drew considerable attention during the Russian Civil War. The *Protocols* depict an alleged conspiratorial international organization dedicated to establishing Jewish world rule. Jewish power is to be achieved primarily through liberal capitalism, which the Jews use to foment revolt and chaos so that they can establish a Jewish despot to rule over the world. The *Protocols* also describe the monstrous world state that the Jews allegedly strive to create.[46]

The *Protocols'* origins remain the subject of controversy. In his work *Warrant for Genocide*, Norman Cohn presents an ultimately unfounded version of the *Protocols'* genesis. Cohn argues that Piotr Rachkovskii, the head of the foreign section of the Okhrana (Tsarist Secret Police), wrote the *Protocols* in French in Paris and then sent them to an Imperial Russian monk, Sergei Nilus, for translation. This supposedly took place as part of an intrigue to eliminate the Tsar's favorite holy man in favor of Nilus.[47] A

---

[43] LGPO report to the RKÜöO from September 9, 1921, RGVA (TsKhIDK), *fond* 772, *opis* 3, *delo* 71, 16, 17.

[44] Bermondt-Avalov, *Im Kampf gegen den Bolschewismus*, 45.

[45] ATsVO report from August 1921, GARF, *fond* 5893, *opis* 1, *delo* 39, 4.

[46] Michael Hagemeister, "Die 'Protokolle der Weisen von Zion' und der Basler Zionistenkongress von 1897," *Der Traum von Israel: Die Ursprünge des modernen Zionismus*, ed. Heiko Haumann (Weinheim: Beltz Athenäum Verlag, 1998), 259; Norman Cohn, *Warrant for Genocide: The Myth of the Jewish World-Conspiracy and the "Protocols of the Elders of Zion"* (Chico, CA: Scholars Press, 1981), 61, 62.

[47] Cohn, *Warrant for Genocide*, 83–87.

German expert on the *Protocols*, Michael Hagemeister, has recently noted that the holy man in question, Monsieur Philippe, had already died in France when Nilus, who was not a monk, though he wrote widely on religious topics, published the *Protocols* during the revolutionary year 1905 in the appendix of one of his devotional books, *The Great in the Small and the Anti-Christ as an Imminent Political Possibility: Notes of an Orthodox Believer.*[48]

Cohn based his version of the *Protocols'* origins primarily on filtered information that the Russian émigré historian Boris Nikolaevskii had given him, as seen in correspondence between Cohn's Russian wife Vera and Nikolaevskii. Nikolaevskii wrote Vera Cohn that already at the beginning of the 1930s he had privately concluded that Rachkovskii had not had anything to do with the fabrication of the *Protocols* nor even could have. Nikolaevskii admitted that he had decided not to present his research findings since this would have damaged the case of anti-Hitler authorities at the Bern Trial of 1934–1935 who sought to prove that the Imperial Russian Okhrana had forged the *Protocols*.

The Slavist Cesare G. De Michelis has recently carried out a detailed textual analysis of early versions of the *Protocols* which demonstrates that the *Protocols* were not fabricated in Paris, but within Imperial Russian borders between April 1902 and August 1903. The earliest versions of the *Protocols* contain pronounced Ukrainian features, whereas later ones were given French overtones to lend them the appearance of a credible foreign account.[49] The fabricator or fabricators of the *Protocols* may well have been influenced by Vladimir Solovev's 1900 story, "A Short Tale of the Anti-Christ," which was included in his *Three Conversations*. This cannot be proven, however, since the author or authors of the *Protocols* remain unknown.[50] As we shall see, despite their suspect origins, the *Protocols* found great credence in right-wing circles.

Traveling to Germany proved the politic action for anti-Semitic White leaders in and just outside the Ukraine to undertake in the summer of 1918. The Great Don Host leader General Krasnov dispatched his representative, Duke Georgii Leuchtenbergskii, a member of the Russian nobility who

---

[48] Hagemeister, "Der Mythos der 'Protokolle der Weisen von Zion,'" *Verschwörungstheorien: Anthropologische Konstanten – historische Varianten*, eds. Ute Caumanns and Matthias Niendorf (Osnabrück: Fibre Verlag, 2001), 97; Hagemeister, "Vladimir Solov'ëv: Reconciler and Polemicist," *Eastern Christian Studies 2: Selected Papers of the International Vladimir Solov'ëv Conference held at the University of Nijmegen, the Netherlands, in September 1998* (Leuven: Peeters, 2000), 288.

[49] Hagemeister, "Der Mythos der 'Protokolle der Weisen von Zion,'" 96, 99.

[50] Hagemeister, "Vladimir Solov'ëv," 293.

possessed an estate in Germany, to Berlin in July 1918.[51] Leuchtenbergskii met with the Kaiser and other Imperial German leaders, including General Ludendorff, with whom he held extensive consultations at the Army High Command in Belgium in August 1918. Leuchtenbergskii secured a trade agreement with the German government whereby the Great Don Host would provide agricultural products in return for German machinery and chemicals.[52] The complementary nature of German industrial production and southern Russian, or Ukrainian, agricultural richness fostered German–White collaboration in the time of the Kaiser's rule and beyond, including during the period of Hitler's Third Reich.

Other Whites left the Ukraine for Germany in the summer of 1918. General Biskupskii of the Ukrainian Volunteer Army journeyed to Berlin to demonstrate his fidelity to Germany.[53] Hetman Skoropadskii arrived in Berlin in early September 1918. The Kaiser assured him that he wished an independent Ukraine. Skoropadskii then met with General Ludendorff at the Army High Command Headquarters in Spa, Belgium. Ludendorff suggested coordinating the Ukrainian Volunteer Army with the Southern Army and Krasnov's Don Cossacks to attack the Bolsheviks. He promised to release Russian prisoners of war to serve in the Ukrainian Volunteer and Southern Armies. He urged this combined anti-Bolshevik force to attack from the south while the German Army marched against the Bolsheviks from the west.[54] With Imperial Germany's deteriorating military position on the Western Front and in the Balkans, however, this strategy of coordinated anti-Bolshevik action ultimately had to be abandoned.

As a sidelight to the major German-backed White endeavors that were focused in and just outside the Ukraine, in September 1918, the former Black Hundred member Lieutenant Piotr Shabelskii-Bork, who had been released from a Bolshevik prison through a May 1, 1918 amnesty, undertook a dangerous undercover mission to help the Tsar and his family, whom he believed to be still alive in Bolshevik captivity. He disguised himself as a Bolshevik and traveled to Ekaterinburg in the Urals while it was still under Bolshevik control. After White troops captured the city later in the month,

---

[51] Robert Williams, *Culture in Exile: Russian Émigrés in Germany, 1881–1941* (Ithaca: Cornell University Press, 1972), 76.

[52] Vsevelikoe Voisko Donskoe, Embassy in Berlin reports from July 5, 1918 and another time in 1918, GARF, *fond* 1261, *opis* 1, *delo* 40, 2, 27; letter from Georgii Leuchtenbergskii to Piotr Krasnov from August 22, 1918, GARF, *fond* 1261, *delo* 40, 24, 25.

[53] DB report from May 22, 1936, RGVA (TsKhIDK), *fond* 7, *opis* 4, *delo* 168, reel 1, 1.

[54] Skoropadskii, *Erinnerungen*, 346, 348, 351, 378.

he participated in the official investigation of the Bolshevik murder of the Tsarist family.[55]

The White investigators discovered that the Tsaritsa had possessed Black Hundred member Sergei Nilus' *The Great in the Small and the Anti-Christ as an Imminent Political Possibility* with a copy of *The Protocols of the Elders of Zion*. They also noted that she had drawn a swastika in her room.[56] The report that the White commission, which included Shabelskii-Bork, compiled eventually appeared in the *Völkischer Beobachter* (*Völkisch Observer*). An article in a September 1920 edition of the newspaper, soon before the paper became the official newspaper of the National Socialist Party, claimed that Jews had murdered the Tsar and his family. The paper concluded this from information in the White commission's report that the walls in which the assassination of the Tsar and his family had taken place had been covered with graffiti in German, Hungarian, and Hebrew.[57]

Shabelskii-Bork had arrived too late to save the Tsar and his family, and time began running out for the Southern Army and Skoropadskii's Hetmanate as well. Count Keller found himself unable to carry out his mission of leading the Southern Army against the Bolsheviks. In September and October 1918, he had to refocus his energies on leading the weak Ukrainian Volunteer Army against an internal revolt under the Ukrainian socialist Simon Petliura, who sought to overthrow Skoropadskii's Hetmanate.[58] Colonel Bermondt was likewise forced to leave his organizational activities for the Southern Army to form a machine-gun unit, which he then deployed in the defense of Kiev under Keller.[59] General Biskupskii also served under Keller against Petliura. Skoropadskii named him the commander of the Ukrainian Volunteer Army's Third Corps.[60]

In his new defensive role, Keller also made use of the services of Shabelskii-Bork's colleague Colonel Fedor Vinberg, who had journeyed to Kiev in the face of considerable danger after being released from Bolshevik incarceration on May 1, 1918. Vinberg commanded a unit composed of approximately 5,000 former Tsarist officers with only 400 to 500 ordinary soldiers. This extremely lopsided ratio demonstrated an acute lack

[55] Piotr Shabelskii-Bork, "Über Mein Leben," March 1926, GSAPKB, *Repositur* 84a, number 14953, 103–105.

[56] Henri Rollin, *L'Apocalypse de notre temps: Les dessous de la propagande allemande d'après des documents inédits* (Paris: Gallimard, 1939), 480, 481.

[57] "Wer waren die Mörder des Zaren?" *Völkischer Beobachter*, September 9, 1920, 2.

[58] DB report from March 6, 1919, RGVA (TsKhIDK), *fond* 198, *opis* 9, *delo* 4474, reel 1, 48; Fedor Vinberg's March 30, 1922 testimony, BHSAM, BSMI 22, number 71624, fiche 4, 1.

[59] Bermondt-Avalov, *Im Kampf gegen den Bolschewismus*, 47.

[60] LGPO report to the RKÜßO from July 20, 1921, RGVA (TsKhIDK), *fond* 772, *opis* 3, *delo* 81a, 35.

of peasant and worker support for White forces in the Ukraine. Keller and Vinberg realized that they could only function with considerable German material assistance, which initially came in abundance.[61]

Vinberg became acquainted with Shabelskii-Bork's comrade Lieutenant Sergei Taboritskii in the fall of 1918, when the latter likewise operated under Keller's command to suppress Petliura's uprising. Taboritskii had earlier fled Bolshevik rule and had journeyed into the "sun[light] of the German occupation." Already in January 1918, he had concluded: "Not Germany, but the Entente is the worst enemy of Russia and . . . only Germany can save Russia. It became clear to me that Russia's future lay in an alliance with Germany, as Germany's future did in an alliance with Russia." In addition to opposing Petliura's troops, Keller ordered Taboritskii to form command units that were to fight in the Baltic region as a counterpart to the Southern Army. Parts of the forces that Taboritskii helped to organize later fought in the 1919 Latvian Intervention under the command of Colonel Bermondt-Avalov.[62]

The outbreak of revolution in Germany on November 9, 1918 overthrew the rule of the Kaiser and undermined German–White collaboration in the Ukraine. Vinberg later claimed that the revolutionary German government's discontinuation of support for the Ukrainian Volunteer Army had led to the defeat of Keller's forces and to the death of Keller himself.[63] Hetman Skoropadskii openly broke with a pro-German policy at the time of the German Revolution. He symbolized his new pro-Entente orientation by ostentatiously replacing a medal that the Kaiser had given him with a French decoration.[64] Skoropadskii subsequently attributed his downfall to the Entente's "gross error" in not sending a representative to Kiev and providing military assistance to demonstrate *de facto* support.[65] Skoropadskii's nominal subordinate Poltavets-Ostranitsa wished to continue a German–Ukrainian alliance. The pro-Entente Skoropadskii ordered him to be arrested, a fate that the Cossack leader avoided by fleeing the Ukraine. He eventually made his way to Germany.[66]

Shabelskii-Bork suffered as well under the chaotic conditions in the Ukraine during the fall of 1918. After discovering the murder of the

[61] Vinberg's March 30, 1922 testimony, BHSAM, BSMI 22, number 71624, fiche 4, 1.
[62] Letter from Sergei Taboritskii to Mrs. Shabelskii-Bork from March 18, 1926, GSAPKB, *Repositur* 84a, number 14953, 78, 79.
[63] Vinberg's March 30, 1922 testimony, BHSAM, BSMI 22, number 71624, fiche 4, 1.
[64] Gestapo report from May 2, 1934, RGVA (TsKhIDK), *fond* 501, *opis* 3, *delo* 496a, 44.
[65] Skoropadskii, *Erinnerungen*, 1, 2.
[66] Poltavets-Ostranitsa's 1926 *curriculum vitae*, RKÜöO, RGVA (TsKhIDK), *fond* 772, *opis* 1, *delo* 105b, 9.

Tsarist family in September, he had carried out conspiratorial counter-revolutionary activities in Bolshevik-controlled Russia for two months. As the Chrezvychainaia Komissia po Borbe s Kontr-revolutsiei (Extraordinary Commission for the Struggle with Counter-revolution, commonly known as the Cheka) had arrested more and more of his accomplices inside Soviet territory, he had traveled to the Ukraine to serve in the Ukrainian Volunteer Army. Troops loyal to Petliura arrested him in late November before he could make it to Kiev, however.[67]

Signs of the approaching collapse of Skoropadskii's Hetmanate appeared, as when Fedor Evaldt became the military commander of Kiev despite the open knowledge that he had embezzled funds intended for the Ukrainian Volunteer Army.[68] Petliura's forces captured the final remnants of the Ukrainian Volunteer Army, only about 2,000 men, on December 17, 1918 and entered Kiev. In addition to Shabelskii-Bork, Petliura's forces in Kiev incarcerated the White officers Keller, Vinberg, Taboritskii, and Bermondt.[69] Some of Petliura's soldiers shot Keller, who had been assigned to take command of the Northern Army in the Baltic region, on the night of December 20/21, 1918.[70] Executions of other White officers, including Vinberg, Shabelskii-Bork, and Taboritskii, were scheduled for the beginning of January.[71]

German forces rescued the remaining White officers that Petliura's forces had incarcerated. On December 29, 1918, General Bronsart von Schellendorf negotiated the White officers' release. German forces transported the officers to Germany beginning on December 31, 1918.[72] The Germans took approximately 3,000 intensely anti-Bolshevik White officers and soldiers with them when they withdrew from the Ukraine.[73] Despite his turn from Germany to the Entente, retreating German forces even took Skoropadskii to Germany by disguising him as a wounded German military surgeon.[74] Vinberg and Shabelskii-Bork met each other once again on the way to the main train station in Kiev, and from that point on they remained inseparable

---

[67] Shabelskii-Bork, "Über Mein Leben," GSAPKB, *Repositur* 84a, number 14953, 109.

[68] MMFT report to the DB from December 24, 1923, RGVA (TsKhIDK), *fond 7, opis 2, delo 2575,* reel 2, 134.

[69] Letter from Taboritskii to Mrs. Shabelskii-Bork from March 18, 1926, GSAPKB, *Repositur* 84a, number 14953, 81; LGPO report to the RKÜöO from September 9, 1921, RGVA (TsKhIDK), *fond 772, opis 3, delo 71,* 17.

[70] Bermondt-Avalov, *Im Kampf gegen den Bolschewismus,* 488.

[71] Vinberg's March 30, 1922 testimony, BHSAM, BSMI 22, number 71624, fiche 4, 2, 25.

[72] DB report from March 6, 1919, RGVA (TsKhIDK), *fond 198, opis 9, delo 4474,* reel 1, 47.

[73] A. V. Smolin, *Beloe dvizhenie na Severo-Zapade Rossii 1918–1920* (Saint Petersburg, Dmitrii Bulanin, 1999), 335.

[74] Interrogation of Ambassador Herbert von Dirksen from October 1945, The National Archives, IZG, number 679, roll 1, 415.

"true friends" in the words of Vinberg. Taboritskii joined them during the train ride to Germany, and the three colleagues began an intense period of anti-Bolshevik and anti-Semitic collaboration in Germany in which they soon supported Hitler's National Socialist cause.[75]

WHITE ÉMIGRÉ IDEOLOGY'S TRANSFER FROM
THE UKRAINE TO GERMANY

After the end of military collaboration between Germans and Whites, primarily officers, in the Ukraine in 1918, the transfer of White émigré ideology westwards, most notably in the form of *The Protocols of the Elders of Zion*, gained crucial significance in internal German affairs. According to a previously unknown Gestapo report from April 1935 that is currently housed in Moscow, Lieutenant Shabelskii-Bork fled the Ukraine under German protection around the turn of the year 1918/1919 with a copy of the 1911 edition of Nilus' *The Great in the Small and the Anti-Christ as an Imminent Political Possibility* that contained the *Protocols*.[76] The *Protocols* soon became known throughout Germany and the world.

After being transported by train from Kiev to Berlin in a three-week journey, Shabelskii-Bork and his comrades Colonel Vinberg and Lieutenant Taboritskii established themselves in the German capital towards the end of January 1919, where they began disseminating anti-Bolshevik and anti-Semitic views.[77] Berlin represented the logical destination for the White officer trio. The number of White émigrés in Germany as a whole reached 600,000 by 1920, and the largest White émigré community in Germany developed in Berlin as the fortunes of the White armies declined.[78] Vinberg, Shabelskii-Bork, and Taboritskii were only three of the approximately two million former citizens of Imperial Russia who had fled Bolshevik rule or who had earlier been held as prisoners of war and did not wish to go to Bolshevik Russia.[79]

Vinberg, Shabelskii-Bork, and Taboritskii propagated anti-Bolshevik and anti-Semitic propaganda in Berlin. Shabelskii-Bork and Taboritskii moved into the same quarters and developed a close friendship while

---

[75] Vinberg's March 30, 1922 testimony, BHSAM, BSMI 22, number 71624, fiche 4, 4, 25.

[76] Gestapo report from April 13, 1935, RGVA (TsKhIDK), *fond* 501, *opis* 3, *delo* 496a, 208.

[77] Vinberg's March 30, 1922 testimony, BHSAM, BSMI 22, number 71624, fiche 3, 92; fiche 4, 2, 5.

[78] Letter from Ludwig von Knorring to the RMI from September 20, 1921, BAB, 1501, number 14139, 47; L. K. Skarenkov, "Eine Chronik der russischen Emigration in Deutschland: Die Materialien des General Aleksej A. von Lampe," *Russische Emigration in Deutschland 1918 bis 1941: Leben im europäischen Bürgerkrieg*, ed. Karl Schlögel (Berlin: Akademie, 1995), 48.

[79] Schlögel, "Russische Emigration in Deutschland 1918–1941: Fragen und Thesen," *Russische Emigration in Deutschland*, 11; RMI report from December 15, 1921, BAB, 1501, number 14139, 58.

coordinating their activities with Vinberg, who founded the monarchist exile newspaper *Prizyv* (*The Call*) in August 1919. *The Call* sought to foster "close friendly relations between Germany and Russia," meaning between these states as restored monarchies. Taboritskii acted as *The Call's* technical editor. Shabelskii-Bork drafted the primarily Russian news that *The Call* dealt with.[80] He also ran the newspaper's feuilleton section.[81] Vinberg, Shabelskii-Bork, and Taboritskii appealed for nationalist Germans and Russians to combine forces against the supposed Judeo–Masonic–Bolshevik world conspiracy.[82] Hitler's early mentor Dietrich Eckart urged nationalist Germans to pay greater attention to *The Call* in a March 1920 edition of his newspaper *Auf gut deutsch: Wochenschrift für Ordnung und Recht* (*In Plain German: Weekly for Law and Order*).[83]

In addition to editing *The Call*, which served as the mouthpiece of the anti-Semitic far right wing of Germany's White émigré population, Vinberg integrated White émigrés with *völkisch* Germans in Berlin.[84] He soon achieved what the French military intelligence agency the Deuxième Bureau (Second Section) described as a "preponderant influence" among White émigré and *völkisch* German circles in the German capital.[85] Vinberg's most important *völkisch* German contact was Ludwig Müller von Hausen, the leader of the Association against the Presumption of Jewry.

Hausen, who could read Russian, read Vinberg, Shabelskii-Bork, and Taboritskii's *The Call* regularly.[86] He marked off articles that he found valuable and sometimes had them translated into German, such as a piece from a November 1919 edition of *The Call*, "Satanists of the Twentieth Century." This essay claimed that the Soviet Commissar for War, the Jew Trotskii, and other high-ranking Soviet leaders had held a black mass within the walls of the Kremlin in Moscow in which they had prayed to the devil for help in defeating their White enemies. The article claimed that the Latvian member of the Red Army who had reported this satanic ritual was executed the next day upon Trotskii's orders.[87]

---

[80] Vinberg's March 30, 1922 testimony, BHSAM, BSMI 22, number 71624, fiche 4, 2, 4, 5, 25.

[81] Shabelskii-Bork, "Über Mein Leben," GSAPKB, *Repositur* 84a, number 14953, 110.

[82] Rollin, *L'Apocalypse de notre temps*, 153.

[83] Dietrich Eckart, "Die Schlacht auf den Katalaunischen Feldern," *Auf gut deutsch: Wochenschrift für Ordnung und Recht*, February 20, 1920.

[84] Rafael Ganelin, "Rossiiskoe chernosotenstvo i germanskii natsional-sotsializm," *Natsionalnaia pravaia prezhde i teper, Istoriko-sotsiologicheskie ocherki, chast 1: Rossiia i russkoe zarubezhe* (Saint Petersburg: Institut Sotsiologii rossiiskoi akademii nauk, 1992), 137.

[85] DB report from March 6, 1919, RGVA (TsKhIDK), *fond* 198, *opis* 9, *delo* 4474, reel 1, 48.

[86] Handwritten note from Müller von Hausen in Cyrillic letters, RGVA (TsKhIDK), *fond* 577, *opis* 2, *delo* 131, 200.

[87] "Satanisten des XX. Jahrhunderts," translated article from November 5, 1919 edition of *Prizyv* in Hausen's possession, RGVA (TsKhIDK), *fond* 577, *opis* 1, *delo* 541, 3.

Hausen also circled an article from the February 6, 1920 edition of *The Call*, "An Interesting Document."[88] This piece dealt with the Zunder Document, a prominent piece of spurious anti-Semitic literature that circulated among White forces during the Russian Civil War. The Zunder Document was purportedly a letter from the Central Committee of the Israelite International League that had been found on the corpse of Zunder, a Jewish Bolshevik leader. This forged letter stressed, "We," the "Sons of Israel," stood "on the threshold of the command of the world" after bringing "the Russian people under the yoke of Jewish power." The supposed Jewish authors stressed that now "we must make an end of the best and leading elements of the Russian people, so that . . . vanquished Russia may not find any leader!"[89] Hausen printed the Zunder Document in his newspaper *Auf Vorposten* (*On Outpost Duty*).

Before it became the official National Socialist newspaper, the *Völkisch Observer* printed the Zunder Document. The paper's editors had perhaps become aware of the letter through Hausen. The newspaper's editors printed the document in the February 25, 1920 edition of the paper under the title, "A Jewish Secret Document." The piece on the spurious text noted that the source of its information was the February 6, 1920 edition of Vinberg's *The Call*. The commentary on the Zunder Document in the *Völkisch Observer* asserted: "Judaism's most secret goals emerge undisguised in this secret circular of the Jews in Russia."[90] For many far rightists, the Zunder Document demonstrated that the Jews had launched the Bolshevik Revolution and sought to eradicate nationalist Russian leaders.

Hausen is best known not for publicizing the Zunder Document, but for publishing *The Protocols of the Elders of Zion*. He printed the *Protocols* for the first time in German in 1919. The precise manner in which the *Protocols* reached Germany from the East earlier remained unknown.[91] As we have seen, Vinberg's colleague Shabelskii-Bork carried a copy of Sergei Nilus' *The Great in the Small and the Anti-Christ as an Imminent Political Possibility* that included the *Protocols* from the Ukraine to Berlin. In February 1919, Shabelskii-Bork gave the *Protocols* to Hausen.[92] Hausen hired someone to translate the *Protocols* from Russian into German.[93]

[88] "Liubopytnyi Dokument," *Prizyv*, February 6, 1920, 2, in Hausen's possession, RGVA (TsKhIDK), *fond* 577, *opis* 1, *delo* 541.

[89] Cohn, *Warrant for Genocide*, 119–121, 139.

[90] "Ein jüdisches Geheimdokument," *Völkischer Beobachter*, February 25, 1920, 1.

[91] Hagemeister, "Die 'Protokolle der Weisen von Zion,'" 261.

[92] Gestapo report from April 13, 1935, RGVA (TsKhIDK), *fond* 501, *opis* 3, *delo* 496a, 208.

[93] Letter from Hausen to Carl März from March 26, 1921, RGVA (TsKhIDK), *fond* 577, *opis* 1, *delo* 853, 32.

Shabelskii-Bork's comrade Vinberg took the *Protocols* very seriously. In his 1922 book translated from Russian into German as *Der Kreuzesweg Russlands* (*Russia's Via Dolorosa*), he warned against "Jewish imperialism" with its goal of "the foundation of Jewish world rule." He argued that the *Protocols* and "other secret documents that have fallen into the hands of Christians by chance" demonstrated that the Jews strove for a "purely Jewish despotic monarchy."[94] In a letter published in a May 1923 edition of the National Socialist newspaper the *Völkisch Observer*, Vinberg stressed that the *Protocols* had "revealed the secret plans of Jewry."[95] Like many other far rightists, Vinberg erroneously believed in the *Protocols'* authenticity as an accurate blueprint of nefarious Jewish designs for world domination.

Hausen received information on Nilus' personality and on the provenance of the *Protocols* from an intelligence agency in Berlin under General Kurlov, who had earlier served as the head of the Imperial Russian Okhrana. Kurlov had abused his post of Assistant to the Interior Minister in the Russian Empire by making unauthorized use of secret funds. He had managed to be expelled from Pavel Skoropadskii's Hetmanate in the Ukraine in 1918 before resurfacing in Berlin and establishing his intelligence organization.[96] Citing a "high official" in the former Tsarist Interior Ministry, almost certainly Kurlov, Hausen claimed that the *Protocols* had originally been drafted in Hebrew and then translated into French. Then the Russian Interior Ministry had received a copy of them and transferred them to Nilus for translation into Russian and publication.[97] While false, Hausen's version of the *Protocols'* origins lent the document a certain allure.

One of Kurlov's collaborators, Lieutenant Iurii Kartsov, also provided Hausen with information on Nilus. While Aufbau's leading personality Max von Scheubner-Richter later praised him as one of many fine "Russian patriots," Kartsov had a reputation as an "utterly undependable" person. He possessed significant connections in Berlin through his work for the German intelligence agency in the Ukraine in 1918.[98] He had dealings with

---

[94] Vinberg, *Der Kreuzesweg Russlands: Teil I: Die Ursachen des Übels*, trans. K. von Jarmersted (Munich: R. Oldenbourg, 1922), 28, 35.

[95] Vinberg, "Der wackere Zentralverein," *Völkischer Beobachter*, May 9, 1923, 3.

[96] LGPO reports to the RKÜöO from June 2 and August 8, 1921, RGVA (TsKhIDK), *fond* 772, *opis* 3, *delo* 81a, 15; *delo* 539, 17, 20.

[97] Letter from Hausen to März from March 26, 1921, RGVA (TsKhIDK), *fond* 577, *opis* 1, *delo* 853, 33.

[98] Iurii Kartsov, "Existiert die Schuldfrage überhaupt?" *Aufbau-Korrespondenz*, October 4, 1922, 3; LGPO report to the RKÜöO from June 2, 1921, RGVA (TsKhIDK), *fond* 772, *opis* 3, *delo* 81a, 16.

Vinberg, Shabelskii-Bork, and Taboritskii, who were close to Hausen.[99] According to an April 1920 report that he submitted to Hausen, Kartsov had known Nilus personally, and he believed that the mystical Russian had already translated the *Protocols* in 1898. Nilus had sent the *Protocols* to Imperial Russian authorities. He had only received the reply that they proved "most interesting," but that it was too late to publish the information.

Of Nilus personally, Kartsov noted in his report to Hausen that the Russian author was approximately seventy-five years old and "completely un-statesmanlike." Nilus was "not concerned with the racial question, regarding the Jewish plague rather from a mere religious standpoint as the wrath of God for sinful humanity. He sees in the rule of the Jews the rule of Satan, which will later be followed by redemption through God."[100] While Kartsov's information on the origins of the *Protocols* was mistaken, his description of Nilus' personal beliefs was accurate.

Hausen was in a good position to spread White émigré ideology, most notably in the form of the *Protocols*, from Berlin to Munich, where the National Socialist movement arose. He served as a prominent leader of the Germanenorden (German Order), a secretive organization dedicated to protecting "Aryan blood."[101] The German Order had founded an extension in Munich in August 1918, the Thule Gesellschaft (Thule Society). The Thule Society sought to serve as the "guardian and reviver of the *völkisch* spirit."[102] The secretive association was named after an old term for Iceland, where Germanic peoples had found refuge from Christianity. The organization used a swastika with a sword as its symbol.[103] The Thule Society possessed around 200 members in 1919, but those who belonged to the association possessed connections that made the organization more powerful than its numbers suggested.[104]

The Thule Society purchased a *völkisch* newspaper, the *Münchener Beobachter* (*Munich Observer*).[105] The *Munich Observer* possessed a

---

[99] Hagemeister, "Sergej Nilus und die 'Protokolle der Weisen von Zion,'" *Jahrbuch für Antisemitismusforschung der Technischen Universität Berlin*, ed. Wolfgang Benz (Frankfurt am Main: Campus Verlag, 1996), 137.

[100] Kartsov's report to Hausen from April 30, 1920, RGVA (TsKhIDK), *fond* 577, *opis* 2, *delo* 9, 36.

[101] Hagemeister, "Die 'Protokolle der Weisen von Zion,'" 262; Martin Sabrow, *Der Rathenaumord: Rekonstruktion einer Verschwörung gegen die Republik von Weimar* (Munich: Oldenbourg, 1994), 45.

[102] Rudolf von Sebottendorff, "Aus der Geschichte der Thule Gesellschaft," *Thule-Bote*, Gilbhart (October) 31, 1933, 1, BSAM, SAM, number 7716, 9.

[103] Detlev Rose, *Die Thule Gesellschaft: Legende – Mythos – Wirklichkeit* (Tübingen: Grabert-Verlag, 1994), 35.

[104] Interview with Johann Hering on August 29, 1951, IZG, ZS 67, 2.

[105] Sebottendorff, "Aus der Geschichte der Thule Gesellschaft," *Thule-Bote*, Gilbhart (October) 31, 1933, 1, BSAM, SAM, number 7716, 9.

circulation of approximately 1,000 readers as of October 1918. A version of the paper was distributed throughout Germany under the title the *Völkisch Observer* for the first time in August 1919, while the *Munich Observer* continued to be distributed locally. As of the beginning of October 1919, the *Munich Observer* had gained 9,000 subscribers, while the *Völkisch Observer* possessed a circulation of 8,800.[106]

Hausen corresponded regularly with the editors of the *Völkisch Observer* in 1919.[107] He sent *The Protocols of the Elders of Zion*, which ultimately found great resonance in Germany and around the world, to the *Völkisch Observer* in November 1919. He mailed the *Protocols* for the immediate purpose of helping the newspaper's editors in a lawsuit that the Jewish United Order Benai Brith Lodge had filed against them.[108] After suggesting some stalling tactics, Hausen noted that he had sent his soon-to-be released work, *Die Geheimnisse der Weisen von Zion* (*The Secrets of the Wise Men of Zion*). He asserted that with the help of this book, "You can probably gather so much material that the judge will need a year to work through it."

Anticipating difficulties, Hausen noted: "The Minutes would make a devastating judgment possible, but we unfortunately do not have the original text, and the Jews will dispute its authenticity." He stressed, "We have therefore provided indirect evidence in the introduction that the Jews have acted according to the same guidelines that we find in the reports of the 'Wise Men of Zion' throughout time and in the most varied lands."[109] Hausen thus harbored misgivings about the *Protocols'* authenticity, but he did believe that they revealed what he regarded as the quintessentially pernicious Jewish essence.

The editors of the *Völkisch Observer* thanked Hausen for his assistance and pledged with regard to the *Protocols*, "We will study them immediately."[110] An April 1920 edition of the *Völkisch Observer* ran a large front-page article, "The Secrets of the Wise Men of Zion." This piece "emphatically" recommended the book on the *Protocols* released by Hausen's On Outpost

---

[106] Sebottendorff, "Die Thule Gesellschaft," *Thule-Bote*, Gilbhart (October) 31, 1933, 2, BSAM, SAM, number 7716, 10.

[107] Hausen's correspondence with the *Völkischer Beobachter* RGVA (TsKhIDK), *fond* 577, *opis* 1, *delo* 479.

[108] Letter from Hanns Müller to Hausen from November 26, 1919, RGVA (TsKhIDK), *fond* 577, *opis* 1, *delo* 479, 32.

[109] Letter from Hausen to Müller from November 29, 1919, RGVA (TsKhIDK), *fond* 577, *opis* 1, *delo* 479, 35.

[110] Letter from Müller to Hausen from December 10, 1919, RGVA (TsKhIDK), *fond* 577, *opis* 1, *delo* 479, 37.

Duty publishing house in 1919. The essay claimed: "There is no book which demonstrates the spirit of Jewry the same way." The editorial stressed that despite the "enormous significance" of Hausen's work, space constraints necessitated the newspaper to print only some key sections to give a "faint picture" of the work as a whole.

The *Völkisch Observer* printed some sections of Hausen's work that alleged to expose sinister Jewish strivings for world domination. "The end justifies the means," the newspaper quoted Hausen's book. In accordance with this motto, Jewish leaders supposedly carried out their evil plans with less attention to "the good and the moral than with the necessary and the useful." Further, the "wise men of Zion" are supposed to have stressed, "Our motto is: power and cunning!" Moreover: "We must not shy away from bribery, deceit, and betrayal as soon as they serve the attainment of our plans." Another passage from Hausen's work printed in the newspaper had Jews claim that they had come "to influence through the press and yet remained in the shadows; thanks to it we have brought mountains of gold into our hands without concerning ourselves that we had to scoop [them] out of streams of blood and tears."

Another section of the *Völkisch Observer* that quoted Hausen's *Protocols* book treated other dastardly means that the "wise men of Zion" used in their drive for world domination. For instance, Jews supposedly only placed bureaucrats with "slavish abilities" in leading positions. These officials could thus be used as "pawns" in the hands of Jewish "schooled and talented advisors, who have been brought up from youth for rule over the entire world." Moreover, the Jews allegedly "alone" controlled "the rule of money," which they upheld through artificial poverty: "Hunger provides the financial power with . . . the rights to the workers. . . . We move the masses through need and the envy and hatred that arise from it and eliminate those who are in our way with their help." When the time was ripe, the Jews were to switch over from cunning and deceit to brutal force: "Our empire . . . must establish a reign of terror . . . in order to force blind and unconditional obedience."[III] The *Völkisch Observer* took the warnings contained in the *Protocols* very seriously.

The *Völkisch Observer* received severe criticism for printing parts of the *Protocols*. A June 1920 article in the newspaper noted that Jews vehemently denied the authenticity of the *Protocols*. Admitting that the origins of the *Protocols* remained suspicious, the piece followed Hausen's tactics, claiming:

[III] "Die Geheimnisse der Weisen von Zion," *Völkischer Beobachter*, April 22, 1920, 1.

Even if the accounts are not historical in the sense of this term, the history books of Jewish authors as well as serious and impartial German researchers prove nothing else than that the contents of the controversial book are a true to life . . . reflection of Jewish lust for power, avarice, and spirit of subversion.[112]

The *Protocols* were a vicious forgery, but they expressed the fears that anti-Semites felt when faced with rapid societal flux in the form of increasing democratization and industrialization. Since they spoke so well to the insecurities of former privileged groups who feared that they were slipping down the social ladder, the *Protocols* possessed an intense immediacy for many far rightists. By presenting a dastardly meta-historical enemy of all peoples, the Jew, the *Protocols* clearly explained the turmoil and upheavals of the modern world that so upset radical right Germans and Russians in particular.

Hitler's most important early mentors, the *völkisch* publicist Dietrich Eckart and his White émigré colleague Alfred Rosenberg, both attended meetings of the Thule Society in Munich as guests, and they became aware of Hausen's translation of the *Protocols* in late 1919, even before sections of it appeared in the *Völkisch Observer*.[113] They were outraged at what they read, the former more than the latter. Through his collaboration with Eckart and Rosenberg beginning in late 1919, Hitler received his most sustained *völkisch* indoctrination as well as his introduction to apocalyptic and anti-Semitic White émigré thought, which warned in the vein of the *Protocols* that a sinister international Jewish conspiracy controlled both finance capitalism and Bolshevism as tools to achieve world rule.

Eckart has been largely overlooked in the historical literature. The only work in English that examines his career in any detail is a doctoral dissertation, Ralph Engelmann's *Dietrich Eckart and the Genesis of Nazism*.[114] The only non-National Socialist German book that concentrates on Eckart's anti-Semitic ideology is Margarete Plewnia's *Auf dem Weg zu Hitler: Der "völkische" Publizist Dietrich Eckart* (*On the Way to Hitler: The "Völkisch" Publicist Dietrich Eckart*).[115] The *Protocols* significantly shaped Eckart's outlook, and Eckart's role in influencing Hitler's anti-Bolshevik, anti-Semitic ideas in league with Rosenberg warrants greater attention.

---

[112] "Die Geheimnisse der Weisen von Zion," *Völkischer Beobachter*, June 27, 1920, 2.

[113] Rose, *Die Thule Gesellschaft*, 79.

[114] Ralph Engelmann, *Dietrich Eckart and the Genesis of Nazism*, diss. Washington University (Ann Arbor: University Microfilms, 1971).

[115] Margarete Plewnia, *Auf dem Weg zu Hitler: Der "völkische" Publizist Dietrich Eckart* (Bremen: Schünemann Universitätsverlag, 1970).

Eckart enjoyed moderate influence as a publicist. He had worked as a journalist in Berlin before co-publishing a nationalist wartime newspaper in Munich, *Unser Vaterland* (*Our Fatherland*), which had opposed defeatist elements in Germany. He had solicited articles for this paper from the *völkisch* theorist Houston Stewart Chamberlain.[116] In December 1918, Eckart used funds from the Thule Society to launch an attack against Jewish left-wing revolutionary forces in Germany by founding the right-wing political newspaper *In Plain German*.[117] He sent 2,500 copies throughout Germany in accordance with an address list that he had drawn up.[118]

Eckart propounded *völkisch* ideology in the pages of *In Plain German*. He called upon the Germans to negate Jewish world-affirmation. In formulating his views, he borrowed from the *völkisch* theories of Arthur Schopenhauer, Richard Wagner, and Chamberlain, in which the primarily world-denying Germans needed to transcend the corrupting influence of the materialistic and world-affirming Jews.[119] Eckart argued that the "true German . . . lives between the two worlds" of world-affirmation and world-negation.[120] On the other hand: "World-affirmation . . . shows itself totally pure in the Jewish people, without any addition of world-negation."[121] Hitler echoed Eckart's reasoning in a November 1922 speech. He asserted, "The purely earthly is Jewish; among us it is an inner distortion . . . The struggle between both poles has been going on for a long time already."[122]

Eckart met Rosenberg through the Thule Society in late 1918.[123] The two men soon became close collaborators. Rosenberg offered his services to Eckart by asking: "Can you use a fighter against Jerusalem?" Eckart responded, "Certainly!"[124] When Eckart repeatedly sank into periods of lethargy in 1919 and 1920, Rosenberg ran *In Plain German* for considerable

---

[116] Geoffrey G. Field, *Evangelist of Race: The Germanic Vision of Houston Stewart Chamberlain* (New York: Columbia University Press, 1981), 390.

[117] Werner Maser, *Der Sturm auf die Republik: Frühgeschichte der* NSDAP (Stuttgart: Deutsche Verlags-Anstalt, 1973), 179; Plewnia, *Auf dem Weg zu Hitler*, 29.

[118] Alfred Rosenberg, Memoirs, KR, BAB, NS 8, number 20, 2.

[119] Eckart, "Das ist der Jude! Laienpredigt über Juden- und Christentum von Dietrich Eckart," *Auf gut deutsch*, [August/September], 1920, 44; Eckart, "In letzter Stunde," *Auf gut deutsch*, March 15, 1921, 7; Eckart, "Das Judentum in und ausser uns: Grundsätzliche Betrachtungen von Dietrich Eckart: I," *Auf gut deutsch*, January 10, 1919, 14, 15.

[120] Eckart, "Theorie und Praxis," *Auf gut deutsch*, September 12, 1919, 2.

[121] Eckart, "Das Judentum in und ausser uns: IV.," *Auf gut deutsch*, January 31, 1919, 15, 16.

[122] "Positiver Antisemitismus," *Völkischer Beobachter*, November 4, 1922, 1.

[123] Maser, *Der Sturm auf die Republik*, 181, 182.

[124] Robert Cecil, *The Myth of the Master Race: Alfred Rosenberg and Nazi Ideology* (London: B. T. Batsford Ltd., 1972), 24.

stretches at a time.[125] Eckart greatly valued Rosenberg. He referred to him in an early edition of *In Plain German* as his "tireless friend."[126] Eckart and Rosenberg began corresponding with Hausen at some point, but he maintained a rather condescending attitude towards them. He noted: "Both have thoroughly attached themselves to the Jewish/Masonic question, but both are newcomers in it after all."[127]

When Hitler met Eckart and Rosenberg in late 1919, he was an obscure agitator for the fledgling Deutsche Arbeiterpartei (German Worker's Party), a subsidiary organization of the Thule Society and the forerunner of the Nationalsozialistische Deutsche Arbeiterpartei (National Socialist German Worker's Party, or NSDAP), which was founded in February 1920.[128] According to Eckart's secretary, Hitler met Eckart in a small Munich pub in the fall of 1919.[129] Rosenberg later recalled meeting Hitler in the company of Eckart in a small Munich bar in the fall of 1919 as well. At the time of their meeting, Hitler already knew of the writings of both Eckart and Rosenberg in *In Plain German*.[130]

Hitler and Eckart quickly developed a relationship of mutual respect, and Hitler and Rosenberg soon admired each other as well. Hitler electrified Eckart with his persuasive power and intensity so that Eckart remarked early on: "That is Germany's coming man, of whom the world will one day speak." The two men began meeting with each other regularly.[131] Hitler later praised Eckart in glowing terms. He dedicated his autobiographical work *Mein Kampf* (*My Struggle*) in part to "that man, one of the best, who devoted his life to the awakening of his, our people, in his writings and his thoughts and finally in his deeds: Dietrich Eckart."[132] The Führer asserted in January 1942 that Eckart had shone for him "like the polar star."[133] Like Eckart, Rosenberg was extremely impressed with Hitler early on.[134] He joined the German Worker's Party as one of its earliest members.[135] Hitler

[125] Rosenberg, Memoirs, KR, BAB, NS 8, number 20, 2.
[126] Eckart, "Das fressende Feuer," *Auf gut deutsch*, August 22, 1919.
[127] Letter from Hausen to März from April 6, 1921, RGVA (TsKhIDK), *fond* 577, *opis* 1, *delo* 853, 41.
[128] Maser, *Der Sturm auf die Republik*, 150; Rose, *Die Thule Gesellschaft*, 79.
[129] Interview with Walburga Reicheneder on January 11, 1952, IZG, ZS 119, 1.
[130] Rosenberg, Memoirs, KR, BAB, NS 8, number 20, 16.
[131] Plewnia, *Auf dem Weg zu Hitler*, 66, 67.
[132] Hitler, *Mein Kampf*, trans. Ralph Mannheim (Boston: Houghton Mifflin, 1943), 687.
[133] Hitler, *Hitler's Table Talk 1941–44: His Private Conversations*, trans. Norman Cameron and R. H. Stevens, second edn. (London: Weidenfeld and Nicolson, 1973), 217.
[134] Rosenberg, "Meine erste Begegnung mit dem Führer," The National Archives, Records of the Reich Ministry for the Occupied Eastern Territories, 1941–45, IZG, number 454, roll 63, 578.
[135] Walter Laqueur, *Russia and Germany: A Century of Conflict* (London: Weidenfeld and Nicolson, 1965), 56.

valued Rosenberg's views greatly, once remarking that Rosenberg was the only man whose ideas he would always listen to.[136]

Eckart and Rosenberg helped to synthesize *völkisch*-redemptive views of German spiritual and racial superiority with conspiratorial-apocalyptic White émigré conceptions of international Jewry as a malevolent force that strove for world domination through dastardly means. In so doing, they greatly influenced early National Socialist ideology. From November 1919 until the summer of 1920, the scope of Hitler's anti-Semitic arguments broadened considerably. Hitler's increasingly virulent anti-Semitism can largely be attributed to his early ideological apprenticeship under Eckart and Rosenberg, both of whom the *The Protocols of the Elders of Zion* influenced.[137]

The precise manner in which Hitler became aware of the *Protocols* remains unknown, but Eckart most likely introduced them to him in late 1919. Eckart first dealt with the *Protocols* in an October 10, 1919 edition of *In Plain German*. He cited what a Protestant British publication printed in Jerusalem had mistakenly termed a "publicity leaflet" proclaiming "Jewish world rule" that the "Jewish lodge 'The Wise Men of Zion'" had distributed in Imperial Russia in 1911. Eckart claimed that the "wise men of Zion" had already announced the destruction of the German and Russian Empires in 1911. He noted that he had seen a map before the war with Germany truncated along the lines of the borders that it currently possessed according to the provisions of the Treaty of Versailles, while the Russian Empire had been labeled a "desert." He lamented that the "Jew Trotskii" presided over a "field of corpses" that had once been Imperial Russia. He bitterly remarked: "Oh, how wise you wise men from Zion are!"[138]

Eckart treated Hausen's translation of the *Protocols* in a December 1919 article in *In Plain German*, "The Midgard Serpent." He asserted that one read Hausen's work on the *Protocols* "again and again and yet does not get to the end of it since with almost every paragraph one lets the book fall as if paralyzed with unspeakable horror." He claimed that Hausen's translation of the *Protocols* and the "publicity leaflet" of the "Jewish lodge 'The Wise Men of Zion'" in Imperial Russia (which he had referred to in October) undoubtedly originated from the same source. Thus, he emphasized: "The Russian Jews already knew in advance of the collapse of the Tsarist Empire as well as the German monarchy in 1911 and just as surely already at that time

[136] Christine Pajouh, "Die Ostpolitik Rosenbergs 1941–1944," *Deutschbalten, Weimarer Republik und Drittes Reich*, ed. Michael Garleff (Köln: Böhlau Verlag, 2001), 167.
[137] Plewnia, *Auf dem Weg zu Hitler*, 95.
[138] Eckart, "Tagebuch," *Auf gut deutsch*, October 10, 1919.

announced Bolshevik chaos with Jewish world domination as background." Eckart then cited some sections of Hausen's *Protocols* translation, noting that these segments "suffice to attest to the authenticity of the entirety."[139]

In a November 1920 essay in *In Plain German*, "'Jewry über alles'" ("'Jewry above Everything'"), Eckart demonstrated the intense impression that the *Protocols* had made on him by quoting a passage from them that had not appeared in his December 1919 article on the *Protocols* or in the *Völkisch Observer*. He reprinted the supposed words of Jewish conspirators: "The world ruler who will take the place of the currently existing governments has the duty to remove such societies even if he has to drown them in their own blood." For Eckart, this assertion represented a dire and legitimate warning of what the peoples of the world faced unless they took decisive anti-Semitic action.

Eckart upheld the *Protocols* as a genuine document. In his "'Jewry above Everything'" article, he noted that the "entire Jewish press" had labeled the *Protocols* a forgery, but he dismissed this as "the usual tactic of the Hebrews. That which one cannot refute, one chalks up as a forgery." Referring to the spread of the *Protocols* around the world, Eckart argued that despite Jewish protests, "In all peoples, in England, France, Greece, Romania, Poland, Hungary, and so on, the scales are beginning to fall from [people's] eyes: everywhere forces are stirring and engaging in the work of the liberation from humanity's mortal enemy."[140] Eckart thus sounded a call to arms for all anti-Semites of the world.

While Eckart unequivocally believed in *The Protocols of the Elders of Zion* as an authentic warning for Gentiles around the world, his White émigré colleague Rosenberg adopted a considerably more skeptical attitude towards the *Protocols*. Konrad Heiden argued in his 1944 book *Der Führer* that Rosenberg received the *Protocols* from a mysterious stranger in Moscow in 1917.[141] Michael Hagemeister, a German expert on the *Protocols*, has stressed that Heiden's undocumented assertion that someone gave Rosenberg a copy of the *Protocols* in Moscow and that he then brought them to Germany belongs in the "realm of legend."[142] After Rosenberg became aware of the *Protocols* in postwar Munich, he maintained a far more critical attitude towards them than historians have often suggested. In his first major work, which was released early in 1920, *Die Spur des Juden im Wandel der Zeiten*

[139] Eckart, "Die Midgardschlange," *Auf gut deutsch*, December 30, 1919.
[140] Eckart, "Jewry über alles,'" *Auf gut deutsch*, November 26, 1920.
[141] Konrad Heiden, *Der Führer: Hitler's Rise to Power*, trans. Ralph Mannheim (Boston: Houghton Mifflin, 1944), 1.
[142] Hagemeister, "Sergej Nilus und die 'Protokolle der Weisen von Zion,'" 136.

(*The Trail of the Jew through the Ages*), he did not refer directly to the *Protocols*.[143]

Rosenberg examined the *Protocols* in his 1923 book *Die Protokolle der Weisen von Zion und die jüdische Weltpolitik* (*The Protocols of the Elders of Zion and Jewish World Politics*), which, according to the *Völkisch Observer*, was the first work to make a "critical" examination of the "problem of the 'Protocols.'"[144] In his work, Rosenberg remained more skeptical towards the *Protocols* than Eckart. He claimed that the Zionist author Asher Ginsburg could very well have written the *Protocols*, but no "conclusive" proof of this existed, so the question of the authorship of the *Protocols* remained "open." He further noted that no "juridicially conclusive proof" existed for the *Protocols* either as absolutely genuine or as a forgery.

In a manner similar to Hausen, the publisher of the first German version of the *Protocols*, Rosenberg noted that in any case, documents from "ancient times as well as from the most recent past" demonstrated "precisely the same sense" as the *Protocols*, from "the *Talmud* to the *Frankfurter Zeitung* [*Frankfurt Times*] and the *Rote Fahne* [*Red Flag*]." Rosenberg further asserted that the *Protocols* stated that which the "Jewish leaders of Bolshevism themselves openly describe as their plan." While he harbored doubts of the *Protocols'* authenticity, Rosenberg agreed with a central point of the *Protocols*: "First subversion, then dictatorship."[145] The belief that the Jews undermined existing state authorities to form a new Jewish-controlled international tyranny found wide credence among White émigré circles and in the ranks of the early National Socialists.

Hitler referred to the *Protocols* as evidence of Jewish plans for world rule. The first indication of Hitler's internalization of the sinister message of the *Protocols* came in his notes for an August 1921 speech:

Starvation as power – (Russia) . . . Starvation in the service of Jewry[.] "Wise Men of Zion[.]" Objection "not every Jew will know this." What the wise man comprehends intellectually the ordinary one does out of instinct . . . Starvation in Russia[:] charitably, 40 mill[ion] are dying.[146]

In an oration a few days later, he cited the *Protocols* as evidence of the age-old and continuing Jewish goal of "the extraction of rule, no matter

[143] Rosenberg, *Die Spur des Juden im Wandel der Zeiten* (Munich: Deutscher Volks-Verlag, 1920).

[144] "Die Protokolle der Weisen von Zion und die jüdische Weltpolitik," *Völkischer Beobachter*, August 21, 1923, 3.

[145] Rosenberg, *Die Protokolle der Weisen von Zion und die Jüdische Weltpolitik* (Munich: Deutscher Volks-Verlag, 1923), 8, 9, 32, 45.

[146] Hitler, notes for a speech on August 12, 1921, *Sämtliche Aufzeichnungen 1905–1924*, eds. Eberhard Jäckel and Axel Kuhn (Stuttgart: Deutsche Verlags-Anstalt, 1980), 451–453.

through which means."[147] In an April 1923 speech, he stressed that the Jews sought "to extend their invisible state as a supreme dictatorial tyranny over the entire world."[148] This was the basic warning contained in the *Protocols*. Hitler again treated the theme of the Jewish use of starvation as a weapon in an August 1923 oration. He asserted, "In the books of the wise men of Zion it is written: 'Hunger must wear down the broad masses and drive them spinelessly into our arms!'"[149]

Finally, in *Mein Kampf*, Hitler stressed the crucial importance of the *Protocols* in both revealing and undermining diabolical Jewish plans for ruthless world domination:

To what an extent the whole existence of this people is based on a continuous lie is shown incomparably by the *Protocols of the Wise Men of Zion*, so infinitely hated by the Jews. They are based on a forgery, the *Frankfurter Zeitung* moans and screams once every week: the best proof that they are authentic. What many Jews may do unconsciously is here consciously exposed. And that is what matters. It is completely indifferent from what Jewish brain these disclosures originate; the important thing is that with positively terrifying certainty they reveal the nature and activity of the Jewish people and expose their inner contexts as well as their ultimate final aims. The best criticism applied to them, however, is reality. Anyone who examines the historical development of the last hundred years from the standpoint of this book will at once understand the screaming of the Jewish press. For once this book has become the property of a people, the Jewish menace may be considered as broken.[150]

In her seminal 1979 work *The Origins of Totalitarianism*, political theorist Hannah Arendt quoted Heinrich Himmler, the head of the Schutzstaffel (SS), as asserting, "We owe the art of government to the Jews," referring primarily to the *Protocols*, which "the *Führer* [had] learned by heart."[151] While this is an exaggeration, the *Protocols* did provide terrifying visions of an all-encompassing Jewish world conspiracy. The warnings in the *Protocols* greatly influenced the ideology of the National Socialist movement. The *Protocols* went through thirty-three editions by the time Hitler came to power in 1933, and they became the most widely distributed work in the world after the Bible.[152]

---

[147] Hitler, speech on August 19, 1921, *Sämtliche Aufzeichnungen*, 458.
[148] "Adolf Hitlers Ehrentag," *Völkischer Beobachter*, April 22/23, 1923, 1.
[149] Hitler, speech on August 1, 1923, *Sämtliche Aufzeichnungen*, 955.
[150] Hitler, *Mein Kampf*, 306, 307.
[151] Hannah Arendt, *The Origins of Totalitarianism* (New York: Hardcourt Brace Jovanovich, 1979), 360.
[152] Cohn, *Warrant for Genocide*, 128, 138; Rollin, *L'Apocalypse de notre temps*, 40.

CONCLUSION

The 1918 Imperial German intervention in the Ukraine, the land "at the extremity," led to the transfer of extremist anti-Bolshevik and anti-Semitic White views to postwar *völkisch* German circles in Berlin and Munich, including the immediate milieu from which the National Socialist movement arose. Most notably, Lieutenant Piotr Shabelskii-Bork carried *The Protocols of the Elders of Zion* from the Ukraine to Berlin and then gave them to Ludwig Müller von Hausen, a *völkisch* publicist, for translation and publication in German. Hitler's early mentors Dietrich Eckart and Alfred Rosenberg internalized the warnings of looming Jewish world rule contained in the *Protocols*. The *Protocols* in turn influenced Hitler's *Weltanschauung* through their graphic portrayal of ruthless Jewish plans to take over the world through insidious means, notably starving resisting peoples. Hitler used the *Protocols* as a powerful weapon against what he perceived as the menace of international Jewry.

As well as facilitating the cross-cultural transfer of dangerous right-wing views, the German Ukrainian Intervention forged enduring pro-nationalist German sentiments among leading White officers who served under Germany's aegis in the Ukraine. Germany's occupation of the Ukraine began a process of right-wing German–White/White émigré collaboration, as it brought together men who shared common enemies: the Entente, the Bolsheviks, and the Jews. Several White officers who had played prominent roles in the Ukraine under German occupation went on to serve the National Socialist movement in Germany, notably General Vladimir Biskupskii, Colonel Ivan Poltavets-Ostranitsa, Colonel Fedor Vinberg, Lieutenant Shabelskii-Bork, Lieutenant Sergei Taboritskii, and Colonel Pavel Bermondt, later known as Bermondt-Avalov.

Germany's Ukrainian adventure set a precedent for further nationalist German-White anti-Bolshevik military cooperation, as German officers learned to value their White officer counterparts as loyal pro-Germans and anti-Bolsheviks. In particular, the German/White alliance established in and just outside the Ukraine in 1918 served as a precedent for the 1919 Latvian Intervention under the leadership of Bermondt-Avalov. In this campaign, German Freikorps (volunteer corps) fought shoulder to shoulder with White formations in an anti-Bolshevik crusade from which many future National Socialists emerged.

CHAPTER 3

"Hand in hand with Germany"

The 1919 Latvian Intervention of a combined anti-Bolshevik German/ White force built upon the international right-wing collaboration that had been established during the German occupation of the Ukraine in 1918. The German/White crusade against Bolshevik forces in the Baltic region is more well known than the German Ukrainian Intervention, notably due to the German author Klaus Theweleit's detailed study of the German Freikorps (volunteer corps) in the Baltic area, *Male Fantasies*.[1] Freikorps in Latvia fought side by side with Whites, including many veterans of previous anti-Bolshevik operations directed from inside and just outside the Ukraine under Germany's aegis. White émigrés played key leadership roles in the Latvian Intervention. Pavel Bermondt-Avalov, who had earlier helped to establish the Southern Army near the Ukraine in 1918, rose to lead the German/White expeditionary force in Latvia. General Vladimir Biskupskii, who had played a leading role in Hetman Pavel Skoropadskii's Ukrainian Volunteer Army, represented Bermondt-Avalov's Western Volunteer Army politically in Berlin.

In addition to spurring the pro-nationalist German careers of Bermondt-Avalov and Biskupskii (both White officers went on to serve Hitler's National Socialist movement), the Latvian Intervention solidified the Baltic German "Rubonia clique" of four determined anti-Bolsheviks from the same Riga fraternity in Imperial Russia. This right-wing quartet consisted of Max von Scheubner-Richter, who had aided the Imperial German advance into the Baltic region during World War I, Otto von Kursell, Arno Schickedanz, and Alfred Rosenberg. All four comrades went on to play important roles in Aufbau, the Munich-based conspiratorial organization that integrated *völkisch* German and White émigré efforts to overthrow both

---

[1] Klaus Theweleit, *Male Fantasies*, 2 vols., trans. Erica Carter and Chris Turner (Minneapolis: University of Minnesota Press, 1989).

the Weimar Republic and the Soviet Union. All four colleagues likewise joined the National Socialist Party early on.

Like Germany's Ukrainian occupation, the Latvian Intervention failed militarily after some early successes. It nonetheless engendered solidarity between alienated *völkisch* Germans and resentful Whites who regarded themselves as trapped by Bolshevism to the East, the Entente to the West, and Germany's perfidious left-wing regime in the middle. Moreover, the Latvian Intervention significantly affected international right-wing collaboration against the Weimar Republic. The Baltic adventure served not only as an anti-Bolshevik crusade abroad, but also as a means of supporting national revolutionary strivings to overthrow the Weimar Republic. German and White soldiers in Latvia backed the nationalist German conspiracy to establish a right-wing German regime under Wolfgang Kapp, who had sought to replace the Kaiser with a military dictatorship under General Erich von Ludendorff, the Chief of the Army General Staff, during World War I.

Kapp and his co-conspirators, most notably General Ludendorff, counted on support for their intended putsch from combined German/White forces after these had defeated the Bolsheviks in Latvia and Russia. After the failure of Latvian Intervention, Kapp and his allies used demobilized German *Baltikumkämpfer* (Baltic fighters) and the remnants of White units to undermine the largely socialist German government. Nationalist German/White émigré counter-revolutionary efforts culminated in the Kapp Putsch of March 1920. While this undertaking failed overall, it succeeded in Bavaria, and it set a precedent for combined *völkisch* German/White émigré action to reconstitute the German state through violent means. The National Socialist Party under Hitler's leadership subsequently drew from this legacy of international right-wing intrigue.

THE LATVIAN INTERVENTION AND PREPARATIONS FOR NATIONAL RENEWAL

The Latvian Intervention of 1919 came after German wartime successes in the Baltic region. During World War I, Imperial German armed forces made significant advances along the east coast of the Baltic Sea before the Bolshevik seizure of power in 1917. German troops captured Riga, the largest and most important city of the Baltic provinces of the former Russian

Empire, in early September 1917.[2] The Riga native First Lieutenant Max von Scheubner-Richter played a leading role in the German occupation of Baltic lands, which many Baltic Germans regarded as an act of liberation. He served as the deputy leader of the Army High Command East VIII Press Office in Riga. More importantly, the Political Section of the German Army General Staff in Riga assigned him to solve political and military problems relating to the planned German advance into Livonia and Estonia.

The German Political Section considered Scheubner-Richter to be an appropriate choice for such important strategic responsibilities because of his upbringing in the Russian Empire along with his studies to become a lecturer in Russian history. Scheubner-Richter had also gathered valuable wartime experience in Eastern matters. He had served as the German vice consul in the Ottoman Empire with the mission of fostering Caucasian and Ukrainian independence movements within the Russian Empire. He had also unsuccessfully pressured the Ottoman government to stop its wartime massacre of Christian Armenians. The Political Section of the Army Chief of Staff had sent him to Stockholm in July 1917, where he had used the haven of neutral territory to initiate contacts with various anti-Bolshevik groups in Russia, most notably with Ukrainians and Georgians.[3] Scheubner-Richter had come to the attention of General Ludendorff, the chief of the Army General Staff, through his daring and initiative. He had subsequently enjoyed the general's patronage.[4]

With the Bolshevik seizure of power in early November 1917, Scheubner-Richter worried that the Baltic Germans still under Bolshevik rule must have it the worst in Bolshevik Russia. He tirelessly planned the German advance into Livonia and Estonia.[5] His commanding officer in Riga, Major General Buchfink, found Scheubner-Richter to possess great intelligence, courage, and initiative. Buchfink later stressed that his operations in the Baltic region would not have been possible without Scheubner-Richter's knowledge of Russian and Baltic conditions. Buchfink further stressed that Scheubner-Richter was well known and appreciated in the German Officer Corps and was one of the most beloved figures in Riga society.[6]

---

[2] Protocol of a Baltischer Vertrauensrat meeting on March 1, 1919, BAB, 8054, number 2, 138.

[3] Max von Scheubner-Richter, "Abriss des Lebens- und Bildungsganges von Dr. Max Erwin von Scheubner-Richter," sent to Walther Nicolai in April 1923, RGVA (TsKhIDK), *fond* 1414, *opis* 1, *delo* 21, 230; Otto von Kursell, "Dr. Ing. Max Erwin von Scheubner-Richter zum Gedächtnis," ed. Henrik Fischer (Munich, 1969), 4, 5, 9, 24.

[4] Max Hildebert Boehm, "Baltische Einflüsse auf die Anfänge des Nationalsozialismus," *Jahrbuch des baltischen Deutschtums*, 1967, 59, 60.

[5] Kursell, "Dr. Ing. Max Erwin von Scheubner-Richter zum Gedächtnis," 9.

[6] Evaluation of Scheubner-Richter from Major-General Buchfink sent to Nicolai on March 20, 1923, RGVA (TsKhIDK), *fond* 1414, *opis* 1, *delo* 21, 228.

Scheubner-Richter's efforts to bring the Baltic region under German control succeeded initially, but he soon experienced frustration. Imperial German troops captured Reval, Estonia's principal city, in late February 1918.[7] Scheubner-Richter earned the Iron Cross, First Class, for his contributions to the German advance into Livonia and Estonia. Aware that the fledgling Bolshevik regime could not offer serious military resistance, he pressed for German forces to advance on Petrograd, then the Soviet capital, to overthrow the Bolshevik regime and to establish a nationalist Russian government friendly to Imperial Germany. The German negotiations with Bolshevik representatives in Brest-Litovsk precluded this course of action, however. Rebuffed in his efforts to convince the German Army High Command to capture Petrograd, the most Scheubner-Richter could do to undermine Bolshevik rule in early 1918 was to establish an anti-Bolshevik secret service that extracted information from sources within Bolshevik Russia.[8]

Years later, Scheubner-Richter wrote articles in the National Socialist newspaper the *Völkisch Observer* that criticized Imperial Germany's failure to overthrow the Bolshevik regime in 1918. In a March 1923 commentary, "The Red Army," he argued that the German High Command's failure to march on Petrograd in 1918 to end the "Bolshevik specter" had allowed the Bolsheviks to consolidate their power in Russia and had led to the outbreak of socialist revolution in Imperial Germany on November 9, 1918.[9] In a September 1923 essay, "Germany's Bolshevization," Scheubner-Richter stressed that despite his advice to capture Petrograd and to install "a Russian national government friendly towards us," the German High Command, under pressure from the Ministry of Foreign Affairs and the Reichstag (Parliament), had agreed to the "insanity" of negotiations in Brest-Litovsk.[10]

Two of Scheubner-Richter's colleagues from the Rubonia Fraternity at the Riga Polytechnic Institute, Alfred Rosenberg and Otto von Kursell, began collaborating with Scheubner-Richter in late 1918. Like Scheubner-Richter, Rosenberg favored a German advance on Petrograd.[11] He had learned to hate Bolshevism through firsthand experience. He had witnessed the Bolshevik Revolution towards the end of his studies at the Polytechnic Institute that had been relocated from Riga to Moscow, and he had received

---

[7] Protocol of a Baltischer Vertrauensrat meeting on March 1, 1919, BAB, 8054, number 2, 138.
[8] Kursell, "Dr. Ing. Max Erwin von Scheubner-Richter zum Gedächtnis," 10, 11.
[9] Scheubner-Richter, "Die Rote Armee," *Völkischer Beobachter*, March 21, 1923, 3.
[10] Scheubner-Richter, "Deutschlands Bolschewisierung," *Völkischer Beobachter*, September 21, 1923, 1.
[11] Alfred Rosenberg, "Von Brest-Litowsk nach Versailles," *Völkischer Beobachter*, May 8, 1921, 5.

his degree in architecture early in 1918 under Bolshevik rule. He had left Moscow for Reval as a convinced opponent of Bolshevism.[12]

German occupying forces in Estonia hired Rosenberg as a German teacher in October 1918, thereby beginning his extensive career in German service.[13] Like Scheubner-Richter, Rosenberg warned of the Bolshevik peril in the rightist newspaper *Das neue Deutschland* (*The New Germany*).[14] He gave his first public speech in the Reval City Hall on "Marxism and Jewry."[15] Even at this early stage of his career, Rosenberg had formed the basis for his later assertions of the menace of "Jewish Bolshevism."

In addition to working with Rosenberg, Scheubner-Richter joined up with his old Rubonia brother Otto von Kursell in late 1918 to help rebuild Baltic German cultural life after the depredations of war. Kursell had served in the Tsarist Army in the Reval Engineering Battalion before the Bolshevik Revolution, and he considered himself lucky to have survived the Bolshevik seizure of power.[16] After German troops had occupied Reval, Kursell had joined the Baltic German Selbstschutz, or Self-Defense League, in that city.[17] He subsequently worked for Scheubner-Richter in the Political Section of Army High Command East VIII. Both colleagues collaborated to rebuild their *alma mater*, the Riga Polytechnic Institute.[18]

In October 1918, the German Army High Command East VIII centered in Riga, for which Scheubner-Richter and Kursell worked, established partially and entirely White military formations. The High Command set up the Baltische Landeswehr (Baltic Defense Force) under Major Alfred Fletcher. Fletcher maintained close relations with Wolfgang Kapp, who led the right-wing German Fatherland Party, which wished to institute a military dictatorship to replace the Kaiser. The High Command organized four formations of the Baltic Defense Force. The first unit comprised Baltic Germans who had fought in the Imperial German Army, the second and third formations were made up of Baltic Germans who had served in the

[12] Woldemar Helb, *Album Rubonorum, 1875–1972*, fourth edn. (Neustadt an der Aisch: Verlag Degener & Co., 1972), 165.

[13] PDM report from January 26, 1931, NSDAPHA, BAB, NS 26, number 1259, 8.

[14] Walter Laqueur, *Russia and Germany: A Century of Conflict* (London: Weidenfeld and Nicolson, 1965), 60; Seppo Kuusisto, *Alfred Rosenberg in der nationalsozialistischen Aussenpolitik 1933–1939*, trans. Christian Krötzl (Helsinki: Finska Historiska Samfundet, 1984), 12, 13, 30.

[15] "Der Kämpfer Alfred Rosenberg: Zur Ernennung des Reichsleiters zum Reichsminister für die besetzten Gebiete," *Parteipresse-Sonderdienst*, Nr. 368, November 17, 1941, KR, BAB, NS 8, number 8, 8.

[16] Wolfgang Frank, "Professor Otto v. Kursell: Wie ich den Führer zeichnete," *Hamburger Illustrierte*, March 6, 1934, BHSAM, *Sammlung Personen*, number 7440, 12.

[17] Helb, *Album Rubonorum*, 141.

[18] Kursell, "Dr. Ing. Max Erwin von Scheubner-Richter zum Gedächtnis," 9, 10.

Imperial Russian Army, and the fourth detachment was composed of men who had not fought in any armed forces.

The Baltic Defense Force initially contained approximately 1,000 soldiers. Arno Schickedanz, the fourth member of the Rubonia clique after Scheubner-Richter, Kursell, and Rosenberg, played a prominent role in the formation.[19] Like Rosenberg, Schickedanz had experienced the Bolshevik Revolution firsthand. He had earned his degree in chemistry at the Polytechnic Institute in Moscow early in 1918 under Bolshevik rule before disassociating himself from the Bolsheviks. He left Bolshevik Russia and then volunteered for service in the cavalry of the Baltic Defense Force in the fall of 1918.[20]

As well as establishing the Baltic Defense Force in October 1918, the German Army High Command East VIII began organizing a White volunteer force called the Northern Army as a complement to the Southern Army based just outside the Ukraine that German authorities supported. The Northern Army was based in northwestern Russia, including the Baltic region. The necessary funds, weapons, clothing, and rations came from the Imperial German government. The Northern Army was to be combat ready in two-and-a-half months and was to swear an oath of loyalty to the Tsar. Finally having agreed to strike directly at the heart of Bolshevism, the German Army High Command charged the Northern Army with capturing Petrograd, overthrowing the Bolshevik regime, and proclaiming a military dictatorship until the monarchy could be reestablished in Russia.[21]

German Fatherland Party leader Kapp supported the Northern Army, which was soon overwhelmed because of worsening political and military circumstances. He believed that German forces had to support monarchists in Russia to bring about a nationalist Russian state that would serve as Germany's ally against the Entente. Kapp personally wrote the chief of staff of the Northern Army, Colonel Heye, and stressed that German troops had to support the Russian monarchists.[22] The outbreak of revolution in Germany in early November severely weakened the position of German occupying forces in the Baltic as well as in the Ukraine. A grand nationalist German–Russian rapprochement in the Baltic region along the lines that

---

[19] Pavel Bermondt-Avalov, *Im Kampf gegen den Bolschewismus: Erinnerungen von General Fürst Awaloff, Oberbefehlshaber der Deutsch-Russischen Westarmee im Baltikum* (Hamburg: Von J. J. Augustin, 1925), 251, 252.

[20] Helb, *Album Rubonorum*, 165.

[21] Bermondt-Avalov, *Im Kampf gegen den Bolschewismus*, 68–70.

[22] Bruno Thoss, *Der Ludendorff-Kreis 1919–1923: München als Zentrum der mitteleuropäischen Gegenrevolution zwischen Revolution und Hitler-Putsch* (Munich: Stadtarchiv München, 1978), 372.

Kapp desired did not materialize in 1918. By the end of November 1918, the Northern Army faced rout at the hand of the advancing Red Army.[23]

Scheubner-Richter had played an important role in German successes in the Baltic region, and he led a rearguard action when faced with a rapidly deteriorating situation in Latvia. He transferred from his recently acquired position as leader of the Press Office of the Army High Command East VIII to the German Embassy in Riga in December 1918.[24] High Command East personnel left Riga on the night of December 29/30, 1918, but Scheubner-Richter volunteered to stay behind as the acting head of the German Embassy in Riga. He negotiated with primarily Latvian Bolshevik forces, which captured the city on January 3, 1919. He secured the evacuation of 2,400 *Reich* Germans and a number of Baltic Germans to Germany before Bolshevik officers arrested him. Bolshevik leaders wished to execute him as a dangerous counter-revolutionary agent, but the German Foreign Office brought sufficient pressure to bear on Latvian Bolshevik leaders to release him.

After his brush with death at the hands of Bolsheviks in Riga, Scheubner-Richter traveled to Königsberg in East Prussia as an even more fiercely determined anti-Bolshevik.[25] He acted as the political advisor of August Winnig, the socialist German government's chargé who served as Reichskommissar (State Commissioner) of the narrow Eastern territories still under German occupation.[26] Scheubner-Richter sent reports of the Bolshevik peril to the new socialist government in Berlin, which distrusted Bolshevism and fostered the formation of German Freikorps to fight against Bolshevik forces in the Baltic region.[27]

Scheubner-Richter's superior Winnig concluded an agreement with the fledgling non-Bolshevik exile Latvian government under Minister President Karlis Ulmanis whereby German volunteers for military service in Latvia would gain the right to receive Latvian citizenship and with it the ability to acquire land.[28] Entente representatives undertook a delicate balancing

[23] Müller-Leibnitz, "V. Der Rückmarsch der 10. Armee im Winter 1918/19," [1937?], RGVA (TsKhIDK), *fond* 1424, *opis* 1, *delo* 13, 39.

[24] Scheubner-Richter, "Abriss des Lebens- und Bildungsganges," April 1923, RGVA (TsKhIDK), *fond* 1414, *opis* 1, *delo* 21, 230, 231.

[25] Kursell, "Dr. Ing. Max Erwin von Scheubner-Richter zum Gedächtnis," 12, 24.

[26] Robert Williams, *Culture in Exile: Russian Émigrés in Germany, 1881–1941* (Ithaca: Cornell University Press, 1972), 165; Rudolf Klatt, *Ostpreussen unter dem Reichskommissariat 1919/1920* (Heidelberg: Quelle & Meyer, 1958), 82.

[27] Scheubner-Richter, "Deutschlands Bolschewisierung," 1; Müller-Leibnitz, "V. Der Rückmarsch der 10. Armee im Winter 1918/19," RGVA (TsKhIDK), *fond* 1424, *opis* 1, *delo* 13, 38.

[28] "Die Ereignisse im Baltikum vom Herbst 1918 bis Ende 1919," January 1920, BA/MF, RWM, *Nachlass* 247, number 91, 4.

act at this time. They were wary of granting the new socialist German government too much leeway, yet they feared the spread of Bolshevism into Germany. Entente authorities ultimately decided to cast a blind eye on the establishment of significant German forces in the Baltic region though this was specifically forbidden according to the terms of the November 11, 1918 Armistice.[29]

Under Winnig's overall supervision, Scheubner-Richter performed organizational and propaganda tasks to further the establishment of Freikorps to fight in Latvia.[30] To intensify anti-Bolshevik propaganda, he founded the Zentralausschuss für den ostpreussischen Heimatdienst (Central Committee for the East Prussian Home Service) in February 1919.[31] This organization was subordinated to the Reichszentrale für Heimatdienst (Central Office for Home Service), which worked for "reconstruction" through the means of disseminating "indisputable facts" about Bolshevism that would lead to the "people's enlightenment."[32] Scheubner-Richter proved one of Bolshevism's greatest opponents.

Hoping to regain the initiative in the Baltic region, where Scheubner-Richter directed his energies, General Rüdiger von der Goltz, the former leader in Wolfgang Kapp's now outlawed German Fatherland Party, set about creating a powerful anti-Bolshevik force in Latvia. Goltz officially took command of German Freikorps in the Baltic region, primarily in the southern portion of Latvia, in the middle of February 1919.[33] He enjoyed great popularity among opponents of Bolshevism in the Baltic region, largely because he had led the German military expedition that had secured Finnish independence from Bolshevik Russia in the spring of 1918.[34] Like Scheubner-Richter and Rosenberg, Goltz had unsuccessfully lobbied the German Army High Command to advance on Petrograd to overthrow the fledgling Bolshevik regime in 1918.[35]

Goltz viewed his struggle against the Bolsheviks in the Baltic region as a fight against a plague that threatened all of Europe. In his 1920 memoirs, Goltz asserted that he had fought against the "Bolshevik *Weltanschauung*

[29] A. V. Smolin, *Beloe dvizhenie na Severo-Zapade Rossii 1918–1920* (Saint Petersburg, Dmitrii Bulanin, 1999), 334.

[30] Kursell, "Dr. Ing. Max Erwin von Scheubner-Richter zum Gedächtnis," 13.

[31] Williams, *Culture in Exile*, 164; Klatt, *Ostpreussen unter dem Reichskommissariat*, 139.

[32] "Reichszentrale für Heimatdienst," a booklet, RKÜöO, BAB, 1507, number 23, 4.

[33] Müller-Leibnitz, "II. Der Feldzug im Baltikum 1919," [1937?], RGVA (TsKhIDK), *fond* 1255, *opis* 2, *delo* 48, 4.

[34] "Hochwohlgeborener Herr Generalmajor Graf von der Goltz!", BA/MF, *Nachlass* 714, number 1, 1; Eduard Freiherr von der Goltz, *Kriegsgedächtnisbuch des Geschlechts der Grafen und Freiherrn von der Goltz* (Potsdam: Stiftungsverlag, 1919), 29.

[35] Rosenberg, "Von Brest-Litowsk nach Versailles," 5.

of Asiatic bondage" in the Latvian Intervention in an effort to prevent the "downfall of the West."[36] A sense of Goltz's missionary spirit can be gained from his 1921 novel *The Guilt*, which is set in the immediate postwar period. The protagonist, Pastor Lange, concludes:

The guilt of our people is that it did not want to fight out this necessary struggle because of its love of peace. Now, for its own good, it is being forced to do so through its irreconcilable enemies, for God Himself wishes this struggle . . . And we clergymen must not stop preaching this holy war . . . Thus let us go forward with God! We follow the cross that shines radiantly before us through terrible struggle, through darkness and affliction . . . We march to the East, from whence the radiance dawns over the West and the entire world – *ex oriente lux* (from the East – light)![37]

Goltz thus employed religiously inspired crusading zeal in his anti-Bolshevik efforts.

In his political views, Goltz favored *Ostpolitik* (Eastern policy) in the form of German–White anti-Bolshevik collaboration on land as a counterweight to the Entente, which primarily demonstrated its power at sea. He advocated an "economic and political rapprochement with the coming Russia." By this he meant that he wished to help overthrow the Bolshevik regime and then "open up broad economic regions and win a new friend in an alliance against the English world empire in the form of the coming bourgeois Russia."[38] Goltz's *Ostpolitik* sought to tip the balance of power into Germany's favor once again through a German–White Russian alliance.

German-sponsored anti-Bolshevik forces in Latvia under Goltz's overall leadership in early 1919 consisted of the Iron Division under Major Josef Bischoff near the Baltic Sea and the Baltic Defense Force under Kapp's colleague Major Fletcher inland. The Baltic Defense Force included a Russian detachment under Prince Anatol Levin composed of infantry and cavalry units. Levin's force consisted entirely of officers at the beginning, but it added common soldiers from Russian prisoner of war camps in Germany. Levin's unit reached a combat strength of 600 men.[39] Lieutenant Sergei Taboritskii, the comrade of Colonel Fedor Vinberg and Lieutenant Piotr

[36] Rüdiger von der Goltz, *Meine Sendung in Finnland und im Baltikum* (Leipzig: Koehler, 1920), V.
[37] Goltz, *Die Schuld* (Greifswald: L. Bamberg, 1921), 288, 292.
[38] Goltz, *Meine Sendung in Finnland und im Baltikum*, 127, 147.
[39] Goltz, *Meine Sendung in Finnland und im Baltikum*, 124, 221; Müller-Leibnitz, "II. Der Feldzug im Baltikum 1919," RGVA (TsKhIDK), *fond* 1255, *opis* 2, *delo* 48, 24.

Shabelskii-Bork, recruited interned Russian soldiers for the Latvian Intervention and organized them into effective combat units from Berlin.[40]

Baltic Defense Force commander Fletcher kept his ultra-nationalist colleague Wolfgang Kapp updated on events in Latvia. Kapp and Fletcher corresponded regularly.[41] In a letter from early March 1919, Fletcher emphasized that he enjoyed good relations with the Baltic Germans under his command as well as the Russian and Latvian formations that served under him. He noted that these units were "composed almost completely of former Russian (Tsarist) officers." He boasted to Kapp, "You can believe that I am creating order with my dazzling 'White Guard' . . . (hated by all Reds in Russia and Germany)." He further stressed:

We have somewhat urgently sent some masters of the "proletariat of all countries" out of the castles and cities and into the Beyond. This is a matter of life and death. There are no prisoners, and that is why these criminals sometimes fight desperately when surrounded.[42]

Fletcher regarded his Baltic Defense Force to be engaged in an all-or-nothing struggle against Bolshevism.

Kapp placed high hopes on Goltz's military formations to which Fletcher's Baltic Defense Force belonged, not only as determined anti-Bolshevik units that were proving their mettle abroad, but also as a source of armed support in his bid to establish a nationalist German regime under his leadership. At the same time that he cultivated ties with forces in the Baltic region that he ultimately hoped to use in a nationalist putsch in Germany, Kapp oversaw the creation of sympathetic nationalist cells inside Germany that would support his bid for power at an auspicious time.[43] In the early months of 1919, Kapp established the Ostpreussischer Heimatbund (East Prussian Home League) to work towards his goal of national renewal. The League officially sought the "repulse of Bolshevism" and the "strengthening of the national idea."[44] Behind the scenes, Kapp planned to overthrow the despised primarily socialist German government.[45]

---

[40] JM charge against Piotr Shabelskii-Bork and Sergei Taboritskii from May 29, 1922, GSAPKB, *Repositur* 84a, number 14953, 16; letter from Taboritskii to Mrs. Shabelskii-Bork from March 18, 1926, GSAPKB, *Repositur* 84a, number 14953, 80.

[41] Wolfgang Kapp correspondence, GSAPKB, *Repositur* 92, number 801.

[42] Letter from Alfred Fletcher to Kapp from March 11, 1919, GSAPKB, *Repositur* 92, number 801, 57.

[43] Kapp, "Zur Vorgeschichte des März-Unternehmens," 1922, BAK, *Nachlass* 309, number 7, 18.

[44] DB report from October 12, 1923, RGVA (TsKhIDK), *fond* 7, *opis* 1, *delo* 878, reel 4, 331, 332.

[45] Kapp, "Zur Vorgeschichte des März-Unternehmens," 1922, BAK, *Nachlass* 309, number 7, 18.

In addition to counting on support from General Goltz, Kapp placed considerable hopes on General Max Hoffmann, who had led the German negotiations with Bolshevik representatives in Brest-Litovsk but had later supported anti-Bolshevik formations in the Ukraine. Kapp and Hoffmann had begun collaborating closely during World War I.[46] In 1919, Hoffmann helped to create dependable military units inside of Germany that Goltz's troops could collaborate with to topple the primarily socialist German government. The overthrow of the German government was to spread from Kapp's East Elbian stronghold to less well-developed western regions with the assistance of power bases in Stuttgart, Darmstadt, and Munich.[47]

Munich, the birthplace of National Socialism, served as the most significant western outpost of Kapp's support. In addition to organizing paramilitary forces under sympathetic officers there, Kapp supported the antigovernmental activities of Dietrich Eckart, Hitler's early mentor. Eckart had seized Kapp's attention through his *völkisch* play *Heinrich der Hohenstaufe* (*Heinrich the Hohenstaufe*) in August 1916.[48] Already at this time, Kapp had argued that Eckart's work needed to be disseminated to "broad circles" to bring about the "awakening of national life."[49] Kapp had subscribed to Eckart's anti-Semitic publication *Auf gut deutsch* (*In Plain German*), immediately upon its appearance in late 1918. Pleased with Eckart's endeavor, Kapp had given him 1,000 marks to further his work.[50]

Eckart thanked Kapp profusely in February 1919 for his considerable financial and moral support, which had come as a "miracle" when he had needed it most. He asserted, "That which lifts me up the most is the certainty you give me that I am running my paper in the right spirit, that I am running it in your spirit."[51] After Eckart received Kapp's moral and financial backing, the number of subscribers to *In Plain German* grew continually yet modestly, reaching 500 by February 1919 and eventually peaking at approximately 5,000.[52]

During the time of his editorship of *In Plain German*, Eckart cooperated with anti-Bolshevik, anti-Semitic members of the Rubonia clique

---

[46] Letter from Max Hoffmann to his wife from January 16, 1917, BA/MF, *Nachlass* 37, number 2, 155.

[47] Kapp, "Zur Vorgeschichte des März-Unternehmens," 1922, BAK, *Nachlass* 309, number 7, 18.

[48] Letter from Karl Graf von Bothmer to Kapp from August 28, 1916, GSAPKB, *Repositur* 92, number 792, 55.

[49] Letter from Kapp to Bothmer from September 8, 1916, GSAPKB, *Repositur* 92, number 792, 73.

[50] Dietrich Eckart's examination at the AGM from July 10, 1920, RGVA (TsKhIDK), *fond* 567, *opis* 1, *delo* 2496, 17.

[51] Letter from Eckart to Kapp from February 11, 1919, BAK, *Nachlass* 309, number 7.

[52] Margarete Plewnia, *Auf dem Weg zu Hitler: Der "völkische" Publizist Dietrich Eckart* (Bremen: Schünemann Universitätsverlag, 1970), 29.

from Riga. We have already noted that Eckart collaborated closely with Rosenberg, who wrote articles for *In Plain German*. Rosenberg's colleague Scheubner-Richter traveled to Munich in 1919 on the urging of the fellow Rubonia Fraternity member Arno Schickedanz, who had already settled in Munich. Once in the Bavarian capital, Scheubner-Richter assessed Rosenberg's efforts to gain financial backing for White forces still fighting in Russia. Rosenberg introduced Scheubner-Richter to industrial circles and White émigrés in Munich society.[53] Scheubner-Richter met Eckart, most likely through Rosenberg, and he in turn introduced Eckart to the former Rubonia member Otto von Kursell, who had settled in Munich earlier in 1919.[54]

Scheubner-Richter soon returned to northern Germany to lead anti-Bolshevik activities there, and Schickedanz seems not to have collaborated closely with Eckart, but Kursell assisted Eckart with *In Plain German*. He specialized in portraying Jewish figures in a sinister manner. In one joint venture, Eckart wrote caustic verses to each of Kursell's drawings of Jewish leaders in Germany. A special edition of *In Plain German* with Kursell's drawings and Eckart's commentary circulated throughout Germany. It provoked a visceral anti-Semitic reaction.[55] In addition to assisting Eckart and Rosenberg with *In Plain German*, Kursell held anti-Bolshevik speeches in Munich. He warned that the propaganda and recruiting methods of revolutionary leaders in Germany followed the pattern set earlier by the Bolsheviks in Russia.[56]

In addition to supporting the anti-Bolshevik, anti-Semitic propaganda activities of Eckart and the largely White émigré circle around him in Munich, Kapp kept in contact with his colleague Ludwig Müller von Hausen, who had published the influential anti-Semitic forgery *The Protocols of the Elders of Zion* in German. Hausen played a shadowy role in the Latvian Intervention. He proved extremely well informed on secret far right German/White plans for closer collaboration. He possessed a detailed outline for an anti-Bolshevik alliance of nationalist Germans and Whites marked "Strictly confidential," and dated from Berlin, March 16, 1919:

---

[53] Paul Leverkühn, *Posten auf ewiger Wache: Aus dem abenteurreichen Leben des Max von Scheubner-Richter* (Essen: Essener Verlagsanstalt, 1938), 184.

[54] Johannes Baur, *Die russische Kolonie in München, 1900–1945: Deutsch–russische Beziehungen im 20. Jahrhundert* (Wiesbaden: Harrassowitz Verlag, 1998), 182, 185; Frank, "Professor Otto v. Kursell: Wie ich den Führer zeichnete," *Hamburger Illustrierte*, March 6, 1934, BHSAM, *Sammlung Personen*, number 7440, 12.

[55] Rosenberg, Memoirs, KR, BAB, NS 8, number 20, 3.

[56] Frank, "Professor Otto v. Kursell: Wie ich den Führer zeichnete," *Hamburger Illustrierte*, March 6, 1934, BHSAM, *Sammlung Personen*, number 7440, 12.

"Draft of a Program for the Activity of an Organization for an Economic Rapprochement between Germany and Russia."

This secretive organization was to provide a "unified direction" and a "headquarters" to the "Russian circles inside as well as outside of Russia who are striving for a close economic-political alliance with Germany." It was also to direct "careful, clever propaganda" towards these Russian elements to prepare them for "energetic action against the Entente." The international organization was to establish a "secret intelligence apparatus" to monitor the mood among the Russian populace and to determine the intentions of the Entente. Moreover, it was to direct "anti-Bolshevik front propaganda" from Germany eastwards in collaboration with the largely anti-governmental Grenzschutz Ost (Frontier Guards East). This conspiratorial German/White association was to establish contacts with White émigré colonies throughout the world and to supervise Russian prisoner of war camps in Germany.

Finally, with regard to organization, the German/Russian entity was to possess both a German and a Russian office in Berlin, with a German representative in the Russian bureau and a Russian representative in the German one. These two offices were to keep in close contact with each other. The central leadership of the entire organization was to be composed of a secret committee of three Germans and two Russians.[57] With further evidence lacking, the degree to which this conspiratorial organization of nationalist Germans and Whites progressed beyond the planning stage remains unclear.

In any case, prospects for a successful German/White anti-Bolshevik campaign in Latvia that could be used as a springboard to establish nationalist regimes in Germany and Russia reached a high point on May 22, 1919. On this date, the roughly 14,000 Baltic and *Reich* Germans and approximately 2,000 Russians and Latvians of Major Fletcher's Baltic Defense Force captured Riga.[58] The Baltic Defense Force's capture of Riga proved the greatest single success of the German-backed Latvian Intervention of 1919. The coup offered White circles throughout the former Russian Empire and abroad the hope of witnessing the overthrow of hated Bolshevik rule.

Baltic Defense Force cavalry officer Arno Schickedanz participated in the capture of Riga. He subsequently submitted a report of conditions in the former hanseatic city to his Rubonia brother Scheubner-Richter, who was

---

[57] Draft in possession of Hausen, March 16, 1919, RGVA (TsKhIDK), *fond* 577, *opis* 2, *delo* 130, 1–5.
[58] Georg Taube, "Der Esten Krieg," [1920], BAB, 8025, number 15, 3.

in Danzig serving as the leader of the Central Committee of the *Ostdeutscher Heimatdienst* (East German Home Service).[59] Schickedanz related how the Baltic Defense Force had successfully stormed the city, but regrettably too late to stop Bolshevik authorities from shooting thirty hostages. He noted that the city's dazed citizens at first had seemed unable to grasp that they had been freed from the "brutality and atrocities of the criminal, bestial Commissars." After the shock of recent events had worn off, however, Riga's population had embraced the Baltic Defense Force for ending Bolshevik terror and accompanying starvation.

Schickedanz asserted that Bolshevik Commissars in Riga had represented "the most depraved criminals one can think of." They had plundered shamelessly. Bolshevik forced labor policies particularly outraged Schickedanz. Bolshevik leaders had collected members of the intelligentsia and the middle class who had become "unemployed" with the "nationalization, that is, closing" of stores and businesses, and "out of pure pleasure in torturing" had forced them to perform degrading tasks such as carrying manure, chopping wood, and cleaning toilets. Schickedanz wrote Scheubner-Richter that Bolsheviks had treated these forced laborers with great brutality, beating them, kicking them, and even dumping excrement over their heads. He asserted: "The Swedes during the 30 Years' War were lenient people in comparison with these beasts."[60] Schickedanz's report demonstrated an intense hatred of the Bolsheviks among White forces in Latvia, and it helped to inflame anti-Bolshevik passions in Germany.

While Arno Schickedanz received considerable credit for his participation in the capture of Riga, the most famous actor in the Baltic Intervention proved to be the White leader Colonel Pavel Bermondt-Avalov. Around the turn of the year 1918/1919, Bermondt, as he then still called himself, traveled to Germany in the third of four German Army convoys from the Ukraine that evacuated White officers and soldiers after Pavel Skoropadskii's Hetmanate had collapsed. Bermondt impressed White leaders with his bravery in volunteering to lead and to protect his particular troop transport. Bermondt arrived at Camp Salzwedel located between Berlin and Hamburg in late January 1919.

Once in Camp Salzwedel, Bermondt used his charisma to attract the attention of rightist German circles around Generals Ludendorff and Hoffmann. These men advocated using White officers from the Ukraine to organize the Russian prisoners of war housed in Germany into

[59] Kursell, "Dr. Ing. Max Erwin von Scheubner-Richter zum Gedächtnis," 25.
[60] Arno Schickedanz, [May] 1919 report to Scheubner-Richter, IZG, ZS 2368, 2–6, 8.

anti-Bolshevik combat units to be employed in Latvia.[61] Nationalist German military leaders involved in this scheme generally regarded White officers who had been evacuated from the Ukraine as dependable pro-Germans who intensely hated the Entente as well as the Bolsheviks.[62] With permission from above, Bermondt organized a mounted machine-gun unit from White internees at Camp Salzwedel in early February 1919.

Bermondt traveled to Berlin in the second half of February 1919 to raise support for his White detachment. Generals Ludendorff and Hoffmann approved Bermondt's proposal to raise an interventionary force of White soldiers for an anti-Bolshevik campaign in the Baltic region. The German generals believed that Bermondt's forces would counterbalance the army of General Nikolai Iudenich in Estonia, which they regarded as fully under the control of the British. The German War Minister Gustav Noske, acting on behalf of the socialist German government, approved using Bermondt's forces in the Baltic at the end of March 1919, thus demonstrating that not only German far rightists sought to drive back the Bolshevik threat from the East.[63]

After a period of organization, Bermondt's White soldiers began leaving Berlin for Latvia on May 30, 1919. British and French representatives learned of these troop movements and ordered them to stop, as they feared an increasing German–Russian rapprochement. Bermondt's men continued to move into the Baltic secretly nonetheless. Bermondt himself arrived in Mitau outside Riga in the middle of June 1919. At the time, his forces numbered approximately 3,500 pro-Tsarist officers and soldiers.[64]

Bermondt immediately held talks with General Goltz, the overall German commander in Latvia. He asked for and received German troops for his White contingent to counteract Entente propaganda that the Germans supported Bolshevism. He assessed relations between members of German Freikorps and the Baltic Defense Force on the one hand and his Whites on the other as the "very best." Bermondt observed that Russians and Germans fraternized on the streets and in cafés, thereby reestablishing bonds of friendship that had been severed during World War I. He noted that the Whites under his command were disappointed at the double-dealings of Britain and France and impressed with the willingness of the

---

[61] RKÜöO report from January 18, 1922, RGVA (TsKhIDK), *fond* 772, *opis* 3, *delo* 71, 91, 92; DB report from March 6, 1919, RGVA (TsKhIDK), *fond* 198, *opis* 9, *delo* 4474, reel 1, 48.

[62] Goltz, *Meine Sendung in Finnland und im Baltikum*, 221.

[63] Bermondt-Avalov, *Im Kampf gegen den Bolschewismus*, 51, 52, 128; LGPO report to the RKÜöO from September 9, 1921, RGVA (TsKhIDK), *fond* 772, *opis* 3, *delo* 71, 18.

[64] Bermondt-Avalov, *Im Kampf gegen den Bolschewismus*, 145, 146, 151; Smolin, *Beloe dvizhenie na Severo-Zapade Rossii*, 337.

Germans to help to rebuild Russia despite the difficult situation that the Entente had placed them in.[65]

Although Bermondt had earlier agreed to serve under the Russian commander Prince Anatol Levin, when Entente representatives ordered Levin to subordinate his forces to General Iudenich in Estonia on July 18, 1919 and Levin complied, Bermondt remained stationed in Mitau, Latvia.[66] He even incorporated White officers traveling north to fight with General Iudenich into the ranks of his own forces.[67] On the whole, Bermondt's troops, both Russians and Germans, supported his decision to defy the Entente. In fact, his men idolized him as a charismatic leader.[68]

While Colonel Bermondt consolidated his power in Latvia in defiance of the Entente, Kapp intensified his putsch preparations. In July 1919, he founded the Nationale Vereinigung (National Union), a conglomeration of counter-revolutionary forces that coordinated preparations centered in Prussia and Bavaria to overthrow the Weimar Republic.[69] The German state was known this way because of the ongoing Constitutional Convention that had been convened in the idyllic Thuringian city of Weimar in February 1919. Kapp's National Union united nationalist German officers, established refuge for Baltic troops in Germany so that they could be mobilized for anti-Weimar Republic undertakings after they victoriously returned from abroad, and disseminated political propaganda against German socialists.[70]

Kapp's National Union included several prominent nationalist German leaders. General Ludendorff played a leading role in the conspiratorial organization.[71] Colonel Karl Bauer, Ludendorff's political representative during World War I and a future member of Aufbau, represented the "soul" of the organization.[72] Captain Waldemar Pabst, who had perceived Bolshevism as a "world danger" in November 1918 and had quashed revolutionary uprisings in such cities as Berlin, Munich, and Braunschweig, served as the secretary of the National Union. This meant that he supervised the organization's administrative affairs.[73] August Winnig, then the minister of

[65] Bermondt-Avalov, *Im Kampf gegen den Bolschewismus*, 151, 152, 164.

[66] Bermondt-Avalov, *Im Kampf gegen den Bolschewismus*, 153, 156; Goltz, *Meine Sendung in Finnland und im Baltikum*, 222, 223.

[67] LGPO report to the RKÜöO from September 9, 1921, RGVA (TsKhIDK), *fond* 772, *opis* 3, *delo* 71, 18.

[68] Goltz, *Meine Sendung in Finnland und im Baltikum*, 224.

[69] Elisabeth Schwarze, "Einleitung," *Nachlass Wolfgang Kapp* (Berlin: GSAPKB, 1997), VIII.

[70] Kapp, "Zur Vorgeschichte des März-Unternehmens," 1922, BAK, *Nachlass* 309, number 7, 19.

[71] Waldemar Pabst, "Das Kapp-Unternehmen," 1952, BA/MF, *Nachlass* 620, number 3, 6; Heinrich Class, *Wider den Strom*, vol. 2, BAK, *Kleine Erwerbung* 499, 233.

[72] RKÜöO report from November 1920, BAB, 1507, number 208, 48.

[73] Pabst, "Auszug aus meinem Lebenslauf," 1954, BA/MF, *Nachlass* 620, number 1, 2; RKÜöO report, [1925?], RGVA (TsKhIDK), *fond* 772, *opis* 3, *delo* 781, 4.

East Prussia, worked with the National Union, as did the Riga native First Lieutenant Scheubner-Richter, who collaborated with Winnig.[74]

Kapp and his co-conspirators in the National Union faced a difficult military situation in Latvia, where Colonel Bermondt played an increasingly prominent role, largely because of Entente demands that the German government cease its support of anti-Bolshevik operations there. Latvian Intervention leader General Goltz obeyed the orders of the German government, which was itself under the increasing pressure of the perfidious Entente, by leaving Latvia in early August 1919. He nevertheless continued to play a key role in the Latvian Intervention from behind the scenes.[75]

Goltz favored creating a Russian volunteer army under Colonel Bermondt to direct combined German/White forces in Latvia, but Bermondt faced serious competition for leadership in Latvia from the former Black Hundred member General Vladimir Biskupskii.[76] Biskupskii had evaded French surveillance after the fall of Skoropadskii's Hetmanate in the Ukraine to travel to Berlin. He possessed staunch pro-German views. In a heated argument on the German–Lithuanian border, a French general accused him of being "more German than the Germans themselves."[77] The Deutsche Legion (German Legion), which now included all the Freikorps in Latvia, as a whole preferred Biskupskii to Bermondt.[78] General Iudenich in Estonia favored Biskupskii as well. He pressured General Goltz to name Biskupskii the leader of all anti-Bolshevik volunteer forces in Latvia. Goltz refused, however, stressing that he would only collaborate with Bermondt.[79]

Goltz formed a competent general staff around Colonel Bermondt to lead what was to be called the Western Volunteer Army. This combined German/White force was to advance into the heartland of Bolshevik Russia in defiance of both the Entente and the German government. Goltz wished Bermondt's forces to act in concert with the White armies of General Anton Denikin in the Ukraine and Admiral Aleksandr Kolchak in Siberia. With their combined strength, these forces were to overthrow the Bolshevik regime and to create a pro-German Russian state that the Germans could ally with against the Entente. On September 21,

---

[74] Pabst, "Nachkriegserlebnisse als 1a und Stabschef der Garde-Kav.- (Schü) Division," BA/MF, *Nachlass* 620, number 2, 136; Williams, *Culture in Exile*, 98, 165.

[75] Goltz, *Meine Sendung in Finnland und im Baltikum*, 245.

[76] Andreas Remmer's testimony from June 1, 1923, BHSAM, BSMÄ 36, number 103009, 12.

[77] RKÜöO report from July 20, 1922, RGVA (TsKhIDK), *fond* 772, *opis* 1, *delo* 96, 150, 151.

[78] Captain Wagener, "Bericht über die augenblickliche Lage in Mitau," Berlin, September 8, 1919, GSAPKB, *Repositur* 92, number 815, 40.

[79] Remmer's testimony from June 1, 1923, BHSAM, BSMÄ 36, number 103009, 12.

1919, Goltz and Bermondt concluded an agreement with the approval of War Minister Noske, who increasingly opposed socialist political leadership in Berlin. This arrangement stipulated that all German forces in Latvia join Bermondt's Western Volunteer Army. This process was completed by October 3, 1919. The army numbered approximately 52,000 men, of which roughly 40,000 were Germans, while the rest came from the former Russian Empire.

Serving under the Imperial Russian flag represented the logical choice for German members of the German Legion and the Baltic Defense Force to make. They felt that the German government had betrayed them. Moreover, they wished to fight for their right to remain in Latvia and to receive land as they had been promised. They were at present not granted the right to settle in Latvia after the cessation of hostilities. Ulmanis' Latvian government, which had established itself in Riga after the Baltic Defense Force's capture of the city the previous May, had reneged on its earlier pledges.[80] German soldiers in Latvia also realized that monarchical Russians represented some of their few allies. Major Josef Bischoff, the leader of the Iron Division in Latvia, told his troops: "We want to help the Russians to liberate their fatherland from the scourge of humanity." He stressed, "By helping our friends the Russians, we are acting for the benefit of Germany."[81]

The German soldiers of the Western Volunteer Army who viewed their interests to be tied in with those of Whites served under a shameless self-promoter. After officially taking control of the Western Volunteer Army in the early autumn of 1919, Colonel Bermondt began to call himself Prince Bermondt-Avalov. He claimed that he had earlier used the simple name Bermondt to protect his wife from Bolshevik reprisals.[82] According to an informant to the State Commissioner for the Supervision of Public Order, Bermondt paid a legitimate Prince Avalov to support his claim that he himself was a Prince Avalov.[83] Bermondt-Avalov's origins remain shrouded in mystery. In the middle of the 1920s, the State Commissioner concluded that it was unclear whether Bermondt-Avalov was justified in using his name and title. It remained possible that he was the illegitimate son of Prince Mikhail Avalov, as a member of the Avalov family had claimed.[84] In

[80] Goltz, *Meine Sendung in Finnland und im Baltikum*, 147, 225.

[81] Bermondt-Avalov, *Im Kampf gegen den Bolschewismus*, 204.

[82] LGPO report to the RKÜöO from September 9, 1921, RGVA (TsKhIDK), *fond* 772, *opis* 3, *delo* 71, 18.

[83] RKÜöO report from January 11, 1922, RGVA (TsKhIDK), *fond* 772, *opis* 3, *delo* 71, 80, 81.

[84] RKÜöO report to the RMI from December 6, 1926, RGVA (TsKhIDK), *fond* 772, *opis* 3, *delo* 71, 196.

any case, the adventurer became famous under the name Bermondt-Avalov, sometimes shortened to Avalov.

Bermondt-Avalov later asserted that he had operated in Latvia under the motto that only "hand in hand with Germany" could White forces save the Russian fatherland.[85] He subsequently stressed of the Latvian Intervention under his leadership: "The foundation stone of the revival of Bismarck's policy was laid in the Baltic," meaning a return to friendship along the lines of the "Holy Alliance" that Imperial Germany and Tsarist Russia had belonged to in the late nineteenth century.[86] A general idea of Bermondt-Avalov's views as the popular commander of German and White forces in Latvia can be gained from his 1921 essay "The Legacy of the Revolution and Bolshevism."

In his treatise, Bermondt-Avalov called for an "army advance into the interior of Russia," followed by a military dictatorship in which "the rights of the military governors are unlimited." All Jews were to be treated as foreigners under the "self-determination of peoples, the motto which the Jews themselves preach." These measures were necessary "to reestablish the mighty, strong organism of a great Russia."[87] Bermondt-Avalov had gained inspiration for his political views from the Imperial Russian Black Hundred movement to which he had belonged.[88]

During the Latvian Intervention in which Colonel Bermondt-Avalov drew the most attention, General Biskupskii had to content himself with acting as Bermondt-Avalov's largely ineffective political representative in Berlin.[89] Biskupskii served as the president of the exile organization the Russian National Political Committee.[90] Kapp's associate Waldemar Pabst, the secretary of the National Union, had established this body.[91] Bermondt-Avalov officially recognized the Committee as the sole governing agency of Western Russia.[92] In practice, however, he circumvented its authority through his personal representative, Andreas Remmer. Remmer, a Baltic

---

[85] Bermondt-Avalov, "Offener Brief an die Engländer," *Deutsches Abendblatt*, May 8, 1921, included in an LGPO report to the RKÜöO from September 9, 1921, RGVA (TsKhIDK), *fond* 772, *opis* 3, *delo* 71, 12.

[86] Letter from Bermondt-Avalov to Karl Werkmann from September 27, 1925, RGVA (TsKhIDK), *fond* 603, *opis* 2, *delo* 30, 2.

[87] Bermondt-Avalov, "Das Erbe der Revolution und des Bolschewismus," included in an RKÜöO report from September 9, 1921, RGVA (TsKhIDK), *fond* 772, *opis* 3, *delo* 71, 22–24, 30.

[88] Letter to the editorial staff of *Volia Rossii* from February 28, 1921, ATsVO, GARF, *fond* 5893, *opis* 1, *delo* 201, 87.

[89] Remmer's testimony from June 1, 1923, BHSAM, BSMÄ 36, number 103009, 12.

[90] Vladimir Biskupskii's testimony included in a PDM report to the BSMÄ from June 2, 1923, BHSAM, BSMÄ 36, number 103009, 7.

[91] Thoss, *Der Ludendorff-Kreis*, 372.

[92] Smolin, *Beloe dvizhenie na Severo-Zapade Rossii*, 345.

German businessman from Latvia who had once held a leading position in the Imperial Russian Interior Ministry, had a reputation for underhanded dealings. Bolsheviks had imprisoned him in the wake of the October Revolution of 1917, but he had managed to emerge from prison in June 1918 after paying a considerable bribe.[93] Bermondt-Avalov named this dubious character his foreign minister and used him to undercut Biskupskii's authority.

Remmer abused Bermondt-Avalov's trust. The Baltic German dissipated the majority of the funds that he received from German authorities for the Western Volunteer Army in pursuit of the high life in the expensive Hotel Continental in Berlin.[94] Despite his questionable morality, Remmer continued to serve as an important White agent. He maintained contacts with both anti-Bolshevik nationalist forces and Bolshevik authorities during the time of intense National Socialist cooperation with White émigré circles from 1920 to 1923. We shall examine this theme in subsequent chapters.

The connected endeavors of Colonel Bermondt-Avalov's bid for victory in Latvia and Russia with political backing in Berlin and Kapp's drive for political leadership in Germany came to a crucial juncture in early October 1919. Bermondt-Avalov planned an assault on Riga, the seat of Latvian Minister President Karlis Ulmanis' government, for the night of October 7/8 to remove a despised political foe and to secure his rear for an advance into the Soviet heartland.[95] On the eve of this venture, Kapp, who presumably knew of Bermondt-Avalov's plans, called a conference of co-conspirators from the National Union. Colonel Bauer and Captain Pabst, among others, attended the meeting. Kapp suggested launching a putsch against the Weimar Republic in the near future.[96] Kapp held detailed discussions with General Ludendorff on a daily basis beginning in October. He allotted the general the post of military dictator in the planned nationalist government.[97]

Kapp's hopes for the military support of Bermondt-Avalov's German/White forces after their triumph in Latvia and beyond soon faded, however. After gaining some initial tactical victories outside Riga, Bermondt-Avalov's Western Volunteer Army faced increasingly effective resistance from

---

[93] RKÜöO report to the PP/AIA from May 30, 1924, RGVA (TsKhIDK), *fond* 772, *opis* 3, *delo* 81a, 58; Remmer testimony from June 1, 1923, BHSAM, BSMÄ 36, number 103009, 10.

[94] RKÜöO report from May 8, 1924 and RKÜöO report to the PP/AIA from May 30, 1924, RGVA (TsKhIDK), *fond* 772, *opis* 3, *delo* 81a, 52, 58.

[95] "Die Ereignisse im Baltikum vom Herbst 1918 bis Ende 1919," January 1920, BA/MF, RWM, *Nachlass* 247, number 91, 6.

[96] Charge against Hermann Ehrhardt from May 5, 1923, RKÜöO, BAB, 1507, number 339, 87/5.

[97] RKÜöO report from March 18, 1920, BAB, 1507, number 214, 9, 12.

Ulmanis' Latvian troops. Moreover, the English fleet opened deadly fire on Bermondt-Avalov's army.[98] Bermondt-Avalov later claimed that English warships had released their salvos on his troops only minutes after one of his subordinates had given an English officer a friendly reception over tea.[99]

The fact that the English fleet had left General Iudenich's army in the lurch by leaving it to attack Bermondt-Avalov's forces in Latvia led to outrage among many Whites. For example, the White émigré and National Socialist ideologue Rosenberg later wrote angrily of the English fleet's assault on the Western Volunteer Army. In the pages of Eckart's newspaper *In Plain German*, Rosenberg claimed that England had wished to play the Whites against the Reds to weaken Russia as a whole while simultaneously protecting "Jewish world criminals" in Russia to obtain valuable economic concessions from them.[100] In a similar vein, he claimed in the pages of the National Socialist periodical the *Völkisch Observer*: "The Entente never seriously fought Bolshevism, but only ensured the starvation and the bleeding white of the Russian people."[101]

Helping to fuel right-wing discontent, the primarily socialist German government, which was under intense pressure from the Entente, acted on its threats to force the German Legion and the Baltic Defense Force to evacuate Latvia. The German government closed the East Prussian border, thereby severing Bermondt-Avalov's lines of communication, and it canceled troop wages and supplies.[102] Scheubner-Richter later claimed in the *Völkisch Observer* that the German government had cut off support for the Freikorps and the allied White Russian formations in Latvia under the pretense of threats from the Entente, "but in actuality because of the pressure of democratic, socialist, and above all Jewish circles" inside of Germany itself in the "sell-out of German honor."[103] He thus gave a sense of the betrayal that Freikorps members and White forces in Latvia felt in the autumn of 1919.

[98] "Die Ereignisse im Baltikum vom Herbst 1918 bis Ende 1919," January 1920, BA/MF, RWM, *Nachlass* 247, number 91, 7.

[99] Bermondt-Avalov, "Offener Brief an die Engländer," *Deutsches Abendblatt*, May 8, 1921, included in an LGPO report to the RKÜöO from September 9, 1921, RGVA (TsKhIDK), *fond* 772, *opis* 3, *delo* 71, 14.

[100] Eckart/Rosenberg, "Zwischen den Schächern," *Auf gut deutsch: Wochenschrift für Ordnung und Recht*, March 5, 1920.

[101] Rosenberg, "Antisemitismus: Eine wirtschaftliche, politische, nationale, religiöse und sittliche Notwendigkeit, (Schluss)," *Völkischer Beobachter*, August 21, 1921, 3.

[102] "Die Ereignisse im Baltikum vom Herbst 1918 bis Ende 1919," January 1920, BA/MF, RWM, *Nachlass* 247, number 91, 6.

[103] Scheubner Richter, "Deutschlands Bolschewisierung," 1.

In this dire military situation, Colonel Bermondt-Avalov received some assistance from First Lieutenant Gerhard Rossbach, the commander of the first German Freikorps established after the November 11, 1918 Armistice. In October 1919, Rossbach ordered his battalion, the Sturmabteilung Rossbach (Storm Section Rossbach), to march from West Prussia to Latvia.[104] Upon arrival in Latvia in early November 1919, Rossbach placed himself and his approximately 1,500 men under Bermondt-Avalov's command.[105] The Storm Section Rossbach joined Major Bischoff's Iron Division, where the German soldiers wore Russian cockades and received their wages in rubles.[106] While Rossbach's daring insubordination did little to alter the overall grim military and political situation that the Western Volunteer Army faced, Rossbach gained General Ludendorff's favor through his illegal march into Latvia.[107] Rossbach later became a prominent National Socialist who played an important role in the November 1923 Hitler/Ludendorff Putsch.

First Lieutenant Rossbach's insubordinate march into Latvia helped Bermondt-Avalov's cause somewhat, but disaster nonetheless struck the Western Volunteer Army on November 3, 1919. Latvian troops under Ulmanis' direction launched a powerful counterattack and broke through the front south of Riga. At the same time, Lithuanian forces attacked Bermondt-Avalov's troops from the rear and cut off their few remaining lines of communication with Germany.[108] Facing rout, Bermondt-Avalov wrote a letter to his colleague Kapp, the head of the conspiratorial National Union, on November 9, 1919, which was the one-year anniversary of Imperial Germany's collapse.

In his letter to Kapp, Bermondt-Avalov stressed that he was devoting all of his energies to the "merciless struggle against Bolshevism," and he asked for the "assistance that is so necessary for our common cause." He argued: "A lasting understanding between Russia and Germany is necessary in the interests of the common fight against Bolsheviks and Spartacists, quite apart from the fact that it is the natural consequence of the geographical situation." In stressing his pro-German credentials to Kapp, Bermondt-Avalov called the "Russo-German War" the "greatest misfortune of our century." He further argued, "In helping us in our struggle against Bolshevism,

---

[104] Gerhard Rossbach's deposition from May 11, 1923, RKÜöO, BAB, 1507, number 211, 149.

[105] RKÜöO report from January 2, 1923, BAB, 1507, number 345, 274.

[106] Interview with Rossbach on December 13, 1951, IZG, ZS 128, 6.

[107] Erich von Ludendorff's deposition from May 16, 1923, RKÜöO, BAB, 1507, number 211, 136.

[108] "Die Ereignisse im Baltikum vom Herbst 1918 bis Ende 1919," January 1920, BA/MF, RWM, *Nachlass* 247, number 91, 7.

Germany combats its own Spartacism with ideas related to Russian Communism as well." He concluded:

I would like to emphasize my unshakeable intention to collaborate with those German circles that support our efforts . . . I willingly commit myself to do everything that serves the common interests of Russia and Germany, which were friends for centuries and should have remained so.[109]

Whatever his faults as a charismatic military leader, Bermondt-Avalov remained committed to the idea of a nationalist German–Russian alliance, and he consistently worked to strengthen what he viewed as an eminently logical and necessary Central and Eastern European strategic partnership against the Entente.

Even in the face of defeat, Colonel Bermondt-Avalov continued to hope for a turnaround in the fortunes of his Western Volunteer Army. The primarily socialist German government, for its part, had tepidly supported and then increasingly outright opposed Bermondt-Avalov's army, yet it did not wish the force's destruction. Socialist leaders therefore arranged for Major General Eberhard to take command of the army and to lead it safely back to Germany. Colonel Bermondt-Avalov ceded command to Eberhard on November 19, 1919. The German government managed to persuade Latvian and Lithuanian forces to suspend major operations to allow for an orderly retreat of the so-called *Baltikumkämpfer* (Baltic fighters).[110]

The Western Volunteer Army evacuated Mitau on the night of November 21/22, 1919. Many members of the force vented their rage at the situation by attacking Jews.[111] During the evacuation, many soldiers beat Jews as perceived enemies. Primarily Russian troops had earlier plundered Jewish stores since the Jews had refused to accept Bermondt-Avalov's currency.[112] The retreating army displayed intense anti-Weimar Republic sentiments as well. General Goltz even conceived a "*Dolchstoss*" or "stab in the back" on the part of the Weimar German government.[113]

Even in this desperate position, Bermondt-Avalov still hoped for an improvement in his fortunes through the assistance of Kapp and the powerful nationalist German collaborators around him. Bermondt-Avalov

[109] Letter from Bermondt-Avalov to Kapp from November 9, 1919, GSAPK, *Repositur* 92, number 815, 88.

[110] "Die Ereignisse im Baltikum vom Herbst 1918 bis Ende 1919," January 1920, BA/MF, RWM, *Nachlass* 247, number 91, 7; Smolin, *Beloe dvizhenie na Severo-Zapade Rossii*, 349.

[111] Bermondt-Avalov, *Im Kampf gegen den Bolschewismus*, 229.

[112] LGPO report from December 1, 1919, GSAPKB, *Repositur* 77, title 1810, number 2, 29, 31.

[113] Johannes Erger, *Der Kapp-Lüttwitz-Putsch: Ein Beitrag zur deutschen Innenpolitik 1919/20* (Düsseldorf: Droste Verlag, 1967), 54.

wrote a letter to Kapp in late November 1919. He noted that he had not achieved the "hoped-for success" in Latvia, but that this was inevitable given his army's lack of wages, clothing, and provisions. He stressed that as soon as his forces received the necessary support, they would again "take up the struggle for the culture and security of Europe" and stop the "wild Bolshevik horde" from "overflowing East Prussia."[114] Even at this late hour, Bermondt-Avalov still hoped for fruitful cooperation with Kapp and his co-conspirators to overthrow the Bolshevik regime.

Despite his fervent desire to continue an anti-Bolshevik struggle in the Baltic region and beyond, Bermondt-Avalov had to back down, at least publicly. He officially relinquished the leadership of the remnants of the White contingents of the Western Volunteer Army in late December 1919. In his last order, he told his men, "You were greeted as friends, not as foreign troops, and you must be grateful to the German people and keep this gratitude in your hearts for ever."[115] Bermondt-Avalov's rival, General Vladimir Biskupskii, sought to keep the Russian units of the Western Volunteer Army under arms as coherent military formations, but under pressure from the Entente, the White soldiers were disarmed and interned.[116]

Even after the disappointing end of the Latvian Intervention, White circles under Biskupskii and Bermondt-Avalov remained dedicated to defeating Bolshevism militarily, and they covertly built up German/Russian formations in Germany to achieve this goal.[117] In another development, General Goltz, the mastermind of the Latvian intervention, worked with Latvian Intervention supporter General Hoffmann behind the scenes to name General Biskupskii, whom they viewed as a strong leader, General-Inspector of the Russian Forces Interned in Germany. While the remnants of Bermondt-Avalov's army, which were interned in Camp Altengrabow not far from Berlin, officially passed under the control of Biskupskii and General Altvater, in fact the demobilized soldiers remained by and large intensely loyal to Bermondt-Avalov.[118]

With the internment of the White remnants of Bermondt-Avalov's Western Volunteer Army, Kapp, General Ludendorff, and their nationalist backers lost significant military support for their political aspirations. They

---

[114] Letter from Bermondt-Avalov to Kapp from November 28, 1919, GSAPKB, *Repositur 92*, number 815, 93.

[115] Bermondt-Avalov's order of resignation from December 24, 1919, RGVA, *fond* 40147, *opis* 1, *delo* 18, 17.

[116] "Tagebuchauszug von General der Infanterie a. D. Hasse," December 2, 1919, RGVA (TsKhIDK), *fond* 1255, *opis* 2, *delo* 42, 10.

[117] LGPOP report from March 9, 1920, GSAPKB, *Repositur 77*, title 1810, number 1, 76.

[118] OKL report from April 8, 1920, RGVA, *fond* 40147, *opis* 1, *delo* 48, 1, 3, 4.

also could not count on the assistance of demobilized Freikorps from the Baltic region, as the primarily socialist German government dissolved such units in January 1920 in an act of self-protection.[119] Kapp's colleague General Goltz nevertheless placed significant numbers of *Baltikumer*, as the German veterans of the Latvian Intervention were known, in East-Elbian military colonies. Here they served as a reserve against Bolshevism in Germany and abroad. Goltz ensured that only politically dependable soldiers joined such establishments, most notably former members of the now legendary Storm Section Rossbach.[120]

NATIONALIST GERMAN–WHITE ÉMIGRÉ COLLABORATION IN THE KAPP PUTSCH

While Goltz placed dependable soldiers from the Baltic Intervention in safe locations throughout East Elbian Prussia so that they could be used in a putsch against the Weimar Republic, General Ludendorff intensified his preparations to establish a right-wing dictatorship in which he would play a leading role. Weimar Germany's secret political police later asserted that Ludendorff had been the "father of the Kapp Putsch."[121] As well as counting upon interned White soldiers, Ludendorff upheld relations with Whites inside the former Russian Empire itself. In particular, he kept in contact with the Narodno-gosudarstvennaia Partiia (People's State Party), a successor organization to Vladimir Purishkevich's Black Hundred association, Michael the Archangel Russian People's Union.[122]

Purishkevich had nationalist and pro-German views. While heading Hetman Pavel Skoropadskii's health service in the Ukraine, he had led a small and yet active group that had desired an autocratic Tsar for a reconstituted Russian state and had admired Germany as a champion of order.[123] He had established the pro-German, anti-Bolshevik, and anti-Semitic People's State Party in late 1918 in Rostov/Don under the aegis of General Piotr Krasnov's Cossack formation, the Great Don Host. Krasnov's Cossacks had continued to fight against Bolshevik forces after Skoropadskii's Hetmanate in the Ukraine had collapsed in December 1918.[124]

---

[119] Interview with Rossbach on December 13, 1951, IZG, ZS 128, 6.

[120] Goltz, "Erste Versuche," BA/MF, *Nachlass* 714, number 14, 1.

[121] RKÜöO report to the BSMÄ from January 31, 1924, BHSAM, BSMÄ 36, number 103456, 7.

[122] Rafael Ganelin, "Beloe dvizhenie i 'Protokoly sionskikh mudretsov,'" *Natsionalnaia pravaia prezhde i teper: Istoriko-sotsiologicheskie ocherki, chast 1: Rossiia i russkoe zarubezhe* (Saint Petersburg: Institut Sotsiologii rossiiskoi akademii nauk, 1992), 127.

[123] ÉMG report to the DB from October 22, 1919, RGVA (TsKhIDK), *fond* 7, *opis* 1, *delo* 953, reel 4, 313.

[124] ATsVO report from September 27, 1921, GARF, *fond* 5893, *opis* 1, *delo* 46, 7.

Purishkevich disseminated his nationalist and anti-Semitic views in his newspaper, *Blagovest: Zhurnal russkoi monarkhicheskoi narodno-gosudarstvennoi mysli* (*The Ringing of the Church Bells: Journal for Russian Monarchical People's-State Thought*). He advocated a "national dictatorship." He further argued that the Jews opposed the "Russian national spirit," and he called for an "open fight against Jewry."[125] *The Ringing of the Church Bells* cited the Russian author Fedor Dostoevskii's assertions, "The Jew and his Kahal" formed a "conspiracy against Russians," and "The Jews are Russia's undoing."[126]

Purishkevich's People's State Party displayed intense anti-Semitism in other ways. The organization believed in *The Protocols of the Elders of Zion*.[127] Moreover, the anti-Semitic Party Program stressed that the Jews had to be separated from Russian society through economic boycott, revocation of their citizenship rights, and severe limitation of their access to secondary education. The Party Program exhibited racist thought. It defined Jews as both those who practiced the Jewish religion and those who had converted to Christianity. The document ended with the assertion about the Jews: "Their role [in social and political life] is over once and for all."[128]

In January 1919, N. N. Fermor, the People's State Party's vice president, received one of General Ludendorff's emissaries while residing in Paris. Fermor left Paris for Berlin at the end of the month carrying a letter for Ludendorff.[129] The contents of this letter remain unknown, but Fermor's actions suggest significant collaboration between the nationalist circle around Kapp and Ludendorff and Purishkevich's People's State Party in the time leading up to the Kapp Putsch of March 1920. In any case, Purishkevich died of typhus in February 1920, and his death led to the decline of the People's State Party.[130]

While the conspiratorial clique around Kapp and General Ludendorff hoped for White assistance to overthrow the Weimar Republic, they relied most heavily upon Captain Hermann Ehrhardt's Second Marine Brigade (commonly known as the Ehrhardt Brigade) for armed support. Ehrhardt, a corvette captain, had founded his brigade in February 1919. The Ehrhardt Brigade had used 2,000 men to help overthrow the Soviet Bavarian

[125] Vladimir Purishkevich, "Bez zabrala," *Blagovest: Zhurnal russkoi monarkhicheskoi narodno-gosudarst-vennoi mysli*, December 1919, 1, 2. GARF.

[126] Nikolai Ismailov, "Chudesnyi son," *Blagovest*, December 1919, 3.

[127] "Sionskie Protokoly," *Chasovoi*, January 23, 1919, 1, GARF.

[128] Henri Rollin, *L'Apocalypse de notre temps: Les dessous de la propagande allemande d'après des documents inédits* (Paris: Gallimard, 1939), 169, 170.

[129] SG report from January 28, 1920, RGVA (TsKhIDK), *fond* 1, *opis* 27, *delo* 12518, 2.

[130] S. A. Stepanov, *Chernaia Sotnia v Rossii 1905–1914* (Moscow: Izdatelstvo Vsesoiuznogo zaochnogo politekhnicheskogo instituta, 1992), 329.

Republic in May 1919 and had subsequently fought Polish invaders in Upper Silesia.[131] Ehrhardt had also kept close tabs on the Latvian Intervention. In September 1919, he had written Kapp from Mitau, the site of Colonel Bermondt-Avalov's Western Volunteer Army Headquarters. Ehrhardt had asked Kapp to use his influence with General Ludendorff on behalf of Captain Heinz Guderian, who later became famous as Hitler's greatest proponent of armored warfare.[132] In 1920, the Ehrhardt Brigade was stationed near Berlin.

The conspiratorial circle around Kapp and Ludendorff faced a critical situation on March 10, 1920, when War Minister Noske ordered the dissolution of the Ehrhardt Brigade.[133] Ehrhardt consulted with Kapp's colleague Captain Pabst at length the next day. Ehrhardt agreed to march his brigade on Berlin during the night of March 12 so that his soldiers would be at the Brandenburg Gate in the center of Berlin the next morning.[134] Ehrhardt appeared as promised on the morning of March 13 with roughly 3,000 men. Hermann Göring, who later became one of the leading figures of the Third Reich, played a key leadership role in the Ehrhardt Brigade's renegade occupation of the German capital on behalf of Kapp.[135] The primarily socialist German government fled Berlin at the appearance of Ehrhardt's troops.[136]

Kapp seized political control in Berlin. He used the specter of Bolshevism to justify his putsch. He issued a proclamation, "To the German People!" in which he stressed that the Weimar Republic had proved unable to fend off the threat of "devastation and murder through belligerent Bolshevism." He stressed that Germany faced "external and internal collapse" and therefore needed a "strong state authority."[137] He established a militaristic regime in which General Ludendorff, Colonel Bauer, and Captain Pabst played important roles.[138] Kapp faced a serious weakness, however, in that he lacked broad popular backing for his undertaking.[139]

Kapp received support for his putsch from *völkisch* Bavarians, including the Munich publicist Eckart and his then little-known pupil Hitler. Eckart

[131] RKÜöO report from September 2, 1921, BAB, 1507, number 568, 24; deposition of Manfred von Killinger from December 22, 1922, RKÜöO, BAB, 1507, number 339, 412.
[132] Letter from Ehrhardt to Kapp from September 12, 1919, GSAPKB, *Repositur* 92, number 815, 43.
[133] Deposition of Killinger from December 22, 1922, RKÜöO, BAB, 1507, number 339, 412.
[134] Charge against Ehrhardt from May 5, 1923, RKÜöO, BAB, 1507, number 339, 87/6, 7.
[135] RKÜöO report from July 13, 1923, BAB, 1507, number 442, 100; deposition of Killinger from December 22, 1922, RKÜöO, BAB, 1507, number 339, 412.
[136] RKÜöO report, [1925?], RGVA (TsKhIDK), *fond* 772, *opis* 3, *delo* 781, 4.
[137] Kapp, "An das deutsche Volk!" [March 1920], BAK, *Nachlass* 309, number 7.
[138] RKÜöO report, [1925?], RGVA (TsKhIDK), *fond* 772, *opis* 3, *delo* 781, 4.
[139] Erger, *Der Kapp-Lüttwitz-Putsch*, 300.

had mobilized his considerable social connections to assist Hitler, including tying him to Kapp.[140] Kapp had met with Eckart in Munich in early 1920.[141] Eckart had then traveled to Berlin to confer with Kapp in Berlin three weeks before the latter's putsch attempt. Eckart had warned Kapp of "Bolshevism," stressing that "the Jews" would use the "easily led masses" to seize power in Germany "as in Russia." To counter this danger, Eckart had proposed imprisoning the Jews, at least the most influential ones, while there was still time.[142] After launching his putsch, Kapp arranged for Eckart and Hitler to be flown up from Munich to Berlin.[143]

In Berlin, Eckart soon despaired of Kapp's chances of leading a successful national revolution. Kapp did not imprison Jews as Eckart had recommended. Instead, he merely confiscated flour for matzos. This insufficient action subsequently led Eckart to comment in *In Plain German*: "One does not provoke wild animals, one locks them up." Kapp had refused to implement such a radical policy, and Eckart later asserted that Kapp's "half measures" had ensured his downfall. The last straw for Eckart came when he witnessed three Jews at Kapp's headquarters, "not groveling, but provocatively impudent."[144] Eckart had wished to help Kapp's undertaking precisely to combat Jewish influence in Germany, and the presence of Jewish representatives in Kapp's vicinity disgusted him.

According to a report that Kapp's pupil Hitler wrote, when he had met with Kapp's press chief on March 17, 1920, he had realized, "This could not be a national revolution" and that the Kapp Putsch would fail, "for the press chief was a Jew."[145] Hitler referred to Ignatz Trebitsch-Lincoln, an adventurer born to Jewish parents in Hungary who had left for Canada at the age of twenty and converted to Christianity, adding the name Lincoln to his original name Trebitsch. After a three-year prison term in England for falsifying documents, he had traveled to Berlin in 1919 and had begun collaborating with Kapp's colleague Colonel Bauer to coordinate a putsch against the Weimar Republic. Trebitsch-Lincoln emerged from behind the scenes in March 1920 to serve as Kapp's press chief.[146] After the Kapp Putsch

---

[140] Rosenberg, "Meine erste Begegnung mit dem Führer," The National Archives, Records of the Reich Ministry for the Occupied Eastern Territories, 1941–45, IZG, number 454, roll 63, 578.

[141] Letter from Karl Mayr to Kapp from September 24, 1920, GSAPKB, *Repositur* 92, number 840/1, 4.

[142] Eckart's examination at the AGM on July 10, 1920, RGVA (TsKhIDK), *fond* 567, *opis* 1, *delo* 2496, 17.

[143] Letter from Wilhelm Kiefer to Anneliese Kapp from June 24, 1958, BAK, *Nachlass* 309, number 20.

[144] Eckart, "Kapp," *Auf gut deutsch*, April 16, 1920, 4.

[145] Adolf Hitler, March 29, 1920 report on the Kapp Putsch, *Sämtliche Aufzeichnungen*, eds. Eberhard Jäckel and Axel Kuhn (Stuttgart: Deutsche Verlags-Anstalt, 1980), 117.

[146] AA report to the RKÜöO from April 23, 1926, RGVA (TsKhIDK), *fond* 772, *opis* 3, *delo* 927, 30, 32, 33.

failed, he fled to Budapest and passed information about monarchical activities in Germany to French intelligence.[147]

While Eckart and Hitler despaired of Kapp's undertaking early on, leading White émigrés supported the undertaking more enthusiastically. The Russian remnants of the Western Volunteer Army unequivocally supported the Kapp Putsch. These men under the official direction of General Biskupskii and the unofficial leadership of Colonel Bermondt-Avalov had long been preparing to support Kapp's bid for power.[148] Shortly before the Kapp Putsch, Bermondt-Avalov wrote General Altvater at the Altengrabow Camp, where most of the former Western Volunteer Army members were interned. Bermondt-Avalov assured Altvater that conditions appeared favorable. He asserted that money, clothing, and munitions would shortly arrive, and he urged Altvater to keep the officers and soldiers together and on alert.[149] Biskupskii, the nominal head of the White elements of Bermondt-Avalov's former army, also supported Kapp's brief seizure of power.[150]

Other White émigrés supported the Kapp Putsch. First Lieutenant Scheubner-Richter appeared in Berlin to assist Kapp's cause. Because of his open support of the Kapp Putsch, he was subsequently forced to give up his position as the secretary of the Ostdeutscher Heimatdienst (East German Home Service).[151] Colonel Fedor Vinberg and his associates Lieutenant Piotr Shabelskii-Bork and Lieutenant Sergei Taboritskii, who published the far right newspaper *The Call*, compromised their position in Berlin by supporting the Kapp Putsch.[152]

Despite the assistance of leading White émigrés in league with key German military figures, Kapp's undertaking collapsed within a week because it lacked popular support.[153] Years later, in an essay titled "Looks Back and Parallels," Scheubner-Richter regarded the Kapp Putsch as an endeavor that "fatherland-loving men" had carried out in the belief that the Germans had opened their eyes. He lamented that this calculation had proved false. He drew parallels between the Kapp Putsch and the Kornilov

[147] RMI report to the RKÜöO from July 16, 1926, RGVA (TsKhIDK), *fond* 772, *opis* 3, *delo* 927, 47; PDB report to the RKÜöO from May 28, 1926, RGVA (TsKhIDK), *fond* 772, *opis* 3, *delo* 927, 40.

[148] DB report from July 23, 1920, RGVA (TsKhIDK), *fond* 7, *opis* 1, *delo* 1255, reel 2, 209.

[149] SKöO report to the AA from April 26, 1920, PAAA, 83377, 62.

[150] Ganelin, "Rossiiskoe chernosotenstvo i germanskii natsional-sotsializm," *Natsionalnaia pravaia*, 142.

[151] Scheubner-Richter, "Abriss des Lebens- und Bildungsganges," April 1923, RGVA (TsKhIDK), *fond* 1414, *opis* 1, *delo* 21, 231.

[152] Aleksandr von Lampe, *Dnevnik* (Diary), Berlin, August 13, 1920, GARF, *fond* 5853, *opis* 1, *delo* 3, 920.

[153] Erger, *Der Kapp-Lüttwitz-Putsch*, 300.

Putsch, in which General Lavr Kornilov and his co-conspirators, including the White trio of Vinberg, Shabelskii-Bork, and Taboritskii, had attempted to overthrow the Provisional Government in Russia in August 1917.[154]

In his own post-putsch assessment of the situation, Kapp indicated the considerable degree to which he had placed his hopes on the assistance of White forces. He wrote a letter from exile in Sweden to a friend after the failure of his putsch. He remarked that East Prussia had lost its ability to serve as the focal point of an "uprising" in Germany. This condition of impotence would last for the foreseeable future unless the "restoration of a strong national Russia" took place.[155] Such a turn of events did not occur, and East Prussia did indeed recede as the center of conservative revolutionary conspiracies in Germany. Bavaria, the birthplace of National Socialism, subsequently assumed this mantle.

CONCLUSION

The intense German–White/White émigré collaboration in 1919 and early 1920 in Latvia and Germany failed to achieve its objectives. The year 1919 witnessed the rise and fall of Colonel Pavel Bermondt-Avalov's Western Volunteer Army, which primarily consisted of German Freikorps and White Russian units. The Latvian Intervention under Bermondt-Avalov built upon the German–White cooperation that had been established in the Ukraine in 1918 as well as German successes in the Baltic region in World War I, in which the Baltic German First Lieutenant Max von Scheubner-Richter had played a prominent role. Bermondt-Avalov sought to work "hand in hand with Germany" to destroy Bolshevik rule. After some initial successes, Bermondt-Avalov's Western Volunteer Army faced rout and had to retreat back to Germany, largely because of increasing pressure from the Entente as well as the Weimar Republic.

Early 1920 saw the ignominious defeat of the first large-scale German–White émigré political alliance in Germany when the far right Kapp Putsch collapsed. The nationalist German conspirators around Kapp used demobilized German and White émigré formations from the Latvian Intervention to support the preparation and execution of their putsch. *Völkisch* German participants in the Kapp Putsch included, in addition to Wolfgang Kapp, General Erich von Ludendorff, his advisor Colonel Karl Bauer, Captain

---

[154] Scheubner-Richter, "Rückblicke und Parallelen," *Wirtschafts-politische Aufbau-Korrespondenz über Ostfragen und ihre Bedeutung für Deutschland*, July 19, 1922, 2.

[155] Letter from Kapp to an East Prussian friend from September 22, 1920, BAK, *Nachlass* 309, number 7.

Hermann Ehrhardt, whose troops deposed the largely socialist German government, as well as Adolf Hitler and his mentor Dietrich Eckart. White émigré supporters of the doomed undertaking included Bermondt-Avalov, General Vladimir Biskupskii, who had represented the Western Volunteer Army politically in Berlin, Scheubner-Richter, Colonel Fedor Vinberg, Lieutenant Piotr Shabelskii-Bork, and Lieutenant Sergei Taboritskii. All of these officers went on to serve the National Socialist cause.

While the Latvian Intervention and the Kapp Putsch failed to achieve their immediate military and political objectives, they nevertheless fostered determined *völkisch* German–White/White émigré collaboration between men who viewed themselves as trapped between Bolshevik expansion from the East, Entente pressure from the West, and the opposition and betrayal of the left-wing political establishment in Germany. The Latvian Intervention in particular granted a powerful sense of anti-Bolshevik, anti-Entente, and anti-Weimar Republic solidarity to its right-wing German and White émigré participants. Many *Baltikumer* (Baltic fighters) went on to join the National Socialist Party.[156]

The collapse of the Kapp Putsch in Berlin following the failure of the Latvian Intervention brought about a low point in the fortunes of the German/White émigré far right. National revolutionary German and White émigré conspirators based in East Elbian Prussia undermined their political position by participating in the Kapp Putsch. They subsequently either had to maintain low profiles or to flee the region altogether. From late March 1920 on, Bavaria in general and Munich in particular, where the Kapp Putsch had succeeded, provided the leading haven for the collaboration of *völkisch* Germans (increasingly under National Socialist leadership) and pro-nationalist German White émigrés. From their power base in Bavaria, National Socialists and their *völkisch* allies conspired with White émigrés in various anti-Weimar Republic, anti-Semitic, and anti-Bolshevik schemes.

---

[156] RKÜöO report from November 24, 1922, BAB, 1507, number 345, 266.

CHAPTER 4

The international radical right's Aufbau
(reconstruction)

Karl Schlögel, a German expert on White émigrés, has noted that Munich ascended to the dynamic crux of *völkisch* German–White émigré collaboration after the Kapp Putsch collapsed in Berlin in March 1920.[1] Leading German and White émigré participants in the Kapp Putsch fled East Elbian Germany for Bavaria, where they quickly reorganized and found new means to further complementary right-wing German/White émigré interests. Former German and White émigré Kapp Putsch conspirators in Bavaria sent a mission under Max von Scheubner-Richter to establish clandestine military and economic relations with General Piotr Vrangel's Southern Russian Armed Forces, which were based on the Crimean Peninsula in the Ukraine. To foster the common struggle against Bolshevism, Vrangel's regime pledged to deliver large amounts of agricultural goods in return for military personnel and supplies from right-wing Bavarian circles.

The cooperation between German and White émigré rightists based in Bavaria and Vrangel proved short-lived because of the Red Army's surprisingly rapid victory over Vrangel's forces. Nonetheless, this brief German-White émigré/White connection spurred the formation of Aufbau, a conspiratorial *völkisch* German/White émigré organization that opposed the Entente, the Weimar Republic, Jewry, and Bolshevism. Aufbau sought to overthrow the Bolshevik regime and to set Grand Prince Kirill Romanov at the head of a pro-German Russian monarchy. Following the low point of right-wing fortunes in Germany that had been reached with the Kapp Putsch's failure, Aufbau demonstrated its resilience by rejuvenating the *völkisch* German/White émigré radical right on German soil in the course of late 1920 and the first half of 1921.

---

[1] Karl Schlögel, *Der grosse Exodus: Die Russische Emigration und ihre Zentren 1917 bis 1941* (Munich: C. H. Beck, 1994), 251.

Aufbau maintained close ties with the National Socialist Party from the beginning. The German Max Amann served both as Aufbau's second secretary and as secretary of the National Socialist Party. Four Baltic German Aufbau colleagues from the same Riga fraternity in the Russian Empire played leading roles in the National Socialist Party: Aufbau's first secretary (and *de facto* leader) Scheubner-Richter, Aufbau's deputy director Arno Schickedanz, and two collaborators with Hitler's early mentor Dietrich Eckart, Alfred Rosenberg and Otto von Kursell. Prominent White émigré members of Aufbau who did not belong to the NSDAP but who nevertheless served its cause included Aufbau's vice president Vladimir Biskupskii, the Ukrainian Cossack Ivan Poltavets-Ostranitsa, who led Aufbau's Ukrainian section, and the close trio of Fedor Vinberg, Piotr Shabelskii-Bork, and Sergei Taboritskii. Scheubner-Richter also introduced Hitler to General Erich von Ludendorff in the context of Aufbau, thereby beginning a political collaboration that led to the disastrous Hitler/Ludendorff Putsch of November 1923.

THE BAVARIAN-CRIMEAN CONNECTION

While the Kapp Putsch failed ignominiously in East Elbian Germany, it succeeded in overthrowing the socialist government in Bavaria. As a result of the Kapp Putsch, a new right-wing regime was installed in Bavaria under Minister President Gustav Ritter von Kahr and Bavarian Police Chief Ernst Pöhner.[2] The National Socialist Party headquartered in Munich in which Hitler played a key role (he only established dictatorial control over the Party in July 1921) began its dramatic rise in rightist German affairs in the favorable new political climate in Bavaria.[3] White émigré Aufbau member and prominent National Socialist Alfred Rosenberg later credited Pöhner, a staunch opponent of the November 1918 Revolution in Germany, with holding a "protective hand" over the National Socialist Party.[4]

In addition to protecting the fledgling National Socialist movement, the new right-wing Bavarian government offered a haven for German nationalist revolutionary officers connected with the Kapp Putsch. Prussian officers implicated in the Kapp Putsch received a warm welcome in Bavaria. General Erich von Ludendorff established cordial relations with

---

[2] Heinrich Class, *Wider den Strom*, vol. 2, BAK, *Kleine Erwerbung* 499, 737.

[3] Werner Maser, *Der Sturm auf die Republik: Frühgeschichte der NSDAP* (Stuttgart: Deutsche Verlags-Anstalt, 1973), 280.

[4] Alfred Rosenberg, Memoirs, KR, BAB, NS 8, number 20, 25, 27.

Police Chief Pöhner after fleeing Berlin for Bavaria.[5] Ludendorff's Kapp Putsch comrades Colonel Karl Bauer, Captain Waldemar Pabst, and Captain Hermann Ehrhardt, the last of whom had led the troops for the failed coup in Berlin, likewise received police protection in Munich and surrounding areas. In general, Bavarian police officers and armed supporters guarded failed conservative revolutionaries from the north.[6] From exile in Sweden, Wolfgang Kapp approved of the move of so many of his former co-conspirators southwards. He noted in a letter to General Ludendorff: "At least in Bavaria there is a bourgeois government in power. The people have come to the correct conclusions from the March Undertaking."[7]

In general, the German Kapp Putsch conspirators who relocated from Prussia to Bavaria favored a monarchical state system. In an April 1921 booklet, "Germany's Future: Tasks and Goals," Captain Ehrhardt presented views that accorded with prevalent *völkisch* sympathy for monarchy as an institution, as opposed to its practice under the last, weak Kaiser. Ehrhardt stressed, "We declare our support for monarchy with pride as the constitution that is in principle the most suitable for us." He further called for the German people to unite with a common will. He noted, "We are a people, but still not a nation . . . We are a people inwardly, among ourselves," but not a "nation outwardly, as a unified power . . . We are a people, united in everything except for the will, and since we do not have a united will, we are not a nation. But this is just what we must become."[8] Ehrhardt thus argued that the inherently powerful German people lacked correspondingly forceful leadership to lead it to greatness.

Like many *völkisch* German officers such as Ehrhardt implicated in the Kapp Putsch, several leading White émigrés who had supported the Kapp Putsch moved to Munich in the spring of 1920. The Kapp Putsch conspirators Scheubner-Richter, Fedor Vinberg, and Piotr Shabelskii-Bork fled Berlin for the Bavarian capital in March 1920. German governmental authorities promptly banned Vinberg's Berlin newspaper *Prizyv* (*The Call*) in the wake of the Kapp Putsch. Vinberg left behind considerable debts from the venture.[9] Once in Munich, Scheubner-Richter, Vinberg, and Shabelskii-Bork collaborated with other White émigrés who had already

[5] Class, *Wider den Strom*, vol. 2, BAK, *Kleine Erwerbung* 499, 738.
[6] RKÜöO report from September 14, 1921, BAB, 1507, number 568, 26, 27.
[7] Letter from Wolfgang Kapp to Erich von Ludendorff from September 25, 1920, GSAPKB, *Repositur* 92, number 839, 6.
[8] Hermann Ehrhardt, *Deutschlands Zukunft: Aufgaben und Ziele* (Munich: J. F. Lehmanns Verlag, 1921), BHSAM, *Sammlung Personen*, number 3678, 1, 34, 36.
[9] Letter from Ludwig von Knorring to the RKÜöO from December 28, 1923, RGVA (TsKhIDK), *fond* 772, *opis* 2, *delo* 179, 69.

established residency in Munich, including the former Rubonia Fraternity colleagues Rosenberg, Arno Schickedanz, and Otto von Kursell.[10]

In the spirit of *The Call*, Vinberg and Shabelskii-Bork edited a newspaper in Munich, *Luch Sveta (A Ray of Light)*.[11] *A Ray of Light* argued that Jews and Freemasons sought to destroy Christianity and to take over the world. The White émigré colleagues wrote their paper from the point of view that no room remained for passive bystanders in the struggle against these forces of evil.[12] Vinberg and Shabelskii-Bork, eventually joined by their colleague Sergei Taboritskii, were extremely destitute in Munich. They only possessed some disposable income immediately after finishing a work for publication. Even then, however, they soon fell back into a state of poverty.[13]

White émigrés who wished to reside in Munich under the Kahr government required the references of two members of the existing Russian refugee community there. The Munich Police under Pöhner thus guarded against leftist Russian expatriates. Munich's White émigré community, which peaked at 1,105 in 1921, contained virtually no Constitutional Democrats, Social Revolutionaries, or Mensheviks. Munich's White émigré population thus differed markedly from Berlin's more leftist Russian refugee community. Nobles, high-level bureaucrats, and leading officers, who were right-wing by virtue of their background, dominated Munich's White émigré landscape. Many members of Munich's White émigré population had belonged to the radical right Black Hundred movement in Imperial Russia. The White exiles in Munich had greater contact with *völkisch* German circles than those Russian refugees who lived in Berlin.[14]

Some prominent White émigrés managed to stay in Berlin after the Kapp Putsch, but Munich, as the rising center of right-wing activity in Germany, held increasing attraction for them. Colonel Pavel Bermondt-Avalov, the former leader of the Western Volunteer Army in the 1919 Latvian

[10] Robert Williams, *Culture in Exile: Russian Émigrés in Germany, 1881–1941* (Ithaca: Cornell University Press, 1972), 98, 165; PDM report to the BSMI from March 30, 1922, BHSAM, BSMI 22, number 71624, fiche 3, 78; Fedor Vinberg's March 30, 1922 testimony, BHSAM, BSMI 22, number 71624, fiche 4, 4.

[11] Piotr Shabelskii-Bork, "Über Mein Leben," March 1926, GSAPKB, *Repositur* 84a, number 14953, 110.

[12] Baur, *Die russische Kolonie in München, 1900–1945: Deutsch–russische Beziehungen im 20. Jahrhundert* (Wiesbaden: Harrassowitz Verlag, 1998), 204, 205.

[13] Josefine Trausenecker's testimony included in a PDM report to the BSMI from March 30, 1922, BHSAM, BSMI 22, number 71624, fiche 4, 13.

[14] Baur, "Russische Emigranten und die bayerische Öffentlichkeit," *Bayern und Osteuropa: Aus der Geschichte der Beziehungen Bayerns, Frankens und Schwabens mit Russland, der Ukraine, und Weissrussland*, ed. Hermann Beyer-Thoma (Wiesbaden: Harrassowitz Verlag, 2000), 462, 463, 471; Henri Rollin, *L'Apocalypse de notre temps: Les dessous de la propagande allemande d'après des documents inédits* (Paris: Gallimard, 1939), 168.

Intervention, kept a low profile in Berlin under constant surveillance. He also traveled regularly to Munich to collaborate with radical right colleagues there.[15] General Vladimir Biskupskii, who had cooperated with German occupying forces in the Ukraine in 1918, had served as the political representative of Bermondt-Avalov's Western Volunteer Army, and had supported the Kapp Putsch, managed to maintain his primary residence in Berlin. He worked diligently behind the scenes to organize paramilitary forces dedicated to reestablishing monarchical regimes in Central and Eastern Europe.[16] He developed contacts with all leading pro-German, anti-Bolshevik White émigré groups in Germany. He spent increasing amounts of time in Bavaria, where he coordinated his activities with rightist German and White émigré circles there.[17]

General Biskupskii increasingly overshadowed his rival Colonel Bermondt-Avalov. After the Kapp Putsch, Bermondt-Avalov steadily lost authority and trust in leading White émigré circles.[18] German agents who shadowed him soon wrote of him derisively as an insignificant braggart. In one report, they asserted that Bermondt-Avalov's "most viable" option for increasing his support was marrying "a rich American," as he did undeniably possess a way with the ladies.[19]

A new destabilizing Russian émigré personage emerged in right-wing Munich society in early 1920. Despite his chronic duplicity and his collaboration with Bolshevik authorities, the former Black Hundred publicist Mikhail Kommissarov managed to gain a position of trust in rightist German and White émigré cliques in Bavaria. He eventually played an important role in the formation of Aufbau, which furthered anti-Entente, anti-Weimar Republic, anti-Semitic, and anti-Bolshevik collaboration between *völkisch* Germans and White émigrés. Kommissarov wormed his way into conspiratorial rightist Munich circles as part of a convoluted career of intrigue and deceit in which he operated as a double agent.

Kommissarov had a dubious past. After losing his post in the Okhrana (Tsarist Secret Police) in Saint Petersburg because he had printed illegal pamphlets that encouraged anti-Semitic pogroms during the Revolution of 1905, he had managed to regain his position. He had demonstrated his

---

[15] MMFP report from October 12, 1921, RGVA (TsKhIDK), *fond* 1703, *opis* 1, *delo* 350, reel 3, 277.

[16] Rafael Ganelin, "Rossiiskoe chernosotenstvo i germanskii natsional-sotsializm," *Natsionalnaia pravaia prezhde i teper, Istoriko-sotsiologicheskie ocherki, chast 1: Rossiia i russkoe zarubezhe* (Saint Petersburg: Institut Sotsiologii rossiiskoi akademii nauk, 1992), 140.

[17] AA report from November 4, 1920, PAAA, 83578, 2.

[18] RKÜöO report from September 9, 1921, RGVA (TsKhIDK), *fond* 772, *opis* 3, *delo* 71, 20.

[19] LGPO report to the RKÜöO from September 9, 1921, RGVA (TsKhIDK), *fond* 772, *opis* 3, *delo* 71, 8.

lack of gratitude to his superior by starting an affair with his wife and then absconding with secret funds. He had subsequently used his drinking friendship with the court mystic Rasputin (whom the Black Hundred leader Vladimir Purishkevich subsequently shot) to acquire the Tsar's favor. Kommissarov had managed to become the mayor of Rostov/Don for three weeks before being removed for gross mismanagement and embezzlement. After disappearing from the landscape for a while, he had resurfaced in Kiev under German occupation in 1918. There he had offered to serve Hetman Pavel Skoropadskii. The Ukrainian leader had understandably replied that he could do without Kommissarov's assistance.[20]

Many Whites correctly suspected Kommissarov of collaborating with Bolshevik leaders. He had traveled through Bolshevik-controlled territory to the Terek Cossacks during the summer of 1919 with no problems, which had proved highly suspicious. He had been elected to the Krug, or leadership circle, of the Terek Cossacks. He had then traveled as an envoy to General Anton Denikin's Southern Army, a White force based in the Ukraine that was engaged in fighting the Bolsheviks with Entente support. Denikin had ordered Kommissarov's arrest as a Soviet agent. According to the French military intelligence agency the Second Section, after being rebuffed from Denikin's forces, Kommissarov had assisted the chief of the Chrezvychainaia Komissia po Borbe s Kontr-revolutsiei (Extraordinary Commission for the Struggle with Counter-revolution, the Cheka) in Petrograd.[21]

In April 1920, Kommissarov began working for the intelligence agency that his old protector in the Tsarist Secret Police, General Kurlov, had recently established in Berlin to provide anti-Bolshevik information to White émigrés in Germany. Despite the mistrust that he had engendered among rightist circles in the past, Kommissarov used his considerable intellectual gifts and social adroitness to find his way quickly into high society wherever he went. He began circulating in right-wing monarchical circles in Munich. He worked especially diligently to gain General Ludendorff's favor. At the same time, however, he initiated contact with Bolshevik representatives in Germany and provided them with information on anti-Soviet activities in Germany.[22]

---

[20] LGPO report to the RKÜöO from August 8, 1921, RGVA (TsKhIDK), *fond* 772, *opis* 3, *delo* 539, 17, 19, 20.

[21] DB reports from June 13, 1922 and October 1922, RGVA (TsKhIDK), *fond* 7, *opis* 2, *delo* 2575, reel 3, 240; reel 2, 200.

[22] RKÜöO report from June 17, 1922, RGVA (TsKhIDK), *fond* 772, *opis* 3, *delo* 539, 21v; LGPO report to the RKÜöO from August 8, 1921, RGVA (TsKhIDK), *fond* 772, *opis* 3, *delo* 539, 20.

As one of his many lies, Kommissarov claimed to serve as the authorized representative of General Piotr Vrangel, a man of noble Estonian/Baltic German ancestry who had taken control of the weakening Southern Russian Armed Forces from General Denikin in April 1920.[23] On the basis of this spurious authority, Kommissarov began collaborating with White émigrés who sought to wrest the Ukraine from Bolshevik rule. In particular, he teamed up with the extreme anti-Semitic right-wing monarchists and Germanophiles Boris Pelikan and Konstantin Scheglovitov.

Kommissarov's Ukrainian associates possessed solid right-wing credentials. Pelikan and Scheglovitov had belonged to the far right Monarchical Bloc in Kiev in 1918 under German occupation.[24] Pelikan, an extremely wealthy individual, had played a prominent role in the Black Hundred movement in Imperial Russia, and he had served as the mayor of Odessa with its large Jewish population.[25] Like Kommissarov, he belonged to the Southern Section of the monarchical Soiuz vernych (Union of the Faithful) under the overall leadership of the former Union of the Russian People faction leader Nikolai Markov II.[26] Scheglovitov had served as the Minister of Justice in Imperial Russia, and he subsequently engaged in shady business deals and acquired large sums of money from rightist organizations in the Ukraine.[27] In 1920, Pelikan and Scheglovitov led a Munich-based grouping that struggled for an independent Ukraine.[28]

Kommissarov, Pelikan, and Scheglovitov helped to form a commercial organization dedicated to fostering trade between rightist elements in Bavaria and General Vrangel's forces on the Crimean Peninsula.[29] A German named Wagner, a former *aide de camp* in the German Army High Command, officially led this venture. Wagner used his influence in the house of Wagner and Furter to foster the Society for Ukrainian–Bavarian Import and Export. This organization possessed 300,000 marks

[23] RKÜöO reports from January 29, 1923 and April 27, 1928, RGVA (TsKhIDK), *fond* 772, *opis* 3, *delo* 539, 34; *opis* 1, *delo* 108, 25; LGPO report to the RKÜöO from August 8, 1921, RGVA (TsKhIDK), *fond* 772, *opis* 3, *delo* 539, 20.

[24] LGPO report to the RKÜöO from November 28, 1921, RGVA (TsKhIDK), *fond* 772, *opis* 1, *delo* 96, 48.

[25] LGPO report from October 27, 1920, GSAPKB, *Repositur* 77, title 1810, number 4, 303; RKÜöO report from January 29, 1923, RGVA (TsKhIDK), *fond* 772, *opis* 3, *delo* 539, 34.

[26] DB report from December 15, 1923, RGVA (TsKhIDK), *fond* 7, *opis* 2, *delo* 2575, reel 2, 140; [FZO] report from October 15, 1920, MMFP, RGVA (TsKhIDK), *fond* 198, *opis* 2, *delo* 1031, reel 2, 73.

[27] DB report from July 17, 1920, RGVA (TsKhIDK), *fond* 7, *opis* 1, *delo* 1255, reel 3, 220; RKÜöO report from June 17, 1922, RGVA (TsKhIDK), *fond* 772, *opis* 3, *delo* 539, 21v.

[28] DB reports from July 17 and 21, 1920, RGVA (TsKhIDK), *fond* 7, *opis* 1, *delo* 1255, reel 3, 220; *opis* 2, *delo* 2575, reel 4, 341.

[29] RKÜöO report from January 29, 1923, RGVA (TsKhIDK), *fond* 772, *opis* 3, *delo* 539, 34; DB report from September 15, 1920, RGVA (TsKhIDK), *fond* 7, *opis* 1, *delo* 953, reel 3, 245.

in venture capital from right-wing firms, most notably from the Münchner–Augsburger Maschinenfabrik (Munich–Augsburg Machine Factory). The Society for Ukrainian–Bavarian Import and Export proposed providing civilian industrial goods, war materials, and German officers for General Vrangel's Southern Russian Armed Forces in return for Crimean agricultural goods.[30]

Germans and White émigrés associated with the Society for Ukrainian–Bavarian Import and Export held May 1920 consultations in Munich and nearby Regensburg. German consultants at these talks included General Ludendorff, his advisor and Kapp Putsch co-conspirator Colonel Bauer, the aforementioned Wagner, and Major Josef Bischoff, the former commander of the Iron Division in the 1919 Latvian Intervention. Bischoff closely followed Ukrainian matters, and he had established a secret anti-Bolshevik propaganda center in Odessa. Kommissarov, Pelikan, and General Biskupskii represented the Russian (more properly Ukrainian) side of the talks. The Baltic Germans Scheubner-Richter and Rosenberg mediated between the German and Russian conspirators.[31]

The German and White émigré plotters adopted Colonel Bauer's program, which called for uniting all those who had fought against the Bolsheviks in the Russian Civil War under the slogan: "The end justifies the means." *The Protocols of the Elders of Zion* had leading Jews use this motto as well, further suggesting the influence of the fabrication on the views of members of the radical right. The conspirators schemed to annul the Paris Peace Treaties concluded after World War I and to overthrow the Bolshevik regime through an alliance of nationalist Germans, Russians, Hungarians, Bulgarians, and Turks. The plotters sought to reestablish monarchies in Central and Eastern Europe, after which an alliance between Germany, Russia, and Hungary would be declared and Poland would be partitioned once again. The rightist participants at these May conferences in Bavaria decided to send a White mission to General Vrangel's forces in the Crimea to specify the terms of mutual assistance.[32]

Although General Vrangel received material assistance from the Entente, most importantly from France, the German and White émigré conspirators based in Bavaria had reason to count on his sympathy with their

---

[30] DB report from September 6, 1920, RGVA (TsKhIDK), *fond* 7, *opis* 2, *delo* 2575, reel 3, 253, 254.

[31] DB reports from September 9, 1920 and March 8, 1921, RGVA (TsKhIDK), *fond* 7, *opis* 2, *delo* 2575, reel 1, 99; *opis* 1, *delo* 953, reel 2, 117; LGPO report from December 11, 1920, GSAPKB, *Repositur* 77, title 1810, number 6, 48.

[32] LGPO report from December 11, 1920, GSAPKB, *Repositur* 77, title 1810, number 6, 48; DB report from September 9, 1920, RGVA (TsKhIDK), *fond* 7, *opis* 2, *delo* 2575, reel 1, 99.

cause. While he would subsequently lean increasingly towards the Entente, at this time, Vrangel wished to cooperate with a monarchical Germany to bring about what he regarded as Russia's renewal. Those who knew Vrangel personally verified that he held staunchly monarchical and pro-German views. His occasional Entente-friendly remarks, Vrangel's associates claimed, arose because of his dependence on French material aid.[33] Vrangel relied on French support largely since the primarily socialist German government had refused to recognize his delegation in order to appease the Soviet regime. Though they aided him, French authorities distrusted Vrangel.[34]

To maintain good relations with both the Entente and Jewish residents in the Crimea, General Vrangel curbed anti-Semitic agitation among his forces.[35] Some men under his command nevertheless campaigned vehemently against Jews, most notably Gregor Schwartz-Bostunich, who ultimately rose in the ranks of Heinrich Himmler's SS.[36] Schwartz-Bostunich had been born in Kiev to a Baltic German father and a mother with the maiden name Bostunich whose own mother had come from the Bavarian nobility. He had received degrees in law and theology in Kiev in 1908. He had traveled from Imperial Germany to the Russian Empire after the outbreak of World War I before acting as what he later described in an SS report as an "agitator and army speaker" for General Vrangel.[37] In the Crimea, Schwartz-Bostunich preached fanatically against Bolsheviks, Freemasons, and Jews. His inflammatory actions led the Soviet secret police, the Cheka, to issue a death warrant for him. The prominent National Socialist and Aufbau leader Scheubner-Richter later employed Schwartz-Bostunich as a speaker on behalf of the NSDAP and sent him to hold talks throughout Germany.[38]

Georgii Nemirovich-Danchenko also worked as a prominent anti-Semitic agitator under Vrangel's White regime on the Crimean Peninsula. Nemirovich-Danchenko had been born in Saint Petersburg in 1889, he

---

[33] LGPO reports from August 20 and October 18, 1920, GSAPKB, *Repositur 77*, title 1810, number 4, III, 330, 331.

[34] DDVL report to the AA from October 31, 1920, PAAA, 83379, 112 ob; Aleksandr von Lampe, *Dnevnik* (Diary), Berlin, August 4, 1920, GARF, *fond* 5853, *opis* 1, *delo* 3, 899.

[35] Georgii Nemirovich-Danchenko, *V Krymu pri Vrangele: Fakty i itogi* (Berlin: Oldenburg, 1922), 41.

[36] *Dienstaltersliste der Schutzstaffel der NSDAP (SS-Obersturmbannführer und SS-Sturmbannführer): Stand vom 1. Oktober 1944* (Berlin: Reichsdruckerei, 1944), RGVA (TsKhIDK), *fond* 1372, *opis* 5, *delo* 89, 6.

[37] Gregor Schwartz-Bostunich, *SS-Personalakten, SS-OStubaf.*, IZG, *Fa* 74, 1.

[38] Michael Hagemeister, "Das Leben des Gregor Schwartz-Bostunich, Teil 2," *Russische Emigration in Deutschland 1918 bis 1941: Leben im europäischen Bürgerkrieg*, ed. Karl Schlögel (Berlin: Akademie, 1995), 209; Schwartz-Bostunich, *SS-Personalakten, SS-OStubaf.*, IZG, *Fa* 74, 1, 2.

had received his law degree as the top student of his class in 1910, and he had worked in the State Council under the Tsar. He had published his first article on the land question in 1917.[39] He became the press chief of Vrangel's regime.[40] Nemirovich-Danchenko managed to disseminate a significant amount of anti-Semitic propaganda in a largely clandestine manner during his service under General Vrangel.[41] Like Schwartz-Bostunich, Nemirovich-Danchenko went on to collaborate with Scheubner-Richter in Aufbau.

Nemirovich-Danchenko became increasingly disappointed with General Vrangel's leadership in the Crimea during the Russian Civil War. While he had hoped to exercise wide-ranging autonomy as Vrangel's press chief, in fact, Vrangel greatly restrained his activities. In September 1920, for example, the first edition of the planned weekly *Russkaia Pravda* (*Russian Truth*) appeared with two anti-Semitic articles based on the assessments of various philosophers and writers. Vrangel immediately banned the newspaper. According to Nemirovich-Danchenko, Vrangel did so because of pressure from the Crimea's Jewish population. Nemirovich-Danchenko strongly protested Vrangel's decision, but to no avail.[42]

The clandestine mission to General Vrangel's regime in which Nemirovich-Danchenko played a leading role, which had been decided upon during the rightist German/White émigré conferences in May 1920, left Munich under Scheubner-Richter's leadership in the middle of June 1920.[43] Other members of the delegation included the double agent Kommissarov, the former important Black Hundred member Pelikan, the economically well-connected German Wagner, and some Hungarian and Austrian representatives. The deputation traveled down the Danube River, first stopping in Austria's capital Vienna and then continuing on to the Hungarian capital Budapest.[44]

Scheubner-Richter's delegation benefited from advance support work in Budapest. The officers Bauer and Biskupskii had earlier left Munich for Budapest to coordinate the mission's activities with the *de facto* Hungarian leader Admiral Nicholas Horthy. Horthy acted as the regent for the

---

[39] SG report from August 1, 1939, RGVA (TsKhIDK), *fond* 1, *opis* 14, *delo* 3242, 2; letter from Nemirovich-Danchenko to Count Iurii Pavlovich from February 7, 1928, RSHA, RGVA (TsKhIDK), *fond* 500, *opis* 1, *delo* 452, 28.

[40] Nemirovich-Danchenko, *V Krymu pri Vrangele*, 32.

[41] Laqueur, *Russia and Germany: A Century of Conflict* (London: Weidenfeld and Nicolson, 1965), 107.

[42] Nemirovich-Danchenko, *V Krymu pri Vrangele*, 33, 41, 42.

[43] DB report from July 17, 1920, RGVA (TsKhIDK), *fond* 7, *opis* 1, *delo* 1255, reel 3, 220.

[44] DB reports from September 9 and October 10, 1920, RGVA (TsKhIDK), *fond* 7, *opis* 2, *delo* 2575, reel 1, 21, 99.

Habsburg Dynasty, which the Hungarian parliament had pledged to return to Hungary (some day) in a May 1920 resolution.[45] General Ludendorff and the former Latvian Intervention mastermind General Count Rüdiger von der Goltz, who resided in Budapest under a false name, had also conducted negotiations with members of Horthy's government on behalf of Scheubner-Richter's delegation to General Vrangel.

Scheubner-Richter's mission achieved considerable success in the Hungarian capital. The delegates to the Crimea under Scheubner-Richter's guidance emphasized the pronounced military component of their undertaking as well as the economic one. Admiral Horthy supported the deputation and its goals of German–White collaboration. Horthy's approval moved Scheubner-Richter to express his profound thanks. General Berzewicsky, the chief of the Hungarian Armed Forces, asserted that he had 70,000 soldiers at his disposal to further the German/White émigré plans to abolish the Paris Peace Treaties.[46]

After its successful layover in Budapest, Scheubner-Richter's mission arrived in the Yugoslavian capital Belgrade in the middle of July 1920. Troubles began there because of Kommissarov's deceit. Scheubner-Richter held talks with members of the local White émigré delegation in Belgrade.[47] Meanwhile, the swindler Kommissarov absconded. Soon afterwards, perhaps on the way to the next stopover in Varna, Bulgaria, the delegation members Wagner and Pelikan realized that Kommissarov had deceived them.[48] Kommissarov had received 115,000 marks for arranging the journey to the Crimea on the false basis of representing General Vrangel in Germany.[49] The Ukrainian nationalist Pelikan later wrote Kommissarov never to show himself in his sight again. In August 1920, Vrangel ordered that Kommissarov never be allowed to gain passage to the Crimea.[50] Kommissarov went on to join the Soviet cause openly as an agent in Bulgaria in March 1921. His reports led to the arrest of numerous White émigré officers throughout the Balkans.[51]

[45] LGPO report from December 11, 1920, GSAPKB, *Repositur 77*, title 1810, number 6, 48.

[46] DB reports from September 9 and October 10, 1920, RGVA (TsKhIDK), *fond 7, opis 2, delo 2575*, reel 1, 21, 99; Otto von Kursell, "Dr. Ing. Max Erwin von Scheubner-Richter zum Gedächtnis," ed. Henrik Fischer (Munich, 1969), 20.

[47] DB reports from July 21 and September 30, 1920, RGVA (TsKhIDK), *fond 7, opis 2, delo 2575*, reel 4, 336, 341.

[48] DB report from October 10, 1920, RGVA (TsKhIDK), *fond 7, opis 2, delo 2575*, reel 1, 21.

[49] RKÜöO report from January 29, 1923, RGVA (TsKhIDK), *fond 772, opis 3, delo 539*, 34.

[50] DB reports from August 25, 1920 and October 1922, RGVA (TsKhIDK), *fond 7, opis 2, delo 2575*, reel 1, 26; reel 2, 200, 201.

[51] RKÜöO report from January 29, 1923, RGVA (TsKhIDK), *fond 772, opis 3, delo 539*, 35.

Despite Kommissarov's duplicity, the international right-wing mission under Scheubner-Richter's leadership managed to evade Bolshevik agents to arrive to a warm welcome in Sevastopol, the site of Vrangel's headquarters on the Crimean Peninsula, in July 1920.[52] The presence of Scheubner-Richter's delegation had to be kept as a diplomatic secret since French authorities in the Crimea had threatened to cut off Vrangel's supplies if he collaborated with Germans.[53] Scheubner-Richter ascertained the views of Vrangel's officers and soldiers. He presented himself as a Russian and engaged in numerous conversations with members of Vrangel's Southern Russian Armed Forces. He concluded that whereas Vrangel's government contained a significant number of Constitutional Democrats, commonly known as "Kadets," who supported the French, Vrangel's armed forces primarily consisted of rightists who openly sympathized with Germany. Vrangel's soldiers and officers jeered at the French Military Mission whenever it appeared.[54]

The Entente proved very unpopular on the Crimean Peninsula. Scheubner-Richter later described the lasting resentments of the Crimean population against the French largely since French troops had fled pell-mell from Bolshevik forces and had abandoned White formations in nearby Odessa to grisly Bolshevik retribution earlier in the Russian Civil War.[55] Vrangel's press chief Nemirovich-Danchenko later noted in his memoirs (which Aufbau published in April 1923) that the residents of the Crimea had harbored considerable anti-English and anti-French sentiments. Inhabitants of the Crimea had blamed the English and French not only for half-heartedly resisting Bolshevik forces, but also for using their power to maintain unfair currency exchange rates. Nemirovich-Danchenko remarked that when word had circulated in Sevastopol that a delegation from Germany had evaded French intelligence agents to arrive in the city, Sevastopol society had greeted the news with "poorly concealed exultation."[56]

Scheubner-Richter's delegation achieved considerable successes in Sevastopol. Despite French anti-German countermeasures in the Crimea, Scheubner-Richter's colleague Wagner established a branch of the house of Wagner and Furter in General Vrangel's capital.[57] Scheubner-Richter, for

[52] DB report from January 10, 1924, RGVA (TsKhIDK), *fond* 7, *opis* 1, *delo* 876, reel 4, 332.

[53] Nemirovich-Danchenko, *V Krymu pri Vrangele*, 81.

[54] AA report from December 15, 1920, PAAA, 83379, 256.

[55] Max von Scheubner-Richter, "Im Eilmarsch zum Abgrund!" *Wirtschafts-politische Aufbau-Korrespondenz über Ostfragen und ihre Bedeutung für Deutschland*, July 26, 1922, 4.

[56] "In der Krim bei Wrangel," *Aufbau-Korrespondenz*, April 19, 1923, 4; Nemirovich-Danchenko, *V Krymu pri Vrangele*, 79, 80.

[57] DB report from September 6, 1920, RGVA (TsKhIDK), *fond* 7, *opis* 2, *delo* 2575, reel 3, 254.

his part, held extensive talks with Vrangel that progressed well.[58] Significant numbers of German technicians and traders subsequently traveled to the Crimea in accord with Scheubner-Richter's designs.[59] By the end of July 1920, Vrangel's approximately 75,000 soldiers included a sizeable number of White and German officers sent from Scheubner-Richter's associates in Bavaria.[60] The French Military Mission in Poland noted with dismay that Vrangel's officer entourage strongly approved of the growing Bavarian–Ukrainian cooperation under Scheubner-Richter's direction.[61]

Despite their increasing collaboration with Vrangel, Scheubner-Richter's financial backers in Bavaria distrusted the White general as too pro-French, largely because of his concessions to the French in including Constitutional Democrats in his government. In order to placate critics in right-wing Bavarian financial circles, Vrangel added far rightists to his regime. Most notably, he gave a post to the former Black Hundred writer Ivan Rodionov.[62] Rodionov was a Ukrainian Cossack who had published *The Protocols of the Elders of Zion* in *The Sentinel*, the official newspaper of General Piotr Krasnov's Great Don Host.[63] Rodionov later had his anti-Bolshevik work, "Victims of Insanity," serialized in the National Socialist newspaper the *Völkischer Beobachter* (*Völkisch Observer*) beginning in October 1923.[64] By including far rightists in his government and stressing that he had first gone to the German government for help in fighting the Bolsheviks, Vrangel stiffened the wavering support of leading White émigrés and Bavarian industrialists by early October 1920.[65]

Another large German-Russian monarchical consultation with key players from the Kapp Putsch took place in Bavaria in early October 1920. The participants discussed fostering closer ties between right-wing Germans and White émigrés based in Germany and Vrangel's regime. The Generals Ludendorff, Goltz of Latvian Intervention fame, and Max Hoffmann, who had negotiated with Soviet Foreign Minister Lev Trotskii in Brest-Litovsk but had subsequently turned against the Bolsheviks, represented the German side of the discussions. Latvian Intervention commander Colonel Bermondt-Avalov and General Biskupskii, the latter of whom

[58] Nemirovich-Danchenko, *V Krymu pri Vrangele*, 81.
[59] DDVL report to the AA from October 31, 1920, PAAA, 83379, 112 ob.
[60] LGPO report from August 1, 1920, GSAPKB, *Repositur 77*, title 1810, number 4, 66.
[61] MMFP report from September 24, 1920, RGVA (TsKhIDK), *fond* 1703, *opis* 1, *delo* 440, reel 2, 88.
[62] LGPO report from October 8, 1920, GSAPK, *Repositur 77*, title 1810, number 4, 240.
[63] Ganelin, "Beloe dvizhenie i 'Protokoly sionskikh mudretsov,'" *Natsionalnaia pravaia*, 127; ATsVO report from August 1921, GARF, *fond* 5893, *opis* 1, *delo* 39, 4.
[64] Ivan Rodionov, "Opfer des Wahnsinns," *Völkischer Beobachter*, October 2–November 9, 1923.
[65] LGPO report from October 10, 1920, GSAPKB, *Repositur 77*, title 1810, number 4, 261.

actually did not possess a mandate to represent General Vrangel as he claimed, represented Russian interests.[66] General Goltz proposed sending 50,000 armed Germans, overwhelmingly officers, to Vrangel's forces in the Crimea via Hungary.[67] Goltz's former collaborator in the Latvian Intervention, Major Bischoff, subsequently recruited German and Austrian officers and soldiers for Vrangel's forces from his new base in Austria.[68]

French military personnel in Hungary noted the effects of increased collaboration between former Kapp Putsch conspirators and General Vrangel's Southern Russian Armed Forces. French authorities soon took action to stop this anti-French cooperation. A French military report from October 1920 complained that large numbers of German officers in possession of valid Russian passports were traveling to Vrangel's forces via Hungary to fulfill the agreement for closer military and economic collaboration that Scheubner-Richter and Vrangel had reached the previous July. Such German officers followed the directives of General Goltz in particular. Goltz operated on the margins of the German government to penetrate Vrangel's army with the goal of overthrowing Bolshevism and creating a right-wing Russian, more properly Ukrainian, state that would cooperate with a nationalist Germany.[69]

In light of the increasing threat that growing right-wing German–White collaboration posed to France's interests, French police in the Crimea supervising Vrangel's forces arrested Scheubner-Richter and the members of his delegation in the middle of October 1920. French authorities released the members of the mission after much wrangling and bribery, but the delegation could not leave the peninsula immediately because of a lack of transportation facilities. The mission remained under strict French police surveillance until it left the Crimea for Germany later in October 1920.[70]

AUFBAU'S GENESIS AND EARLY DEVELOPMENT

Upon his return to Munich from his dangerous mission to General Vrangel's forces in the Crimea in late October 1920, Scheubner-Richter, who was

[66] MMFP report from October 12, 1921, RGVA (TsKhIDK), *fond* 1703, *opis* 1, *delo* 350, reel 3, 277; DB report to the ÉMMF from November 18, 1920, RGVA (TsKhIDK), *fond* 7, *opis* 2, *delo* 2575, reel 3, 269.

[67] MMFH report to the DB from October 25, 1920, RGVA (TsKhIDK), *fond* 198, *opis* 17, *delo* 203, reel 2, 160.

[68] DDVL report to the AA from October 31, 1920, PAAA, 83379, 112 ob.

[69] MMFH reports to the DB from October 30 and November 1, 1920, RGVA (TsKhIDK), *fond* 198, *opis* 17, *delo* 203, reel 3, 173, 185.

[70] LGPO report from October 27, 1920, GSAPKB, *Repositur* 77, title 1810, number 4, 303, 304.

widely regarded as an authority on Russian matters among *völkisch* German circles, set about organizing Aufbau.[71] This conspiratorial organization developed into the center of cooperation between *völkisch* Germans, notably including Hitler and General Ludendorff, and pro-German White émigrés. Despite Aufbau's crucial influence on the genesis and growth of National Socialism, historians have neglected to subject the secretive association to a thorough analysis.[72]

According to Aufbau's statutes, the organization fostered the "national interests of Germany and the Russian area of reconstruction." Aufbau sought the "promotion of an energetic national economic policy with regard to the Eastern states, especially those states that have formed on the territory of the former Russian Empire, for the reconstruction of the economic life of these states or the Russian Empire."[73] The imprecise language of Aufbau's statutes sidestepped the crucial issue of whether the Russian Empire was to be reconstructed as a unified whole, or whether the Ukraine and the Baltic regions, for instance, were to be granted autonomy. This lack of clarity was most likely intended to render the organization palatable both to Great Russians and to minorities, most notably Ukrainians and Baltic Germans who came from the margins of the former Russian Empire.

Aufbau closely controlled its membership, which tended to be wealthy, and the organization carried out its activities in a strictly conspiratorial manner. Aufbau sought fiercely determined anti-Bolshevik Germans and White émigrés, notably Russians, Ukrainians, and Baltic Germans, as ordinary members. Interested people of other nationalities could join as extraordinary members if they could demonstrate their commitment to furthering Aufbau's goals of far right German–Russian collaboration. Ordinary members had to pay 100,000 marks upon admission into the association and 20,000 marks in annual dues, whereas extraordinary members had to disburse 10,000 marks to enter the organization and had to contribute 50,000 marks annually. Aufbau's leaders carefully checked the background of prospective associates and could accept or reject applicants without offering any explanation for their decision. Aufbau's organizational work was carried out in complete secrecy.[74]

[71] Scheubner-Richter, "Abriss des Lebens- und Bildungsganges von Dr. Max Erwin von Scheubner-Richter," sent to Walther Nicolai in April 1923, RGVA (TsKhIDK), *fond* 1414, *opis* 1, *delo* 21, 231; DB report from November 11, 1922, RGVA (TsKhIDK), *fond* 7, *opis* 1, *delo* 386, reel 2, 156, 157.

[72] Baur, *Die russische Kolonie in München*, 253.

[73] "Auszug aus den Satzungen," *Aufbau: Zeitschrift für wirtschafts-politische Fragen Ost-Europas*, Number 2/3, August 1921, RKÜöO, BAB, 43/I, number 131, 498.

[74] DB reports from November 11, 1922 and July 3, 1923, RGVA (TsKhIDK), *fond* 7, *opis* 1, *delo* 876, reel 4, 367, 368, 378.

The former Tsarist general Aleksandr von Lampe observed the genesis of Aufbau. As a moderate monarchist, a sympathizer with the Entente, and a man who disapproved of what he termed Fedor Vinberg's "hysterical cries," Lampe regarded the decidedly pro-German Aufbau suspiciously.[75] He noted in his extensive Russian diary that Aufbau professed the official goal of establishing waterway trading and industrial relations with southern Russia (the Ukraine) after the overthrow of Soviet power. He also wrote of Aufbau's unofficial goals, most notably to bring about the rapprochement of right-wing German and White émigré circles to reestablish monarchical regimes in Germany and Russia and to defeat "Jewish dominance."[76]

Hitler developed close ties with Scheubner-Richter's Aufbau early on. In the course of November 1920, Hitler met Scheubner-Richter through the agency of Rosenberg. This meeting initiated an intense period of collaboration between the *völkisch* leaders, both of whom came from outside Germany's borders.[77] Hitler demonstrated his agreement with Aufbau's anti-Bolshevik, anti-Semitic views in a November 19, 1920 speech. He argued that the Soviet Union was an agrarian state, but it could not even feed its own people "as long as the Bolsheviks govern under Jewish rule." He stressed that the Jews were in control in Moscow, Vienna, and Berlin, and he argued, "There can be no talk of reconstruction" because of the fact that the Jews, as servants of international capital, "sell us Germans."[78] Scheubner-Richter heard Hitler speak publicly for the first time a few days later, on November 22, 1920.[79] Impressed with the experience, he joined the National Socialist Party soon after.[80] From this time on, the fortunes of Aufbau and the National Socialist movement become ever more closely entwined.

While alliance with Hitler's National Socialists furthered Aufbau's cause, Scheubner-Richter had to overcome a serious setback during his early direction of the conspiratorial right-wing organization. During the initial period of Aufbau's anti-Bolshevik activities, he placed significant hopes on General Vrangel's Southern Russian Armed Forces. He counted on the complete fulfillment of the agreement that he had concluded with Vrangel

[75] Lampe, *Dnevnik* (Diary), Berlin, August 26, 1920, GARF, *fond* 5853, *opis* 1, *delo* 3, reel 1, 921; MMFT report to the DB from December 24, 1923, RGVA (TsKhIDK), *fond* 7, *opis* 2, *delo* 2575, reel 2, 131.

[76] Lampe, *Dnevnik* (Diary), Berlin, June 5, 1923, GARF, *fond* 5853, *opis* 1, *delo* 11, reel 3, 4851/190.

[77] Paul Leverkühn, *Posten auf ewiger Wache: Aus dem abenteurreichen Leben des Max von Scheubner-Richter* (Essen: Essener Verlagsanstalt, 1938), 191.

[78] Adolf Hitler, speech on November 19, 1920 as reported by the PDM, BSAM, PDM, number 6698, 256.

[79] Leverkühn, *Posten auf ewiger Wache*, 191.   [80] Williams, *Culture in Exile*, 167.

for close military and economic cooperation. Expectations of sizeable support from Vrangel's forces in the Crimea nevertheless disappeared early on. The Red Army routed Vrangel's Southern Russian Armed Forces in the course of late November 1920. Vrangel's men evacuated the Crimea in order to escape death or incarceration at the hands of the victorious Bolshevik forces.[81] After his defeat, Vrangel stressed that he had fought against the "fundamental causes of the destruction that threatens the entire world."[82]

In a November 1921 article in the *Völkisch Observer*, "Jewish Bolshevism," Aufbau member and National Socialist ideologue Rosenberg asserted: "Vrangel was left in the lurch by the French, just as Iudenich was by England." As we have seen, the English fleet had stopped covering General Nikolai Iudenich's advance on Petrograd in 1919 in order to fire on Colonel Bermondt-Avalov's Western Volunteer Army. Rosenberg claimed that in the span of seven months, Vrangel's forces had only received three shipments of antiquated French military supplies. In return, the French had taken great amounts of grain. He also complained that the "'French' military mission" to Vrangel was composed of seven Jews and only three Gentiles. He concluded, "The Russian generals were supported only as long as they did not have dominance over the Red Army, just long enough to be able to pursue the process of tearing the Russian people to pieces with the greatest success."[83] Rosenberg's hatred of the Entente found great resonance in *völkisch* German and White émigré circles.

After Vrangel's anti-Bolshevik undertaking in the Crimea collapsed, Scheubner-Richter had to concentrate on using *völkisch* Germans and White émigrés centered in Bavaria to build Aufbau into a powerful conspiratorial organization. He regarded White émigrés in Germany from whom he drew support as "pro-German and pro-culture."[84] Through Aufbau, he sought to undermine socialists in Germany and the Bolshevik regime, both of which he regarded as under the control of Jews. He acted as the *de facto* leader of Aufbau, though officially he only held the post of first secretary of the organization. He could devote himself completely to directing right-wing German and White émigré elements for conspiratorial

---

[81] Bruno Thoss, *Der Ludendorff-Kreis 1919–1923: München als Zentrum der mitteleuropäischen Gegenrevolution zwischen Revolution und Hitler-Putsch* (Munich: Stadtarchiv München, 1978), 401.

[82] W. Dawatz, *Fünf Stürmjahre mit General Wrangel*, trans. Georg von Leuchtenberg (Berlin: Verlag für Kulturpolitik, 1927), iii.

[83] Rosenberg, "Der jüdische Bolschewismus," *Völkischer Beobachter*, November 26, 1921, 1, 2.

[84] Max von Scheubner-Richter, "Dem Bolschewismus entgegen," *Aufbau-Korrespondenz*, September 9, 1921, 1.

undertakings, for he possessed considerable personal wealth that he had acquired through his marriage into the German nobility.

Scheubner-Richter won over Baron Theodor von Cramer-Klett to serve as Aufbau's official president. Cramer-Klett was a fantastically wealthy individual with vast industrial enterprises and agricultural lands who possessed many connections to high places in Germany and abroad.[85] He proved Aufbau's most important German financial contributor. He placed large sums of money at the organization's disposal in return for future concessions in a planned independent nationalist Ukrainian state. He received particularly large funds for Aufbau from the German company Mannesmann. Cramer-Klett was allied with General Ludendorff through marriage. Moreover, he maintained a close friendship with Prince Ruprecht von Wittelsbach of Bavaria, whom Scheubner-Richter initially envisioned as the future German Kaiser.[86]

While Cramer-Klett officially led Aufbau by virtue of his wealth and connections, General Biskupskii served as Scheubner-Richter's truly indispensable collaborator in the association.[87] Biskupskii held the post of vice president. He brought valuable military and financial clout to the organization. He used his proud martial bearing and his elegant military costumes to ingratiate himself in the higher echelons of Bavarian society. His considerable intellect, adroitness, versatility, and language abilities allowed him to secure a leading role in the White émigré community in Munich. He also used his social skills to establish relations between Aufbau and leading aristocrats, landowners, industrialists, and military officers in Bavaria.[88] Biskupskii gradually developed a close relationship with Hitler himself.[89]

At the time of Aufbau's foundation in late 1920, Biskupskii led the Pan-Russian People's Military League, which sought to establish a popular

[85] DB report from July 3, 1923, RGVA (TsKhIDK), *fond* 7, *opis* 1, *delo* 876, reel 4, 366; Max Hildebert Boehm, "Baltische Einflüsse auf die Anfänge des Nationalsozialismus," *Jahrbuch des baltischen Deutschtums*, 1967, 59; Baur, *Die russische Kolonie in München*, 258.

[86] DB report from July 3, 1923, RGVA (TsKhIDK), *fond* 7, *opis* 1, *delo* 876, reel 4, 366; Karsten Brüggemann, "Max Erwin von Scheubner-Richter (1884–1923) – der 'Führer der Führers'?" *Deutschbalten, Weimarer Republik und Drittes Reich*, ed. Michael Garleff (Cologne: Böhlau Verlag, 2001), 129; Boehm, "Baltische Einflüsse," 60.

[87] DB reports from November 11, 1922 and July 3, 1923, RGVA (TsKhIDK), *fond* 7, *opis* 1, *delo* 386, reel 2, 157; *delo* 876, reel 4, 367.

[88] DB report from November 4, 1922, RGVA (TsKhIDK), *fond* 7, *opis* 1, *delo* 876, reel 4, 371; report from Stuttgart [Baron von Delingshausen?] to the RKÜöO from July 11, 1923, RGVA (TsKhIDK), *fond* 772, *opis* 1, *delo* 96, 222.

[89] Ganelin, "Rossiiskoe chernosotenstvo i germanskii natsional-sotsializm," 143.

federal monarchy on the territory of the former Russian Empire. Each segment of the confederation, such as the Ukraine and the Baltic region, was to enjoy substantial autonomy, initially under dictatorial military leaders. The organization used the mottos: "Federal monarchy," "The land to the people as property," "Power to the Tsar," and "Tsar and people." Biskupskii thus did not pursue purely "reactionary" political goals. He promised peripheral peoples substantial autonomy in a new Russian confederation. Moreover, realizing the popularity of Bolshevik land reforms among the peasants, he sought to win support for a new Russian monarchy by pledging to respect peasant land ownership.

Although the German Foreign Office consistently collaborated with the Bolshevik regime, a Foreign Office report from early November 1920 asserted that Biskupskii was

the right personality to lead the intended [anti-Bolshevik military] action to a fortunate solution. B[iskupskii] is clever, energetic, adroit, without political prejudices, and has a name that is in no way politically handicapped. For this last reason, B[iskupskii] also will not run into resistance on principle among any Russian group. A special advantage of General B[iskupskii]'s is the correct recognition of the ideas that always take root in the consciousness of the Russian people. At that time, Lenin also only attained victory since he correctly assessed the people's psyche at the given moment.[90]

Scheubner-Richter sought to transfer the German Foreign Office's positive assessment of Biskupskii personally into material support for Aufbau's anti-Bolshevik cause. He submitted a report to the Foreign Office in December 1920 which suggested that, while the agency's representatives officially had to deal with the Soviet Union, they should secretly support the White émigré activities that Aufbau coordinated.[91] The Foreign Office did not support Aufbau's endeavors, however. Instead, it maintained its fundamentally pro-Soviet stance. Scheubner-Richter became increasingly irate at the Foreign Office's close relations with Soviet leadership.[92]

While Aufbau failed to gain the support it desired from the German Foreign Office, the organization did attain considerable prestige by winning over General Ludendorff, who had been Germany's most valuable military strategist during World War I and a driving force behind the Kapp Putsch. Biskupskii established a close relationship with Ludendorff and helped

---

[90] AA report from November 4, 1920, PAAA, 83578, 3–5.
[91] AA report from December 15, 1920, PAAA, 83379, 256.
[92] Scheubner-Richter, "Zum fünften Jahrestag der Revolution," *Aufbau-Korrespondenz*, November 9, 1923, 1.

to gain him for Aufbau's cause.[93] Scheubner-Richter had long enjoyed Ludendorff's patronage, and he also played an important role in winning the general for Aufbau.[94] Ludendorff found Aufbau with its marked anti-Bolshevism and bold solutions to the "Eastern question" appealing. Scheubner-Richter introduced Ludendorff to Hitler in the framework of Aufbau in March 1921. Aufbau's *de facto* leader thereby initiated a political collaboration that culminated in the Hitler/Ludendorff Putsch of November 1923.[95]

Ludendorff contributed significantly to Hitler's militaristic *Weltanschauung*. In 1921, the general released a book, *Kriegsführung und Politik* (*War Leadership and Politics*). In this work, he claimed along the lines of *The Protocols of the Elders of Zion*: "The supreme government of the Jewish people was working hand in hand with France and England. Perhaps it was leading them both." He further stressed that peace was only a period of preparation for war. War brought "front-line socialism" that stabilized a warrior community whose energies were directed outwards.[96] Hitler later claimed that Ludendorff's book "clearly pointed out where it was practical to search [for the mistakes of the past and the possibilities for the future] in Germany."[97]

Another important collaborator in Aufbau was Arno Schickedanz, Scheubner-Richter's former Rubonia Fraternity brother in Riga, a veteran of the 1919 Latvian Intervention, and an enthusiastic National Socialist.[98] Schickedanz served as Aufbau's deputy director and also acted as Vice President Biskupskii's secretary.[99] Scheubner-Richter, Biskupskii, and Schickedanz ran Aufbau's daily affairs as a triumvirate. They alone had desks in Aufbau's main office.[100] Schickedanz also helped Scheubner-Richter to publish the organization's official weekly, which was originally titled *Aufbau: Zeitschrift für wirtschafts-politische Fragen Ost-Europas* (*Reconstruction: Journal for Economic-Political Questions of Eastern Europe*). Scheubner-Richter soon renamed the newspaper *Wirtschafts-politische Aufbau-Korrespondenz*

[93] DB reports from November 4 and 11, 1922, RGVA (TsKhIDK), *fond* 7, *opis* 1, *delo* 876, reel 4, 371; *delo* 386, reel 2, 157.

[94] Boehm, "Baltische Einflüsse," 59, 60.

[95] Nicolai's commentary on his article "Ludendorff" from April 9, 1921, *Tagebuch* (Diary), RGVA (TsKhIDK), *fond* 1414, *opis* 1, *delo* 19, 125, 126.

[96] Quoted from Norman Cohn, *Warrant for Genocide: The Myth of the Jewish World-Conspiracy and the "Protocols of the Elders of Zion"* (Chico, CA: Scholars Press, 1981), 134.

[97] Quoted from Thoss, *Der Ludendorff-Kreis*, 8.

[98] RKÜöO report from April 25, 1924, RGVA (TsKhIDK), *fond* 772, *opis* 3, *delo* 81a, 55.

[99] Baur, *Die russische Kolonie in München*, 259; RKÜöO report from April 25, 1924, (TsKhIDK), *fond* 772, *opis* 3, *delo* 81a, 55.

[100] DB report from July 3, 1923, RGVA (TsKhIDK), *fond* 7, *opis* 1, *delo* 876, reel 4, 369.

über Ostfragen und ihre Bedeutung für Deutschland (*Economic-Political Reconstruction Correspondence on Eastern Questions and Their Significance for Germany*).[101] Many *Aufbau Correspondence* editions were subsequently preserved in the NSDAP Archives.[102]

In addition to Schickedanz, Aufbau and Hitler's NSDAP shared several other common members. Hitler's close colleague from World War I, National Socialist Party Secretary Max Amann, also served as Aufbau's second secretary.[103] Amann worked in tandem with Scheubner-Richter to handle Aufbau's financial and organizational affairs.[104] Moreover, Scheubner-Richter and Schickedanz's Rubonia Fraternity colleagues Rosenberg and Otto von Kursell, who both collaborated with Hitler's early mentor Dietrich Eckart, served as prominent members of both Aufbau and the National Socialist Party.[105] In addition to participating in Aufbau's activities, Rosenberg acted as the primary National Socialist ideologue after Hitler himself.

Kursell worked closely with Scheubner-Richter in Aufbau, much as he had earlier collaborated with him during the German occupation of the Baltic region. In the early 1930s, Kursell stressed that while he had not officially joined the National Socialist Party until 1922, he had begun working in the vanguard of the movement in 1919 through his cooperation with Scheubner-Richter, Eckart, and Rosenberg.[106] Kursell also served as the vice president of the Munich branch of the Baltenverband (Baltic League).[107] The Baltic League's Munich subdivision originally had roughly forty-five members, but it achieved a membership of 530 by 1923.[108] The Baltic League possessed approximately 2,200 members nationally in 1920.[109] Baltic League leadership regarded Bolshevism as the "tyranny of a small clique consisting mostly of Jewish elements that wishes to prepare a

---

[101] Leverkühn, *Posten auf ewiger Wache*, 185.

[102] *Aufbau-Korrespondenz* editions are preserved in the NSDAPHA, BAB, NS 26, number 1263.

[103] DB report from July 3, 1923, RGVA (TsKhIDK), *fond* 7, *opis* 1, *delo* 876, reel 4, 367.

[104] LGPO *report* to the RKÜöO from December 24, 1921, RGVA (TsKhIDK), *fond* 772, *opis* 1, *delo* 96, 62.

[105] Nicolai's commentary on his article "Ludendorff" from April 9, 1921, *Tagebuch* (Diary), RGVA (TsKhIDK), *fond* 1414, *opis* 1, *delo* 19, 125.

[106] Wolfgang Frank, "Professor Otto v. Kursell: Wie ich den Führer zeichnete," *Hamburger Illustrierte*, March 6, 1934, BHSAM, *Sammlung Personen*, number 7440, 12.

[107] Protocol of a Baltenverband leadership meeting on March 24, 1920, BAB, 8012, number 4, 284.

[108] Membership list of the Baltenverband from October 1921, BAB, 8012, number 9, 53; letter from the Baltenverband Gau München to the Baltenverband headquarters in Berlin from October 25, 1923, BAB, 8012, number 11, 88.

[109] Protocol of a Gau Neubrandenburg Baltenverband meeting on October 4, 1920, BAB, 8012, number 7, 59.

springboard from which to extend its rule over Europe."[110] Kursell regarded Aufbau as a suitable tool for struggle against what he regarded as the Jewish Bolshevik threat.

While the virulently anti-Bolshevik Aufbau vaguely promoted the return of the monarchy to a future Russian confederation, the association strongly represented nationalist Ukrainian interests. As the Bolsheviks consolidated their power in the Ukraine during the Russian Civil War, the most important Ukrainian émigré community arose in Germany.[111] Colonel Ivan Poltavets-Ostranitsa, who had collaborated with German armed forces during their occupation of the Ukraine during World War I, joined Aufbau in 1921 after coming to Munich from Berlin.[112] He led the Ukrainian faction of Aufbau, and he worked to expand his military league dedicated to Ukrainian independence, the Ukrainian Cossack Organization.[113] He even held detailed negotiations with rightist officers in Bavaria in March 1921.[114] Moreover, Nemirovich-Danchenko, General Piotr Vrangel's former press chief on the Crimean Peninsula, joined Aufbau, where he acted as an expert on Ukrainian affairs.[115]

Other prominent White émigré Aufbau members included the comrades Colonel Vinberg, Lieutenant Shabelskii-Bork, and Lieutenant Taboritskii. These exiles had collaborated on the far right newspaper *The Call* in Berlin, had transferred *The Protocols of the Elders of Zion* to Ludwig Müller von Hausen for translation into German in 1919, and had supported the Kapp Putsch in 1920. Vinberg served as a leading Aufbau ideologue. He ultimately engaged in lengthy theoretical discussions with Hitler himself.[116] Vinberg's close colleagues Shabelskii-Bork and Taboritskii became infamous for their attempted assassination of the exiled Russian Constitutional Democratic leader Pavel Miliukov. This Aufbau-led assassination attempt formed one of a string of acts of political terrorism that rocked the early Weimar Republic.

Some White émigré Aufbau members possessed valuable American connections. Colonel Boris Brazol resided in New York, where he played a leading role in the Russkoe natsionalnoe obschestvo (Russian National

---

[110] Speech of Landrat A. v. Oettingen at a Baltenverband meeting on October 15, 1920, BAB, 8012, number 2, 128.

[111] RKÜöO report from December 4, 1925, RGVA (TsKhIDK), *fond* 772, *opis* 1, *delo* 101, 2.

[112] PDM report to the RKÜöO from September 14, 1926, RGVA (TsKhIDK), *fond* 772, *opis* 1, *delo* 101, 22.

[113] DB report from July 3, 1923, RGVA (TsKhIDK), *fond* 7, *opis* 1, *delo* 876, reel 4, 366; Horbaniuk, "*Zur ukrainischen Führerfrage*," 1926, RKÜöO, RGVA (TsKhIDK), *fond* 772, *opis* 1, *delo* 105b, 5.

[114] RKÜöO report from July 20, 1922, RGVA (TsKhIDK), *fond* 772, *opis* 1, *delo* 96, 151.

[115] DB report from May 15, 1923, RGVA (TsKhIDK), *fond* 7, *opis* 1, *delo* 954, reel 1, 55.

[116] DB report from November 11, 1922, RGVA (TsKhIDK), *fond* 7, *opis* 1, *delo* 386, reel 2, 160.

Society).[117] This organization supported Grand Prince Kirill Romanov's candidacy for Tsar.[118] As we shall see, Aufbau increasingly backed Kirill for Tsar. Brazol also worked on the staff of the American industrialist and politician Henry Ford's anti-Semitic newspaper, *The Dearborn Independent*. In particular, Brazol provided information on the "Jewish question."[119] Scheubner-Richter praised Brazol as "one of the leading personalities in the Russian émigré circles of America."[120] Brazol also spent much time in Munich, though he was not officially registered there. He collaborated with Scheubner-Richter and furthered Aufbau's cause by writing anti-Semitic literature.[121]

At least two other White émigré Aufbau members possessed important American ties. General Biskupskii's cousin Vladimir Keppen received a $500,000 fortune from a parent in America, and he put much of this money at Aufbau's disposal.[122] General Konstantin Sakharov also possessed connections with America. After making a name for himself as an extraordinarily capable Tsarist officer, he had served as the chief of the General Staff of General Aleksandr Kolchak's White army in Siberia during the Russian Civil War.[123] From Siberia, he had maintained relations with the German General Staff.[124] After the Bolsheviks had captured and executed General Kolchak, Sakharov had led the remains of the latter's White army over Lake Baikal into the Russian Far East.[125] Sakharov had tried to travel to Europe as a representative of the White cause, but the Entente had refused to allow him entry because of his pro-German views. He had left for America instead.[126] He arrived in Munich from America in 1921 and immediately joined Aufbau.[127]

[117] Letter from Müller to the Gestapo from July 12, 1938, RGVA (TsKhIDK), *fond* 500, *opis* 1, *delo* 677, 1.
[118] ROVS report from 1925, GARF, *fond* 5826, *opis* 1, *delo* 123, 301.
[119] James and Suzanne Pool, *Hitlers Wegbereiter zur Macht*, trans. Hans Thomas (New York: The Dial Press, 1978), 105.
[120] Scheubner-Richter, "Fürst Lwow, der Expremier – als Defraudant," *Aufbau-Korrespondenz*, October 27, 1921, 4.
[121] Letter from Müller to Heinrich Himmler from August 29, 1938, RGVA (TsKhIDK), *fond* 500, *opis* 1, *delo* 677, 3.
[122] Vladimir Biskupskii's subpoena from March 11, 1930, APA, BAB, NS 43, number 35, 129; DB report from June 18, 1922, RGVA (TsKhIDK), *fond* 7, *opis* 2, *delo* 2575, reel 3, 233.
[123] RMI report to the AA from June 9, 1931, PAAA, 31665, 136; letter from Wagner, Federal Chancellor of the Steel Helmet, to Duesterberg from January 20, 1931, BAB, 72, number 261, 24.
[124] SG report from March 11, 1924, RGVA (TsKhIDK), *fond* 1, *opis* 18, *delo* 2381, 2.
[125] HSKPA report to the APA/AO from November 22, 1937, RGVA (TsKhIDK), *fond* 1358, *opis* 2, *delo* 643, 125.
[126] Lampe, *Dnevnik* (Diary), Berlin, November 17, 18, 1922, GARF, *fond* 5853, *opis* 1, *delo* 9, reel 2, 3343.
[127] DB report from November 11, 1922, RGVA (TsKhIDK), *fond* 7, *opis* 1, *delo* 386, reel 2, 157.

Two influential Germans played important roles in Aufbau. Ludendorff's political advisor and Kapp Putsch co-conspirator Colonel Bauer joined Aufbau along with the general.[128] Dr. A. Glaser, a Reichstag (Parliament) member, served as Aufbau's second vice president. In 1919 and 1920, before Aufbau's establishment, he had edited a right-wing newspaper: *Aufbau, Bayerischer Zeitungskorrespondenz für nationalen und wirtschaftlichen Wiederaufbau* (*Reconstruction, Bavarian Newspaper Correspondence for National and Economic Reconstruction*).

Available records do not indicate whether Hitler's mentor Eckart officially belonged to Aufbau, but it is clear that he worked closely with the Aufbau members Rosenberg and Kursell, and he knew of the organization's activities. As we have seen, Eckart collaborated directly with Rosenberg and Kursell in the framework of the *völkisch* newspaper *Auf gut deutsch* (*In Plain German*). An article in the November 1920 edition of *In Plain German* indicates that Eckart cultivated close relations with Scheubner-Richter as well.

In his essay "'Jewry über alles'" ("'Jewry above Everything'"), Eckart related a long discussion that he had held with a "friend" who had recently returned from the Crimean Peninsula, where he had led a "certain mission" under the "greatest difficulties." Eckart noted that General Vrangel's forces had still not collapsed at the time that he had spoken with his "friend." His comrade had told him that the English and French officers in the Crimea were almost all Jews, whereas Vrangel's officers and the majority of his soldiers were "full of indignation" at the Jews.[129] This article demonstrates that Eckart and Scheubner-Richter held detailed political conversations of an anti-Semitic nature at an early date.

Other figures in Aufbau cannot be identified with certainty since the organization's leadership sought to keep its membership secret.[130] Moreover, documentation is lacking. The State Commissioner for the Supervision of Public Order file dedicated specifically to Aufbau that could shed light on Aufbau's membership is most likely held under wraps in Moscow at the Sluzhba vneshnoi razvetki (Foreign Intelligence Service), a successor organization to the Komitet gosudarstvennoi bezopasnosti (State Security Committee, KGB). If so, this valuable document is inaccessible to historians and will remain so indefinitely.

---

[128] DB report from November 11, 1922, RGVA (TsKhIDK), *fond* 7, *opis* 1, *delo* 386, reel 2, 163.

[129] Dietrich Eckart, "'Jewry über alles,'" *Auf gut deutsch: Wochenschrift für Ordnung und Recht*, November 26, 1920.

[130] DB report from July 3, 1923, RGVA (TsKhIDK), *fond* 7, *opis* 1, *delo* 876, reel 4, 367.

Aufbau's fortunes improved in the spring of 1921, when the organization gained many valuable new members. In late April 1921, Scheubner-Richter attended a general meeting of the Deutsch–Russische Gesellschaft (German–Russian Society). This organization sought to achieve "cultural understanding" between Germany, including German Austria, and the "coming Russia." Scheubner-Richter stressed that the association should become part of Aufbau. The German–Russian Society renamed itself Erneuerung: neue deutsch–russische Gesellschaft (Renewal: New German–Russian Society).[131] It officially became a subsection of Aufbau on May 1, 1921.[132] Renewal's statutes stressed that all nationalist Germans and Russians could join the organization. All leading pro-German White émigré monarchists in Munich joined Renewal, bringing its total membership in May to approximately 150 members.[133] Renewal eventually advertised in the pages of the National Socialist newspaper the *Völkisch Observer*.[134]

In the context of Renewal, Scheubner-Richter gained a valuable connection with Grand Prince Kirill Romanov, a claimant to the Tsarist throne, for Aufbau. Kirill displayed marked pro-German sympathies. His mother was the Duchess of Mecklenburg, and he had grown up in constant contact with German teachers and relatives.[135] His wife, Grand Princess Viktoria Romanov, was the daughter of Duke Alfred of Saxe-Coburg and the granddaughter of Queen Victoria of England.[136] Viktoria was a strong-willed and energetic woman who overshadowed her somewhat staid husband.[137] Scheubner-Richter arranged for her to serve as Renewal's honorary president.[138] Renewal's parent organization Aufbau increasingly benefited from financial assistance and prestige emanating from its association with the Russian throne claimants Kirill and Viktoria. In return, Aufbau supported Kirill's bid to become Tsar.

[131] Article from the *Münchner Neueste Nachrichten* from May 10, 1921, RMI, BAB, 1501, number 14139, 9.

[132] Schlögel, Katharina Kucher, Bernhard Suchy, and Gregor Thum, *Chronik russischen Lebens in Deutschland 1918–1941* (Berlin: Akademie Verlag, 1999), 23.

[133] Letter from Knorring to the RKÜöO from October 18, 1922, RGVA (TsKhIDK), *fond* 772, *opis* 1, *delo* 96, 196; article from the *Münchner Neueste Nachrichten* from May 10,1921, RMI, BAB, 1501, number 14139, 9.

[134] "Erneuerung," *Völkischer Beobachter*, May 4, 1923, 4.

[135] Pool, *Hitlers Wegbereiter zur Macht*, 60.

[136] Report from Stuttgart [Baron von Delingshausen?] to the RKÜöO from July 11, 1923, RGVA (TsKhIDK), *fond* 772, *opis* 1, *delo* 96, 222; Pool, *Hitlers Wegbereiter zur Macht*, 60.

[137] Nicolai's commentary on his letter to Ludendorff from February 18, 1922, *Tagebuch* (Diary), RGVA (TsKhIDK), *fond* 1414, *opis* 1, *delo* 20, 171.

[138] Baur, "Russische Emigranten und die bayerische Öffentlichkeit," 472.

CONCLUSION

After the Kapp Putsch collapsed in Berlin in March 1920, Munich rose to become the new hub of *völkisch* German–White émigré alliance. Former nationalist German and White émigré Kapp Putsch conspirators, notably General Erich von Ludendorff, his advisor Colonel Karl Bauer, Max von Scheubner-Richter, and Vladimir Biskupskii, did not waste time in setting up fresh intrigues from their new base in Bavaria. With the backing of Bavarian industrialists, they sent a mission under Scheubner-Richter to the Crimea to establish economic and military relations with General Piotr Vrangel's Southern Russian Armed Forces, which were based there. Scheubner-Richter's delegation gained the desired terms of mutual support, but this alliance proved brief, as the Red Army soon overran the Crimean Peninsula. Nonetheless, this short-lived German–White émigré/White connection inspired the creation of Aufbau, a secretive organization based in Munich that sought to collect *völkisch* Germans and White émigrés for joint action against the Weimar Republic and Bolshevik Russia.

With Aufbau's consolidation as a powerful conspiratorial force composed of *völkisch* Germans and White émigrés who backed the Tsarist candidate Grand Prince Kirill Romanov in the first half of 1921, far right German–White émigré collaboration recovered from the low point that it had reached with the embarrassing failure of the Kapp Putsch. Aufbau's rise to prominence in far right Bavarian politics marked the resurgence of the combined German/White émigré radical right in Germany, with Bavaria instead of East-Elbian Prussia serving as the center of *völkisch* German–White émigré partnership.

Aufbau supported Hitler's National Socialist Party from the beginning. Several of Aufbau's members belonged to the NSDAP, including four colleagues from the Rubonia Fraternity in Riga in Imperial Russia: Scheubner-Richter, Alfred Rosenberg, Arno Schickedanz, and Otto von Kursell. Other Aufbau White émigrés supported the National Socialist Party though they did not belong to it, including Biskupskii, Ivan Poltavets-Ostranitsa, Fedor Vinberg, Piotr Shabelskii-Bork, Sergei Taboritskii, and Konstantin Sakharov. The German Max Amann served both as Aufbau's second secretary and as National Socialist Party secretary. Scheubner-Richter also brought the *völkisch* leaders Hitler and Ludendorff together in the framework of Aufbau, thereby starting a political alliance that was to have fateful consequences for the National Socialist Party, as Hitler and Ludendorff led a doomed putsch against the Weimar Republic along with Scheubner-Richter in November 1923.

Under the direction of Scheubner-Richter, a prominent National Socialist, Aufbau was poised to exert ever-increasing influence over the domestic and foreign policies of Hitler's fledgling National Socialist Party as of 1921. Aufbau guided a common National Socialist/White émigré crusade against the Weimar Republic and the Soviet Union. As we shall see, while Aufbau convinced Hitler of the necessity for an alliance of nationalist Germans and Russians, the conspiratorial organization could not overcome internecine struggle among White émigrés in Germany to forge a united German/White émigré anti-Semitic and anti-Bolshevik front.

CHAPTER 5

"Germany–Russia above everything"

In his memoirs, the influential *völkisch* leader and former Aufbau member General Erich von Ludendorff complained bitterly that it had proven impossible to combine all White monarchical crosscurrents in Germany into one stream.[1] Ludendorff's assessment of the situation had merit. While Aufbau convinced Hitler of the complementary nature of German and Russian anti-Entente, anti-Weimar Republic, anti-Bolshevik, and anti-Semitic interests, the conspiratorial organization could not consolidate all White émigrés in Germany (and beyond) under its leadership to form a common front against the Weimar Republic and "Jewish Bolshevism." White émigrés seemed united at the May–June 1921 Monarchical Congress at Bad Reichenhall in Bavaria that Aufbau had organized, but appearances proved deceiving.

In an increasingly acrimonious power struggle, Aufbau and Nikolai Markov II's Supreme Monarchical Council, which had been established at the Bad Reichenhall Congress, offered divergent visions of how to overthrow Bolshevism in the course of 1921–1923. Aufbau fostered National Socialist–White émigré collaboration to place Grand Prince Kirill Romanov at the head of a Russian monarchy that would be allied with autonomous Ukrainian and Baltic states. Markov II's Council opposed Aufbau's pro-German designs for reorganizing the East. Despite operating from Berlin, the Council increasingly vehemently backed the Tsarist candidacy of Grand Prince Nikolai Nikolaevich Romanov, Kirill's cousin, who lived in Paris and had close ties with the French government. The Supreme Monarchical Council counted on French military assistance in its schemes to topple the Bolshevik regime. The Council favored a Great Russian solution, meaning

---

[1] Erich von Ludendorff, *Meine Lebenserinnerungen*, 204, cited from Johannes Baur, "Russische Emigranten und die bayerische Öffentlichkeit," *Bayern und Osteuropa: Aus der Geschichte der Beziehungen Bayerns, Frankens und Schwabens mit Russland, der Ukraine, und Weissrussland*, ed. Hermann Beyer-Thoma (Wiesbaden: Harrassowitz Verlag, 2000), 472.

that the Ukraine and the Baltic region would be subsumed under Russia as they had been in the Russian Empire.

No White émigré-backed invasion of the Soviet Union materialized in the early 1920s, largely because of the jealous rivalries among White émigrés in Germany and Europe as a whole. In the end, Aufbau's increasingly bitter struggle against Markov II's Supreme Monarchical Council sapped the energy of Germany's White émigré community. Aufbau even contemplated a hazardous tactical alliance with the Red Army to thwart French-led designs to invade the Soviet Union with the support of White émigrés who backed Nikolai Nikolaevich for Tsar. This desperate contingency plan demonstrated the fragile nature of the apparent White unity that had been established in 1921 at the Monarchical Congress at Bad Reichenhall. White émigré discord provided a valuable respite to the still unstable Bolshevik regime.

Hitler's National Socialist Party came down clearly on Aufbau's side in internecine White émigré struggle. Hitler allied himself with Kirill's candidacy for the Tsarist throne in return for Kirill's considerable financial support of the NSDAP. The key Aufbau ideologues Max von Scheubner-Richter, Alfred Rosenberg, Fedor Vinberg, and their *völkisch* colleague Dietrich Eckart, Hitler's early mentor, provided a theoretical basis for National Socialist–White émigré collaboration against Bolshevism and Jewry in league with Kirill. They emphasized the complementary nature of the Germans and Russians, generally not differentiating between Russians and Ukrainians. They further argued that Jewry consistently undermined the German and Russian peoples. In his early political career, Hitler repeatedly urged nationalist Germans and Russians to cooperate to overthrow what he perceived as "Jewish Bolshevism."

AUFBAU'S CALL FOR A NATIONALIST GERMAN–RUSSIAN ALLIANCE

In the early 1920s, the Aufbau ideologues Rosenberg, Scheubner-Richter, and Vinberg convinced Hitler's mentor Eckart and Hitler himself that nationalist Germans and Russians needed to cooperate to overcome alleged Jewish preponderance in the world. They presented a view of history in which Imperial Germany and the Russian Empire should never have gone to war against each other, but rather should have allied with each other against Britain and France. They argued that insidious Jewish conspirators had pitted the two powerful empires against each other in order to weaken them both, thereby setting the stage for an international Jewish dictatorship. Aufbau's views of the complementary anti-Bolshevik and anti-Semitic interests of nationalist Germans and Russians (in the broad sense of the term) engendered a surprisingly pro-Russian attitude in Hitler's early ideological views.

While historians often regard the National Socialist ideologue Rosenberg, one of Hitler's early mentors, as thoroughly anti-Russian in his outlook, the Baltic German expressed decidedly pro-Russian sentiments in his early writings. In an April 1919 article in Eckart's newspaper *Auf gut deutsch* (*In Plain German*), "Russian and German," Rosenberg drew a favorable parallel between Russians and Germans as found in the attitudes of their "great men" towards the "Jewish question." He mentioned the Russian authors Lev Tolstoi and Fedor Dostoevskii as well as the German philosopher Johann Gottlieb Fichte as opponents of the alleged Jewish exploitation of others. He noted another similarity between the German and Russian peoples in that "Jewish bands" had caused both to face the "broken structure of their state and culture."[2]

Rosenberg again compared Russians and Germans favorably in his 1920 work *Die Spur des Juden im Wandel der Zeiten* (*The Trail of the Jew through the Ages*). He alleged a Jewish "hatred" of all non-Jews, but particularly of the "Russian and German" peoples. He stressed that the Germans had investigated "the inner secret of mankind" more than any other people and therefore constituted "the spiritual antithesis of the Jew." The "Russian soul," for its part, possessed "tones closely related to the German one that, it is true, almost never bring themselves to a synthesis, but stand no less contrasting opposite the tendency of the Jew."[3] Rosenberg's first book thus conceived a basic correspondence between the exalted spiritual natures of the German and Russian peoples as opposed to alleged Jewish shallowness.

In a February 1921 article in Eckart's newspaper *In Plain German*, Rosenberg wrote in a similarly pro-Russian manner. He urged national Russia to draw from the "old Slavic force that is related to the Germanic one." He asserted: "Right now chaos and force are struggling on the Russian plains from the Gulf of Finland to the mountains of the Caucasus. The future will depend on this decision." Here Rosenberg placed the internal fight against Bolshevism in the very center of world events. Then he offered a highly favorable comparison between Germans and Russians. He

---

[2] Alfred Rosenberg, "Russe und Deutscher," *Auf gut deutsch: Wochenschrift für Ordnung und Recht*, April 4, 1919.

[3] Rosenberg, *Die Spur des Juden im Wandel der Zeiten* (Munich: Deutscher Volks-Verlag, 1920), 82.

claimed, "By nature, through their eternal searching for the light (Faust and the Karamazovs) . . . Russians and Germans are the noblest peoples of Europe; . . . they will be dependent on each other not only politically, but culturally as well."[4] In his early political career, Rosenberg placed the spiritual and cultural capabilities of Russians only slightly below those of Germans, and he called for nationalist German–Russian collaboration.

Rosenberg strongly advocated German–Russian cooperation against international Jewry. In a January 1921 article in *In Plain German*, he presented a view of history in which Zionist leaders in Imperial Russia had helped to overthrow the Tsar "just at the moment when he thought of making peace with Germany." Rosenberg argued that sinister Jews in league with Freemasons had sown discord between the German and Russian peoples in order to have them "bleed each other to death," thereby clearing the way for an international "Jewish dictatorship." Rosenberg believed that popular knowledge of these Jewish machinations would lead to the creation of a "German–Russian national (that is, anti-Jewish) united block. At this moment Jewry with allied Freemasonry will stand powerless opposite us. This day must and will come."[5] In the spirit of Aufbau, Rosenberg envisioned nationalist German–Russian might overcoming the twin evils of Jewry and Freemasonry.

Borrowing from Rosenberg, his highly valued collaborator in *In Plain German*, Eckart supported nationalist German–Russian cooperation. In a March 1919 article in *In Plain German*, "Russian Voices," which both he and Rosenberg wrote, Eckart argued, "German politics hardly has another choice than to enter an alliance with a new Russia after the elimination of the Bolshevik regime."[6] In an *In Plain German* article from February 1920 that warned of the Bolshevik peril, Eckart emphasized: "That Germany and Russia are dependent upon each other is not open to any doubt." He stressed that Germans had to seek connections with the "Russian people" and not with its "current Jewish regime." If Germans worked with this "current Jewish regime" in Russia, then the "lightning inundation of our native country with the entire Bolshevik chaos" would follow.[7] Eckart thus distinguished between nefarious Jewish Bolshevik leaders and the oppressed Russian people, the latter of whom were the natural allies of the Germans.

---

[4] Rosenberg, "Das Verbrechen der Freimaurerei: Judentum, Jesuitismus, deutsches Christentum: VIII. Deutsches Christentum," *Auf gut deutsch*, February 28, 1921.

[5] Rosenberg, "Das Verbrechen der Freimaurerei: IV. Freimaurerei und Judentum," *Auf gut deutsch*, January 15, 1921.

[6] Rosenberg, "Russische Stimmen," *Auf gut deutsch*, March 28, 1919.

[7] Dietrich Eckart, "Die Schlacht auf den Katalaunischen Feldern," *Auf gut deutsch*, February 20, 1920.

Eckart's friend Scheubner-Richter, Aufbau's mastermind and ultimately Hitler's closest advisor, advocated nationalist German–Russian partnership in the pages of his *Aufbau-Korrespondenz* (*Aufbau Correspondence*). In a July 1922 article, he presented a view of history in which the German and Russian Empires had had complementary interests. He claimed that the empires had possessed "no serious conflict" before World War I. Both states had "soared high above" all other countries and had proved "respected, envied, and, because of their strength, hated."[8] In a later essay, he alleged a plot of the "international Jewish press" working for "Jewish-international Marxism" to pit the two "mutually complementary" states against each other, despite the fact that they had been "naturally dependent upon each other."[9] Scheubner-Richter thus presented Germans and Russians as the primary victims of international Jewish machinations.

Scheubner-Richter remained true to his vision of a nationalist German–Russian alliance to the end, as seen in the last lead editorial that he wrote for *Aufbau Correspondence*, "On the Fifth Anniversary of the Revolution." This article was released on November 9, 1923, the day that he was fatally shot while marching at Hitler's side in the Hitler/Ludendorff Putsch. In his essay, Scheubner-Richter stressed that Aufbau had always operated on the principle: "The national Germany and the national Russia must find a common path for the future, and . . . it is therefore necessary that the *völkisch* circles of both countries already meet today."[10] Hitler's close collaborator and political advisor thus tirelessly stressed the fundamentally complementary interests of nationalist Germans and Russians up until his death.

Scheubner-Richter's fervently religious Aufbau colleague Vinberg similarly believed in the necessity of nationalist German–Russian collaboration. In March 1922, Vinberg truthfully assured the Munich Police that his "entire literary activities, pamphlets, books, and other writings, culminated in the intention to bring monarchical Russia closer to the Germany of the time, especially to bring the economic and political relations of both countries in line."[11] Like Scheubner-Richter, Vinberg offered a view of history in which the German and Russian Empires had not possessed serious differences with each other. In his 1922 work translated into German as *Der Kreuzesweg*

[8] Max von Scheubner-Richter, "Rückblicke und Parallelen," *Aufbau-Korrespondenz*, July 19, 1922, 1.

[9] Scheubner-Richter, "Klarheit," *Aufbau-Korrespondenz*, January 17, 1923, 1.

[10] Scheubner-Richter, "Zum fünften Jahrestag der Revolution," *Aufbau-Korrespondenz*, November 9, 1923, 1.

[11] Fedor Vinberg's March 30, 1922 testimony, BHSAM, BSMI 22, number 71624, fiche 4, 5.

Russlands (*Russia's Via Dolorosa*), he portrayed the German–Russian conflict on the Eastern Front in World War I as the result of a "Jewish-Masonic policy" directed towards the "carving up and destruction of Russia and Germany."

In another passage in *Russia's Via Dolorosa*, Vinberg asserted that for "true harmony," the *Deutschlandlied* (German national anthem) needed "two choirs," those of "two united and allied peoples, the German and the Russian." The song should therefore have its refrain changed from "Germany above everything, above everything in the world" to "Germany–Russia above everything, above everything in the world." He stressed, "Under the chord of this song, both of these peoples will fulfill their true purpose" of engendering "peace on earth, as the Christian Church intends."[12] Vinberg, one of Hitler's close ideological advisors, thus singled out Germans and Russians as chosen peoples destined to bring about the world's salvation.[13]

Aufbau's emphasis on the complementary nature of nationalist Germans and Russians (in the broad sense of the term) in opposition to Jewry strongly influenced Hitler's early views. While he later developed more derogatory views towards Russians, in his notes for an August 1921 oration, Hitler placed Russians on the same basic level as Germans. He wrote of "creative working" people with the note, "Aryans, Germans, Russians."[14] He also expressed a harmonious view of pre-World War I German–Russian relations along the lines of Aufbau thought. He asserted in another August 1921 speech:

The war turned out especially tragic for two countries: Germany and Russia. Instead of entering into a natural alliance with one another, both states concluded sham alliances to their detriment. Thus, Germany had to bleed for an incompetent Austria-Hungary, and Russia had to pull the chestnuts out of the fire for the Entente.[15]

In a similar vein, Hitler asserted in an April 1923 oration that the German and Russian peoples had originally been "friendly towards each other." Moreover, "not the German had a reason" for Imperial Germany's 1914 mobilization against the Russian Empire, "but the Jew." He asserted,

---

[12] Vinberg, *Der Kreuzesweg Russlands: Teil I: Die Ursachen des Übels*, trans. K. von Jarmersted (Munich: R. Oldenbourg, 1922), 32, 40, 41.

[13] DB report from November 11, 1922, RGVA (TsKhIDK), *fond* 7, *opis* 1, *delo* 386, reel 2, 160.

[14] Adolf Hitler, notes for a speech on August 12, 1921, *Sämtliche Aufzeichnungen 1905–1924*, eds. Eberhard Jäckel and Axel Kuhn (Stuttgart: Deutsche Verlags-Anstalt, 1980), 453.

[15] Hitler, speech on August 4, 1921, *Sämtliche Aufzeichnungen*, 450, 451.

"Liberalism, our press, the stock market, and Freemasonry" together represented nothing but "instrument[s] of the Jews" that they had used to stir "hatred of the Russian people among the German people." The Jews had schemed in this manner since they had realized that while they were already "absolute rulers in the other states," there remained

antitheses in only two more states: in Germany and Russia. They knew that as long as a monarch was in existence, the state would not be entirely at the mercy of the parliamentary economy. Thus the Jews became revolutionaries at the moment in which they knew that the revolution would bring the rise of their own power.[16]

Hitler's allegation of a Jewish *Dolchstoss* (stab in the back) against nationalist Germans and Russians appeared on the front page of a May 1923 edition of *Aufbau Correspondence*.[17] This prominent location proved a fitting place for his anti-Semitic assertion, given that Aufbau leadership had influenced Hitler's early ideas on the complementary nature of nationalist Germans and Russians in opposition to international Jewry.

In the spirit of Aufbau, Hitler frequently called for nationalist Germans to ally themselves with like-minded Russians against the Jews. In July 1920, even before Aufbau's inception, he stressed, "Our deliverance will never come from the West. We must seek friendship with national, anti-Semitic Russia. Not with the Soviet [one] . . . The Jew rules there."[18] In an August 1921 speech, he stressed that the Germans must give "no support to the Jewish usurpers, in order to help the Russian people finally to freedom."[19] In an April 1922 oration, he called on the "Russian people to shake off their tormentors," meaning the Jews, after which the Germans could "get closer" to the Russians.[20] While he ordered brutal policies towards Russians during World War II, in his early career, Hitler upheld the fundamental Aufbau goal of securing the cooperation of nationalist Germans and Russians against the alleged international Jewish peril.

Hitler continued to view Germans and Russians as the primary victims of international Jewish plotters after 1923. In his unpublished 1928 sequel to *Mein Kampf*, he expressed a view of history in which insidious Jewish conspirators had pitted Germans and Russians against each other. He warned of "the Jew's" drive to dominate Europe. As part of this scheme, the

---

[16] Hitler, "Die Urschuldigen am Weltkriege: Weltjude und Weltbörse," *Völkischer Beobachter*, April 15/16, 1923, 1.

[17] Georgii Nemirovich-Danchenko, "Russland und Deutschland: Gedanken eines russischen Emigranten," *Aufbau-Korrespondenz*, May 24, 1923, 1.

[18] Hitler, speech on July 21, 1920, *Sämtliche Aufzeichnungen*, 163.

[19] Hitler, speech on August 4, 1921, *Sämtliche Aufzeichnungen*, 451.

[20] Hitler, speech on April 21, 1922, *Sämtliche Aufzeichnungen*, 631.

Jew "methodically agitates for world war" with the aim of "the destruction of inwardly anti-Semitic Russia as well as the destruction of the German Empire, which in administration and the army still offered resistance to the Jew." Hitler lamented the partial success of "this Jewish battle aim," noting that both "Tsarism and Kaiserism in Germany were done away with."[21] Even in the late 1920s, Hitler upheld the basic Aufbau philosophy that the Jews concentrated their nefarious actions against two complementary peoples, the Germans and the Russians.

AUFBAU'S ATTEMPT TO UNITE ALL WHITE ÉMIGRÉS IN CONCERT WITH HITLER

Aufbau proved less successful in combining all White émigrés in Germany (and beyond) under its aegis than in convincing Hitler of the need for German-Russian collaboration against international Jewry. While it never tired of trying, Aufbau could not unite all of Europe's White émigrés under its banner. Despite early cooperation, as witnessed at the May–June 1921 Monarchical Congress at Bad Reichenhall, Aufbau and Nikolai Markov II's Union of the Faithful drifted further and further apart. Both factions grew increasingly vindictive, and Aufbau even contemplated a perilous tactical alliance with the Red Army to oppose Markov II's pro-French designs to invade Bolshevik Russia. White émigrés in 1921–1923 offered a powerful example of the disastrous consequences of engaging in infighting instead of uniting for a common cause.

In the early 1920s, Markov II, the former leader of a faction of the far right Union of the Russian People in Imperial Russia and the current head of the pro-monarchical Union of the Faithful, wished to unite all White émigrés under his leadership. Unlike the solidly pro-German members of Aufbau, Markov II had displayed marked pro-Entente tendencies in the recent past. During the German–White Latvian Intervention under Colonel Pavel Bermondt-Avalov in 1919, he had backed General Nikolai Iudenich in Estonia, who had relied on English support. Markov II had regarded Bermondt-Avalov's Western Volunteer Army with extreme suspicion. He had even claimed that Germany always secretly worked to help the Bolsheviks, intending the Latvian Intervention to dissipate White offensive power so that General Iudenich could not capture Petrograd.[22]

---

[21] Hitler, *Hitlers Zweites Buch: Ein Dokument aus dem Jahr 1928* (Stuttgart: Deutsche Verlags-Anstalt, 1961), 221.

[22] LGPO report from June 3, 1921, GSAPKB, *Repositur 77*, title 1813, number 2, 9.

Despite his pro-Entente leanings and his suspicion that the Germans supported Bolshevism, in May 1920, Markov II left Estonia for Berlin to lead the Union of the Faithful from there. He traveled with Fedor Evaldt, who had earlier served as the military commander of Kiev under Pavel Skoropadskii's Hetmanate in the Ukraine in 1918.[23] Once in Berlin, Markov II and Evaldt joined up with Union of the Faithful members already established in the German capital, most notably Nikolai Talberg, a Baltic German who had served Skoropadskii as the head of the Kiev Police Department.[24] From Berlin, Markov II, Evaldt, and Talberg led the Union of the Faithful, commonly referred to as the "Markov Group," as a strictly disciplined conspiratorial organization dedicated to restoring the monarchy to Russia.[25] The Union of the Faithful established numerous agents among the peasantry and in the Red Army in the Soviet Union. The Union especially made its presence felt in the Red Army's officer corps.[26]

Markov II wished to hold a general congress to work out a common program for all leading White émigré monarchical groups in the spring of 1921. Markov II's Union of the Faithful desired to lead the White movement as a whole, but it did not possess the financial means for a grandiose conference, nor could such a meeting be held in Berlin, the seat of the mistrustful primarily socialist German government.[27] The Union of the Faithful soon received substantial assistance from Aufbau. In the spring of 1921, the prospects for White émigré unity appeared bright, as the Union of the Faithful and Aufbau were able to collaborate effectively with each other to advance the White émigré cause.

While the two groups would become fierce enemies, Aufbau supported the Union of the Faithful early on. Aufbau's *de facto* leader Scheubner-Richter received word of Markov II's desire for a large-scale monarchical White émigré congress, perhaps through General Vladimir Biskupskii, who, in addition to acting as Aufbau's vice president, often aided Markov II's Union of the Faithful in Berlin early on.[28] Scheubner-Richter developed the idea of holding a general White émigré monarchical congress

---

[23] LGPO report to the RKÜöO from December 24, 1921, RGVA (TsKhIDK), *fond* 772, *opis* 1, *delo* 96, 57, 58; MMFT report to the DB from December 24, 1923, RGVA (TsKhIDK), *fond* 7, *opis* 2, *delo* 2575, reel 2, 134.

[24] LGPO report from March 16, 1922, GSAPKB, *Repositur* 77, title 1813, number 8, 11.

[25] LGPO reports to the RKÜöO from November 28 and December 24, 1921, RGVA (TsKhIDK), *fond* 772, *opis* 1, *delo* 96, 39, 41, 58.

[26] [FZO] report from October 15, 1920, MMFP, RGVA (TsKhIDK), *fond* 198, *opis* 2, *delo* 1031, reel 2, 72.

[27] LGPO report to the RKÜöO from December 24, 1921, RGVA (TsKhIDK), *fond* 772, *opis* 1, *delo* 96, 58, 60.

[28] DB report from November 4, 1922, RGVA (TsKhIDK), *fond* 7, *opis* 1, *delo* 876, reel 4, 371.

in the picturesque (and remote) Bavarian alpine resort town of Bad Reichenhall.[29] He toiled throughout May 1921 as the key practical organizer of the planned monarchical congress. Moreover, he channeled the majority of the means for the undertaking, roughly 12,000 marks.[30]

Some of Scheubner-Richter's colleagues in Aufbau gave considerable financial assistance to the organization of the monarchical émigré congress in Bad Reichenhall. Baron Theodor von Cramer-Klett, Aufbau's official president, raised funds from Bavarian industrialists and contributed substantial money of his own.[31] As always, Biskupskii proved Scheubner-Richter's invaluable partner. He used his entrée into wealthy Bavarian circles to raise significant funds for the White émigré congress.[32] Max Amann, the secretary of the NSDAP and Aufbau's second secretary, collaborated with Scheubner-Richter to raise funds for the congress from right-wing Bavarian circles.[33]

While Aufbau in general and Scheubner-Richter in particular laid the groundwork for the White émigré assembly in Bad Reichenhall, Markov II, Evaldt, and Talberg of the Union of the Faithful ran the Organizational Committee that invited the Congress participants.[34] Latvian Intervention leader Colonel Bermondt-Avalov, who had aroused Markov II's distrust in the past, pointedly did not receive an invitation.[35] Markov II also excluded those émigrés who opposed the Great Russian stance of his Organizational Committee, most notably the Ukrainian Cossack separatist and Aufbau member Colonel Ivan Poltavets-Ostranitsa.[36]

A total of 106 White émigrés from Europe, Africa, Asia, and North America representing 24 different organizations attended the Monarchical Congress at Bad Reichenhall, which lasted from May 29 to June 5, 1921.[37] The members of the Congress had come from the upper strata of Imperial Russia. Congress participants had predominantly served as officers and

---

[29] Aleksandr von Lampe, *Dnevnik* (Diary), Budapest, October 8–22, 1921, GARF, *fond* 5853, *opis* 1, *delo* 7, reel 1, 1998.

[30] RKÜöO report from June 20, 1921, RGVA (TsKhIDK), *fond* 772, *opis* 3, *delo* 81a, 16.

[31] RKÜöO report from June 11, 1921, RGVA (TsKhIDK), *fond* 772, *opis* 2, *delo* 129b, 230.

[32] DB report from November 4, 1922, RGVA (TsKhIDK), *fond* 7, *opis* 1, *delo* 876, reel 4, 371.

[33] LGPO report to the RKÜöO from December 24, 1921, RGVA (TsKhIDK), *fond* 772, *opis* 1, *delo* 96, 62.

[34] LGPO report to the RKÜöO from December 24, 1921, RGVA (TsKhIDK), *fond* 772, *opis* 1, *delo* 96, 61.

[35] RKÜöO report from September 9, 1921, RGVA (TsKhIDK), *fond* 772, *opis* 3, *delo* 71, 20, 21.

[36] LGPO report to the RKÜöO from July 11, 1921, RGVA (TsKhIDK), *fond* 772, *opis* 2, *delo* 129b, 254.

[37] "Der I. Kongress zum wirtschaftlichen Wiederaufbau Russlands in Reichenhall: Erster Tag, 29 Mai 1921," *Aufbau: Zeitschrift für wirtschafts-politische Fragen Ost-Europas*, Number 2/3, August 1921, 5, RKÜöO, BAB, 43/I, number 131, 503; LGPO report to the RKÜöO from July 11, 1921, RGVA (TsKhIDK), *fond* 772, *opis* 2, *delo* 129b, 253, 263.

high-ranking governmental officials.[38] The majority of the Congress members had been active in the Black Hundred movement, having belonged to Aleksandr Dubrovin's Union of the Russian People, Vladimir Purishkevich's Michael the Archangel Russian People's Union, or both.[39]

Several prominent members of Aufbau attended the Monarchical Congress at Bad Reichenhall, including the organization's guiding figure Scheubner-Richter, Vice President Biskupskii, Vinberg, a strident anti-Bolshevik and anti-Semitic ideologue, Georgii Nemirovich-Danchenko, General Piotr Vrangel's former press chief in the Crimea who served as an authority on Ukrainian matters, Piotr Shabelskii-Bork, the carrier of *The Protocols of the Elders of Zion* from the Ukraine to Germany, and General Konstantin Sakharov, a representative from America.[40]

The Monarchical Congress at Bad Reichenhall displayed a pronounced religious aura. Archbishop Eulogius, who had earlier served in the second Imperial Russian Duma (Parliament) from the Lublin region as a Black Hundred representative, and who had long belonged to the Markov Group, led an Orthodox Christian ceremony that climaxed with a solemn group prayer to bless the proceedings.[41] Eulogius subsequently led the Congress' Religious Committee.[42]

Markov II, the head of the Organizational Committee, gave a welcoming address to the assembled White émigrés at the Monarchical Congress at Bad Reichenhall. He assured the Congress participants that after so much suffering, their time had come. He noted that mainly because of financial difficulties, it had not been possible to hold a large-scale monarchical congress earlier. He thanked Scheubner-Richter's Aufbau for providing the funding for the Congress.

After Markov II's speech, Scheubner-Richter gave a rousing address to the Congress participants in German and then in Russian. He welcomed the delegates on behalf of Aufbau and other "German, national, and monarchical circles." He expressed his particular satisfaction that "Russian national circles from all regions of the world" had gathered on "Bavarian soil." He lamented the "unfortunate" war between the Russian and German peoples. He argued that both peoples had not possessed any serious conflicting interests with each other, and he noted that the war had led to the "fall

---

[38] RKÜöO report from June 11, 1921, RGVA (TsKhIDK), *fond* 772, *opis* 2, *delo* 129b, 229.

[39] Report from Ludwig von Knorring to the AA from June 30, 1921, PAAA, 31490, K096232.

[40] LGPO report to the RKÜöO from December 24, 1921, RGVA (TsKhIDK), *fond* 772, *opis* 1, *delo* 96, 62, 65.

[41] S. A. Stepanov, *Chernaia Sotnia v Rossii 1905–1914* (Moscow: Izdatelstvo Vsesoiuznogo zaochnogo politekhnicheskogo instituta, 1992), 243; LGPO reports to the RKÜöO from July 11 and December 4, 1921, RGVA (TsKhIDK), *fond* 772, *opis* 2, *delo* 129b, 263; *opis* 1, *delo* 96, 66.

[42] LGPO report to the RKÜöO from July 11, 1921, RGVA (TsKhIDK), *fond* 772, *opis* 2, *delo* 129b, 261.

of the two most powerful empires." He stressed that Germany and Russia could only rise to greatness again through "joint reconstruction work." He gained thunderous applause at the end of his speech for his assertion that the Congress would serve as the "cornerstone of the reconstruction of a great and powerful Russia."[43]

While Scheubner-Richter acted as an organizer and crowd-pleaser at the Monarchical Congress at Bad Reichenhall, Markov II displayed himself as a forceful leader. He denounced the Treaty of Versailles in a fiery speech, claiming that it had "betrayed and sold Russia."[44] He concluded to loud applause: "Russia does not recognize the Treaty of Versailles. We must give back to the Russian people what the Russian Tsars accumulated over the centuries."[45] The Congress members decided to create a governing body, the Supreme Monarchical Council, which was to be located in Berlin under Markov II's leadership.[46] Markov II's close colleague Talberg was elected to serve as the Supreme Monarchical Council's secretary as well as the leader of the Council's intelligence service.[47]

Markov II gained another victory at the Congress by having his Cossack colleague General Piotr Krasnov charged with coordinating White émigré military forces in Germany.[48] Krasnov, the former leader of the pro-German Great Don Host just outside of the Ukraine during the Russian Civil War, currently played a leading role in the Military Section of Markov II's Union of the Faithful.[49] He was to lead White forces against the Bolsheviks after internal revolts in the Soviet Union had sufficiently weakened Soviet rule.[50] The general was best known for his popular 1921 novel, *From the Double-Headed Eagle to the Red Banner*. In this work, the protagonist discovers the "terrible secret" of the Bolshevik Revolution, namely that the Jews had eradicated the best of the Russian Gentiles.[51]

---

[43] LGPO report to the RKÜöO from July 11, 1921, RGVA (TsKhIDK), *fond* 772, *opis* 2, *delo* 129b, 257–259.

[44] Scheubner-Richter, "Der russische Wiederaufbaukongress in Bad Reichenhall: Ein Rückblick und Ausblick von Dr. M. E. von Scheubner-Richter," *Aufbau*, Number 2/3 August 1921, 1, RKÜöO, BAB, 43/I, number 131, 499.

[45] "Der I. Kongress zum wirtschaftlichen Wiederaufbau Russlands in Reichenhall: Sechster Tag, 3. Juni 1921," *Aufbau*, Number 2/3, August 1921, 14, RKÜöO, BAB, 43/I, number 131, 514.

[46] PDM report to the BSMÄ from June 7, 1923, BHSAM, BSMÄ 36, number 103009, 29; LGPO report to the RKÜöO from July 11, 1921, RGVA (TsKhIDK), *fond* 772, *opis* 2, *delo* 129b, 253.

[47] LGPO report from March 16, 1922, GSAPKB, *Repositur* 77, title 1813, number 8, 11.

[48] DB report from August [11], 1921, RGVA (TsKhIDK), *fond* 7, *opis* 2, *delo* 2575, reel 2, 109.

[49] [FZO] report from October 15, 1920, MMFP, RGVA (TsKhIDK), *fond* 198, *opis* 2, *delo* 1031, reel 2, 70.

[50] DB report from August [11], 1921, RGVA (TsKhIDK), *fond* 7, *opis* 2, *delo* 2575, reel 2, 109.

[51] Matthias Vetter, "Die Russische Emigration und ihre 'Judenfrage,'" *Russische Emigration in Deutschland 1918 bis 1941: Leben im europäischen Bürgerkrieg*, ed. Karl Schlögel (Berlin: Akademie, 1995), 111.

At the Congress, members of Markov II's Union of the Faithful were officially slated for the leading White émigré political roles, whereas Aufbau members largely had to content themselves with important ideological functions. Shabelskii-Bork served as the secretary of the Propaganda Committee, while his comrade Vinberg acted as an assistant to it.[52] Nemirovich-Danchenko appealed for German–Russian collaboration. He argued that the war between the German and Russian Empires had been mutual suicide, and he stressed that Germans and Russians had to collaborate to overthrow the Bolsheviks.[53] He subsequently wrote of the efforts of himself and other Congress members to free the future Russia from the "capitalist yoke."[54] He thus believed in a conspiratorial alliance between finance capitalism and Bolshevism, a popular White émigré theme that became part of National Socialist ideology.

After the conclusion of the anti-Bolshevik Monarchical Congress at Bad Reichenhall, Scheubner-Richter wrote an article about the proceedings in his weekly newspaper, *Aufbau: Zeitschrift für wirtschafts-politische Fragen Ost-Europas* (*Reconstruction: Journal for Economic-Political Questions of Eastern Europe*). He included a thinly veiled anti-Semitic argument in his essay, and he expressed an exaggerated view of fundamental political agreement among the Congress participants. He asserted that the Russian people viewed "God's scourge in the rule of the racial foreigners," meaning the Jews, and saw "their deliverance only in the return of the rule of the church and the Tsar."[55]

In fact, the question of the Tsarist succession had not been clarified at the Monarchical Congress at Bad Reichenhall. While the majority of the Congress participants recognized Grand Prince Kirill Romanov's official right to the throne on the basis of the rules of heredity, many Congress members disapproved of Kirill personally. Kirill had sullied his reputation among Russian far rightists by paying homage to Aleksandr Kerenskii's Provisional Government in March 1917 before the Tsar had abdicated.[56] As we shall see, the question of who possessed the legitimate right to ascend the Russian throne turned into an acute source of discord between White émigré factions.

---

[52] LGPO report to the RKÜöO from July 11, 1921, RGVA (TsKhIDK), *fond* 772, *opis* 2, *delo* 129b, 261.

[53] Report from the French Ambassador in Berlin, Laurent, to the MAÉ from June 25, 1921, SG, RGVA (TsKhIDK), *fond* 1, *opis* 27, *delo* 12523, 52.

[54] Nemirovich-Danchenko, "Der wirtschaftliche Aufbau Russlands," *Aufbau*, Number 2/3, August 1921, 2, RKÜöO, BAB, 43/I, number 131, 500.

[55] Scheubner-Richter, "Der russische Wiederaufbaukongress in Bad Reichenhall," *Aufbau*, Number 2/3, August 1921, 2, RKÜöO, BAB, 43/I, number 131, 500.

[56] LGPO report to the RKÜöO from August 24, 1921, RGVA (TsKhIDK), *fond* 772, *opis* 1, *delo* 96, 7.

In addition to papering over political differences at the Congress in his *Aufbau* article, Scheubner-Richter stressed the harmony of interests between White émigrés and right-wing Germans. He praised Bavaria for demonstrating, "There are broad circles in Germany that reject the Moscow pseudo-Russiandom and are gladly willing to help with the reconstruction of a national Russian state." He extolled the Congress' anti-Entente tone. He noted of the Treaty of Versailles, "National Russiandom sees in it an ignominious act of violence and a disgrace for humanity." He further argued that the firm resolution of the Congress participants to reestablish the monarchy in Russia possessed the "greatest importance" for "those German national circles who see the basis of the economic and cultural rebirth of Germany in a firm state authority independent of parliamentary whims."[57] Scheubner-Richter thus sounded a clarion call for right-wing German and White émigré collaboration.

In organizing the Monarchical Congress at Bad Reichenhall, Scheubner-Richter gained an impressive triumph for Aufbau. The Congress lent White émigrés the appearance of cohesion and unity. The proceedings were generally hailed as a great success that had spurred the Russian monarchical movement worldwide.[58] While the Markov Group had left the Congress with the official leadership of the White émigré community in Germany, Aufbau under Scheubner-Richter and Biskupskii had gained a great deal of prestige by holding the Congress in Bavaria, the organization's own sphere of influence. The French military intelligence agency the Second Section even wrote of a "union" of the Bavarian and White émigré monarchical right in the wake of the Bad Reichenhall Congress.[59]

The Monarchical Congress at Bad Reichenhall appeared to demonstrate White émigré unity and determination to drive the Bolsheviks from power in league with right-wing German allies. In reality, however, serious differences had been glossed over regarding the means of toppling Bolshevik Russia. Relations between Aufbau under Scheubner-Richter and Biskupskii and the Supreme Monarchical Council under Markov II grew increasingly strained in the course of 1921–1923.[60] While both Aufbau and the Supreme Monarchical Council wished to overthrow the Bolshevik regime, they disagreed significantly on how to do so, where the new borders in the East should be drawn, and who should rule after the defeat of Bolshevism.

[57] Scheubner-Richter, "Der russische Wiederaufbaukongress in Bad Reichenhall," *Aufbau*, Number 2/3, August 1921, 1, RKÜöO, BAB, 43/I, number 131, 499.
[58] LGPO report to the RKÜöO from December 24, 1921, RGVA (TsKhIDK), *fond* 772, *opis* 1, *delo* 96, 61.
[59] DB report from November 11, 1922, RGVA (TsKhIDK), *fond* 7, *opis* 1, *delo* 386, reel 2, 157.
[60] Baur, "Russische Emigranten und die bayerische Öffentlichkeit," 463.

In the course of the summer of 1921, serious differences became evident between Aufbau and the Supreme Monarchical Council, notably regarding the Ukrainian question. Several members of Markov II's Union of the Faithful with Great Russian views reproached General Biskupskii with relying excessively on Ukrainian émigré circles and with establishing a Ukrainian officer league in opposition to the existing Russian one.[61] Markov II and some of his Union allies began openly disparaging Biskupskii, and the Union forbade its members from serving in any military formations associated with him.[62] A State Commissioner for the Supervision of Public Order report written shortly after the Monarchical Congress at Bad Reichenhall noted that White émigrés held widely differing views of Biskupskii. Some hoped that he would unite White émigrés, whereas others regarded him as a "political pest."

Drawing upon Union of the Faithful sources, the State Commissioner report asserted that Biskupskii constantly set up damaging intrigues and demonstrated "unreliability," as he was only led by "personal motives." The report admitted, "Energy, cunning, and a certain cleverness cannot be denied him." Nonetheless, "Boundless ambition, vanity, and egoism comprise the greatest part of his nature." The report concluded:

Although one cannot directly prove him to favor the Entente, it is nevertheless conspicuous that for all of his activity and energy, he has not achieved anything positive for Russian–German cooperation, and that everywhere he is involved, intrigues and grousings begin that have a destructive and subversive effect.[63]

Biskupskii had powerful enemies, and he was not able to unite all White émigrés in Germany and the rest of Europe under his leadership.

In the course of internecine White émigré struggle, Biskupskii scored a coup against the increasingly hostile Markov Group. He won over Evaldt, an important member of Markov II's Union of the Faithful, to Aufbau. Evaldt left Berlin for Munich in September 1921.[64] He also established a residence in Bad Reichenhall, where he received considerable funding from Bavarian monarchists.[65] He rose quickly in Aufbau's hierarchy, reaching the post of assessor.[66] Aufbau leadership rewarded Evaldt for his *de facto* defection,

---

[61] RKÜöO report from July 20, 1922, RGVA (TsKhIDK), *fond* 772, *opis* 1, *delo* 96, 150.

[62] LGPO report to the RKÜöO from November 28, 1921, RGVA (TsKhIDK), *fond* 772, *opis* 1, *delo* 96, 45.

[63] RKÜöO report from June 20, 1921, RGVA (TsKhIDK), *fond* 772, *opis* 3, *delo* 81a, 11, 14.

[64] MMFT report to the DB from December 24, 1923, RGVA (TsKhIDK), *fond* 7, *opis* 2, *delo* 2575, reel 2, 134; LGPO report from September 21, 1921, GSAPKB, *Repositur* 77, title 1813, number 2, 65.

[65] ATsVO report from October 8, 1921, GARF, *fond* 5893, *opis* 1, *delo* 70, 64.

[66] DB report from July 3, 1923, RGVA (TsKhIDK), *fond* 7, *opis* 1, *delo* 876, reel 4, 367.

though officially he continued to belong to the Union of the Faithful, by placing him at the head of the Russisches Komitée für Flüchtlingsfürsorge in Bayern (Russian Committee for Refugee Welfare in Bavaria).[67]

The Bavarian government under Minister President Gustav Ritter von Kahr allowed Evaldt's Refugee Committee to decide which Russian émigrés could settle in Bavaria and which ones would be expelled from the existing refugee community.[68] Biskupskii collaborated with Evaldt to determine which politically undesirable Russian exiles were to be barred entrance to Bavaria. In addition to Bolsheviks, socialists and liberals, even moderate monarchists were refused admittance.[69] Scheubner-Richter, who enjoyed friendly relations with the Bavarian Chief of Police Ernst Pöhner, also played a leading role in Evaldt's refugee organization. He worked behind the scenes to coordinate the Committee's activities with those of Aufbau.[70]

Strengthened by Evaldt's defection to Aufbau, Scheubner-Richter traveled to Budapest in early October 1921 to raise support for an autonomous Ukraine. He met with the right-wing Hungarian Minister President Gyula Gömbös as well as Aleksandr von Lampe, the former Tsarist general who represented the Russkii obshii-voinskii soiuz (Russian Universal Military Union, or ROVS). General Piotr Vrangel, who had lost to the Red Army on the Crimean Peninsula during the Russian Civil War, led ROVS.[71] Unlike Aufbau, ROVS favored the pro-French Grand Prince Nikolai Nikolaevich Romanov, who lived in Paris, over Kirill for Tsar.[72]

At the talks in Budapest, Scheubner-Richter expressed marked pro-Ukrainian views. He argued that Germany's renewal could only take place after a Russian nationalist rebirth, but he stressed that the Ukraine represented the most vital Russian region for the struggle against Bolshevism. He advocated uniting all anti-Bolsheviks there. He emphasized the need for wide-ranging Ukrainian autonomy, noting that the Russian Empire could not be reconstituted in its old form in any case. To sweeten the prospect of an independent Ukraine, he stressed that the industrial and financial circles

---

[67] LGPO report to the RKÜöO from November 28, 1921, RGVA (TsKhIDK), *fond* 772, *opis* 1, *delo* 96, 39, 42; Nikolai von Epanchin's testimony included in a PDM report to the BSMI from April 15, 1922, BHSAM, BSMI 22, number 71624, fiche 5, 3.

[68] DB report from November 4, 1922, RGVA (TsKhIDK), *fond* 7, *opis* 1, *delo* 876, reel 4, 373.

[69] Baur, "Russische Emigranten und die bayerische Öffentlichkeit," 471.

[70] Walther Nicolai's commentary on his telegraph to Ludendorff from November 10, 1923, *Tagebuch* (Diary), RGVA (TsKhIDK), *fond* 1414, *opis* 1, *delo* 22, 98; DB report from November 4, 1922, RGVA (TsKhIDK), *fond* 7, *opis* 1, *delo* 876, reel 4, 373.

[71] Lampe, *Dnevnik* (Diary), Budapest, Berlin, October 8–22, 1921, November 11, 12, 1923, GARF, *fond* 5853, *opis* 1, *delo* 7, reel 1, 1993; *delo* 13, reel 1, 5769.

[72] Baur, "Russische Emigranten und die bayerische Öffentlichkeit," 463.

he represented were prepared to guarantee German capital and technology for a variety of projects throughout the former Russian Empire after the overthrow of the Bolsheviks.

General Lampe did not swallow the bait. He placed more faith in French support. He brusquely rejected Scheubner-Richter's proposals as excessively pro-Ukrainian. The failed talks between Scheubner-Richter and Lampe in Budapest led to a clean break between the two men in particular and Aufbau and ROVS in general. Scheubner-Richter subsequently kept the Aufbau member General Ludendorff away from General Lampe and ROVS.[73] At the end of October 1921, Scheubner-Richter staged an ostentatious re-founding of Aufbau with revised statutes.[74] He allotted a role in the lime-light to Ludendorff at the ceremony to signal that the *völkisch* general stood firmly in the Aufbau camp.[75]

After Aufbau's re-founding, the organization strongly supported Kir-ill's claim to the Tsarist throne in opposition to Markov II's increasingly pro-French Supreme Monarchical Council. In February 1922, the Aufbau leaders Scheubner-Richter, Biskupskii, and Ludendorff urged Kirill to move from the French Riviera to Bavaria so that he could act in the center of his German base of support. Kirill and his wife Viktoria discussed this relo-cation with German officials.[76] Anticipating Kirill's arrival in Germany, General Ludendorff worked to establish an intelligence service for Kirill and his allies under Walther Nicolai in early April 1922. Nicolai had served Ludendorff as the head of the German Army High Command Intelli-gence Service during World War I. Ludendorff asked Nicolai to use his considerable experience and connections to establish a reliable pro-Kirill intelligence agency for the struggle against Bolshevism.[77] This bureau was to replace the more modest agency that General Kurlov and Lieutenant Iurii Kartsov had earlier established to support the legitimist movement behind Kirill.[78]

Nicolai was eminently qualified to lead such an intelligence service. In addition to possessing impressive intelligence credentials from World

[73] Lampe, *Dnevnik* (Diary), Budapest, October 8–22, 1921 and Berlin, November 11–17, 1923, GARF, *fond* 5853, *opis* 1, *delo* 7, reel 1, 1994–1997; *delo* 13, reel 1, 5769, 5773.

[74] DB report from November 11, 1922, RGVA (TsKhIDK), *fond* 7, *opis* 1, *delo* 876, reel 4, 379.

[75] Schlögel, Katharina Kucher, Bernhard Suchy, and Gregor Thum, *Chronik russischen Lebens in Deutschland 1918–1941* (Berlin: Akademie Verlag, 1999), 80.

[76] Lampe, *Dnevnik* (Diary), Berlin, June 5, 1923, GARF, *fond* 5853, *opis* 1, *delo* 11, reel 3, 4851/180; RKÜöO report from February 21, 1922, RGVA (TsKhIDK), *fond* 772, *opis* 1, *delo* 96, 115.

[77] Nicolai's commentary on a letter from Ludendorff from early April 1922; letter from Hans von Seekt to Nicolai from March 9, 1920, *Tagebuch* (Diary), RGVA (TsKhIDK), *fond* 1414, *opis* 1, *delo* 20, 172; *delo* 18, 539.

[78] RKÜöO report from February 21, 1922, RGVA (TsKhIDK), *fond* 772, *opis* 1, *delo* 96, 115.

War I, he enjoyed considerable influence in contemporary right-wing German circles. In February 1921, he had taken over the leadership of the Kartell nationaler Zeitungen im Reich (Cartel of National Newspapers in the State). The Cartel propagated nationalist policies, notably rejecting the provisions of the Treaty of Versailles, which had truncated Germany, severely limited its armed forces, and subjected it to immense reparations.[79]

Nicolai met with Scheubner-Richter and Ludendorff in the middle of April 1922 to discuss matters in greater detail. He agreed to establish an anti-Bolshevik intelligence agency so that Ludendorff and his allies, including Scheubner-Richter, Kirill, and Hitler, would have a reliable source of information on events in the Soviet Union. The money for the intelligence service, code-named Project S, came from Kirill. Nicolai began sending regular reports to Scheubner-Richter in the first half of July 1922.[80] Scheubner-Richter expressed satisfaction with Aufbau's intelligence information in an October 1922 edition of *Aufbau Correspondence*. He noted that agents were sending reports from Vienna, Budapest, the Balkans, Kiev, and "other" cities in the Soviet Union.[81] In addition to using information from Project S for Aufbau's purposes, Scheubner-Richter passed intelligence on to Hitler's National Socialist Party, to which he belonged and with which Aufbau was ever increasingly allied.[82]

In addition to establishing a pro-Kirill intelligence bureau, Aufbau increased its military and economic ties with Hungary and strengthened the pro-Kirill movement there in the spring and summer of 1922. In April 1922, the Aufbau leaders Scheubner-Richter, Biskupskii, and Ludendorff journeyed to Budapest to arrange for the transfer of Cossacks from Poland to Hungary to supplement White forces there.[83] In May 1922, Ludendorff and Biskupskii formed a German-Southern Russian, i.e. Ukrainian, trade organization within Aufbau, the Eugen Hoffmann & Co. Aussenhandels-Aktiengesellschaft (Eugen Hoffmann & Co. Foreign Trade Joint-Stock Company). Before the (anticipated) overthrow of Bolshevik rule in the Ukraine, this association concentrated on business matters in Eastern Europe, most importantly in Hungary.

---

[79] Nicolai's commentary on Heye's letter to him from March 12, 1921, *Tagebuch* (Diary), RGVA (TsKhIDK), *fond* 1414, *opis* 1, *delo* 18, 351.

[80] Nicolai's commentary on his letter to Ludendorff from April 19, 1922; Nicolai's letter to Ludendorff from August 21, 1923; Nicolai's commentary on his "Mitteilung Nr. 8" from early July 1922, *Tagebuch* (Diary), RGVA (TsKhIDK), *fond* 1414, *opis* 1, *delo* 20, 174, 356; *delo* 22, 91.

[81] Scheubner-Richter, "Allgemeine Wirtschaft und Politik," *Aufbau-Korrespondenz*, October 11, 1922, 3.

[82] DB report from May 15, 1923, RGVA (TsKhIDK), *fond* 7, *opis* 1, *delo* 954, reel 1, 56.

[83] Lampe, *Dnevnik* (Diary), Budapest, April 4, 1922, GARF, *fond* 5853, *opis* 1, *delo* 7, reel 2, 2119.

The venture capital for this company, six million paper marks, had come from German and White émigré sources. German backers had provided four million marks, and Biskupskii had raised two million marks from White émigré sources. He had secured one million marks from Grand Duchess Viktoria Romanov and the other million from his cousin, the wealthy Aufbau member Vladimir Keppen who had inherited a fortune from American relatives. The Eugen Hoffmann & Co. Foreign Trade Joint-Stock Company speculated in Hungarian wool production in particular under the premise of tremendous profits.[84] Aufbau's strong economic ties with Hungary helped to unite far rightists in both Germany and Hungary.

In late June 1922, Scheubner-Richter, Biskupskii, and Poltavets-Ostranitsa, the leader of Aufbau's Ukrainian faction, traveled to Budapest. Whatever secret agenda they may have followed regarding German Foreign Minister Walther Rathenau's assassination, their open goal consisted of planning a pro-Kirill White émigré congress in Budapest along the lines of the Monarchical Congress at Bad Reichenhall. The uproar caused by Aufbau's suspected involvement in Rathenau's murder, however, persuaded Scheubner-Richter and his colleagues to break off the negotiations in favor of a more suitable time and place.[85]

Despite the truncated nature of the talks in Budapest that Aufbau leaders participated in, the Aufbau contingent did manage to hold detailed discussions with Prince Mirza Kazem Bek, the president of the Russian Monarchical Club, which represented Hungary's approximately 3,500 White émigrés. Kazem Bek had long cultivated close ties with Aufbau.[86] Kazem Bek agreed to create an organization along the lines of Aufbau in Budapest that would serve as a Hungarian–Russian society. Scheubner-Richter announced that Aufbau would organize an economic representation in Hungary under the leadership of von Krause, a White émigré. Scheubner-Richter also spoke of negotiating with the Hungarian Agricultural Ministry to regulate trade in livestock and grain between Hungary and Bavaria.[87]

During his trip to Hungary, Scheubner-Richter placed great hopes on the power of Kirill and his supporters to undermine Soviet rule. In a July

[84] Vladimir Biskupskii's subpoena from March 11, 1930, APA, BAB, NS 43, number 35, 129, 131 ob.

[85] DGBud report to the AA from July 18, 1922, PAAA, 83580, 20 ob.

[86] DGBud report to the AA from July 5, 1922, PAAA, 83579, 130; "Die russischen Emigranten in Ungarn und Deutschland bereiten sich zum Aufbau ihres Vaterlandes vor," translated article from *Nemzeti Ujsag* that Scheubner-Richter sent to the DGBud on July 6, 1922, forwarded to the AA, PAAA, 83580, 26, 27.

[87] "Die russischen Emigranten in Ungarn und Deutschland," 29; DGBud report to the AA from July 5, 1922, PAAA, 83580, 130 ob.

1922 interview with the German Embassy in Budapest, he claimed that the Soviet regime would collapse in the near future because of three factors. First, the heir to the Tsarist throne would soon be announced, by which he meant Kirill. Second, the Tsarist claimant would win the farmers of the Soviet Union over to his side by proclaiming that he would respect Bolshevik land reforms and pardon those who had served in the Red Army. Third, an "anti-Jewish movement" would break out "in elementary force" that would "end Soviet rule with one blow."[88] Scheubner-Richter clearly possessed an overly optimistic view of the situation, as the Soviet Union did not collapse in 1922.

Whereas Aufbau operated in Germany and Hungary to gain support for Kirill as the future Tsar who would unite all White émigrés, Markov II's Supreme Monarchical Council favored Grand Prince Nikolai Nikolaevich's candidacy and increasingly adopted a pro-French policy. After initial reservations, Markov II called for a White army under General Vrangel to invade the Soviet Union with French support through Poland and Romania in the summer of 1922.[89] After this White army had toppled the Bolsheviks, Nikolai Nikolaevich was to become the Tsar of the restored Russian Empire in its old borders. Acting on the advice of the Markov Group, Nikolai Nikolaevich arrived in Munich, the center of Kirill's support, in late July 1922. Largely to coordinate its activities with Nikolai Nikolaevich, Markov II's Supreme Monarchical Council resolved to relocate from Berlin to Munich.[90]

In the face of the Supreme Monarchical Council's support of Nikolai Nikolaevich, Aufbau launched a pro-Kirill offensive. Kirill had learned that Nikolai Nikolaevich planned to promulgate a declaration to the Russian people. Urged on by his energetic wife, Viktoria, the honorary president of the Aufbau subsection Renewal, Kirill forestalled Nikolai Nikolaevich by releasing manifestos on August 8, 1922.[91] Aufbau printed Kirill's appeals, in which the Tsarist candidate proclaimed himself the legitimate head of all Russian monarchical forces both inside and outside the Soviet Union.[92]

Scheubner-Richter dedicated the entire August 16, 1922 edition of *Aufbau Correspondence* to Kirill's declarations to the "Russian people"

[88] DGBud report to the AA from July 18, 1922, PAAA, 83580, 21.

[89] DGBer report to the AA from July 3, 1922, PAAA, 83579, 102; RKÜöO report from July 29, 1922, RGVA (TsKhIDK), *fond 772, opis 1, delo 96*, 154.

[90] DB reports from August 4 and 6, 1922, RGVA (TsKhIDK), *fond 7, opis 1, delo 386*, reel 3, 197; reel 2, 185.

[91] Letter from Knorring to the AA from August 16, 1922, PAAA, 83580, 112, 112 ob.

[92] Kirill Romanov, "An das russische Volk!", included in Scheubner-Richter, "Zwei bedeutsame Deklarationen," *Aufbau-Korrespondenz*, August 16, 1922, 3.

and the "Russian army." Scheubner-Richter translated these appeals into German for the first time. In his opening commentary on Kirill's manifestos, he claimed that neither "imported parliamentarism" nor "Asiatic, Jewish Bolshevism" could establish firm roots in Russia, for monarchy was the "*völkisch* more well-founded" system. He thus advocated a well-run monarchy for Russia. This idea did not contradict *völkisch* thought, which had rejected Kaiser Wilhelm Hohenzollern II as a weak leader, but had approved of a powerful monarchy as a system.

Scheubner-Richter further stressed in his article on Kirill's declarations that the Monarchical Congress at Bad Reichenhall had represented the "first start" towards the "collection of Russian patriots," and now Kirill's appeals, coming from the "legitimate nearest heir to the Tsar's throne," represented the "second fanfare" towards this goal. He enthused: "The entire Russian patriotic movement finally has a leader." He concluded, "From a national German standpoint, we can . . . only hope that the coming to the fore of Grand Prince Kirill will be successful" so that "the future will grant us a national Russia that will work hand in hand with a national Germany to heal the wounds that the World War and the Revolution dealt."[93] Scheubner-Richter again expressed his firm conviction that the German and Russian peoples needed to collaborate closely with each other in order to regain greatness.

Aufbau had firmly backed Kirill's claim to the Russian throne. After Scheubner-Richter printed Kirill's manifestos, some White émigrés gave his newspaper *Aufbau Correspondence* the moniker of the "organ of the Kirill-supporters."[94] Baron Ludwig von Knorring, a noble Baltic German proponent of a moderate constitutional monarchy for Russia who led the White émigré community in Baden-Baden, noted to German authorities in October 1922 that with Aufbau's printing and distributing of Kirill's declarations in German, Munich had to be regarded as the center of White émigré monarchical agitation in Germany.[95]

Aufbau under Scheubner-Richter's guidance used Kirill's declarations to undermine Soviet authority. Aufbau smuggled Kirill's manifestos into the Soviet Union. This subversive action elicited a memorandum from Feliks Dzerzhinskii, the head of the Narodnyi komissariat vnutrennikh del (People's Commissariat for Internal Affairs, NKVD), which stressed that

---

[93] Scheubner-Richter, "Zwei bedeutsame Deklarationen," *Aufbau-Korrespondenz*, 2, 4.

[94] Report from Knorring to the RKÜöO from December 28, 1923, RGVA (TsKhIDK), *fond* 772, *opis* 2, *delo* 179, 69.

[95] Report from Knorring to the AA from June 30, 1921, PAAA, 31490, K096232; report from Knorring to the RKÜöO from October 18, 1922, RGVA (TsKhIDK), *fond* 772, *opis* 1, *delo* 96, 192.

Soviet censorship of foreign mail was doing a poor job, as evidenced by the widespread presence of Kirill's declarations in the Soviet Union.[96]

Largely because of the urgings of Aufbau leadership, the increasingly important couple Kirill and Viktoria Romanov moved to Bavaria in August 1922. They divided their time between a Munich hotel and the northern Bavarian city of Coburg, where they possessed an estate. Scheubner-Richter regularly held talks with Kirill and Viktoria, who possessed considerable financial means. Kirill had 50 million francs for the raising of White forces as of August, and he was hoping for more money from American sources, presumably most importantly from the right-wing politician and industrialist Henry Ford. Viktoria, as the daughter of Duke Alfred of Saxe-Coburg, who was related to the English royal family, also possessed significant financial resources in the form of English money. She financially supported many of Kirill's backers from her own funds, which included money that she acquired by selling parts of her extensive jewelry collection.[97]

Aufbau's vice president, Biskupskii, played the leading role in the circle around Kirill and Viktoria. He channeled General Ludendorff's energies into furthering Kirill's cause.[98] Biskupskii greatly influenced Viktoria, who had a far more dynamic personality than her somewhat drab husband.[99] Biskupskii acted as her closest advisor.[100] Viktoria ardently supported the dashing general. She granted him considerable funding for his activities in Aufbau in 1922, and she continually praised Aufbau to her husband.[101] Biskupskii later engendered a great deal of antipathy in the German White émigré community when it became known that he had long been having an affair with Viktoria and mainly owed his leading role in Kirill's shadow government to his lover's recommendations.[102]

General Biskupskii's colleagues Generals Piotr Glasenap and Konstantin Sakharov also supported Kirill's claim to the Russian throne. They

---

[96] Feliks Dzerzhinskii, NKVD memorandum from September 1, 1922, RGASPI, *fond* 76, *opis* 3, *delo* 400, 54.

[97] Lampe, *Dnevnik* (Diary), Berlin, September 12, 13, 1922, April 16–20, 1923, June 5, 1923, GARF, *fond* 5853, *opis* 1, *delo* 9, reel 1, 3270; *delo* 11, reel 1, 4698; reel 3, 4851/180, 191; report from Stuttgart [Baron von Delingshausen?] to the RKÜöO from July 11, 1923, RGVA (TsKhIDK), *fond* 772, *opis* 1, *delo* 96, 222; Nicolai's commentary on his letter to Ludendorff from February 18, 1922, *Tagebuch* (Diary), RGVA (TsKhIDK), *fond* 1414, *opis* 1, *delo* 20, 171.

[98] Lampe, *Dnevnik* (Diary), Munich, May 26, 1923 and Berlin, June 5, 1923, GARF, *fond* 5853, *opis* 1, *delo* 11, reel 1, 4722; reel 3, 4851/181.

[99] Nicolai's commentary on his letter to Ludendorff from February 18, 1922, *Tagebuch* (Diary), RGVA (TsKhIDK), *fond* 1414, *opis* 1, *delo* 20, 171.

[100] Report from Stuttgart [Baron von Delingshausen?] to the RKÜöO from July 11, 1923, RGVA (TsKhIDK), *fond* 772, *opis* 1, *delo* 96, 223.

[101] Lampe, *Dnevnik* (Diary), Berlin, June 5, 1923, GARF, *fond* 5853, *opis* 1, *delo* 11, reel 3, 4851/190, 191.

[102] RKÜöO report from July 1927, RGVA (TsKhIDK), *fond* 772, *opis* 1, *delo* 91, 51.

intensified their collaboration with Kirill in August 1922, a month after Viktoria had given 100,000 francs to Glasenap via Sakharov for anti-Bolshevik
activities.[103] Sakharov acted as a key intermediary between Kirill and General Ludendorff.[104] Sakharov also directed intelligence operations on Kirill's
behalf. Every month, the White émigré Aufbau member sent questionnaires
to Kirill's representatives in diverse European cities. The forms dealt with
such topics as the general economic and political conditions in the countries in which Kirill's agents were stationed as well as the activities of local
Bolshevik organizations and the private lives of their members.[105]

Hitler's National Socialist Party supported Kirill and his backers in the
dispute over who should become the next Tsar. A September 1921 edition of the National Socialist newspaper the *Völkischer Beobachter* (*Völkisch
Observer*) noted unanimous support for Kirill's claim to the throne among
the Don Cossack exile community.[106] After Kirill's proclamations to the
"Russian people" and the "Russian army" that Aufbau had translated into
German in August 1922, Aufbau leadership under Scheubner-Richter and
Biskupskii cooperated increasingly closely with Hitler's NSDAP.[107] Biskupskii viewed Hitler as an admirable "strong man," and he developed close
ties with him.[108] Biskupskii began to transfer large sums of money that he
received from Kirill and Viktoria to Hitler in 1922.[109]

The first major National Socialist expedition, a trip to Coburg to participate in a German Day on October 14 and 15, 1922, suggests the increasing
convergence of Aufbau and National Socialist policies behind the legitimist
movement around Kirill.[110] Hitler and his mentors Eckart and the Aufbau
ideologue Rosenberg, among others, arrived in Coburg, the seat of Kirill's
shadow government, with 800 members of the paramilitary Sturmabteilung
(Storm Section, SA). In addition to fighting against leftists in pitched street
battles, members of the National Socialist contingent distributed copies of
Eckart and Rosenberg's *In Plain German* with caricatures of leftist, primarily Jewish leaders drawn by the Aufbau member Otto von Kursell. Members
of the Coburg expedition received a Coburg Medal that National Socialists

[103] Lampe, *Dnevnik* (Diary), Berlin, July 27, 1922, August 9–10, 1922, June 5, 1923, GARF, *fond* 5853,
  opis 1, *delo* 8, reel 1, 2947; *delo* 9, reel 1, 3230; *delo* 11, reel 3, 4851/179.
[104] RMI report to the AA from June 9, 1931, PAAA, 31665, 136.
[105] DB report from September 19, 1923, RGVA (TsKhIDK), *fond* 7, *opis* 1, *delo* 386, reel 2, 113, 116, 117.
[106] "Die Kosaken und Grossfürst Kyrill," *Völkischer Beobachter*, September 20, 1922, 4.
[107] DB report from November 11, 1922, RGVA (TsKhIDK), *fond* 7, *opis* 1, *delo* 386, reel 2, 160.
[108] Rafael Ganelin, "Rossiiskoe chernosotenstvo i germanskii natsional-sotsializm," *Natsionalnaia pravaia prezhde i teper, Istoriko-sotsiologicheskie ocherki, chast 1: Rossiia i russkoe zarubezhe* (Saint
  Petersburg: Institut Sotsiologii rossiiskoi akademii nauk, 1992), 142.
[109] 2. SAUV report from October 6, 1927, BHSAM, BSMÄ 36, number 103476/1, 113.
[110] RKÜöO report from November 1, 1922, BAB, 134, number 68, 142.

ultimately prized only less than an award for participating in the November 1923 Hitler/Ludendorff Putsch.[111]

In the second half of 1922, around the time of the Coburg action, Aufbau continued to strengthen the pro-Kirill movement in Hungary. Aufbau's Vice President Biskupskii and his colleague Evaldt, the head of the Russian Committee for Refugee Welfare in Bavaria, won Prince D. P. Golitsyn, the representative of the Supreme Monarchical Council in Hungary, over to Kirill's cause.[112] Golitsyn had led the original Black Hundred organization in Imperial Russia, the Russian Assembly.[113] Aufbau also improved its ties with Prince Mikhail Volkonskii, another former leading member of the Russian Assembly who currently led the Russian Delegation in Hungary. Volkonskii possessed the power to decide which Russian exiles could reside in Hungary.[114] He edited the newspaper *Rossiia* (*Russia*) in Budapest, a paper that was dedicated to Kirill, the "guardian of the throne." Volkonskii received funding for this newspaper from Kirill and the Hungarian leader Admiral Nicholas Horthy, who also strongly supported Kirill's bid to become Tsar.[115]

While Aufbau succeeded in strengthening the pro-Kirill movement in Hungary in the second part of 1922, it could not unite all White émigrés in Germany (and beyond) behind Kirill. Instead, the White émigré community remained deeply divided. On the one side, Aufbau-led White émigrés backed Kirill for Tsar and collaborated closely with *völkisch* Germans, most importantly National Socialists, to establish successor Russian, Ukrainian, and Baltic states.[116] As we shall see in the next chapter, these entities were to be organized along National Socialist lines. On the other side, the Supreme Monarchical Council supported Nikolai Nikolaevich for Tsar of a Russian state in its pre-World War I borders, and they increasingly viewed France as their patron.[117]

As the president of the Russian Committee for Refugee Welfare in Bavaria, Evaldt, with the behind-the-scenes direction of Scheubner-Richter,

---

[111] Robert Cecil, *The Myth of the Master Race: Alfred Rosenberg and Nazi Ideology* (London: B. T. Batsford Ltd., 1972), 35, 36; RKÜöO report from October 22, 1922, BAB, 1507, number 327, 207.

[112] DB report from November 11, 1922, RGVA (TsKhIDK), *fond* 7, *opis* 1, *delo* 386, reel 2, 159;

[113] Stepanov, *Chernaia Sotnia v Rossii*, 33.

[114] DB reports from May 15, 1922 and June 8, 1923, RGVA (TsKhIDK), *fond* 7, *opis* 1, *delo* 386, reel 3, 217; reel 2, 131; *Spisok chlenov Russkogo Sobraniia s prilozheniem istoricheskogo ocherky sobraniia* (Saint Petersburg: Tip. Spb. Gradonachalstva, 1906), 21.

[115] DB reports from August 19, 1922 and April 9, 1923, RGVA (TsKhIDK), *fond* 7, *opis* 1, *delo* 386, reel 3, 192; reel 4, 334.

[116] DB report from November 11, 1922, RGVA (TsKhIDK), *fond* 7, *opis* 1, *delo* 386, reel 2, 161, 163, 164.

[117] MMFT report to the DB from December 24, 1923, RGVA (TsKhIDK), *fond* 7, *opis* 2, *delo* 2575, reel 2, 135; DB report from November 11, 1922, RGVA (TsKhIDK), *fond* 7, *opis* 1, *delo* 386, reel 2, 157.

primarily used loyalty to Kirill in deciding who was to be allowed into or expelled from Munich's White émigré community.[118] The Munich Police closely cooperated with the pro-Kirill legitimists to keep pro-French elements out of Bavaria.[119] While in Bavaria in 1922, Markov II and his followers in the pro-French majority faction of the Supreme Monarchical Council kept a relatively low profile. They recognized that they were in a perilous position because of the determination of the Munich Police to remove the residency permits of anti-German foreigners.[120]

White émigré backers of both Kirill and Nikolai Nikolaevich tried to win converts to their cause. Markov II tried to convert the established members of the Bavarian White émigré community under the direction of Aufbau to the side of Nikolai Nikolaevich, but without success.[121] Boris Brazol, an Aufbau member and the White émigré contact man with the right-wing American industrialist and politician Henry Ford, sought to convince Markov II to back Kirill, but likewise to no avail.

In November 1922, relations snapped between Markov II's Supreme Monarchical Council and the White émigrés who backed Kirill under Aufbau's direction.[122] A second White monarchical congress shattered any semblance of White émigré unity that had been presented at the Monarchical Congress at Bad Reichenhall in the late spring of 1921. This second assembly met in Paris from November 16 to November 23, 1922 under the direction of the Supreme Monarchical Council. Seventy delegates representing 125 organizations attended the proceedings.[123] The Munich White émigré community under Aufbau's leadership rejected the authority of the increasingly pro-French Supreme Monarchical Council.[124] Aufbau members rejected the guidelines set down at the Paris Congress, and they openly broke with what pretensions of obedience to the Supreme Monarchical Council that they had maintained. Other Russian monarchical émigré communities followed their example, notably those in Prague, Budapest, and Belgrade.[125] White émigré disunity had reached critical dimensions.

The apparent White émigré unity that had been established at the Monarchical Congress at Bad Reichenhall in May–June 1921 collapsed in

[118] Lampe, *Dnevnik* (Diary), Berlin, June 5, 1923, GARF, *fond* 5853, *opis* 1, *delo* 11, reel 3, 4851/183.
[119] Baur, "Russische Emigranten und die bayerische Öffentlichkeit," *Bayern und Osteuropa*, 471.
[120] PDM report to the BSMÄ from June 7, 1923, BHSAM, BSMÄ 36, number 103009, 29.
[121] DB report from November 11, 1922, RGVA (TsKhIDK), *fond* 7, *opis* 1, *delo* 386, reel 2, 159.
[122] SG report from November 4, 1922, RGVA (TsKhIDK), *fond* 1, *opis* 27, *delo* 12523, 39.
[123] PDM report from May 25, 1923, BSAM, PDM, number 6708, 129; SG report from November 25, 1922, RGVA (TsKhIDK), *fond* 1, *opis* 27, *delo* 12523, 9.
[124] DB report from November 11, 1922, RGVA (TsKhIDK), *fond* 7, *opis* 1, *delo* 386, reel 2, 157.
[125] PDM report from May 25, 1923, BSAM, PDM, number 6708, 129.

1922, but in 1923, Aufbau's distrust and even hatred of the pro-Nikolai Nikolaevich actions of Markov II's Supreme Monarchical Council intensified even more markedly. Aufbau's leadership even carried out contingency planning for a temporary alliance with the Red Army in the case of a French-led invasion of the Soviet Union launched in the name of Nikolai Nikolaevich. White émigré disunity granted the fledgling Soviet state a measure of respite.

Amid continuing internecine White émigré struggle, Kirill enjoyed rising popularity in the spring of 1923 both among nationalists inside the Soviet Union and in White émigré circles in Europe. At the same time, Nikolai Nikolaevich and the pro-French Markov II saw their influence wane, especially in Germany.[126] General Biskupskii aided Kirill by denouncing Nikolai Nikolaevich and his supporters. For instance, Biskupskii spread slanderous rumors that Nikolai Nikolaevich was old and feeble, virtually at death's door, and thus could not be expected to play any considerable future political role. Markov II's close associate Talberg retaliated in coin. He maintained that Biskupskii secretly served as a Bolshevik agent.[127]

In a striking manifestation of the intense animosity between White émigré factions, upon receiving the news that French leaders were intensifying their preparations to invade the Soviet Union in May 1923, Aufbau leadership indefinitely shelved its plans to foment revolt inside the Soviet Union and to lead a White military intervention against the Bolsheviks. The French-coordinated assault that Aufbau feared was to rely on Polish and Romanian support in addition to assistance from pro-French White émigrés behind Nikolai Nikolaevich, most notably Markov II and Talberg of the Supreme Monarchical Council. The French planned to establish a pro-French regime in the territory of the Soviet Union in the middle of the summer of 1923.[128] Markov II had held a meeting at the beginning of May 1923 in which he had discussed the advanced French-backed preparations for an anti-Bolshevik front under Nikolai Nikolaevich.[129]

Nikolai Nikolaevich himself was reluctant to collaborate with Polish troops, and he did not wish for a military campaign against the Soviet Union unless Russians there and not just White émigrés called for him to claim the throne.[130] Aufbau's leading figure Scheubner-Richter nonetheless perceived

---

[126] PDM report to the BSMÄ from June 7, 1923, BHSAM, BSMÄ 36, number 103009, 31.

[127] RKÜöO report from January 28, 1924, RGVA (TsKhIDK), *fond* 772, *opis* 3, *delo* 81a, 45.

[128] Andreas Remmer's testimony from June 2, 1923, BHSAM, BSMÄ 36, number 103009, 8; PDM report to the BSMÄ from June 7, 1923, BHSAM, BSMÄ 36, number 103009, 31.

[129] LGPO report from May 7, 1923, GSAPKB, *Repositur* 77, title 1809, number 9, 121.

[130] SKöO report to the AA from August 22, 1923, PAAA, 83582, 94.

a great threat to Aufbau's interests in the French-led plans for an invasion of the Soviet Union. In a May 1923 edition of *Aufbau Correspondence*, he warned of advanced French preparations to topple Bolshevism. He asked what "German national circles" were doing to prepare for the moment that "Bolshevik-Jewish rule in Moscow collapses and a national Russia takes its place." He stressed that this course of events "does not lie outside of the realm of the possible."[131] Scheubner-Richter believed that the Soviet regime was ripe for dissolution, and he tried to keep the "wrong" White émigrés from seizing power in Russia.

In its drive to thwart a French-led invasion of the Soviet Union in the name of Nikolai Nikolaevich, Aufbau went so far as to negotiate with Bolshevik leaders through intermediaries. Aufbau had a contact man with the Soviet Great Russian heartland, Andreas Remmer. Remmer had served as Western Volunteer Army leader Colonel Pavel Bermondt-Avalov's Foreign Minister in Berlin during the 1919 Latvian Intervention. Remmer traveled from Berlin to Munich to consult with General Biskupskii in late May 1923. The two colleagues were to meet with Kirill to discuss important strategic questions, but the Munich Police arrested Remmer, whom they suspected of serving as a Soviet agent, before these talks could take place. Biskupskii was able to convince Munich authorities that while Remmer maintained contacts with various members of the Soviet government through middlemen, he used the information that he received for nationalist purposes.[132]

Remmer told the Munich Police that the planned French-led invasion of the Soviet Union would either fail miserably or bring about the "complete enslavement of Russia." He claimed that Nikolai Nikolaevich and those White émigrés who supported him played the "most despicable role" of serving the "plans and goals of . . . Jewish high finance." Remmer emphasized that if the French launched a military intervention against the Soviet Union with Polish and Romanian assistance, then the pro-German White émigré faction behind Kirill under Aufbau's leadership and the nationalist forces that it collaborated with in the Soviet Union would be forced to fight along with the Red Army. Once the attackers had been defeated, pro-German Whites would launch a putsch in the ranks of the Red Army and destroy the Soviet government.[133] According to Remmer, Aufbau had

[131] Scheubner-Richter, "Russland und England," *Aufbau-Korrespondenz,* May 17, 1923, 2.
[132] Remmer's testimony from June 1, 1923, BHSAM, BSMÄ 36, number 103009, 10; Biskupskii's testimony from June 2, 1923, BHSAM, BSMÄ 36, number 103009, 7.
[133] Remmer's testimony from June 1 and 2, 1923, BHSAM, BSMÄ 36, number 103009, 8, 9; Remmer's letter from May 7, 1923, BHSAM, BSMÄ 36, number 103009, 14, 15.

come to regard French invasion plans that Markov II supported as a threat great enough to warrant a hazardous tactical alliance with the Red Army.

In a June article in *Aufbau Correspondence*, "Intervention Intentions against Soviet Russia," Scheubner-Richter attacked pro-French White émigrés. He asserted: "We cannot believe that France is serious with the fight against Jewish world Communism." He stressed that Kirill's backers rejected a French-led offensive. He further argued that a French-led intervention with Poland's participation would strengthen the Soviet Union, for nationalist circles inside the Great Russian heartland would be forced to fight on behalf of the Bolshevik regime against foreign invaders.[134]

In the summer of 1923, the chasm between Aufbau and the Supreme Monarchical Council continued to widen. Scheubner-Richter criticized Markov II in a July edition of *Aufbau Correspondence* by running an article, "From the Russian-Monarchical Movement." This piece stressed that Kirill's supporters had formed a legitimist alliance centered in Munich that opposed Markov II's Supreme Monarchical Council. The article claimed that the Council had not submitted to Kirill's leadership as it had pledged at Bad Reichenhall. (Actually, the question of the Tsarist succession had been left open then.) Scheubner-Richter also included a translated essay from the newspaper that the Aufbau ideologue Vinberg edited on Kirill's behalf, *Vestnik russkago monarkhicheskago obedineniia v Bavarii* (*Bulletin of the Russian Monarchical Union in Bavaria*). Vinberg's article urged all White émigrés to unite behind Kirill and to foster the "active struggle for the liberation of the homeland."[135]

An August article in *Aufbau Correspondence* lamented the strife between White émigré factions. The essay noted, "We, the Russian anti-Semites" acted as "fighters for the national cause in its purest form," but the "'wise men of Zion' are laughing up their sleeves" regarding the disunity among the White émigré groups who aspired to be the "'saviors of the fatherland.'"[136] The aversion of pro-Kirill backers under Aufbau's direction to Markov II, Talberg, and other White émigrés who supported a pro-French policy had reached critical extremes. Internecine strife among White émigrés helped the Bolshevik regime to consolidate its power at a critical time when Soviet leader Vladimir Lenin's health was deteriorating rapidly.

---

[134] Scheubner-Richter, "Interventionsabsichten gegen Sowjetrussland," *Aufbau-Korrespondenz*, June 14, 1923, 2.

[135] "Aus der russisch-monarchistischen Bewegung," *Aufbau-Korrespondenz*, July 20, 1923, 2.

[136] "Die 'Russische Tribüne' über die Regierungsformen in Russland," *Aufbau-Korrespondenz*, August 25, 1923, 3.

The Munich Police determined during August 1923 that Kirill's supporters under Aufbau's direction were truly determined to restore Kirill to the Russian throne even at the cost of temporarily collaborating with the Bolsheviks. In the case of such an alliance, Kirill's faction hoped to instill the Red Army with pro-monarchical views and to win it over for a putsch against the Bolshevik state.[137] The summer of 1923 thus witnessed extreme political fluidity between members of the radical right and the radical left. It is worth noting in this context that already in May 1922, the Aufbau member Colonel Karl Bauer had traveled to the Soviet Union with the mission of establishing the terms for a potential German–Soviet military agreement.[138]

In another example of tentative far right German–Bolshevik rapprochement, the State Commissioner for the Supervision of Public Order noted an increasing "exchange of ideas" between *völkisch* Germans and Communists in August 1923. A State Commissioner report described "certain parallels" of a "negative nature" between members of the radical right and the radical left. Both far rightists and far leftists opposed democracy and parliamentarism, wished to institute a dictatorship, and believed in using violent means to achieve their goals. Certain *völkisch* Germans and Communists proposed seizing power together and then defeating France.[139] Hitler opposed cooperating with Communists, however. He stressed in a speech at this time: "Swastika and Soviet star tolerate each other like fire and water and cannot be brought together even on tactical grounds."[140]

Tentative *völkisch*/Bolshevik peace feelers did not lead to a solid political alliance in 1923. Moreover, largely because of the intense discord among White émigrés, no military intervention against the Soviet Union took place that year either. In September 1923, the Pro-French faction of the Munich White émigré community under Markov II's Supreme Monarchical Council left for Wiesbaden, close to the French border. This occurred after Aufbau leaders had made it absolutely clear that they would go to extreme lengths to foil any French-led intervention in Russia, including temporarily allying with the Bolshevik regime.[141] White émigré disunity proved a boon to the early Soviet Union, which generally faced deep suspicion if not outright hostility in the world political arena.

---

[137] PDM report to the BSMI from September 3, 1923, BHSAM, BSMÄ 36, number 103009, 36.
[138] MAÉ report to Ferdinand Foch from May 31, 1922, RGVA (TsKhIDK), *fond* 198, *opis* 17, delo 406, reel 1, 82.
[139] RKÜöO report from August 6, 1923, BAB, 134, number 76, 76.
[140] Hitler, speech on August 19, 1923, *Sämtliche Aufzeichnungen*, 975.
[141] BSMÄ report to the RKÜöO from September 26, 1923, BHSAM, BSMÄ 36, number 103009, 35.

CONCLUSION

The prominent Aufbau White émigré ideologues Max von Scheubner-Richter, Alfred Rosenberg, Fedor Vinberg, and their *völkisch* German associate Dietrich Eckart provided a theoretical basis for German–White émigré collaboration against the Entente, the Weimar Republic, the Soviet Union, and international Jewish conspirators. They called for "Germany–Russia above everything, above everything in the world." They emphasized the complementary nature of the German and Russian peoples against their Jewish foes. Hitler seized upon the Aufbau and Eckartian notions of a Jewish *Dolchstoss* (stab in the back) of both Imperial Russia and the German Empire. In his early political career, he repeatedly called for nationalist Germans and Russians to ally against "Jewish Bolshevism."

Aufbau envisioned large-scale nationalist German–Russian collaboration in which *völkisch* Germans, most notably National Socialists, and White émigrés would play the leading roles. With Aufbau's successful organization of the May–June 1921 Monarchical Congress at Bad Reichenhall, White émigrés in Europe in general and in Germany in particular seemed ready for a coordinated anti-Bolshevik campaign. Appearances nonetheless proved deceiving. Aufbau could not unite all White émigrés behind its candidate for the Tsarist throne, Grand Prince Kirill Romanov. Instead, Aufbau fought against Nikolai Markov II's pro-French Supreme Monarchical Council, which supported Grand Prince Nikolai Nikolaevich Romanov for Tsar.

Aufbau's antipathy towards Markov II's Supreme Monarchical Council reached such a degree that Aufbau planned a dangerous tactical alliance with the Red Army in the case of a French-led invasion of the Soviet Union that would be conducted in Nikolai Nikolaevich's name. In the end, Aufbau's increasingly bitter conflict with the Supreme Monarchical Council sapped the energy of the White émigré community in Europe and provided some respite to the fledgling Soviet Union. As we shall see, although much of its energy was directed towards its increasingly vicious rivalry with Markov II's Supreme Monarchical Council, Aufbau sought to undermine the Weimar Republic through terrorism and to topple the Bolshevik regime through subversion and military force from 1921 to 1923.

CHAPTER 6

Conspiracies of fire and the sword

While Aufbau failed to unite all White émigrés in Europe behind the Tsarist candidate Grand Prince Kirill Romanov in league with National Socialists, the *völkisch* German/White émigré organization did use political terror and covert military operations to undermine the Weimar Republic and the Soviet Union. As the first known example of Aufbau's participation in terrorism, Vice President Vladimir Biskupskii tried to arrange the murder of Aleksandr Kerenskii, who had led the Provisional Government in Russia in 1917 before the Bolsheviks had seized power. In other terrorist undertakings, Aufbau coordinated its activities with those of Organization C, a conspiratorial far right association under the leading Kapp Putsch figure Captain Hermann Ehrhardt, which possessed considerable connections with the NSDAP.

Aufbau participated in at least two prominent terrorist acts in league with Organization C. The Aufbau colleagues Piotr Shabelskii-Bork and Sergei Taboritskii, who possessed ties with Ehrhardt's secretive organization, mistakenly killed a prominent Russian Constitutional Democrat, Vladimir Nabokov, in their attempt to assassinate the Constitutional Democratic leader Pavel Miliukov. The evidence suggests that at least three Aufbau members, General Biskupskii, General Erich von Ludendorff, and his advisor Colonel Karl Bauer colluded in Organization C's shocking assassination of Walther Rathenau, who served as Germany's Foreign Minister. Aufbau thus clearly acted as a terrorist organization.

In its anti-Bolshevik military schemes, Aufbau adopted a three-pronged approach. Building upon the precedent of earlier German/White anti-Bolshevik campaigns in the Ukraine and the Baltic region, Aufbau raised armed forces for operations in these areas. Early Aufbau plans called for an army under Archduke Vasily Vyshivannyi to advance into the Ukraine while troops under the 1919 Latvian Intervention commander Colonel Pavel Bermondt-Avalov struck in the Baltic area. Aufbau later planned to foment revolt inside Soviet borders and then to launch an attack on the Russian heartland of the Soviet Union under the direction of Biskupskii. Aufbau sought to destroy Bolshevik rule and then to establish close political and economic ties between a National Socialist Germany and National Socialist Russian, Ukrainian, and Baltic states.

Aufbau's guiding figure, First Lieutenant Max von Scheubner-Richter, greatly influenced Adolf Hitler's Eastern designs as his leading foreign policy advisor and as one of his closest counselors in general. Aufbau's ideas of reconstructing the Soviet Union along National Socialist lines appealed to Hitler. He had not yet developed his view that the Germans needed to conquer *Lebensraum* (living space) in the East. Before the Hitler/Ludendorff Putsch of November 1923, Hitler did not envision annexing former Soviet territories to Germany. He still sought to establish an alliance between a National Socialist Germany and National Socialist Eastern states. While none of Aufbau's anti-Bolshevik military schemes came to fruition, the organization's position on the "Eastern question" significantly influenced Hitler's early views.

While Hitler approved of Aufbau's Eastern designs in general, he especially supported the conspiratorial organization's efforts to establish an independent National Socialist Ukraine. After Vyshivannyi's Ukrainian intervention failed to materialize, Aufbau envisioned an autonomous Ukraine under Colonel Ivan Poltavets-Ostranitsa, the head of the organization's Ukrainian section. Poltavets-Ostranitsa directed a National Socialist Ukrainian Cossack association that sought to establish a National Socialist Ukraine that would head a powerful Black Sea League. Hitler collaborated closely with Poltavets-Ostranitsa. He desired a National Socialist Ukraine as a provider of agricultural and mineral supplies as well as a springboard for future military operations against both the Soviet Union and France's ally Poland.

AUFBAU'S ENGAGEMENT IN TERRORISM

Despite its benign statutes, Aufbau participated in and supported political terrorism on German soil. In May 1921, General Biskupskii and his Aufbau colleague and Kapp Putsch co-conspirator Colonel Bauer received 12 million Hungarian crowns in Budapest from the Hungarian regent Admiral Nicholas Horthy's regime. Biskupskii and Bauer used some of these funds to place a contract for the assassination of Aleksandr Kerenskii, the former leader of the 1917 Provisional Government in Russia. Biskupskii and other

White émigrés blamed Kerenskii for having undermined Imperial Russia.[1] In the pages of *Aufbau-Korrespondenz* (*Aufbau Correspondence*), for instance, Scheubner-Richter accused Kerenskii of having brought "chaos" to Russia, and he even named him the "greatest enemy of the Germans."[2] Despite trying, Scheubner-Richter's Aufbau comrades Biskupskii and Bauer failed to bring about Kerenskii's death.

Aufbau did not succeed in having Kerenskii murdered, but Aufbau members did execute one of a series of high-profile assassinations that plagued the early Weimar Republic. Aufbau thereby helped to establish terror as a means of political pressure from the radical right. On March 28, 1922, the Aufbau members Lieutenant Piotr Shabelskii-Bork, who had transferred *The Protocols of the Elders of Zion* from the Ukraine to Germany, and his comrade Lieutenant Sergei Taboritskii traveled from Munich to Berlin. There they intended to assassinate Pavel Miliukov, the leader of the Constitutional Democrats, whom they blamed for helping to topple the Tsar.[3] When the critical moment arrived, they instead shot and killed Vladimir Nabokov, who was also a Constitutional Democratic leader and the father of the famous novelist, in the heat of the scuffle.[4] Shabelskii-Bork and Taboritskii were eventually sentenced to twelve and fourteen years' jail time respectively.[5]

The details of the planning for Miliukov's assassination remain unclear because of the covert nature of the operation. It is known that Taboritskii had moved in with the leading Aufbau ideologue Fedor Vinberg and Aufbau member Shabelskii-Bork in the Munich pension Modern in January 1922 and had joined Aufbau.[6] The three comrades since the time of the German occupation of the Ukraine in 1918 formed a terrorist cell based along the lines of the Black Hundreds in Imperial Russia.[7] Taboritskii lived with

[1] ATsVO report from May 23, 1921, GARF, *fond* 5893, *opis* 1, *delo* 47, 2.

[2] Max von Scheubner-Richter, "Deutsche Wirtschaftspolitik," *Wirtschafis-politische Aufbau-Korrespondenz über Ostfragen und ihre Bedeutung für Deutschland,* October 13, 1921, 1, 2.

[3] JM charge against Piotr Shabelskii-Bork and Sergei Taboritskii from May 29, 1922, GSAPKB, *Repositur* 84a, number 14953, 16.

[4] Norman Cohn, *Warrant for Genocide: The Myth of the Jewish World-Conspiracy and the "Protocols of the Elders of Zion"* (Chico, CA: Scholars Press, 1981), 141.

[5] Karl Schlögel, Katharina Kucher, Bernhard Suchy, and Gregor Thum, *Chronik russischen Lebens in Deutschland 1918–1941* (Berlin: Akademie Verlag, 1999), 112.

[6] PDM report to the BSMI from March 30, 1922, BHSAM, BSMI 22, number 71624, fiche 3, 89; letter from Ludwig von Knorring to the RKÜöO from December 28, 1923, RGVA (TsKhIDK), *fond* 772, *opis* 2, *delo* 179, 69.

[7] Rafael Ganelin, "Rossiiskoe chernosotenstvo i germanskii natsional-sotsializm," *Natsionalnaia pravaia prezhde i teper, Istoriko-sotsiologicheskie ocherki, chast 1: Rossiia i russkoe zarubezhe* (Saint Petersburg: Institut Sotsiologii rossiiskoi akademii nauk, 1992), 142.

Vinberg for a while, and they frequently met with Shabelskii-Bork to discuss politics and to conspire against common enemies.[8]

Vinberg in particular passionately detested Miliukov for his claim in a November 1916 speech before the Imperial Russian Duma (Parliament) that Tsaritsa Aleksandra Romanov, who was of German descent, harbored anti-Russian intentions. Vinberg had comforted his intimate royal friend and quite possibly lover (the Tsar was consistently away at the front throughout this period) when she had burst into tears in his presence upon receiving word of the charges.[9] Because of his known hatred of Miliukov and his close connections with the perpetrators Shabelskii-Bork and Taboritskii, Vinberg was suspected of having masterminded the assassination attempt against the Constitutional Democratic leader.

In his testimony to the Munich Police, Vinberg admitted that he had traveled to Berlin on March 23, 1922 and had left early on March 28, the day of Nabokov's assassination. He noted that his actions appeared "very suspicious," but that he had stayed in Berlin to arrange for the distribution of his new book translated into German as *Der Kreuzesweg Russlands* (*Russia's Via Dolorosa*).[10] Vinberg's alibi proved highly suspect indeed, but he managed to avoid prosecution. He was eventually implicated in Nabokov's murder, however, and he later fled Germany largely as a result of this.[11]

The State Commissioner for the Supervision of Public Order concluded that Aufbau leadership had colluded in the Miliukov assassination attempt.[12] General Biskupskii, Aufbau's number two man, had also left Munich for Berlin at the time of the attempted murder. Like Vinberg, he became the object of intense suspicion. Also like Vinberg, Biskupskii managed to escape prosecution.[13] Later, Weimar Germany's secret intelligence agency concluded that the Munich branch of Nikolai Markov II's Union of the Faithful, which had been formed in February 1922, had also helped to organize the attempted assassination of Miliukov.[14] While Aufbau and

---

[8] Harald Gustav Graf's testimony included in a PDM report to the BSMI from March 30, 1922, BHSAM, BSMI 22, number 71624, fiche 4, 8.

[9] Letter from Shabelskii-Bork to his wife from December 31, 1925, GSAPKB, *Repositur* 84a, number 14953, 65.

[10] Fedor Vinberg's March 30, 1922 testimony, BHSAM, BSMI 22, number 71624, fiche 4, 18.

[11] Cohn, *Warrant for Genocide*, 141.

[12] RKÜöO report from March 30, 1922, RGVA (TsKhIDK), *fond* 772, *opis* 1, *delo* 96, 100.

[13] Vinberg's testimony included in a PDM report to the BSMI from April 15, 1922, BHSAM, BSMI 22, number 71624, fiche 4, 64.

[14] RKÜöO report from [August?] 1922, RGVA (TsKhIDK), *fond* 772, *opis* 1, *delo* 96, 167, 169.

the Union of the Faithful possessed many political differences, they agreed on the use of terror as a means of political pressure.

Scheubner-Richter wrote an article maligning Miliukov that appeared in *Aufbau Correspondence* soon after the assassination attempt. Scheubner-Richter actually wrote his piece shortly before the attempted murder, which strongly suggests that he knew of Shabelskii-Bork and Taboritskii's murderous undertaking. Scheubner-Richter's essay incited hatred against Miliukov, most likely to justify the Constitutional Democrat's murder. Scheubner-Richter accused Miliukov of working for the "final suppression of Germany." He further asked if the German government's permission for Miliukov to publish an Entente-friendly newspaper in Germany represented "stupidity or a crime."[15]

Scheubner-Richter condoned the attempted assassination of Miliukov in an April 1922 *Aufbau Correspondence* article, "Russian Terrorists." The piece did not mention that Shabelskii-Bork, Taboritskii, and their mentor Vinberg all played active roles in Aufbau. As "distressing" as the recent assassination attempt against Miliukov proved, the article noted the prevailing poverty among White émigrés as a mitigating factor. Scheubner-Richter condemned the "brazen gourmet existence" of Bolshevik leaders, who lived off of "plundered Russia," and the substantial wealth among Constitutional Democratic leaders such as Miliukov that came from Entente sources. Given such material disparity, it remained "surprising" that White émigrés had not carried out more violent acts.

Scheubner-Richter's article also pointed out a certain Constitutional Democratic hypocrisy regarding the use of terrorism. The piece noted that in 1907 the Constitutional Democrats under the leadership of Miliukov and Nabokov had rejected a Duma proposal to censure terrorist acts as morally reprehensible.[16] Indeed, the use of political terror was by no means the sole property of the far right. The radical right attracted a great deal of negative attention for its use of assassination as a means of political pressure, however. The lead article of *Aufbau Correspondence* cast the attempted murder of Miliukov in a somewhat positive light while seeking to keep Aufbau's name away from the undertaking.

The official National Socialist response to the assassination attempt against Miliukov as presented in the *Völkischer Beobachter* (*Völkisch Observer*) attempted to mitigate Shabelskii-Bork and Taboritskii's deed. An early April 1922 article in the National Socialist periodical accused

[15] Scheubner-Richter, "Miljukow in Berlin," *Aufbau-Korrespondenz*, March 31, 1922, 1.
[16] Scheubner Richter, "Russische Terroristen," *Aufbau-Korrespondenz*, April 14, 1922, 1.

Miliukov of agitating for war against Imperial Germany, leading the February Revolution in Russia with English support, and seeking to undermine Germany.[17] Direct evidence is lacking that Hitler had concrete knowledge of the Aufbau plans to assassinate Miliukov, however.

It is known that the Aufbau terrorist cell of Vinberg, Shabelskii-Bork, and Taboritskii possessed connections with Organization C. This conspiratorial organization under the key Kapp Putsch participant Captain Hermann Ehrhardt committed terrorist acts, carried out covert anti-Bolshevik and anti-Weimar Republic military preparations, and possessed close links with Hitler's NSDAP.[18] Ehrhardt's secretive alliance arose in June 1921, when officers of the disbanded Ehrhardt Brigade who had participated in the Kapp Putsch of March 1920 formed Organization Consul, commonly known as Organization C. "Consul" stood for Ehrhardt himself.[19] Organization C became infamous for its attempted and successful assassinations of leftist, often Jewish, leaders in the early years of the Weimar Republic.[20] Aufbau increasingly coordinated its activities with those of Organization C. Like Aufbau, Organization C rejected the Treaty of Versailles and the Weimar Constitution. Organization C dedicated itself to fighting socialism, Bolshevism, and "Jewry" under the motto: "Struggle for Germany's rebirth."[21]

Like the National Socialist Party and Aufbau, Organization C based its operations in Munich. It also possessed many branches throughout Germany. Captain Ehrhardt led Organization C from exile, most of the time from Austria. He headed approximately 5,000 active members who could call further men to action if necessary.[22] Organization C possessed several subdivisions. Section C of Organization C directed right-wing press and propaganda.[23] Lieutenant-Commander Eberhard Kautter led Section C. Kautter served as Captain Ehrhardt's political advisor and intelligence officer.

While Aufbau's guiding figure and the prominent National Socialist leader Scheubner-Richter assured the Bavarian Interior Ministry that only White émigrés had participated in the Monarchical Congress at Bad Reichenhall in May–June 1921, in fact, he had allowed Kautter to negotiate

---

[17] "Das Attentat in Berlin," *Völkischer Beobachter*, April 1, 1922, 2.
[18] Ganelin, "Rossiiskoe chernosotenstvo i germanskii natsional-sotsializm," 142.
[19] RKÜöO reports from September 29 and November 12, 1921, BAB, 1507, number 339, 2; number 325, 29;
[20] RKÜöO report from September 23, 1923, BAB, 1507, number 442, 126.
[21] RKÜöO reports from November 4 and 12, 1921, BAB, 1507, number 557, 105, 106; number 325, 29.
[22] RKÜöO report from November 4 and 12, 1921, BAB, 1507, number 557, 76; number 325, 29, 30.
[23] RKÜöO report from November 12, 1921, BAB, 1507, number 325, 29.

with Congress members. Kautter had helped Congress participants to secure a substantial loan from German industrialists, including Aufbau's President Baron Theodor von Cramer-Klett and representatives of the company Mannesmann. In return, Congress members had pledged to grant the industrialists railway and mining concessions in the planned future monarchical Russian state.[24] Kautter's clandestine activities at the Congress demonstrated significant coordination between White émigré circles and Organization C.

Scheubner-Richter supported Organization C. Lieutenant-Commander Paul Werber of Organization C became acquainted with Dr. Rüthenick of the Deutschvölkischer Schutz- und Trutzbund (German *Völkisch* Protection League) in Bremen, who raised money for nationalist causes in Germany from far right American sources. Werber arranged for Dr. Rüthenick to hold talks with the "leading personalities" in Munich. In late August 1921, Dr. Rüthenick met with Scheubner-Richter. Another member of Organization C, Dr. Börner, assured Dr. Rüthenick that he had "come to the right person" in Scheubner-Richter, who had written a letter that had aided Dr. Rüthenick in raising $5,000. Dr. Börner used this money for a mission to America to gain financial support for far right German activities.[25] The primary American connection to the German far right was most likely the anti-Semitic industrialist and politician Henry Ford.

The Munich Police established a high level of collaboration between the well-connected Organization C and the National Socialist Party. Hitler communicated regularly with Ehrhardt and tried to gain as many of Ehrhardt's followers for the NSDAP as he could.[26] Seized letters demonstrated that even before Organization C had existed, the future Organization C leader Captain Alfred Hoffmann had written Hitler personally with regard to personnel matters in the NSDAP. He had also worked to "prepare the ground for Hitler" in the city of Wilhelmshaven on the North Sea.[27] Moreover, Hoffmann's colleague Lieutenant-Commander Werber, who represented Organization C in northwestern Germany, carried out propaganda for the NSDAP and its periodical, the *Völkisch Observer*.

---

[24] Letter from Scheubner-Richter to the BSMI from September 19, 1921, BHSAM, BSMI 22, number 71624, fiche 3, 54; Heinrich Class, *Wider den Strom*, vol. II, BAK, *Kleine Erwerburg* 499, 508; LGPO report to the RKÜöO from July 11, 1921, RGVA (TsKhIDK), *fond* 772, *opis* 2, *delo* 129b, 266, 267.
[25] Questioning of Paul Werber, RKÜöO, BAB, 1507, number 441, 10; letters from Ludwig Neeb to Alfred Hoffmann from August 21 and 22, 1921, RKÜöO, BAB, 1507, number 441, 4, 87.
[26] RKÜöO report to the PDM from October 20, 1921, BSAM, PDM, number 6803, 34.
[27] Situation reports from Hoffmann from January 17, 1921, and February 23, 1921, RKÜöO, BAB, 1507, number 441, 127, 231.

He even opened branches of the National Socialist Party in northwestern Germany.[28]

In an example of the "fight fire with fire" philosophy, Organization C operated along the lines of the Communist Party by using influential men to build cells that inconspicuously influenced the opinions of rank and file members of radical right organizations, including the National Socialist Party.[29] During the summer of 1921, Ehrhardt sent the student Hans Ulrich Klintzsch to lead the paramilitary Sturmabteilung (Storm Section, SA) of the NSDAP and to coordinate its activities with those of Organization C.[30] Klintzsch later sent Franz Jaenicke, the co-founder of the Deutsch–Russischer Club (German–Russian Club) in Berlin, to found a branch of the National Socialist Party in the German capital.[31] Jaenicke's high position in the German–Russian Club indicates another connection between White émigrés and the NSDAP. Ehrhardt later sent the prominent Organization C leader Hermann Göring to the SA to gain control of it. Göring nonetheless switched his loyalties from Ehrhardt to Hitler as the leader of the SA beginning in February 1923.[32]

Organization C possessed more military might than the National Socialist Party. The secretive alliance combated overt and subversive threats from the Soviet Union and also fought against Polish invaders in Upper Silesia. The conspiratorial association coordinated its anti-Bolshevik activities with White émigrés. Section A of Organization C under Captain Hoffmann led an anti-Bolshevik counter-intelligence service and cultivated contacts with nationalist Germans and White émigrés.[33] Already in November 1920, the time of Aufbau's foundation, Hoffmann had stressed in a speech that the far right's "emergence" in Bavaria could only occur after the "shattering of the Treaty of Versailles," which itself would only be possible after the "successful German orientation of the coming Russia."[34] Organization C thus connected Germany's welfare with that of a restored nationalist Russian state.

---

[28] RKÜöO report from December 1, 1922, BAB, 134, number 69, 153.

[29] RKÜöO report from August 4, 1922, BAB, 134, number 66, 6, 7.

[30] PDM report from June 1, 1923, BSAM, PDM, number 6697, 322.

[31] Franz Jaenicke, "Lebenslauf," Luckenwalde, July 1, 1923, RKÜöO, BAB, 1507, number 329, 331.

[32] Interview with Gerhard Rossbach on October 31, 1951, IZG, ZS 128, 1; PDM report from June 1, 1923, BSAM, PDM, number 6697, 322.

[33] RKÜöO reports from September 29 and November 12, 1921, BAB, 1507, number 339, 2; number 325, 29.

[34] Situation report from Hoffmann from November 12, 1920, RKÜöO, BAB, 1507, number 441, 218.

Section B of Organization C under Lieutenant Manfred von Killinger oversaw military matters. Section B supported German self-defense organizations in Upper Silesia, most importantly Freikorps Oberland (Uplands Volunteer Corps), the only fully armed formation of the roughly 80,000 German soldiers who opposed Polish invaders in 1921.[35] The Thule Society, which had helped to spawn the National Socialist Party, had overseen the formation of Freikorps Uplands.[36] The former Latvian Intervention commander Colonel Pavel Bermondt-Avalov possessed connections with Freikorps Uplands in the fall of 1921. In another example of nationalist German–White émigré collaboration, he raised volunteers from Russian internment camps in Germany for action against the Poles in Upper Silesia.[37] Freikorps Uplands held ideological views similar to those of White forces in the Russian Civil War. The formation advertised for members with the assertion: "We fight Jewish-Russian Bolshevism and American–Jewish capitalism, both of which are diseased outgrowths of economic life."[38]

Hitler admired Freikorps Uplands, which had connections to Organization C and White émigrés. He used the formation as a model for National Socialist paramilitary forces that had begun with the creation of a Turn- und Sportabteilung (Gymnastics and Sport Section), actually a large-scale armed bodyguard, in the fall of 1920.[39] In his March 1921 deposition on behalf of members of Freikorps Uplands, he noted that when "the concept of self-protection is taken up, then this self-protection cannot effectively be achieved in the form of weak local defense, but only in the form of shock and strike-ready organizations roughly of the type Uplands."[40]

Section B of Organization C feared the Bolshevik specter. Section B's leader, Lieutenant Killinger, stressed that Organization C had been formed with the urgent sense that it had to be "avoided above all else that Germany become a Soviet republic and such conditions as in Russia should enter the country."[41] Section B worked to overthrow Bolshevik rule. It received one million gold Marks in April 1922 from American sources,

[35] RKÜöO report from November 12, 1921, BAB, 1507, number 325, 29; questioning of Friedrich Wilhelm von Plodowski from March 17, 1922, RKÜöO, BAB, 1507, number 339, 217.

[36] Letter from the *Sicherheitsdienst des Reichsführers – SS, der SD-Führer des SS Oberabschnittes Ost* to the RSHA from October 5, 1938, RGVA (TsKhIDK), *fond* 500, *opis* 1, *delo* 504, 24.

[37] LGPO report from September 1921, GSAPKB, *Repositur* 77, title 1813, number 6, 25, 26.

[38] "Verpflichtung," BSMI, BHSAM, BSMI 22, number 73675, fiche 4, 89.

[39] PDM report from June 1, 1923, BSAM, PDM, number 6697, 320.

[40] Case against Joseph Römer at the LGMI, RKÜöO report from November 21, 1922, BAB, 1507, number 343, 148.

[41] Deposition of Manfred von Killinger from October 20, 1921, BAB, 1507, number 339, 15.

most likely primarily from Ford, to defeat Communism in Germany and Russia in cooperation with White émigrés the next summer. After military success, right-wing governments in Germany and Russia were to be established.[42]

Section B of Organization C gained the loyalty of the fierce anti-Bolshevik First Lieutenant Gerhard Rossbach, who had led a Freikorps in the 1919 Latvian Intervention and had afterwards established the Rossbach Corps, an illegal paramilitary formation in northern Germany with 8,000 combat-ready men.[43] Rossbach maintained the determined anti-Bolshevik spirit of the Latvian Intervention. He used two Baltic German officers who had followed him back from Latvia in 1919 as his assistants. In April 1922, he traveled to Prague to discuss an operation against the Soviet Union under the leadership of General Piotr Vrangel, the former head of the Southern Russian Armed Forces in the Crimea during the Russian Civil War.

At these talks, Rossbach agreed to lead a troop contingent in the planned undertaking, for which Vrangel was organizing troops on Yugoslavian soil.[44] The intervention, which enjoyed French backing, was to be carried out officially in Grand Prince Kirill Romanov's name with Grand Prince Nikolai Nikolaevich Romanov playing a leading military role alongside Vrangel.[45] As we have seen, no military intervention against the Soviet Union took place in 1922, largely because of internecine White émigré strife between Scheubner-Richter's Aufbau and Nikolai Markov II's Supreme Monarchical Council.

Hitler's National Socialist Party drew strength from the Freikorps movement that conspired with Organization C. Rossbach became acquainted with Hitler at a National Socialist meeting in Munich in the summer of 1922. He joined the Munich branch of the NSDAP soon after.[46] His intense anti-Semitism and his belief in using *Sturmtruppen* (storm troops) for political purposes accorded with fundamental National Socialist ideas.[47] In late 1922, Hitler created the Grossdeutsche Arbeiterpartei (Greater German Worker's Party) with Rossbach's assistance to expand National Socialism's influence in northern Germany. Hitler did not achieve the success he had hoped for, but this initiative under Rossbach's immediate supervision improved

[42] RMI report to the SKöO from April 3, 1922, GSAPKB, *Repositur 77*, title 1812, number 25, 2.
[43] RKÜöO report from September 11, 1921, BAB, 1507, number 339, 410; questioning of Plodowski from March 17, 1922, RKÜöO, BAB, 1507, number 339, 222.
[44] RKÜöO reports from April 7, another date in April, and November 25, 1922, BAB, 1507, number 345, 186, 242, 249; DGBel report to the AA from March 14, 1922, PAAA, 83578, 15.
[45] DGBer report to the AA from June 20, 1922, PAAA, 83579, 57.
[46] Rossbach's deposition from May 11, 1923, RKÜöO, BAB, 1507, number 211, 153.
[47] RKÜöO report from December 16, 1922, BAB, 134, number 69, 170.

collaboration between the southern National Socialist and northern *völkisch* movements.[48]

Years after the Hitler/Ludendorff Putsch of November 1923, the State Commissioner for the Supervision of Public Order stressed the key role that Freikorps-type organizations had played in the early "radical right movement" in Germany. In particular, the agency noted that Rossbach, Uplands, and Ehrhardt (Including Organization C) had "stood at the center of the different putsch undertakings." The report further noted: "The National Socialists were strongly infiltrated by Freikorps leaders and Freikorps ideas in the first years of their existence up until 1923."[49]

Freikorps formations that influenced the early NSDAP upheld the Russian Civil War spirit of cooperation between nationalist Germans and Russians. For instance, Lieutenant Edmund Heines, who led the Munich branch of Rossbach Corps, stressed in a speech at a National Socialist congress in November 1922 that everyone present shared the ethos of the "*Baltikumer*" (Baltic fighters) whether they had served in Latvia under Colonel Bermondt-Avalov's command or not.[50] Freikorps members who shared a common spirit and drive with White émigrés tended to be anti-Semitic. In late 1922, members of the NSDAP were heard singing a Freikorps song, "The Republic Asked Us."[51] This song includes the lines: "We do not want a Jew republic / Phooey! Jew republic, / For it is to blame. / For they yelled: Bow-wow-wow! / And we yelled: Throw them out! Throw them out! Throw them out!"[52]

The intensely anti-Semitic Organization C with which Aufbau and the NSDAP were allied became best known for assassinating the prominent Jewish politician Walther Rathenau in Berlin on June 24, 1922.[53] Rathenau had become Germany's Foreign Minister in January 1922. On April 16, 1922, he had signed the Treaty of Rapallo with the Soviet Foreign Minister Georgii Chicherin, thereby making Germany the first Western country to recognize the Soviet Union officially.[54] Already in early April 1922, Organization C had sent agents to Genoa, Italy, where an international conference

[48] RKÜöO report from January 24, 1925, BAB, 134, number 170, 151.
[49] RKÜöO report from April 27, 1928, BAB, 134, number 173, 117, 118.
[50] RKÜöO reports from November 24, 1922 and March 25, 1923, BAB, 1507, number 345, 266; number 211, 2.
[51] PDM report to the RKÜöO from August 1, 1922, BAB, 1507, number 440, 172.
[52] "Die Republik hat uns gefragt," a Freikorps song, RKÜöO, July 25, 1922, BAB, 1507, number 440, 162.
[53] RKÜöO report from September 23, 1923, BAB, 1507, number 442, 126.
[54] Martin Sabrow, *Der Rathenaumord: Rekonstruktion einer Verschwörung gegen die Republik von Weimar* (Munich: Oldenbourg, 1994), 70.

was taking place from which the Rapallo Treaty emerged, with the mission of assassinating Soviet representatives.[55] This assignment demonstrates the high degree to which Organization C's leadership despised German governmental efforts to seek rapprochement with the Soviet Union. Rightist Germans and White émigrés hated Rathenau for signing the Treaty of Rapallo, and his action sealed his doom.

The degree to which Aufbau members participated in the conspiracy to assassinate German Foreign Minister Rathenau is not entirely clear, but Aufbau leaders drew unwelcome attention to themselves through their known hatred of Rathenau. Already in a September 1921 edition of *Aufbau Correspondence*, for instance, the *de facto* Aufbau leader Scheubner-Richter wrote of Rathenau as a man who did not serve German interests but who rather sought to bring Bolshevism to Germany. Scheubner-Richter expressed his amazement that such a dangerous person could serve in the German government instead of being imprisoned for treason.[56] Baron Ludwig von Knorring, the leader of the White émigré community in Baden Baden, who favored a constitutional monarchy for Russia, wrote the German Foreign Office in the wake of the Rathenau assassination and lamented the "suggestive force" that members of "Russian far right groups" exerted on "calm German types."[57]

Aufbau leaders came under suspicion of complicity in Rathenau's murder while they were outside Germany. Shortly before Rathenau's assassination on June 24, 1922, a high-level Aufbau delegation that included First Lieutenant Scheubner-Richter, General Biskupskii, and the Ukrainian Cossack leader Colonel Ivan Poltavets-Ostranitsa arrived in Budapest to hold talks with the president of the Russian Monarchical Club there, Prince Mirza Kazem Bek, who had supported Aufbau for some time.

Kazem Bek drew unwelcome attention to Aufbau's high-level delegates by giving a fiery speech in their presence in which he denounced Rathenau soon after the latter's assassination. Kazem Bek noted that the politician's murder had "cleared many obstacles out of the way of the German nationalists." He hoped: "German policy, which had gone astray, will now be directed in a better path." He further stressed, "It goes completely without saying that Rathenau's death will also strengthen our connection with Germany, for it has given rise to a strengthening of the national idea."[58]

[55] RMI report to the SKöO from April 3, 1922, GSAPKB, *Repositur 77*, title 1812, number 25, 2.
[56] Scheubner-Richter, "Worum es sich handelt," *Aufbau-Korrespondenz*, September 17, 1921, 1.
[57] Letter from Knorring to the AA from June 26, 1922, PAAA, 83579, 61 ob.
[58] DGBud report to the AA from July 5, 1922, PAAA, 83579, 130; "Die russischen Emigranten in Ungarn und Deutschland," *Nemzeti Ujsag*, AA, PAAA, 83580, 26–28.

The *Wiener Morgenzeitung* (*Vienna Morning Newspaper*) caused a furor in its July 1, 1922 edition by releasing an article on the Budapest talks under the provocative title, "A Conference of Murderers in Budapest."[59]

Scheubner-Richter termed the *Vienna Morning Newspaper* article a "provocation."[60] He claimed that it put words into his mouth, cast him in a negative light with regard to Rathenau's assassination, and associated him with "all possible political adventurers."[61] The *Vienna Morning Newspaper* article did indeed fabricate an incendiary speech of Scheubner-Richter's. The newspaper was correct, however, in asserting that the Aufbau member and former Kapp Putsch conspirator Colonel Karl Bauer, whose adjutant Lieutenant Alfred Günther had been arrested in connection with the Rathenau murder, maintained close connections with various White émigrés and Hungarian rightists, including many present at the conference in Budapest.[62]

In his own defense, Scheubner-Richter assured the German Embassy in Budapest that his arrival date of June 22, 1922, two days before Rathenau's assassination, demonstrated that he had not come to discuss the changed political situation that had arisen after Rathenau's death.[63] While hard evidence is lacking, it is quite possible that Scheubner-Richter and his colleagues Biskupskii and Poltavets-Ostranitsa had possessed advance knowledge of Rathenau's impending assassination and had left Munich both to distance themselves from suspicion of complicity in the crime and to strengthen ties with Hungarian rightists in light of the soon-to-be altered political situation. In any case, Biskupskii and others around him in Aufbau praised Rathenau's assassination, thereby drawing suspicion of their involvement in the conspiracy to murder the controversial politician.[64]

As a further indication of Aufbau's complicity in Rathenau's murder, Colonel Bauer, who served as Aufbau's contact man in Vienna, was implicated in Rathenau's assassination. Bauer's arrest threw suspicion on, among others, his close colleague General Biskupskii and the contact man whom he and Biskupskii used in Budapest, the White émigré General Piotr Glasenap.[65] Moreover, Bauer's adjutant and General Ludendorff's secretary

59 "Ein Mörderkongress in Budapest," *Wiener Morgenzeitung*, July 1, 1922, DGBud, forwarded to the AA, PAAA, 83580, 32.
60 Letter from Scheubner-Richter to the DGBud from July 6, 1922, PAAA, 83580, 19.
61 Letter from Scheubner-Richter to *Nemzeti Ujsag* from July 6, 1922 that Scheubner-Richter sent to the DGBud on July 6, 1922, PAAA, 83580, 34.
62 "Ein Mörderkongress in Budapest," 32.
63 Letter from Scheubner-Richter to *Nemzeti Ujsag* from June 29, 1922, PAAA, 83580, 33.
64 DB report from July 17, 1922, RGVA (TsKhIDK), *fond* 7, *opis* 1, *delo* 386, reel 3, 199.
65 DB reports from November 11, 1922 and June 8, 1923, RGVA (TsKhIDK), *fond* 7, *opis* 1, *delo* 386, reel 2, 134, 163; ATsVO report [1921 or 1922], GARF, *fond* 5893, *opis* 1, *delo* 46, 24.

during the Kapp Putsch, Lieutenant Günther, a *Gruppenleiter* (group leader) in Organization C, was suspected of conspiring in Rathenau's murder. Authorities found recent suspicious letters from the Aufbau members Ludendorff and Bauer at Günther's residence.[66]

Like Walther Steinbeck, a prominent member of Organization C who was arrested in connection with Rathenau's assassination, Günther had close links with Hitler's NSDAP. This demonstrates a connection between Aufbau and the National Socialist Party in conspiratorial terrorist operations. After his brush with the authorities, Günther traveled to Munich, where he was well acquainted with the SA leader Hans Ulrich Klintzsch and Hitler as well. Günther began working for the NSDAP.[67] He served in the *Fahndungsabteilung* (Detective Department) that observed the political police. He was later sought in connection with the June 4, 1922 assassination attempt on Phillip Scheidemann, who had proclaimed the German Republic on November 9, 1918.[68]

Despite the evidence against him and his close associates, the Aufbau member Colonel Bauer was able to avoid prosecution for Rathenau's assassination. He was able to continue his subversive activities for Aufbau's cause for a while. In the summer of 1922, he transferred large sums of money to Aufbau in general and General Biskupskii in particular, perhaps some of which was intended to fund terrorist operations.[69] Bauer threw more suspicion on Aufbau as a terrorist organization when he was later arrested for planning the assassination of Scheidemann.[70]

Because of a lack of hard evidence, the precise degree that Aufbau participated in the wave of assassinations that rocked the early Weimar Republic cannot be determined. It is clear, however, that Aufbau supported and engaged in political terrorism. The attempted assassination of the Constitutional Democratic leader Miliukov, which led to the death of Nabokov instead, can be attributed to Aufbau with great certainty, for the culprits Shabelskii-Bork and Taboritskii as well as their mentor Vinberg all belonged to the conspiratorial organization. With regard to Rathenau's murder, compelling circumstantial evidence implicates Aufbau members, most notably Biskupskii, Ludendorff, and Bauer, of at least abetting the crime, while Scheubner-Richter and Poltavets-Ostranitsa seem to have known of the

---

[66] RKÜöO report from [August?] 1922, RGVA (TsKhIDK), *fond* 772, *opis* 1, *delo* 96, 169; PVE report to the PDM from September 1, 1922, BSAM, PDM, number 6708, 49.

[67] RKÜöO reports from June 4 and November 1923, BAB, 1507, number 442, 93, 199; PVE report to the PDM from September 21, 1922, BSAM, PDM, number 6708, 48.

[68] PDM report to the RKÜöO from January 16, 1923, BHSAM, BSMI 22, number 71525, fiche 1, 34.

[69] RKÜöO report from [August?] 1922, RGVA (TsKhIDK), *fond* 772, *opis* 1, *delo* 96, 169.

[70] RKÜöO report from March 25, 1923, BAB, 1507, number 211, 2.

assassination plans beforehand. The two most prominent assassinations that Aufbau members carried out or conspired in dealt with politicians who had staunchly opposed Aufbau's policy of fostering *völkisch* German–White émigré collaboration to establish right-wing regimes in both Germany and Russia.

AUFBAU'S MILITARY PLANS AGAINST THE SOVIET UNION

In addition to participating in political terrorism on German soil, Aufbau planned large-scale military operations against the Soviet Union in league with Hitler's NSDAP in the course of 1921–1923. Continuing in the tradition of earlier German–White Russian Civil War campaigns, where regular German Army units and Freikorps had collaborated with White forces against the Red Army on the flanks of the Soviet Union, Aufbau planned armed operations in the Baltic region and the Ukraine. Aufbau particularly emphasized wresting the Ukraine from Soviet control. Aufbau also planned a military intervention for the Soviet heartland itself under General Biskupskii to overthrow Bolshevik rule. Hitler approved of Aufbau's goals of reorganizing the Soviet Union into National Socialist Russian, Ukrainian, and Baltic states that would ally with Germany against the Entente. He especially wished the creation of a National Socialist Ukraine under the Ukrainian Cossack and Aufbau member Colonel Poltavets-Ostranitsa.

In the course of 1921, Poltavets-Ostranitsa's collegue General Biskupskii, Aufbau's vice president and Scheubner-Richter's most important White émigré collaborator, intensified his efforts to form a "League of the Defeated" composed of nationalist Germans, Hungarians, and Russians (actually primarily Ukrainians) under his leadership.[71] Soon after the end of the Monarchical Congress at Bad Reichenhall in June 1921, Biskupskii's efforts at alliance building bore fruit. German (Prussian and Bavarian), Russian, and Hungarian monarchists concluded a pact of mutual assistance to restore monarchical regimes to their respective countries. After this restoration, the three nations were to ally along the lines of the Holy Alliance of the nineteenth century.[72]

In the late summer of 1921, after Biskupskii's success in right-wing alliance building, Aufbau supported a Ukrainian separatist, the young Archduke Wilhelm von Habsburg, who called himself Vasily Vyshivannyi in

---

[71] LGPO report to the RKÜöO from June 2, 1921, RGVA (TsKhIDK), *fond* 772, *opis* 3, *delo* 81a, 12.
[72] DB report from August [11], 1921, RGVA (TsKhIDK), *fond* 7, *opis* 2, *delo* 2575, reel 2, 108.

Ukrainian. Aufbau under the direction of Scheubner-Richter and Biskupskii backed Vyshivannyi in part to return Habsburg rule to Austria.[73]
Vyshivannyi had served as a lieutenant in the Austro-Hungarian Army
during the German/Austro-Hungarian occupation of the Ukraine late in
World War I. He had received Austro-Hungarian support in a failed bid
to replace Pavel Skoropadskii as hetman, or leader, of the Ukraine in July
1918. In 1920, Vyshivannyi had begun to lead the most influential group
of Galician nationalists based in Vienna who sought to separate Galicia
from Poland and to join it with an independent Ukraine. Vyshivannyi
was to serve as the hetman of the new state. While Vyshivannyi's supporters generally opposed Skoropadskii, Vyshivannyi had helped to mend old
animosities by marrying Skoropadskii's daughter.[74]

Scheubner-Richter and Biskupskii aroused considerable right-wing
interest in Vyshivannyi's bid for an independent Ukraine.[75] They secured
approximately two million Marks in financing for Vyshivannyi's cause from
Aufbau members and sympathetic Bavarian parties. The wealthy President
of Aufbau, Baron Theodor von Cramer-Klett, granted Vyshivannyi particularly substantial subsidies.[76] The Aufbau member Vladimir Keppen,
Biskupskii's cousin, contributed 60,000 Swiss francs to support Vyshivannyi's cause.[77] General Ludendorff lent his name to Vyshivannyi's efforts.[78]
Aufbau's leading Ukrainian representative, Poltavets-Ostranitsa, served in
Vyshivannyi's Supreme Council in Vienna.[79]

In the summer of 1921, Vyshivannyi signed an agreement with
Scheubner-Richter and Biskupskii whereby he officially commissioned
Biskupskii with forming his army in Bavaria for use in the Ukraine.
In return, Vyshivannyi granted Biskupskii, Scheubner-Richter, and their
wealthy Aufbau associates trading and industrial concessions in the planned
autonomous Ukrainian state. At the beginning of September 1921, Biskupskii sent an agent to Hungary to purchase horses for Vyshivannyi's nascent
army stationed in Bavaria. Vyshivannyi established recruiting centers for
his interventionary force outside his Bavarian base, most notably in Berlin.

---

[73] DB report from November 11, 1922, RGVA (TKhIDK), *fond* 7, *opis* 1, *delo* 386, reel 2, 163, 164.
[74] ATsVO report from October 10, 1921, GARF, *fond* 5893, *opis* 1, *delo* 47, 9, 10; MMFH report to the
DB from May 1, 1921, RGVA (TKhIDK), *fond* 198, *opis* 17, *delo* 203, reel 5, 479.
[75] ATsVO report from October 10, 1921, GARF, *fond* 5893, *opis* 1, *delo* 47, 10.
[76] DB report from January 3, 1922, RGVA (TKhIDK), *fond* 7, *opis* 1, *delo* 953, reel 1, 81.
[77] ATsVO report from October 10, 1921, GARF, *fond* 5893, *opis* 1, *delo* 47, 11.
[78] MMFH report to the DB from May 1, 1921, RGVA (TsKhIDK), *fond* 198, *opis* 17, *delo* 203, reel 5,
479.
[79] RKÜöO report from July 20, 1922, RGVA (TsKhIDK), *fond* 772, *opis* 1, *delo* 96, 152.

Volunteers were paid for their trip to Bavaria. Once there, they were given a horse and a rifle, and they were disguised as equestrian forest wardens.[80]

General Biskupskii planned a two-pronged campaign against the Soviet Union with a northern theater of operation as well as a southern one. In addition to supervising the creation of Vyshivannyi's army that was to operate in the Ukraine, he organized a White émigré interventionary force for the Baltic region that was to succeed where Colonel Bermondt-Avalov's Western Volunteer Army had failed in the 1919 Latvian Intervention. In this endeavor, Biskupskii collaborated with his old comrade General Piotr Glasenap, who had taken over command of the Russian Northwestern Army in Estonia from General Nikolai Iudenich in 1919. Biskupskii also cooperated with Bermondt-Avalov. With General Ludendorff's backing, the three White émigré officers organized armed White émigré formations backed with German Freikorps support. This White émigré/German interventionary force was to engage Soviet troops in the north while Vyshivannyi's army invaded the Ukraine.[81]

Biskupskii's collaboration with Bermondt-Avalov aroused the suspicion of the State Commissioner for the Supervision of Public Order. The agency asserted in September 1921 that Bermondt-Avalov, with his "adventurous nature" and the "poor insight" he demonstrated in his "dealings with Russian and German hotheads," proved "just as detrimental as a paid agent of the Entente." The report noted that Bermondt-Avalov nevertheless

was and still is a sincere sponsor of German–Russian rapprochement; he hates the Entente with his entire soul, and he perceives an alliance between Germany and Russia to be the only possibility to overthrow the Bolsheviks and to take revenge together against the Entente.

The secret political police concluded that Bermondt-Avalov had laudable intentions, which, driven by "morbid vanity," he could not carry out.[82] Incidentally, it is not clear if Bermondt-Avalov officially belonged to Aufbau, but he conspired with Aufbau leaders and he supported Grand Prince Kirill Romanov, Aufbau's candidate for the Tsarist throne.[83]

The southern and northern military offensives against the Soviet Union that Biskupskii planned with his colleagues Vyshivannyi, Bermondt-Avalov, and Glasenap failed to progress past the organizational stage. The planned

---

[80] ATsVO report from October 10, 1921, GARF, *fond* 5893, *opis* 1, *delo* 47, 9, 11.

[81] MMFT report to the DB from December 24, 1923, RGVA (TsKhIDK), *fond* 7, *opis* 2, *delo* 2575, reel 2, 133; RKÜöO report from December 8, 1921, RGVA (TsKhIDK), *fond* 772, *opis* 3, *delo* 71, 40.

[82] RKÜöO report from September 9, 1921, RGVA (TsKhIDK), *fond* 772, *opis* 3, *delo* 71, 5, 6, 19.

[83] SKöO report to the AA from March 20, 1923, PAAA, 83581, 239 ob.

southern offensive under Vyshivannyi lost initiative in the fall of 1921, largely because of a lack of funding.[84] While Bermondt-Avalov established recruiting centers for a new Baltic intervention, the anti-Bolshevik advance in the north he planned in league with Generals Biskupskii and Glasenap likewise did not materialize.[85] In January 1922, the socialist Prussian government exiled Bermondt-Avalov from Prussian territory on the grounds that he was a troublesome foreign adventurer.[86]

After experiencing disappointments, Aufbau downscaled its anti-Bolshevik military planning in the first half of 1922, but it continued to envision a sweeping reorganization of Europe and the Soviet Union. The foreign policy views of Aufbau's guiding figure Scheubner-Richter are particularly important since by the fall of 1922, the Baltic German served as Hitler's chief advisor on foreign policy matters and one of his closest counselors in general.[87] A Munich Police report from November 1922 noted that since the primary National Socialist foreign policy advisor represented White émigré interests, he was bound to act according to the desires of his constituency. It was therefore questionable if he could mesh White émigré desires with nationalist German concerns. The report noted that the direction of National Socialist foreign policy through a representative of exile Russian interests gave rise to serious reservations both in Germany and abroad.[88]

French intelligence from November 1922 indicated that Scheubner-Richter and his indispensable Aufbau colleague Biskupskii sought monarchical restoration. First of all, Aufbau policy called for the return of Habsburg rule to Austria. Colonel Bauer, who engaged in political terrorism and acted as Aufbau's contact man in Vienna, in particular worked towards this goal. Aufbau leadership organized combat groups in Austria under the direction of Bavarian officers and strove to include the South Tyrol, which had come under Italian control after World War I, in the planned Austrian state. Aufbau strategy then sought to unite Austria and Hungary under the Habsburg crown. Aufbau also sought to reestablish the Wittelsbach Dynasty in Bavaria as a step towards giving Germany a monarchical state system.

[84] DB report from March 22, 1922, RGVA (TsKhIDK), *fond* 7, *opis* 1, *delo* 954, reel 7, 583.

[85] RKÜöO report from January 17, 1922, RGVA (TsKhIDK), *fond* 772, *opis* 3, *delo* 71, 77.

[86] RKÜöO report to the PDB from January 13, 1922, RGVA (TsKhIDK), *fond* 772, *opis* 3, *delo* 71, 70.

[87] PDM report from November 26, 1922, BSAM, PDM, number 6697, 183; Johannes Baur, *Die russische Kolonie in München, 1900–1945: Deutsch–russische Beziehungen im 20. Jahrhundert* (Wiesbaden: Harrassowitz Verlag, 1998), 268.

[88] PDM report from November 26, 1922, BSAM, PDM, number 6697, 182, 183.

French intelligence further specified that Aufbau foreign policy, which set the tone of National Socialist strategy, sought to detach huge regions from the Soviet Union and to establish friendly governments in the East. Specifically, Aufbau envisioned the creation of Southern (Ukrainian), Baltic, and Siberian states in addition to a rump Russia. The Southern state was to take the form of a Black Sea League under Ukrainian leadership. This new entity would include the Don, Kuban, and Terek Cossack nations. The Black Sea League was to form the most important of the planned successor states to the Soviet Union. The League was to come under the control of Poltavets-Ostranitsa, the head of Aufbau's Ukrainian faction who led what was known in German as the Ukrainische Nationale Kosakenvereinigung (Ukrainian National Cossack Organization). Poltavets-Ostranitsa had already envisioned a Black Sea League during the German occupation of the Ukraine in late World War I.[89]

By late December 1922, when Poltavets-Ostranitsa's superior Scheubner-Richter had already established himself as Hitler's leading foreign policy advisor, Hitler seems to have begun developing his notion of gaining *Lebensraum* (living space) in the East, but only in embryonic form. Hitler's early *Lebensraum* ideas reflected the prevailing Aufbau policies of the time. In a conversation with the journalist Eduard Scharrer towards the end of December 1922, Hitler called for the "vigilant" observation of the Soviet Union. He warned that as soon as the Bolsheviks had solidified their power internally, they could turn against Germany. He called for the "smashing of Russia with the help of England" to gain room for German settlers and to establish a wide field of activity for German industry.[90]

Since its inception in late 1920, Aufbau had emphasized the complementary nature of German industrial production and Russian (or Ukrainian) agricultural supplies and raw materials. Where economic domination develops, settlement follows. Hitler gradually formed his plans to gain *Lebensraum* in the East as a more aggressive outgrowth of fundamental Aufbau Eastern policy. Yet it is important to note that Hitler's *Lebensraum* ideas did not fully take shape until after the failed Hitler/Ludendorff Putsch of November 1923. Hitler did not treat the *Lebensraum* theme in his pre-Putsch speeches.[91]

[89] DB report from November 11, 1922, RGVA (TsKhIDK), *fond* 7, *opis* 1, *delo* 386, reel 2, 161, 163, 164.
[90] Adolf Hitler, notes of a conversation with Eduard Scharrer towards the end of December 1922, *Sämtliche Aufzeichnungen 1905–1924*, eds. Eberhard Jäckel and Axel Kuhn (Stuttgart: Deutsche Verlags-Anstalt, 1980), 773.
[91] Ian Kershaw, *Hitler 1889–1936: Hubris* (London: Penguin Press, 1998), 649.

Hitler only made a powerful case for Germany's need to drive eastwards in Volume II of *Mein Kampf,* which was published in December 1926. He stressed in a famous passage:

And so we National Socialists consciously draw a line beneath the foreign policy tendency of our pre-War period. We take up where we broke off six hundred years ago. We stop the endless German movement to the south and west, and turn out gaze toward the land in the east. At long last we break off the colonial and commercial policy of the pre-War period and shift to the soil policy of the future. If we speak of soil in Europe today, we can primarily have in mind only Russia and her vassal border states.[92]

In the pre-Putsch period, Hitler conspired with White émigrés to overthrow both the Weimar Republic and the Soviet Union, and he tried not to alienate his Eastern allies by openly scheming to conquer their homeland. He only developed aggressive *Lebensraum* ideas after the National Socialist/Aufbau bid for power in Germany and Russia had collapsed in November 1923.

In the spring of 1923, Aufbau leadership in alliance with Hitler increased its preparations to invade the Soviet Union by directing subversive activities within the Great Russian center of the state. Aufbau possessed a significant number of contacts with anti-Bolshevik and pro-Kirill Romanov elements inside the Great Russian core of the Soviet Union.[93] Hitler seems to have favored Aufbau's plan of weakening Bolshevism through internal revolt. In 1921, he had told the National Socialist ideologue and Aufbau member Alfred Rosenberg that those inside a country made revolutions, not those who had been exiled.[94]

In the spring of 1923, Andreas Remmer, who had served as the Foreign Minister of Bermondt-Avalov's Western Volunteer Army during the 1919 Latvian Intervention, increased his activities as an intermediary between Kirill's supporters under Aufbau and nationalist groupings in the Great Russian heartland. After the failure of the Latvian Intervention, Remmer had led an anti-Bolshevik intelligence operation in Berlin that had smuggled White propaganda into the Soviet Union. By the spring of 1923, he had established significant contacts with nationalist organizations inside the Soviet Union composed largely of merchants and Orthodox clergy. Remmer helped to coordinate preparations for a nationalist Russian coup

---

[92] Hitler, *Mein Kampf,* trans. Ralph Mannheim (Boston: Houghton Mifflin, 1943), 654.
[93] Otto von Kursell, "Dr. Ing. Max Erwin von Scheubner-Richter zum Gedächtnis," ed. Henrik Fischer (Munich, 1969), 19, 20.
[94] Ganelin, "Rossiiskoe chernosotenstvo i germanskii natsional-sotsializm," 146.

that Kirill Romanov, Scheubner-Richter, Biskupskii, and, judging by his regular correspondence with Biskupskii, Bermondt-Avalov planned for the beginning of July 1923.[95]

Remmer outlined the planned nationalist Russian state in a May 1923 report that he drafted for Biskupskii and other Aufbau leaders. Remmer stressed that the intended coup in the Soviet heartland would create an "all-Russian national soviet (council) state." This country would encompass a "league of all Christian national soviets" in Russia, which other entities could join if they possessed the "same Christian and governmental goals." This new federation was to be ruled by a "national dictatorship," but local soviets would nonetheless possess considerable autonomy. The Orthodox religion was to serve as the "basis of legislation and morality." An economic recovery was to be brought about "with the help of national forces" that would effect the "expulsion of the foreigners and their exploitative system," referring primarily to Jews.[96]

When questioned by the Munich Police in early June 1923, Remmer stated that if the pro-German Whites succeeded in overthrowing Bolshevism, they would not immediately restore the monarchy, but would instead establish a "Russian national farmers' dictatorship" and only set a Tsar upon the throne a few years later. He stressed that this new Russian state would maintain friendly relations with Germany and reject cooperation with the Entente.[97]

With the waning support for the pro-French Russian throne claimant Grand Prince Nikolai Nikolaevich Romanov among White émigrés during the spring of 1923, Aufbau intensified its preparations to direct an internal revolt inside the Great Russian heartland of the Soviet Union that was to be coupled with an anti-Bolshevik military intervention from abroad. From June 1 to June 15, 1923, the Aufbau leaders Scheubner-Richter and Biskupskii left Munich for Finland, where propaganda and military preparations for a White offensive against the core of the Soviet Union were already well advanced. The Aufbau-coordinated intervention was to use many German officers and troops already placed in Finland, including units from Freikorps Uplands that had fought against Polish invaders in Upper Silesia and which Hitler so admired.

Scheubner-Richter noted on the day of his departure for Finland that, conditions willing, the anti-Bolshevik offensive in harness with a revolt

---

[95] Andreas Remmer's testimony from June 1 and 2, 1923 and Remmer's letter from May 7, 1923, BHSAM, BSMÄ 36, number 103009, 8, 10, 12, 14.

[96] Remmer's letter from May 7, 1923, BHSAM, BSMÄ 36, number 103009, 22, 23.

[97] Remmer's testimony from June 2, 1923, BHSAM, BSMÄ 36, number 103009, 9.

of nationalist Russian circles inside the Soviet Union would begin during the first half of August under the direction of Generals Biskupskii and Piotr Krasnov.[98] Krasnov, the former leader of the pro-German Great Don Host during the Russian Civil War, had frequent dealings with pro-Kirill Aufbau.[99] He managed to skirt White émigré infighting between Aufbau and Nikolai Markov II's pro-Nikolai Nikolaevich Supreme Monarchical Council in that he personally favored neither Kirill nor Nikolai Nikolaevich for Tsar. Instead, he advocated the candidacy of Grand Prince Dmitrii Romanov, who enjoyed little support among White émigrés as a whole.[100]

Scheubner-Richter referred to Aufbau's policy of fomenting anti-Semitic internal revolt in the heartland of the Soviet Union in a June 1923 article in *Aufbau Correspondence*, "Intervention Intentions against Soviet Russia." He wrote of the "rise of the anti-Semitic movement and religious currents in Russia" that supported Kirill Romanov as the legitimate heir to the Tsarist throne. Scheubner-Richter further noted that circles of "national Russians" believed that they themselves could overthrow their "racially foreign tormentors," meaning the Jews.[101]

Despite all its talk of restoring the monarchy to Russia, Aufbau planned a National Socialist Russian state. The French military intelligence agency the Second Section concluded in June 1923 that Aufbau sought to make General Biskupskii the dictator of a Russian federation who would place Kirill or Kirill's son Vladimir, who was more popular, on the throne as a symbolic figurehead. Aufbau's support of the pro-Kirill movement in Russia thus truly aimed at establishing a dictatorship in Russia along National Socialist lines. This National Socialist Russian state would ally itself closely with a National Socialist Germany.[102] The planned German–Russian National Socialist alliance was to direct itself against the fledgling Polish state. General Ludendorff in particular and Aufbau leadership in general wished to attack France's ally Poland to win back areas that Germany had lost to the new state after World War I, most notably parts of Upper Silesia and Posen Province.[103]

The precise timing is unclear, but some time in 1923, the Aufbau Generals Ludendorff and Biskupskii signed a pact regulating relations between the

---

[98] DB report from June 8, 1923, RGVA (TsKhIDK), *fond* 7, *opis* 1, *delo* 386, reel 2, 129.

[99] DB reports from November 11, 1922 and December 6, 1938, RGVA (TsKhIDK), *fond* 7, *opis* 1, *delo* 386, reel 2, 159; *delo* 299, reel 1, 76.

[100] SKöO report to the AA from July 4, 1923, PAAA, 83582, 56 ob.

[101] Scheubner-Richter, "Interventionsabsichten gegen Sowjetrussland," *Aufbau-Korrespondenz*, June 14, 1923, 2.

[102] DB reports from June 6 and 8, 1923, RGVA (TsKhIDK), *fond* 7, *opis* 1, *delo* 386, reel 2, 125, 130.

[103] SKöO report to the AA from August 22, 1923, PAAA, 83582, 96.

planned National Socialist German and Russian states. The agreement specified that after the overthrow of the Bolshevik regime, a Romanov monarchy would be established in Russia in which Biskupskii would *de facto* play the leading role. The new regime would represent a Russian form of National Socialism. The accord also stipulated Austria's *Anschluss* (incorporation) into Germany as well as Poland's partition between Germany and Russia according to the borders of 1914.[104] Aufbau's plans for an alliance between National Socialist German and Russian states, while never fulfilled, largely because of White émigré disunity, nonetheless reached a high degree of specificity.

In addition to planning an offensive against the Great Russian heartland of the Soviet Union in 1923, Aufbau sought to establish an independent National Socialist Ukraine in the course of that year. Hitler showed considerable interest in Aufbau's designs to create an autonomous Ukrainian state. In early 1923, Aufbau under the direction of Scheubner-Richter and Biskupskii intensified its support of Ukrainian independence. Scheubner-Richter and Biskupskii increasingly relied on the advice of Georgii Nemirovich-Danchenko, the former press chief of General Piotr Vrangel's Southern Russian Armed Forces on the Crimean Peninsula during the Russian Civil War. Nemirovich-Danchenko acted as an expert on Ukrainian matters in both Aufbau and Aufbau's subsidiary organization, Renewal, which opposed what it regarded as the Jewish imperialism of Moscow.[105]

A March 1923 article in the National Socialist newspaper the *Völkisch Observer* that dealt with an anti-Bolshevik uprising in the Ukraine demonstrated Aufbau's success in interesting National Socialist leadership in Ukrainian affairs. The article's commentary, which the Aufbau member and National Socialist ideologue Rosenberg most likely wrote, wished that

the desperate struggle of the Ukrainians may end with the defeat and extermination of Russia's executioner. Then Germany could breathe a sigh of relief as well. As long as the plague in Russia holds sway, however, there will never be peace in the German people.[106]

In league with Hitler's National Socialists, Aufbau undermined Soviet authority in the Ukraine by employing agents in the two largest Ukrainian cities, Kiev and Kharkov. In April 1923, Soviet authorities made numerous arrests and confiscated massive amounts of White émigré propaganda

---

[104] Translation of Vladimir Biskupskii's September 7, 1939 comments, APA, BAB, NS 43, number 35, 47, 48.

[105] DB reports from May 15 and 23, 1923, RGVA (TsKhIDK), *fond* 7, *opis* 1, *delo* 954, reel 1, 55; *delo* 876, reel 4, 349.

[106] "Aufstand in der Ukraine," *Völkischer Beobachter*, March 14, 1923, 3.

material, primarily Grand Prince Kirill Romanov's declarations to the "Russian people" and the "Russian army." These texts had been distributed in Kiev and Kharkov with Aufbau's assistance. Aufbau transmitted the information it received regarding Ukrainian matters to the National Socialist Party. For instance, Aufbau informed the NSDAP of the Bolshevik arrest of intellectuals in Kiev and Kharkov because they had propagated anti-Soviet literature.[107]

Further evidence of National Socialist/Aufbau support of Ukrainian independence appeared in the case of Hustevych Bohdan. Bohdan, a Ukrainian, was discovered to possess detailed military sketches in his Munich apartment in May 1923.[108] He was called in for police questioning. He related that he belonged to a secret alliance, the Military Organization of Eastern Galicia. This group fought for a Greater Ukraine consisting of lands currently under Bolshevik, Polish, Romanian, and Czechoslovakian rule.[109] Aufbau in general and Biskupskii in particular supported this pro-Kirill organization since it strove for an independent Ukraine that could serve as a base of operations for offensives against both Poland and the Soviet Union.[110]

Bohdan admitted that he received military instruction from former active German officers.[111] Captain Ernst Röhm in particular had arranged military training for Ukrainian independence fighters such as Bohdan. Röhm is best known as the SA leader who made an unsuccessful grab for power in 1934. In 1923, he was a prominent leader in the Reichsflagge (Imperial Flag), an organization that had joined the Vereinigte vaterländische Verbände Bayerns (United Patriotic Associations of Bavaria) under Hitler's leadership. Röhm had used his position in the Wehrkreiskommando (District Defense Command) to establish a course to train dependable pro-German Ukrainians, including Bohdan. All course participants had fought on the side of the Central Powers during World War I. The class Bohdan presently attended was the second of three that were planned with a total of thirteen participants, all of whom were to leave Germany for the East to foster the establishment of a powerful, independent Ukraine.[112]

[107] DB reports from May 1 and 15, 1923, RGVA (TsKhIDK), *fond* 7, *opis* 1, *delo* 386, reel 1, 4; *delo* 954, reel 1, 55, 56.
[108] FA/AFK report to the BSMI from May 23, 1923, BHSAM, BSMI 22, number 71625, fiche 2, 60.
[109] Hustevych Bohdan's testimony included in an FA/AFK report to the BSMI from May 23, 1923, BHSAM, BSMI 22, number 71625, fiche 2, 63.
[110] SKöO report to the AA from March 20, 1923, PAAA, 83581, 240.
[111] Bohdan's testimony from May 23, 1923, BHSAM, BSMI 22, number 71625, fiche 2, 63.
[112] RKÜöO report to the RWM from May 15, 1923 presented at the 4. SAUV on October 12, 1927, BHSAM, BSMÄ 36, number 103476/1, 41; Nikolai Derezynskii's testimony included in an FA/AFK report to the BSMI from May 23, 1923, BHSAM, BSMI 22, number 71625, fiche 2, 66.

The Munich Police received further information about the secret military courses for Ukrainian nationalists from Friedrich Preitner, one of the officer instructors. Preitner told the Munich Police that the Ukrainian independence movement would serve as Germany's ally in case Poland attacked in East Prussia or in Upper Silesia. The clandestine military lessons in which Bohdan and other Ukrainian nationalists participated took place in the office of the Bund Bayern und Reich (Bavaria and the Empire League). Like the Imperial Flag, this organization had joined the United Patriotic Associations of Bavaria under Hitler's leadership in November 1922. The Bavaria and the Empire League sought to unite "all Christian-*völkisch* thinking men of German blood for the reconstruction of the Fatherland."[113] Preitner noted that he advised the Ukrainian course participants to listen to Hitler speak so that they could learn how an orator seized an audience. This fact further demonstrated National Socialist-nationalist Ukrainian collaboration.[114]

As another indication of National Socialist interest in Aufbau's efforts to detach the Ukraine from Soviet control, Hitler strongly supported Colonel Poltavets-Ostranitsa's Ukrainian National Cossack Organization as of spring 1923. Hitler viewed Poltavets-Ostranitsa's association as a national independence movement along the lines of his own National Socialist Party. Both groupings opposed Bolshevism, sought to weaken Polish power, worked to intensify anti-Semitism, and strove for national revolutions that would lead to dictatorship. Hitler sent directives to Poltavets-Ostranitsa's supporters in the Ukraine via Vienna and Budapest and supplied them with National Socialist propaganda materials.[115]

Poltavets-Ostranitsa hoped that a National Socialist Germany would help to establish an independent Ukraine under his leadership in the historical form of the hetman state.[116] He even developed his Ukrainian National Cossack Organization along National Socialist lines. The official periodical of his organization, the newspaper translated into German as *Der Ukrainische Kosak* (*The Ukrainian Cossack*), glorified German National Socialism and used the swastika as its symbol.[117] Poltavets-Ostranitsa's newspaper released an article, "Our View," in March 1923 that asserted: "The time of a productive National Socialist revolution that will seize

---

[113] PDM report to the BSMI from November 14, 1922, BHSAM, BSMI 22, number 73685, fiche 1, 5.

[114] Friedrich Preitner's testimony included in an FA/AFK report to the BSMI from May 24, 1923, BHSAM, BSMI 22, number 71625, fiche 2, 68, 69.

[115] DB reports from March 21 and May 15, 1923, RGVA (TsKhIDK), *fond* 7, *opis* 1, *delo* 953, reel 1, 53; *delo* 954, reel 1, 55, 56.

[116] Letter from Kursell to the APA from April 21, 1934, RGVA (TsKhIDK), *fond* 519, *opis* 3, *delo* 11b, 31.

[117] DB report from May 15, 1923, RGVA (TsKhIDK), *fond* 7, *opis* 1, *delo* 954, reel 1, 56.

all countries . . . has drawn near."[118] Poltavets-Ostranitsa thus regarded National Socialism as the wave of the future.

An April 1923 edition of the *Völkisch Observer* printed "Our View" from Poltavets-Ostranitsa's newspaper, *The Ukrainian Cossack*. Commentary on the piece from Rosenberg, the *de facto* editor-in-chief of the National Socialist paper in place of the ailing Dietrich Eckart, noted: "This essay shows us that the National Socialist idea . . . hovers over the world like an aura." Further, "We already know today that the democrat is dead, the Marxist is decayed, and the Bolshevik goes over the land in convulsions, but the future in Europe belongs to the National Socialist idea."[119] Somewhat later, Scheubner-Richter ran the essay "Our View" in *Aufbau Correspondence* with favorable commentary under the title, "The Ukraine and National Socialism."[120] Poltavets-Ostranitsa's National Socialist views found great favor in the early German National Socialist Party and Aufbau.

In an article in an August 1923 edition of the *Völkisch Observer*, "The Ukraine and Russia," Rosenberg, presumably, on behalf of the "editorial staff," drew attention to Poltavets-Ostranitsa's newspaper *The Ukrainian Cossack*. The essay argued: "We believe that Great Russians and Ukrainians will finally decide for a more federal arrangement of their empire after the smashing of Jewish-Bolshevik Moscow." The piece emphasized that the Ukraine, where "patriots" were struggling against a "centralized dictatorship," occupied a similar position to Bavaria, where rightists were opposing the "November Republic."[121] In addition to supporting Poltavets-Ostranitsa's campaign to create a National Socialist Ukraine, by drawing parallels between the Ukraine and Bavaria, this essay hinted that the NSDAP was drawing up plans to destroy "centralized dictatorship," meaning the Weimar Republic. As we shall see, Aufbau supported Hitler and General Ludendorff in their bid to overthrow the Weimar Republic.

CONCLUSION

In the years 1921–1923, Aufbau engaged in political terrorism in Germany and sought to overthrow the Soviet Union through both subversion and military force. Aufbau's Vice President General Vladimir Biskupskii used some of the funds at his disposal to support terrorist activities. The Aufbau comrades Piotr Shabelskii-Bork and Sergei Taboritskii attempted to murder

---

[118] "Ukraine und Nationalsozialismus," *Aufbau-Korrespondenz*, May 17, 1923, 4.
[119] Alfred Rosenberg, "Nationalsozialismus im Weltkampf," *Völkischer Beobachter*, April 7, 1923, 3.
[120] "Ukraine und Nationalsozialismus," May 17, 1923, 4.
[121] "Die Ukraine und Russland," *Völkischer Beobachter*, August 29, 1923, 3.

the Russian Constitutional Democratic leader Pavel Miliukov, but they accidentally killed Miliukov's associate Vladimir Nabokov instead. The Aufbau members Biskupskii, General Erich von Ludendorff, and Colonel Karl Bauer, at the least, colluded with Organization C under the important Kapp Putsch figure Captain Hermann Ehrhardt in the assassination of the German Foreign Minister, Walther Rathenau. Aufbau's *de facto* leader Max von Scheubner-Richter seems to have had advance warning of this crime.

In their anti-Bolshevik military schemes, Aufbau leaders initially planned armed offensives in the Ukraine and the Baltic region along the lines of earlier German/White interventions there. Scheubner-Richter and Biskupskii originally planned for an army under Archduke Vasily Vyshivannyi to march into the Ukraine while the Latvian Intervention leader Colonel Pavel Bermondt-Avalov led an expeditionary force into the Baltic region. Later on, Aufbau tried to direct the creation of an autonomous National Socialist Ukraine under the Cossack leader Ivan Poltavets-Ostranitsa. Finally, Aufbau planned a military strike against the Great Russian heartland of the Soviet Union after the outbreak of revolt there. Biskupskii was to wield *de facto* power over a rump Russian state that would be organized along National Socialist lines. Hitler supported Aufbau's Eastern policies, as Scheubner-Richter acted as his leading foreign policy advisor. Hitler particularly approved of Aufbau's designs to create an autonomous National Socialist Ukraine. He had not yet developed his conception that the German people needed *Lebensraum* in the East.

In its campaign to assert its supremacy in right-wing German/White émigré affairs through the means of political terrorism and anti-Bolshevik military plots, Aufbau increasingly allied itself with and influenced Hitler's rising National Socialist movement. By the fall of 1922, the fortunes of the National Socialist Party and Aufbau had become inextricably intertwined. The two anti-Entente, anti-Weimar Republic, anti-Bolshevik, and anti-Semitic entities were linked most strongly through the Baltic German Scheubner-Richter, Aufbau's driving force and one of Hitler's most trusted counselors. The National Socialist Party and Aufbau had developed into close conspiratorial allies. As we shall see, as of late 1922, the NSDAP and Aufbau were poised for a joint drive to overthrow the Weimar Republic and to place Hitler and General Ludendorff in charge of Germany through the use of paramilitary force.

CHAPTER 7

"In Quick March to the Abyss!"

Late 1922 through November 1923 witnessed both the acme and the almost total collapse of the collaboration between Hitler's National Socialist Party and Aufbau to topple the Weimar Republic. In his newspaper *Aufbau-Korrespondenz (Aufbau Correspondence)*, Aufbau's leading figure and the prominent National Socialist policy maker First Lieutenant Max von Scheubner-Richter stressed: "Today Bavaria's historical mission consists of safeguarding German unity in the face of the international solidarity of the Soviets and the stock exchange people." If Bavaria failed to fulfill its calling, "then Germany's downfall and with it Bavaria's is sealed."[1] Scheubner-Richter titled his essay "In Quick March to the Abyss!" thereby indicating his belief that the Bavarian-based National Socialist/White émigré radical right invited disaster by not forcefully resisting both Bolshevism and the Weimar Republic.

Scheubner-Richter's aggressive political views deserve particular attention since he acted as the closest advisor of both Adolf Hitler and General Erich von Ludendorff, who led anti-Weimar Republic paramilitary groupings in Bavaria that grew increasingly powerful under the stimulus of the French/Belgian occupation of the Ruhr Basin beginning in early 1923. Scheubner-Richter despised Bolshevism, and he spent much of his energies combating its spread. He nonetheless appreciated some of its aspects. In particular, he admired what he regarded as the Bolshevik lesson that a few determined men could shape world history, and he stressed that the National Socialist movement should adopt the Bolshevik tactics of subversion followed by strict centralization and militarization to defeat its political enemies.

Inspired by the Bolshevik model, Scheubner-Richter advocated using paramilitary forces based in Bavaria under himself, Hitler, and Ludendorff

---

[1] Max von Scheubner-Richter, "Im Eilmarsch zum Abgrund!" *Wirtschafts-politische Aufbau-Korrespondenz über Ostfragen und ihre Bedeutung für Deutschland*, July 26, 1922, 3.

to overthrow the Weimar Republic. To a significant degree, he planned a repeat of the March 1920 Kapp Putsch in which he, Hitler, and Ludendorff had participated, with similar White émigré support, only this time from the south. Scheubner-Richter's combative policy of seeking to topple the Weimar Republic by force, in addition to costing him his life in the November 1923 Hitler/Ludendorff Putsch, helped to cause the near-collapse of the National Socialist movement, the termination of Aufbau as a significant political force, and the nadir of *völkisch* German–White émigré collaboration.

THE MILITANT RADICAL RIGHT'S CRYSTALLIZATION
IN BAVARIA

Aufbau's guiding figure Scheubner-Richter served as the pivotal contact man for the Bavarian radical right in the period leading up to the Hitler/Ludendorff Putsch. He officially began serving as the chief advisor of the *völkisch* leader and Aufbau member General Ludendorff in August 1922. In the fall of 1922, Scheubner-Richter acted as the primary liaison man between Hitler and Ludendorff. He coordinated their activities and brought the two far rightists ever closer politically.[2] Scheubner-Richter met with Hitler, Ludendorff, and Walther Nicolai, the head of the pro-Kirill Romanov intelligence service code named Project S, towards the end of October 1922. The four conspirators agreed that Hitler should lead an alliance of radical right paramilitary forces, the Vereinigte vaterländische Verbände (United Patriotic Associations of Bavaria). At this meeting, Hitler argued convincingly in favor of a legal rise to power. Nicolai agreed with Hitler's position, and, for the time being, the four plotters adopted this plan of action.[3]

The seizure of power of Benito Mussolini's Fascists in Italy in late October 1922 inspired Scheubner-Richter and his allies Hitler and Ludendorff to undertake increasingly aggressive measures in Germany. Scheubner-Richter's article in the November 1, 1922 edition of *Aufbau Correspondence*, "The Fascists as Masters in Italy," indicated the spur that Mussolini's March on Rome had given to radical rightists centered in Bavaria. Scheubner-Richter stressed that Communism could only be defeated through its own

[2] Bruno Thoss, *Der Ludendorff-Kreis 1919–1923: München als Zentrum der mitteleuropäischen Gegenrevolution zwischen Revolution und Hitler-Putsch* (Munich: Stadtarchiv München, 1978), 237, 323, 324, 451.
[3] Walther Nicolai's commentary on his letter to Erich von Ludendorff from October 26, 1922, *Tagebuch* (Diary), RGVA (TsKhIDK), *fond* 1414, *opis* 1, *delo* 20, 422, 423.

violent methods. He noted: "That which the German Freikorps did half-heartedly was done passionately in Italy." He praised Mussolini for demonstrating that "bold personalities" could master a "scourge" that held the world in fear. While he asserted that pan-Germans could see "no friend" in Fascism since difficult days lay ahead for the ethnic Germans of the South Tyrol under Italian rule, he hoped that the "principle that the Fascists represent" would become "universal and self-evident in Germany."[4]

Bolstered by Fascism's spectacular rise in Italy, the United Patriotic Associations of Bavaria under Hitler's leadership made their first official appearance on November 9, 1922, the three-year anniversary of the November Revolution that had toppled the German Empire.[5] Among the nineteen organizations that belonged to the far right alliance were the National Socialist Party, the Bavarian branch of *völkisch* leader Heinrich Class' Alldeutscher Verband (Pan-German League), and the Bavarian section of the allied Deutschvölkischer Schutz- und Trutzbund (German *Völkisch* Protection League).[6] General Ludendorff called for the United Patriotic Associations of Bavaria to adopt an audacious national revolutionary offensive. He openly promoted the most dynamic segment of the *völkisch* movement, Hitler's National Socialists. He assisted the NSDAP with his extensive knowledge of organizational and propaganda tactics.[7] As of the autumn of 1922, the radical right centered in Bavaria had coalesced into a dangerous opponent of the Weimar Republic.

The early Weimar Republic, which was never entirely stable at the best of times, received an extreme shock in early January 1923 that aided far rightists. French and Belgian authorities, claiming that the German government had reneged on its obligations under the Treaty of Versailles, sent in troops to occupy Germany's leading industrial region, the Ruhr Basin. The French-Belgian advance into the Ruhr Basin worsened the already ruinous inflation that plagued the Weimar Republic, and it spurred the increasingly vigorous activities of the radical right centered in the National Socialist/Aufbau nexus of Bavaria. In the middle of January 1923, the United Patriotic Associations of Bavaria under Hitler and the Aufbau members Ludendorff and Scheubner-Richter held a mass protest rally against the French/Belgian occupation of the Ruhr Basin.[8]

---

[4] Scheubner-Richter, "Die Faszisten als Herren in Italien," *Aufbau-Korrespondenz*, November 1, 1922, 2.

[5] "Vaterländische Feier," *Völkischer Beobachter*, November 8, 1922, 4.

[6] PDM report to the BSMI from November 14, 1922, BHSAM, BSMI 22, number 73685, fiche 1, 4, 5, 8.

[7] RKÜöO report to the BSMÄ from January 31, 1924, BHSAM, BSMÄ 36, number 103456, 7.

[8] PDM report to the BSMI from January 22, 1923, BHSAM, BSMI 25, number 81592, 10.

Around this time, the Aufbau leaders Scheubner-Richter and General Vladimir Biskupskii urged White émigrés in Germany to repay the Germans for their hospitality by helping them against foreign enemies. Aufbau called on all able-bodied White émigrés either to assist German paramilitary units opposing French and Belgian troops in the Ruhr Basin, or to participate in anti-Bolshevik and anti-Polish operations in the East along the lines undertaken by Biskupskii's close colleague General Piotr Glasenap. Glasenap, who coordinated his activities with Aufbau and presumably belonged to the secretive organization, formed White émigré combat units in East Prussia that he pledged to use to aid rightist Germans in their disputes with the Poles, who were allied with the hated French.[9]

Glasenap soon furthered right-wing German and White émigré interests in Hungary. He transferred his activities to the Danubian state in the course of February 1923. He collaborated with Prince Mikhail Volkonskii, an Aufbau ally and Kirill-supporter who headed the Provisional Senate of White émigrés in Hungary, to lead a military academy in Budapest.[10] Glasenap prepared an armed White émigré formation in Hungary that was to collaborate with German paramilitary forces against foes in both the West and the East.[11] Aufbau's earlier attention to right-wing Hungarian affairs, which had been most recently manifested in Scheubner-Richter's talks with the *de facto* Hungarian dictator Admiral Nicholas Horthy at the beginning of 1923, had paved the way for ever closer military collaboration between Aufbau and Hungarian rightists and White émigrés in Hungary.[12]

SCHEUBNER-RICHTER'S LESSONS FROM BOLSHEVISM

As the year 1923 progressed, Hitler developed an ever-closer political and personal relationship with Aufbau's guiding figure, Scheubner-Richter, who acted as the leading contact man in the radical right German/White émigré milieu in Bavaria. The pro-Kirill, anti-Bolshevik intelligence leader Nicolai noted the extensive degree to which Scheubner-Richter influenced Hitler's political ideas. Nicolai valued Scheubner-Richter highly as a clever and politically talented man, but he nevertheless believed that the Baltic German

[9] Aleksandr von Lampe, *Dnevnik* (Diary), Berlin, February 11–14, March 5– 6, November 21, 1923, GARF, *fond* 5853, *opis* 1, *delo* 10, reel 1, 4102; reel 2, 4120; *delo* 13, reel 2, 5861.

[10] DB report from April 9, 1923, RGVA (TsKhIDK), *fond* 7, *opis* 1, *delo* 386, reel 4, 334.

[11] Lampe, *Dnevnik* (Diary), Berlin, March 5–6, 1923, GARF, *fond* 5853, *opis* 1, *delo* 10, reel 2, 4120.

[12] PDM report to the BSMÄ from December 12, 1923, BHSAM, BSMA 36, number 103472, 50.

lacked the necessary grasp of German conditions because of his formative experiences in Imperial Russia.[13]

In addition to relying on Scheubner-Richter for political counsel, Hitler enjoyed a close personal connection with him and his wife Mathilde. Despite the fact that Mathilde was almost thirty years older than Scheubner-Richter, the couple had a happy marriage. Hitler had his home away from home at Scheubner-Richter's house, and he honored Mathilde like his mother (his own mother was long since dead). She, for her part, adored him. Mathilde had been unable to bear children because of a venereal disease contracted in her first marriage, and she seems to have regarded Hitler as a replacement son.[14]

Although Hitler's close advisor Scheubner-Richter despised Bolshevism, he nonetheless learned from it. In the pages of his newspaper *Aufbau Correspondence*, he argued both that the Weimar Republic had borrowed strict centralizing practices from the Soviet Union, and that National Socialism itself should emulate intense Bolshevik centralization. He addressed the first point in a July 1922 article, "Looks Back and Parallels." He noted similarities between recent German and Russian history, and he warned the German people of the "abyss" that it was in danger of falling into. He asserted that at the German Constitutional Convention in Weimar and Berlin in 1919, the primary goal had been to replace the "creation of the German Bismarck" with that of "the Jew Preuss." The new Constitution authored by Hugo Preuss stressed "centralism and uniformity." This formulation had arisen "consciously with some, unconsciously with the majority, according to Moscow recipe."

In his essay, Scheubner-Richter further argued that primarily Jewish Bolshevik leaders had learned from the Russian Civil War: "Only in a centrally governed state can a small, racially foreign minority rule and violate large national majorities in the long term." He charged the "fathers of the Weimar Constitution" with holding "trains of thought" close to Soviet leaders:

The centralist spirit of the Weimar Constitution, which eliminated the national independent existence of the German tribes and made everything dependent upon Berlin, was the un-German product of Moscow governmental wisdom and was supposed to make Germany ready for the instillation of a Soviet dictatorship.

[13] Nicolai's commentary on Ludendorff's letter to him from March 20, 1923, *Tagebuch* (Diary), RGVA (TsKhIDK), *fond* 1414, *opis* 1, *delo* 22, 26.

[14] Nicolai's commentary on Ludendorff's letter to him from March 20, 1923, *Tagebuch* (Diary), RGVA (TsKhIDK), *fond* 1414, *opis* 1, *delo* 22, 26; Julia Hass (Otto von Kursell's daughter), personal interview, January 21, 2003.

Scheubner-Richter further asserted, "The democratic-socialist majority in the German Parliament" of the Weimar Republic was currently striving "to break the resistance of national circles and to destroy the individuality and self-reliance of the Germans once and for all" so that "a small racially foreign minority can dominate and terrorize large national majorities." He ended his article by appealing: "German people, reflect and learn from the sad experiences of the Russian people! Bavarian people, defend yourself!"[15] Scheubner-Richter portrayed the intense centralization of the Soviet Union that the Weimar Republic had allegedly imitated as a threat to *völkisch* Germany's existence.

On the other hand, Scheubner-Richter viewed ruthless centralization as a positive factor when carried out by the "right" people. Despite his opposition to "Jewish Bolshevism," he admired the strict centralization and militarization of the Soviet Union as directed by the (Jewish) Soviet Commissar for War Lev Trotskii. In a January 1922 article in *Aufbau Correspondence*, "What We Can Learn from Our Enemies!", Scheubner-Richter stressed: "God grant us a national German dictator with the energy of a Trotskii!"[16] In another provocative article in a March 1923 edition of *Aufbau Correspondence*, "The Red Army: What We Can Learn From Soviet Russia!", Scheubner-Richter praised some of Trotskii's recent observations. Scheubner-Richter argued that National Socialism could only defeat Bolshevism by applying the latter's own methods of subversion followed by ruthless centralization and repression.[17] His essay was published along with some editing changes, mostly cuts, in installments in the *Völkischer Beobachter* (*Völkisch Observer*) from March 21–23, 1923 under the more subtle title, "The Red Army."

In his essay, Scheubner-Richter treated Trotskii's "very instructional" description of the "subversion of an army that is not in the hands of the International, and the glorification of the same [old-style] military principles when they serve the purposes of the International." He asserted: "The expositions of Lev Trotskii are consistent, clear, and expedient."[18] Scheubner-Richter intended his article to serve as a lesson on how, as he worded it in a passage in the original *Aufbau Correspondence* article that did not appear in the *Völkisch Observer*, "One should learn from one's enemies."[19]

---

[15] Scheubner-Richter, "Rückblicke und Parallelen," *Aufbau-Korrespondenz*, July 19, 1922, 2–4.
[16] Scheubner-Richter, "Was wir von unseren Feinden lernen können!", *Aufbau-Korrespondenz*, January 14, 1922, 1.
[17] Scheubner-Richter, "Die Rote Armee: Was wir von Sowjetrussland lernen können!", *Aufbau-Korrespondenz*, March 22, 1923, 1–3.
[18] Scheubner-Richter, "Die Rote Armee," *Völkischer Beobachter*, March 21, 1923, 3; March 22, 1923, 2.
[19] Scheubner-Richter, "Die Rote Armee," *Aufbau-Korrespondenz*, March 22, 1923, 3.

Regarding Trotskii's treatment of army propaganda, Scheubner-Richter asserted: "We cannot recommend it urgently enough for the attention of our leading political and military authorities." He stressed the "open secret" that Bolshevik propaganda operated with "non-material slogans" and had succeeded in granting Bolshevism the guise of a "spiritual movement." He noted that unlike troops of the Red Army, German soldiers lacked a clear "unifying idea." He stressed, "An army without ideals is not a fighting force and is not resistant to subversive propaganda." Scheubner-Richter here primarily referred to the catastrophic outcome of World War I for nationalist German and Russian concerns, but then he drew lessons for the future.

At the end of his essay, Scheubner-Richter asked, "What, then, are the practical applications that we must draw from the remarks of Trotskii . . . which are most educational for every German politician and officer?" He listed five principles before offering his own conclusion:

1. Communism first undermines the armies and military institutions of national states through its propaganda to create its own armies from their ruins in accordance with precisely the same military principles. 2. Communism, in contrast to likewise revolutionary Social Democracy and democracy, clearly recognizes that military might constitutes the basis of each state, just as political goals can only be achieved and maintained through the ruthless application of military instruments of power. 3. The economy or civic welfare does not constitute the main thing. If necessary, one can manage without industry and commerce if one has a military power apparatus at one's disposal. 4. Superior leadership qualities cannot be learned in military crash courses, rather these call for tradition and training; that is why it is not possible to create even a proletarian army without giving it the necessary military backbone through an old officer and non-commissioned officer corps. 5. World history is made not through parliaments and majority decisions, but through the energy of a few men who know how to evaluate the realities of life. At a time when Germany in its most difficult hour is being ruled by parliamentary buffoons, pacifistic idiots, and democratic ideologues, it is direly necessary that the few men whose sense has not yet been clouded over by newspaper twaddle and phrase-mongering learn from Russia's example what is necessary for us and how one must act. If they do not do this, then the time must not be far when French chauvinism marching from the West and Russian military Bolshevism marching from the East meet in the heart of Germany and come to an agreement about the division of the spoils.[20]

Scheubner-Richter's reasoning supports the German historian Ernst Nolte's idea that Bolshevism represented "both nightmare and example for

---

[20] Scheubner-Richter, "Die Rote Armee," *Völkischer Beobachter*, March 23, 1923, 3.

National Socialism."[21] Scheubner-Richter's essay demonstrated that the early National Socialist movement borrowed from Bolshevism in stressing the importance of the determination of a few men to carry out subversion followed by ruthless centralization and militarization to achieve political ends. In effect, Scheubner-Richter wished to play Trotskii to Hitler's Lenin. At the time that he wrote his article, Scheubner-Richter was undermining Bolshevik rule by disseminating nationalist, anti-Semitic propaganda among the Red Army and in broad segments of the Soviet population. Some months after the publication of his essay, he marched at the head of strictly organized and highly indoctrinated radical rightists along with Hitler and General Ludendorff. Scheubner-Richter co-led an idealistic putsch against the Weimar Republic that, as it overemphasized the power of a few determined men, failed utterly.

THE HITLER/LUDENDORFF (SCHEUBNER-RICHTER) PUTSCH

As Hitler grew closer to Scheubner-Richter in the course of 1923, his policies became increasingly aggressive. Hitler, Ludendorff, and Scheubner-Richter, the leaders of the United Patriotic Associations of Bavaria, decided to demonstrate their strength in early April 1923. They organized large-scale military exercises in Munich in which approximately 6,000 men participated.[22] The United Patriotic Associations of Bavaria increasingly displayed their paramilitary formations, including the NSDAP Sturmabteilung (Storm Section, SA), the Reichsflagge (Imperial Flag), and the Bund Oberland (Uplands League), a successor to Freikorps Uplands, which had joined the Associations in February.[23] The Munich Police estimated the membership of these three paramilitary groups in Munich at between 1,000 and 1,500 for the SA, 150 to 200 for the Imperial Flag, and 680 to 1,000 for the Uplands League.[24]

In keeping with aggressive far right policies, the paramilitary contingent of the United Patriotic Associations of Bavaria, known as the Vaterländische Kampfverbände (Patriotic Combat Associations), held a massive demonstration on May 1, 1923 under the slogan: "Defense against a leftist putsch."[25] In so doing, the Patriotic Combat Associations demonstrated their adherence

---

[21] Ernst Nolte, *Der europäische Bürgerkrieg 1917–1945: Nationalsozialismus und Bolschewismus* (Frankfurt am Main: Propyläen Verlag, 1987), 21,22.

[22] PDM report to the BSMI from April 11, 1923, BSAM, PDM, number 6707, 16.

[23] PDM report from April 28, 1923, BSAM, PDM, number 6697, 288; RKÜöO report from June 21, 1923, BAB, 1507, number 344, 8.

[24] PDM report from January 15, 1923, BSAM, PDM, number 6697, 405, 406.

[25] PDM report to the BSMI from May 3, 1923, BHSAM, BSMI 25, number 81594, 6.

to the increasingly confrontational policies of Hitler, Ludendorff, and their advisors Scheubner-Richter and General Biskupskii of Aufbau.[26] Early in the morning of May 1, approximately 3,000 men gathered under Hitler's supervision with arms acquired from Army barracks. They threatened to foil the state-approved Communist gathering in the center of Munich by force if necessary.[27]

While Hitler stressed in a fiery speech around this time that he sought a Germany united not "under the Soviet star, the Star of David of the Jews, but under . . . the swastika," he and his militant followers ironically ended up aiding the Communist cause.[28] By occupying most of Munich's security forces on May 1, 1923, they allowed Communist leaders to seize the initiative by holding their march in an aggressive manner with banners flying though they had been specifically forbidden to do so. After an uncomfortable standoff with Munich security forces, Hitler's supporters finally laid down their weapons in return for permission to march into the city center with music blaring.[29]

Scheubner-Richter asserted in the pages of his *Aufbau Correspondence* soon after the tumultuous events of May 1 that the Bavarian government had "put Bavaria's reputation as a national state at stake."[30] Whatever damage the Bavarian government may have caused its reputation, it is clear that the National Socialist movement and Aufbau, both of which Scheubner-Richter represented, had attracted the fury of the previously sympathetic Bavarian government, the Munich Police, and the Army through their insubordination.

Theodor Endres, the chief of staff of Wehrkreiskommando VII (District Defense Command VII), later asserted, "We officers all had 'rightist' leanings" before May 1, 1923 and had supported the militant policies of Hitler, Ludendorff, and Scheubner-Richter. Entire Army companies had joined the National Socialist SA and had proudly participated in Hitler's punitive expeditions, such as the one to Coburg. As we have seen, Army soldiers had also stored the arms of the SA and other rightist paramilitary units in Army barracks. Nonetheless, the insubordination of May 1 "brought a decisive turn in the conduct of the rightist Bavarian government towards the right-wing Associations." Endres asserted: "The

[26] RKÜöO report to the BSMÄ from January 31, 1924, BHSAM, BSMÄ 36, number 103456, 7; Lampe, *Dnevnik* (Diary), Berlin, April 16–20, 1923, GARF, *fond* 5853, *opis* 1, *delo* 11, reel 1, 4698.

[27] Theodor Endres, "Aufzeichnungen über den Hitlerputsch 1923," 1945, BHSAM/AK, *Handschriftensammlung*, number 925, 20.

[28] "Deutsche Maifeier," *Völkischer Beobachter*, May 3, 1923, 2.

[29] Endres, "Aufzeichnungen über den Hitlerputsch," BHSAM/AK, *Handschriftensammlung*, number 925, 22, 23.

[30] Scheubner-Richter, "Bittere Betrachtungen," *Aufbau-Korrespondenz*, April 19, 1923, 2.

day had opened the eyes of the government and clearly shown it where the path of toleration and compromise with the National Socialists led."[31]

Bavarian authorities regarded the events of the next day, May 2, 1923, with distrust as the NSDAP and other right-wing organizations in Bavaria formed the Kampfgemeinschaft nationaler Verbände (Action Group of National Associations). The Action Group came under the overall leadership of Hitler and Ludendorff.[32] Scheubner-Richter served as secretary.[33] Associations that joined the Action Group included the Vereinigung deutscher Grenzmärker (Union of Frontier Area Germans) under the 1919 Latvian Intervention veteran First Lieutenant Gerhard Rossbach, the Wikingbund (Viking League), a successor organization to the conspiratorial Organization C under the 1920 Kapp Putsch participant Captain Hermann Ehrhardt, the German *Völkisch* Protection League, and the Uplands League.[34]

Hitler, urged on by his close advisor Scheubner-Richter, pursued an increasingly militaristic course of action in May 1923 that drew strength from former Freikorps members of Colonel Pavel Bermondt-Avalov's Western Volunteer Army in the Latvian Intervention. Hitler created a new NSDAP Sturmabteilung Hundertschaft (Storm Section Hundred), the Arbeitsgemeinschaft Rossbach- und die Baltikumkämpfer (Rossbach and the Baltic Fighters Association). This formation was named after Rossbach, the prominent former Freikorps leader and ardent National Socialist.[35] The National Socialist movement later adopted the brown shirts of Storm Section Rossbach.[36] Hitler's NSDAP also increased its ties to the Latvian Intervention mastermind General Count Rüdiger von der Goltz.[37] A May 1923 report from the State Commissioner for the Supervision of Public Order grimly noted that the National Socialists and their allies, including many former Freikorps elements, were systematically preparing for a putsch against the Weimar Republic.[38]

[31] Endres, "Aufzeichnungen über den Hitlerputsch," BHSAM/AK, *Handschriftensammlung*, number 925, 3, 4, 10, 22, 23.

[32] RKÜöO reports from May 2 and 23, 1923, BAB, 1507, number 388, 2; number 343, 261.

[33] Johannes Baur, *Die russische Kolonie in München, 1900–1945: Deutsch–russische Beziehungen im 20. Jahrhundert* (Wiesbaden: Harrassowitz Verlag, 1998), 268.

[34] RKÜöO reports from May 23 and October 5, 1923, BAB, 1507, number 343, 261; number 388, 40.

[35] PDM report from June 1, 1923, BSAM, PDM, number 6697, 322.

[36] Karl Dietrich Bracher, *The German Dictatorship: The Origins, Structure, and Effects of National Socialism*, trans. Jean Steinberg (New York: Holt, Rinehart and Winston, 1970), 87.

[37] RKÜöO report from November 18, 1923, BAB, 134, number 78, 14.

[38] RKÜöO report from May 15, 1923 presented at 4. SAUV report on October 12, 1927, BHSAM, BSMÄ 36, number 103476/1, 41.

Hitler and his collaborators possessed a large war chest for their putsch preparations. Aufbau enjoyed a favorable financial situation.[39] General Ludendorff in particular had access to considerable funds. Although Ludendorff claimed in his memoirs that money had been sorely lacking among White émigrés in Germany, the intelligence leader Nicolai stressed in his diary that the general had only possessed substantial funding for his operations during his period of activity in Aufbau.[40] In May 1922, General Biskupskii and his White émigré personal secretary, the enthusiastic National Socialist Arno Schickedanz, had made an arrangement with Ludendorff whereby the latter was to use funds from the Russian throne claimants Kirill and Viktoria Romanov to further the "German–Russian national cause" in the framework of Aufbau. Ludendorff had pledged to return the money as soon as he was able to, presumably when he held a position of authority in Germany after helping to overthrow the Weimar Republic.

Beginning in May 1922 and continuing through 1923, Kirill and Viktoria channeled approximately 500,000 gold marks to Ludendorff to support nationalist German–Russian undertakings.[41] Since this amount of money exceeded the discretionary means of Kirill and Viktoria, wealthy as they were, substantial funding had to have come from outside sources. Most importantly, the right wing, anti-Semitic American industrialist and politician Henry Ford gave considerable sums of money to Kirill's representative in America, the Aufbau member Boris Brazol. Brazol then transferred funds to Kirill and Viktoria for use in financing far right organizations in Germany, notably the National Socialist Party and Aufbau.[42] Hitler praised Ford in *Mein Kampf* as "a single great man" who "still maintains full independence," much to the "fury" of the "Jews who govern the stock exchange forces of the American Union."[43]

The Aufbau leaders Scheubner-Richter and Biskupskii also played key fund-raising roles for Hitler's NSDAP. Scheubner-Richter ostentatiously displayed his wealth by driving an expensive Benz automobile.[44] He was a

[39] DB report from July 3, 1923, RGVA (TsKhIDK), *fond* 7, *opis* 1, *delo* 876, reel 4, 368.

[40] Ludendorff, *Meine Lebenserinnerungen*, 204, cited from Baur, "Russische Emigranten und die bayerische Öffentlichkeit," *Bayern und Osteuropa: Aus der Geschichte der Beziehungen Bayerns, Frankens und Schwabens mit Russland, der Ukraine, und Weissrussland*, ed. Hermann Beyer-Thoma (Wiesbaden: Harrassowitz Verlag, 2000), 472; Nicolai's commentary on his letter to Ludendorff from February 18, 1922, *Tagebuch* (Diary), RGVA (TsKhIDK), *fond* 1414, *opis* 1, *delo* 20, 171.

[41] Letter from Vladimir Biskupskii to Arno Schickedanz from October 21, 1939, APA, BAB, NS 43, number 35, 12, 13.

[42] James and Suzanne Pool, *Hitlers Wegbereiter zur Macht*, trans. Hans Thomas (New York: The Dial Press, 1978), 107.

[43] Adolf Hitler, *Mein Kampf*, trans. Ralph Mannheim (Boston: Houghton Mifflin, 1943), 639.

[44] DB report from July 3, 1923, RGVA (TsKhIDK), *fond* 7, *opis* 1, *delo* 876, reel 4, 370.

rich man through his marriage into the German nobility, and he channeled considerable financial resources to the National Socialist Party from White émigré sources, notably Russian industrialists, especially former oilmen. Moreover, he raised funds for the National Socialist Party from Bavarian aristocrats, businessmen and bankers, and from leading German industrialists such as August Thyssen.[45] General Biskupskii also routed funds from White émigré sources to the NSDAP. In particular, he used the Reichstag (Parliament) member and Aufbau Second Vice President Dr. A. Glaser for this purpose.[46] Hitler benefited a great deal financially from his association with Aufbau.

Hitler received backing from sources other than Aufbau. In the summer of 1923, he obtained increasing support for his anti-Weimar Republic putsch preparations from White émigrés and right-wing Hungarians. French intelligence warned in July 1923 that Bavarian-based White émigrés were preparing for a coup against the German government along the lines of the 1920 Kapp Putsch. In particular, a leader of Ukrainian independence activities in Munich, Konstantin Scheglovitov, who had helped to organize Scheubner-Richter's 1920 mission to General Piotr Vrangel's Southern Russian Armed Forces in the Crimea, was coordinating armed White émigré formations for action against the Weimar Republic.[47]

Other prominent White émigrés backed Hitler's campaign for power. Most likely to help organize a right-wing putsch from the *völkisch* German/White émigré power base in Bavaria, the Latvian Intervention leader Colonel Pavel Bermondt-Avalov, who corresponded regularly with Aufbau Vice President Biskupskii, left Hamburg for Munich in July 1923.[48] Colonel Ivan Poltavets-Ostranitsa, the Ukrainian Cossack leader whom Aufbau intended to rule a National Socialist Ukraine, wrote Hitler in early September 1923. He expressed his confidence that Hitler would soon come to power in Germany, and then the strivings for an independent Ukraine would have excellent chances of success.[49]

Also in the first half of September 1923, Hitler received a pledge of support from the anti-Semitic, nationalist Hungarian movement known in German as *Erwachende Ungarn* (Awakening Hungary). Awakening Hungary conspired with Aufbau, stood in contact with Ludwig Müller von Hausen, the

[45] Pool, *Hitlers Wegbereiter zur Macht*, 53.

[46] 2. SAUV report from October 6, 1927, BHSAM, BSMÄ 36, number 103476/1, 113; DB report from July 3, 1923, RGVA (TsKhIDK), *fond* 7, *opis* 1, *delo* 876, reel 4, 367.

[47] DB report from July 23, 1920, RGVA (TsKhIDK), *fond* 7, *opis* 1, *delo* 1255, reel 2, 209.

[48] Andreas Remmer's testimony from June 1, 1923, BHSAM, BSMÄ 36, number 103009, 12; PBH/AII report to the RKÜöO from July 24, 1922, RGVA (TsKhIDK), *fond* 772, *opis* 3, *delo* 71, 157.

[49] RKÜöO report from August 14, 1925, RGVA (TsKhIDK), *fond* 772, *opis* 1, *delo* 105b, 99.

German publisher of *The Protocols of the Elders of Zion*, and had begun collaborating with the National Socialist Party in 1921.[50] Josef Gaal, an associate of Ulain, the leader of Awakening Hungary, wrote Hitler in early September 1923.[51] Gaal promised Hitler support for any bid for power in Germany that he undertook.

In his letter, Gaal also expressed his hopes of having the honor to greet personally both Hitler and the Aufbau member Colonel Karl Bauer (who was infamous for his involvement in the assassination of the German Foreign Minster Walther Rathenau) in Budapest. Bauer's intermediary role demonstrated that Aufbau served as a liaison between the NSDAP and Awakening Hungary. Gaal assured Hitler that violent action against the postwar European order was impending. He wrote of the present "historical moment, which is so important for the fate of both of our peoples."[52] The radical right in Bavaria and Hungary was gearing up to challenge the existing European order.

Bolstered by increasing support from White émigrés and right-wing Hungarians, Hitler, Ludendorff, and Scheubner-Richter intensified their preparations to overthrow the Weimar Republic in the course of September 1923. On September 17, the National Socialist SA, the Uplands League, and the Imperial Flag formed the Kampfgemeinschaft Bayern (Action Group Bavaria), commonly known as the Kampfbund (Combat League).[53] Friedrich Weber, the leader of the Uplands League in Munich, stressed that all Combat League members subordinated themselves to the "political leadership of Herr Adolf Hitler . . . in complete agreement with the method and goal" that he had set forward.[54] Ludendorff influenced the affairs of the Combat League primarily in an unofficial capacity. Scheubner-Richter served as Hitler's plenipotentiary in the Combat League, once again demonstrating considerable Aufbau influence over National Socialist policies.[55]

In another example of his admiration of Bolshevik tactics, as opposed to Bolshevism as a system, Scheubner-Richter had earlier warned in the pages of the National Socialist newspaper the *Völkisch Observer* that the

[50] Letter from the organizers of the "First World Congress for the Protection of the Christian Nations" to Ludwig Müller von Hausen from April 26, 1921, RGVA (TsKhIDK), *fond* 577, *opis* 2, *delo* 10, 7; PDM report to the BSMÄ from December 12, 1923, BHSAM, BSMÄ 36, number 103472, 50.

[51] BSMI report to the BSMÄ from March 22, 1924, BHSAM, BSMÄ 36, number 103472, 47.

[52] Letter from Josef Gaal to NSDAP Headquarters from September 8, 1923 included in a PDM report to the BSMÄ from December 12, 1923, BHSAM, BSMÄ 36, number 103472, 51.

[53] Letter from Weiss to Hitler from September 17, 1923, IZG, Fa 88, 30; PDM report from September 18, 1923, BSAM, PDM, number 6697, 439.

[54] Friedrich Weber, "An die Herren Landes- und Kreisleiter!", September 26, 1923, included in a RKÜöO report from November 9, 1923, BAB, 1507, number 343, 314.

[55] PDM report from September 18, 1923, BSAM, PDM, number 6697, 439.

"supporters of the independent German Freikorps spirit" and the "political advocates of federal ideas" in Germany would be "swept away by the strict, centrally united Red Armies" if they did not learn "to submit to a unified leadership."[56] He thus had reason to be pleased with the unification of right-wing forces in the Combat League under himself, Hitler, and Ludendorff.

Scheubner-Richter stressed the confrontational goals of the Combat League in an article in the September 21, 1923 edition of the *Völkisch Observer*, "Germany's Bolshevization." He emphasized that Hitler had arisen as a "prophet" of the "German people" who knew how "to jolt the German soul awake and to free it from the chains of Marxist thinking." He argued that the new *"völkisch* Germany" had recognized that its greatest enemy lay in internal dissension, and it had therefore created the Combat League. All those who wished a "free Germany" should join this alliance. He stressed that the Combat League had embarked on an all-out endeavor: "And the struggle will be fought under the motto, 'On the one side the Soviet star, on the other side the swastika.' And the swastika will – triumph!"[57] Scheubner-Richter thus expressed his faith in the ability of Hitler's National Socialist movement and its allies, including Aufbau, to overcome the Bolshevik menace he perceived both inside and outside Germany.

In the midst of his preparations to overthrow the Weimar Republic with the assistance of Scheubner-Richter's Aufbau, Hitler found time in September 1923 to visit Wahnfried in Bayreuth, the former villa of the German composer and *völkisch* philosopher Richard Wagner. He met with the leading *völkisch* theorist Houston Stewart Chamberlain, who currently lived there. Hitler took the Aufbau member and leading National Socialist ideologue Alfred Rosenberg along with him on this pilgrimage.[58] Hitler and Rosenberg's meeting with the partially paralyzed *völkisch* philosopher went extremely well. A week later, Chamberlain wrote Hitler: "My faith in Germandom has never wavered for a moment, though my hopes had, I confess, reached a low ebb. At one blow you have transformed the state of my soul." Hitler rejoiced "like a child" upon receiving this message.[59]

Chamberlain wrote an essay for the *Völkisch Observer* soon after his meeting with Hitler and Rosenberg, "God Wills It! Reflection on Germany's

---

[56] Scheubner-Richter, "Die Rote Armee," *Völkischer Beobachter*, March 22, 1923, 3.
[57] Scheubner-Richter, "Deutschlands Bolschewisierung," *Völkischer Beobachter*, September 21, 1923, 1.
[58] Robert Cecil, *The Myth of the Master Race: Alfred Rosenberg and Nazi Ideology* (London: B. T. Batsford Ltd., 1972), 13.
[59] Geoffrey G. Field, *Evangelist of Race: The Germanic Vision of Houston Stewart Chamberlain* (New York: Columbia University Press, 1981), 435–438.

Current State of Affairs." He supported Hitler during the present "world-historical turning point." He praised Hitler without mentioning him by name, noting that the times called for "the born Führer." Word on the street had it that "the man has appeared and is awaiting his hour among us."[60] Hitler returned praise to Chamberlain. He later referred to Bayreuth as the city in which "the spiritual sword with which we fight today was forged, first by the *Meister* [Wagner] and then by Chamberlain."[61] In *Mein Kampf*, he criticized Imperial Germany, where "official governmental authorities passed by the observations of Houston Stewart Chamberlain with the same indifference as still occurs today."[62] Despite a charged political situation in Bavaria, Hitler found time to strengthen his *völkisch* roots along with the White émigré Rosenberg in September 1923.

Around the time that Hitler and Rosenberg established a personal connection with Chamberlain, the greatest living *völkisch* theorist, relations deteriorated rapidly between the Kahr government in Bavaria and the Combat League under Hitler, Ludendorff, and Scheubner-Richter. In September 1923, Gustav Ritter von Kahr, now the virtual dictator of Bavaria with the title of General State Commissioner, forbade mass gatherings of the NSDAP. Kahr took this drastic step after Scheubner-Richter, Hitler's "influential political advisor," had refused to guarantee him that no complications would arise from such meetings.[63] Scheubner-Richter clearly opposed Kahr, who earlier had helped to turn Bavaria into a haven for *völkisch* German–White émigré collaboration. Scheubner-Richter's negative attitude towards Kahr influenced Hitler.

The dispute between the Kahr government on one side and Hitler, Ludendorff, Scheubner-Richter, and Biskupskii on the other helped to worsen the already deteriorating relations between Hitler and Captain Ehrhardt, the former leader of the now outlawed Organization C. Kahr asked Ehrhardt to visit him in Munich in late September 1923.[64] Ehrhardt left his refuge in the Austrian Tyrol for this meeting. He traveled to Munich in an Army car.[65] Largely as a result of these secret talks, Ehrhardt's Viking League publicly disassociated itself from the NSDAP-led Combat League at the beginning of October 1923. Ehrhardt justified this action by claiming

[60] Houston Stewart Chamberlain, "Gott will es! Betrachtung über den gegenwärtigen Zustand Deutschlands," *Völkischer Beobachter*, November 9, 1923, 1.

[61] Hartmut Zelinsky, *Sieg oder Untergang: Sieg und Untergang. Kaiser Wilhelm II., die Werk-Idee Richard Wagners und der "Weltkampf"* (Munich: Keyser, 1990), 12.

[62] Hitler, *Mein Kampf*, 269.

[63] RP report from November 6, 1923, BHSAM, BSMI 22, number 73694, fiche 2, 18.

[64] Heinrich Class, *Wider den Strom*, vol. 2, BAK, *Kleine Erwerbung* 499, 698.

[65] II. SAUV report, [September–November] 1927, BHSAM, BSMÄ 36, number 103476/2, 634, 639.

that the National Socialist struggle against Kahr's government was dividing nationalist circles instead of uniting them.[66]

The State Commissioner for the Supervision of Public Order noted in early October 1923 that the friendship between Ehrhardt on one side and Hitler, Ludendorff, and Scheubner-Richter on the other had greatly deteriorated as of late.[67] Ludendorff stressed at the time that he had nothing to do with the remnants of Ehrhardt's Organization C. He noted that this grouping was working against him. Ludendorff even openly belittled Ehrhardt as a "pest" in right-wing Munich circles in the course of the month, thereby deepening the rift between himself and Ehrhardt.[68]

Despite the intensifying dispute between Kahr and Ehrhardt on one side and Hitler, Ludendorff, and himself on the other, Scheubner-Richter expressed confidence in the ability of the Combat League to master events on its own. In early October 1923, an agent reported to the State Commissioner that Scheubner-Richter had recently assured him that the entire Bavarian Combat League would march into neighboring Thuringia and Saxony to strike down the powerful Communist movements there within a matter of days. After this, the Combat League would continue on to Berlin to overthrow the German government.

Scheubner-Richter had further told the government informant that the Germans had to fight against the French in the Ruhr Basin, and that it would be better to die in the struggle against the French than to vegetate in the face of such ignominy. Finally, Scheubner-Richter had claimed that the mood amongst the men of the Combat League was even more enthusiastic than among German soldiers in August 1914, at the outbreak of World War I.[69] Scheubner-Richter overestimated the strength of the forces at his disposal. This error would soon cost him his life.

Relations between General State Commissioner Kahr and the Combat League under Hitler, Ludendorff, and Scheubner-Richter steadily deteriorated in late October and early November 1923. At a crucial Combat League leadership meeting on October 23, 1923, Hitler stressed that Kahr could not lead a successful putsch against Berlin since he had already failed during the 1920 Kapp Putsch.[70] On November 5, 1923, Kahr called Combat League leaders to his presence to give them an official protocol stating that

[66] "Ausnahmezustand im Reich und in Bayern. Eine deutliche Absage," *Bayerischer Kurier*, October 4, 1923, reprinted in a PDM report from October 30, 1923, BSAM, PDM, number 6708, 151.

[67] RKÜöO report from October 4, 1923, RGVA (TsKhIDK), *fond* 772, *opis* 2, *delo* 189, 78.

[68] RKÜöO reports from October 18 and November 18, 1923, BAB, 1507, number 558, 116; 134, number 78, 13.

[69] RKÜöO report from October 9, 1923, RGVA (TsKhIDK), *fond* 772, *opis* 4, *delo* 13, 164.

[70] RKÜöO report to the BSMÄ from January 31, 1924, BHSAM, BSMÄ 36, number 103456, 8.

the Bavarian government, the Army, and the Bavarian Police would not participate in any Combat League putsch. Hitler himself did not attend this meeting. Instead, he sent Scheubner-Richter as his representative.[71] Hitler met with Scheubner-Richter the next day. Although Scheubner-Richter had repeatedly assured his intelligence colleague Nicolai that he would prevent a rash action on the part of the Combat League, he advised Hitler to undertake a show of force to begin Germany's "liberation."[72] This plan of action led to debacle.

Hitler launched his bid for power in Bavaria and beyond on November 8, 1923. He came to Scheubner-Richter's dwelling in the afternoon just after General Ludendorff had left. Scheubner-Richter gave Hitler a situation report and urged immediate action. Hitler told Scheubner-Richter to accompany him to the beer hall *Bürgerbräukeller* in uniform, which he did.[73] When Hitler entered the beer hall, where many Bavarian leaders were gathered, including Kahr, the Aufbau member Rosenberg was at his side.[74] Hitler fired his pistol at the ceiling and announced the outbreak of a national revolution. He stressed in a fiery speech that the coup did not oppose the Bavarian Police and the Army, but sought to overthrow the "Berlin Jewish government and the November criminals of 1918."[75] The putschists released an appeal, "To the Population of Munich!", which asserted that the "November Revolution" had met its end that day and that therefore "one of the most ignominious periods in German history has ended and the way has been cleared for the *völkisch* German freedom movement."[76]

Hitler and Scheubner-Richter worked together in the putsch. While Hitler negotiated with Kahr and other Bavarian leaders in a side room of the beer hall while pointing a gun at them, Scheubner-Richter carried out his own, ultimately unsuccessful, talks with high-ranking members of the Bavarian Police.[77] He then drove Hitler's car to pick up General Ludendorff, who had been left out of the loop and had not participated in

---

[71] Endres, "Aufzeichnungen über den Hitlerputsch," BHSAM/AK, *Handschriftensammlung*, number 925, 35.

[72] Nicolai's commentary on his telegraph to Ludendorff from November 10, 1923, *Tagebuch* (Diary), RGVA (TsKhIDK), *fond* 1414, *opis* 1, *delo* 22, 99; Thoss, *Der Ludendorff-Kreis*, 342, 343.

[73] Interview with Mathilde Scheubner-Richter on April 3, 1936, NSDAPHA, BAB, NS 26, number 1263, 5.

[74] Konrad Heiden, *Der Führer: Hitler's Rise to Power*, trans. Ralph Mannheim (Boston: Houghton Mifflin, 1944), 186.

[75] Hitler, speech on November 8, 1923, *Sämtliche Aufzeichnungen 1905–1924*, eds. Eberhard Jäckel and Axel Kuhn (Stuttgart: Deutsche Verlags-Anstalt, 1980), 1054.

[76] "An die Münchener Bevölkerung!", leaflet in possession of the PDM, BSAM, PDM, number 6711, 5.

[77] Deposition of Georg Rauh to the PDM on November 19, 1923, BSAM, PDM, number 6709, 3.

the negotiations in the *Bürgerbräukeller*. Scheubner-Richter came home in the early morning of November 9 and told his wife Mathilde that things had gone "wonderfully," without the shedding of blood.[78]

Actually, while the first day of the putsch did not lead to bloodshed, serious problems arose early on. When approximately 250 members of the Uplands League appeared at an Army barracks at 7:00 in the evening on November 8 and demanded weapons and munitions, the commanding officers there arrested them instead.[79] Former Latvian Intervention Freikorps leader First Lieutenant Gerhard Rossbach failed in his mission to provide the putschists with large-scale armed support as well. Rossbach took some of his followers adorned with swastika armbands to the Bavarian Infantry School, assembled the cadets there, and marched them to the *Bürgerbräukeller*.[80] Then he attempted to use the cadets to occupy the seat of the government in Munich. This endeavor failed at around 1:00 in the morning of November 9, 1923, as Munich Police members threatened to use force against Rossbach and the cadets he had assembled, and Rossbach backed down.[81]

The support that Hitler, Ludendorff, and Scheubner-Richter hoped for from Awakening Hungary ultimately fell through as well. Ulain, the leader of the right-wing Hungarian organization, was arrested on November 9 on the Austro-Hungarian border with a treaty between the Combat League and Awakening Hungary that he wished Hitler and Ludendorff to sign.[82] One of Hitler's representatives had visited Ulain on November 2, 1923 and given him the pact. Ulain planned to use Hungarian "patriotic organizations" to overthrow the Hungarian government and to restore Hungary's 1914 borders with the Combat League's assistance.[83] According to the terms of the treaty, the new Hitler/Ludendorff government was to deliver weapons for Ulain's Awakening Hungary movement in return for substantial agricultural deliveries.[84] This proposed agreement represented a basic variation of Aufbau policy.

Creating more problems for Hitler, Ludendorff, and Scheubner-Richter, the former Organization C leader Captain Ehrhardt ordered his followers in Munich not to join the Hitler/Ludendorff Putsch, largely

[78] Interview with Mathilde Scheubner-Richter on April 3, 1936, NSDAPHA, BAB, NS 26, number 1263, 5.

[79] Endres, "Aufzeichnungen über den Hitlerputsch," BHSAM/AK, *Handschriftensammlung*, number 925, 46, 47.

[80] Interview with Gerhard Rossbach on December 13, 1951, IZG, ZS 128, 9.

[81] Endres, "Aufzeichnungen über den Hitlerputsch," BHSAM/AK, *Handschriftensammlung*, number 925, 40, 44, 45.

[82] KI report on the Hitler Putsch, RGASPI, *fond* 495, *opis* 33, *delo* 306, 108.

[83] DGBud reports to the BSMÄ from November 10, 1923 and January 16, 1924, BHSAM, BSMÄ 36, number 103472, 49, 53.

[84] SALM report to the PDM from November 29, 1923, BSAM, PDM, number 6707, 67.

because of his differences with Ludendorff.[85] Ehrhardt fundamentally agreed with National Socialist ideology, but, as he stressed in a speech soon after the failure of the Hitler/Ludendorff Putsch, Hitler had attempted to overthrow the Weimar Republic too soon. He should have ordered things in Bavaria first and only then prepared for a march on Berlin.[86]

Faced with disappointment on multiple fronts, Hitler, Ludendorff, and Scheubner-Richter decided to march through the streets of Munich with their backers on November 9, 1923 in a show of determination that they hoped would raise popular support for their putsch. Hitler marched to the *Feldherrnhalle* (Commander's Hall) in central Munich arm in arm with Scheubner-Richter at his right, while Ludendorff strode to the right and somewhat ahead of Scheubner-Richter.[87] Arno Schickedanz, Aufbau's deputy director, Aufbau Vice President Biskupskii's secretary, and a fervent National Socialist, marched in the second row of the leading group of putschists. Rosenberg marched farther back.[88]

When pro-Kahr forces opened fire on the marchers after Kahr had withdrawn the support that he had earlier pledged Hitler at the point of a pistol, a bullet struck Scheubner-Richter in the heart and sent him reeling, mortally wounded. According to the version of events that Hitler subsequently told Scheubner-Richter's widow Mathilde, since he had been marching arm in arm with Scheubner-Richter, he had been pulled down when her husband had fallen. Then Scheubner-Richter in his dying convulsions had pinned him down so that he could not get back up.[89] Theodor Endres of District Defense Command VII offered a more plausible version of events, namely that Hitler had thrown himself to the ground with the firing of the first shots, thereby dislocating his shoulder. Endres stressed that Hitler's act had been the correct mode of action for a former active soldier to take and had not been at all unheroic. Endres asserted that claims that Hitler had only gone to the ground as a result of being pulled there were "as dumb as alien to the front [lines in battle]."[90]

Hitler's disastrous bid for power in Germany with the support of Scheubner-Richter's Aufbau failed far more dramatically than the Kapp Putsch of March 1920 had. Hitler himself asserted melodramatically during

---

[85] RKÜöO report from November 18, 1923, BAB, 134, number 78, 13.

[86] RKÜöO report from December 13, 1923, BAB, 1507, number 558, 147.

[87] Interview with Mathilde Scheubner-Richter on April 3, 1936, NSDAPHA, BAB, NS 26, number 1263, 6.

[88] APA report to the A9N from November 2, 1937, RGVA (TsKhIDK), *fond* 519, *opis* 4, *delo* 26, 134.

[89] Interview with Mathilde Scheubner-Richter on April 3, 1936, NSDAPHA, BAB, NS 26, number 1263, 7.

[90] Endres, "Aufzeichnungen über den Hitlerputsch," BHSAM/AK, *Handschriftensammlung*, number 925, 56.

his 1924 court testimony for the putsch that he had believed even before-hand that the undertaking had been "doomed to failure."[91] The State Commissioner for the Supervision of Public Order asserted that the Hitler/Ludendorff Putsch had fundamentally represented a repeat of the Kapp Putsch from the south. Reserve actions had been prepared in Austria and Hungary under the leadership of key players in the Kapp Putsch, most notably Major Waldemar Pabst, who collaborated with Aufbau from the Austrian Tyrol, and the conspiratorial Aufbau member Colonel Bauer, who operated from Vienna.[92]

As had occurred after the Kapp Putsch in March 1920, right-wing forces dispersed in the wake of the failed Hitler/Ludendorff Putsch. Hitler was imprisoned, and other prominent National Socialists such as Hermann Göring and Gerhard Rossbach went into hiding.[93] Many White émigrés left Germany for France. The Aufbau ideologue Fedor Vinberg, for example, traveled to Paris both because of the failure of the Hitler/Ludendorff Putsch, in which he was implicated by association, and as a result of mounting suspicion that he had masterminded the March 1922 assassination attempt on the Constitutional Democratic leader Pavel Miliukov.[94] The Munich White émigré community shrank dramatically in late 1923 and 1924. This process occurred not only because of the failure of the Hitler/Ludendorff Putsch and the death of Scheubner-Richter, who had guided National Socialist–White émigré cooperation, but also since, with the stabilization of the German mark, France with its high inflation rate offered more favorable living conditions for Russian exiles.[95]

The death of the most important White émigré in Bavarian affairs, Scheubner-Richter, in the Hitler/Ludendorff Putsch proved a tremendous blow to National Socialist–White émigré collaboration. Aufbau's guiding figure had displayed remarkable courage throughout his military and polit-ical career. He had asserted in a January 1923 *Aufbau Correspondence* article: "It is not necessary that I live! But it is necessary that the German nation lives in a free, great German Reich!"[96] His words had been based on genuine

---

[91] *The Hitler Trial: Before the People's Court in Munich*, vol. 1, trans. H. Francis Freniere, eds. Lucie Karcic and Philip Fandek (Arlington: University Publications of America, 1976), 59.

[92] RKÜöO report [1925?], RGVA (TsKhIDK), *fond* 772, *opis* 3, *delo* 781, 4; RKÜöO report to the BSMÄ from January 31, 1924, BHSAM, BSMÄ 36, number 103456, 8.

[93] RKÜöO report from February 9, 1924, BAB, 1507, number 442, 210.

[94] Baur, *Die russische Kolonie in München*, 204; Norman Cohn, *Warrant for Genocide: The Myth of the Jewish World-Conspiracy and the "Protocols of the Elders of Zion"* (Chico, CA: Scholars Press, 1981), 141.

[95] PPS report to the AA from November 14, 1924, PAAA, 83584, 168, 170; RKÜöO report from July 1927, RGVA (TsKhIDK), *fond* 772, *opis* 1, *delo* 91, 51.

[96] Scheubner-Richter, "Klarheit," *Aufbau-Korrespondenz*, January 17, 1923, 2.

conviction and had not been mere bravado. Hitler fully appreciated the magnitude of the loss of his closest political advisor. He subsequently lamented, "Everyone is replaceable, with the exception of one: Scheubner-Richter!"[97] Scheubner-Richter had proved truly indispensable in both the National Socialist movement and Aufbau.

Aufbau's remaining leadership gained ideological capital by portraying Scheubner-Richter as a fallen hero of the right-wing German/White émigré cause. Aufbau's new leader, Scheubner-Richter's old Rubonia Fraternity colleague Otto von Kursell, dedicated a manuscript to the memory of Aufbau's former *de facto* leader, "Dr. Engineer M. E. von Scheubner-Richter, Killed in Action on November 9, 1923." Kursell drew a heroic picture of his former comrade on the cover of his dedication, and he related the events of Scheubner-Richter's funeral. At this ceremony, Kursell had given a speech on behalf of the Rubonia Fraternity in Riga. Schickedanz, another Rubonia member and Scheubner-Richter's close ally, had spoken in the name of Aufbau. Georgii Nemirovich-Danchenko, one of Aufbau's Ukrainian experts, had made remarks as a "Russian émigré who has been thrown abroad."[98] Kursell also wrote a retrospective essay praising Scheubner-Richter's struggle against "Marxism and its Jewish heads."[99]

Nemirovich-Danchenko contributed an essay in Kursell's publication in honor of Scheubner-Richter titled, "A Splendid Death." He argued that Scheubner-Richter had fulfilled his dream of attaining a worthy end by falling as a "good German who covered his honored leader and friend, the pride of nationalist Germany," meaning Hitler, "with his breast." Nemirovich-Danchenko concluded: "In these times of cowardice, betrayal, and disgrace, this heroic death will be inscribed with golden letters into Germany's martyr history."[100] He thus eulogized Scheubner-Richter as a self-sacrificing hero whose death served the cause of German greatness. As we will see in Chapter Nine, Hitler also subsequently emphasized this theme.

Scheubner-Richter's death greatly affected Hitler. He partially dedicated *Mein Kampf* to "those eighteen heroes," of whom Scheubner-Richter was

[97] Georg Franz-Willing, *Ursprung der Hitlerbewegung 1919–1922* (Preussisch Oldendorf: K. W. Schütz KG, 1974), 198.

[98] Otto von Kursell, "Die Trauerfeierlichkeiten: Einäschung auf dem Münchner Ostfriedhof am 17. November 10 Uhr früh," *Dr. Ing. M. E. von Scheubner-Richter gefallen am 9. November 1923* (Munich: Müller und Sohn, November 1923), NSDAPHA, BAB, NS 26, number 1263, 3.

[99] Kursell, "Die Linie im Leben Max von Scheubner-Richters," *Dr. Ing. M. E. von Scheubner-Richter gefallen am 9. November 1923*, NSDAPHA, BAB, NS 26, number 1263, 4.

[100] Georgii Nemirovich-Danchenko, "Ein schöner Tod," *Dr. Ing. M. E. von Scheubner-Richter gefallen am 9. November 1923*, NSDAPHA, BAB, NS 26, number 1263, 4.

the most prominent, "who sacrificed themselves for us all with the clearest consciousness. They must forever recall the wavering and the weak to the fulfillment of his duty, a duty which they themselves in the best faith carried to its final consequences."[101] During January 1942, he reminisced of the early days of the National Socialist Party: "Thinking of that time reminds me of Scheubner-Richter's sacrifice."[102] Scheubner-Richter truly proved to have been an irreplaceable comrade and advisor for Hitler.

Biskupskii, who had been Aufbau's leading figure after Scheubner-Richter, experienced serious difficulties after the Hitler/Ludendorff Putsch. Bavarian authorities suspected him of complicity in the failed undertaking. Schickedanz, Biskupskii's secretary in Aufbau, had prominently participated in the events of November 8/9. Moreover, Biskupskii was known to have advised Ludendorff in the fall of 1923. Despite the compelling evidence that Biskupskii had played a key behind-the-scenes role in the buildup to and execution of the Hitler/Ludendorff Putsch, Bavarian authorities were not able to prove that he had worked to incite Hitler, Ludendorff, and Scheubner-Richter to rise against the Bavarian government with the ultimate goal of marching on Berlin.[103]

After the failure of the Hitler/Ludendorff Putsch, the death of Scheubner-Richter, and the marginalization of Biskupskii, Aufbau lost in stature and soon disbanded. After the catastrophic events of November 8/9, 1923, Aufbau officially continued to exist under the direction of Kursell, who headed the editorial staff of *Aufbau Correspondence*.[104] Aufbau soon faded out, however.[105] The last issue of *Aufbau Correspondence* appeared on June 15, 1924.

While National Socialist–White émigré collaboration reached its nadir towards the end of 1923, Hitler granted the leadership of the NSDAP for the duration of his imprisonment to the White émigré, Aufbau member, and Party philosopher Rosenberg. Hitler scrawled a note shortly before his arrest stating that Rosenberg should "lead the movement from now on."[106] Hitler charged Aufbau's second secretary and the secretary of the NSDAP, Max Amann, with serving as Rosenberg's deputy.[107] Hitler thus placed the

[101] Hitler, *Mein Kampf*, 687.
[102] Hitler, *Hitler's Table Talk 1941–44: His Private Conversations*, trans. Norman Cameron and R. H. Stevens, second edn. (London: Weidenfeld and Nicolson, 1973), 173.
[103] RKÜöO reports from April 25, 1924, September 17, 1923, and January 24, 1923 RGVA (TsKhIDK), *fond* 772, *opis* 3, *delo* 81a, 38, 45, 54.
[104] RKÜöO report from May 7, 1925, RGVA (TsKhIDK), *fond* 772, *opis* 4, *delo* 52, 145.
[105] PDM report to the RKÜöO from September 14, 1926, RGVA (TsKhIDK), *fond* 772, *opis* 1, *delo* 101, 22.
[106] Cecil, *The Myth of the Master Race*, 42.
[107] Ian Kershaw, *Hitler 1889–1936: Hubris* (London: Penguin Press, 1998), 211.

direction of the National Socialist Party in the hands of two Aufbau members who had worked for nationalist German–Russian rapprochement.

CONCLUSION

Just as Aufbau could not unite all White émigrés in Europe, the conspiratorial organization failed to place Adolf Hitler and General Erich von Ludendorff in power in Germany in 1923. Aufbau's leading figure, Max von Scheubner-Richter, coordinated the activities of Hitler and Ludendorff in various paramilitary associations that finally crystallized as the Combat League. Scheubner-Richter brought Hitler and Ludendorff together for a Combat League putsch that he largely modeled along Bolshevik lines. While he abhorred Bolshevism, Scheubner-Richter nonetheless admired its example that a few determined men could alter world history, and he learned from the Bolshevik methods of subversion followed by ruthless centralization and militarization to neutralize political enemies. He appreciated the "energy" of the Soviet Commissar for War Lev Trotskii, and he wished to play Trotskii to Hitler's Lenin.

On November 8, 1923, Scheubner-Richter goaded Hitler to undertake what became known as the Hitler/Ludendorff Putsch. While the coup began auspiciously, problems soon arose, as the hoped for support from far right Germans and Hungarians fell short. In an effort to regain mastery of the situation, Scheubner-Richter marched with Hitler and Ludendorff at the head of a radical right contingent that also included the Aufbau members Alfred Rosenberg and Arno Schickedanz. Scheubner-Richter was shot fatally in the heart while marching at Hitler's side. His death proved an irreplaceable loss for Hitler.

National Socialist–White émigré collaboration reached a low point after the Hitler/Ludendorff Putsch collapsed, though two Aufbau members led the NSDAP during Hitler's imprisonment. The Hitler/Ludendorff Putsch that Aufbau supported failed even more spectacularly than the Kapp Putsch of March 1920, in which Hitler, Ludendorff, and Scheubner-Richter had also participated. Right-wing forces dispersed in the aftermath of the Hitler/Ludendorff Putsch, just as they had after the Kapp Putsch had collapsed in Berlin. Without its guiding figure Scheubner-Richter, Aufbau sank into political insignificance and then faded out entirely. Nonetheless, two Aufbau colleagues led the National Socialist movement while Hitler was incarcerated: the White émigré Rosenberg and the German Max Amann.

While Aufbau's political aspirations to place Hitler and Ludendorff in charge in Germany miscarried in the course of 1923, Aufbau did succeed in making crucial ideological contributions to National Socialism from 1920 to 1923. The Aufbau ideologues Scheubner-Richter, Rosenberg, and Fedor Vinberg, acting in league with the *völkisch* publicist Dietrich Eckart, influenced Hitler's early anti-Bolshevik, anti-Semitic views considerably. These four ideological comrades inspired Hitler's notion of a looming descent into apocalyptic struggle against conspiratorial Jewish forces behind predatory finance capitalism and murderous Bolshevism. Aufbau's fundamental ideological contributions to Hitler's anti-Bolshevik and anti-Semitic *Weltanschauung* forms the subject of the following chapter.

CHAPTER 8

The four writers of the apocalypse

The early National Socialist preoccupation with the "Jewish Bolshevik" peril manifested itself in the lead article of a July 1922 edition of the Party newspaper the *Völkischer Beobachter* (*Völkisch Observer*). This essay asserted that the National Socialist movement had begun by warning: "Germany is rushing towards Bolshevism with giant strides." The article, signed by the "Party leadership," asked, "Do you want to wait until, as in Russia, a Bolshevik murder squad comes into operation in every city and bumps off everyone who does not want to bow to the Jewish dictatorship as a 'counter-revolutionary?'" The Party leadership stressed that this and worse would "occur with the same methodicalness as in Russia" unless the Germans realized that "one has to fight now if one wants to live."[1] Resistance to "Jewish Bolshevism," cast in terms of a life and death struggle, formed a central tenet of early National Socialist ideology.

In his book *The Occult Establishment*, the historian James Webb asserts that exiled "Russian idealists" served "as witnesses to the national tragedy and reminders of the insecurity which also troubled the West; as bearers of an illuminated culture that was preoccupied with Apocalypse; and as carriers of the plague of conspiracy-theory politics."[2] Webb correctly assesses the destabilizing influence of Russian expatriates. Several White émigrés significantly affected the virulently anti-Bolshevik and anti-Semitic National Socialist *Weltanschauung*. Adolf Hitler, who only began to develop strong anti-Bolshevik and anti-Semitic views in the second half of 1919, learned extensively from some White émigrés. This chapter examines influential written sources of Aufbau views grouped thematically (including some passages printed before Aufbau's official inception in the fall of 1920) and assesses their impact on Hitler's ideas.

---

[1] National Socialist Party leadership, "Grundsätzliches Programm der national-sozialistischen Deutschen Arbeiterpartei," *Völkischer Beobachter*, July 19, 1922, 1.
[2] James Webb, *The Occult Establishment* (La Salle, IL: Open Court, 1976), 175.

In his groundbreaking 1939 work *The Apocalypse of Our Times*, the French scholar Henri Rollin noted the crucial roles that three White émigré Aufbau members, Max von Scheubner-Richter, Fedor Vinberg, and Alfred Rosenberg, played in shaping National Socialism. In particular, Rollin asserted that the three colleagues were astounded at the success that the Bolshevik leader Vladimir Lenin, who had himself been an obscure émigré, had achieved by using mass propaganda and brutally destroying his adversaries after seizing power. The White émigré trio, Rollin claimed, sought to fight fire with fire by using Lenin's own methods to defeat him.[3] While Bolshevism appalled them, Scheubner-Richter, Vinberg, and Rosenberg nonetheless learned from its ruthless tactics.

Building upon the anti-Semitic ideas of the Imperial Russian author Fedor Dostoevskii, fundamental Aufbau views as expressed by Scheubner-Richter, Vinberg, and Rosenberg maintained that an insidious Jewish world conspiracy manipulated an unholy alliance between rapacious finance capitalism and bloodthirsty Bolshevism. This subversive and destructive phenomenon manifested itself most terribly in the Soviet Union. "Jewish Bolshevism" there, according to Aufbau ideology, not only caused the death of millions of Russians through war, starvation, disease, and misrule, but deliberately worked to annihilate the Russian nationalist Christian intelligentsia. "Jewish Bolsheviks" threatened to spread their terrifying acts of eradication to Germany and beyond in the near future.

The White émigré Aufbau members Vinberg, Rosenberg, and Scheubner-Richter (the last two of whom also served as important National Socialists) transmitted anti-Bolshevik and anti-Semitic White émigré thought with its conspiratorial and apocalyptic overtones to Hitler both directly and indirectly through Hitler's early *völkisch* mentor, Dietrich Eckart. Eckart collaborated with Rosenberg and the Aufbau artist Otto von Kursell in the *völkisch* newspaper *Auf gut deutsch* (*In Plain German*) from 1919 to 1921, he may well have belonged to Aufbau himself, and he edited the *Völkisch Observer* from 1921 until Rosenberg *de facto* replaced him in May 1923. He played a formative role in the genesis of National Socialist ideology. The *Völkisch Observer* praised him as the "champion and intellectual forerunner of the National Socialist movement."[4]

Scheubner-Richter, Vinberg, and Rosenberg warned apocalyptically of the threatened perdition of Germany and the rest of Europe and even the

[3] Henri Rollin, *L'Apocalypse de notre temps: Les dessous de la propagande allemande d'après des documents inédits* (Paris: Gallimard, 1939), 168.
[4] "Dietrich Eckart," *Völkischer Beobachter*, March 23, 1923, 5.

world through "Jewish Bolshevism," and Eckart borrowed from Aufbau's apocalyptic standpoint in his writings. He equated the perceived apocalyptic Jewish world menace with "Jewish Bolshevism." He thus served as the fourth "writer of the apocalypse." While General Count Rüdiger von der Goltz had directed the anti-Bolshevik Latvian Intervention of 1919 in the spirit of "*ex oriente lux!*" ("from the East – light!"), White émigré Aufbau ideologues and their *völkisch* comrade Eckart emphasized the negative corollary of this motto, namely *ex oriente obscuritas!* (from the East – darkness!).

THE "JEWISH BOLSHEVIK" PERIL

In developing his intensely anti-Bolshevik and anti-Semitic outlook, Hitler borrowed extensively from the ideas of Eckart and Aufbau White émigrés, although he later tried to minimize the importance of outside influences on his ideas in Munich. In *Mein Kampf*, he claimed of his time in Vienna (1908–1913): "There took shape within me a world picture and a philosophy which became the granite foundation of all my acts. In addition to what I then created, I have had to learn little; and I have had to alter nothing."[5] As we noted in the Introduction, Brigitte Hamann's 1996 work, *Hitler's Vienna: Apprentice Years of a Dictator*, convincingly refutes notions of Hitler's early anti-Semitic ideological development.[6] Moreover, while Hitler claimed in *Mein Kampf* that one should not enter politics until the age of thirty, for it is only then that one possesses a firm *Weltanschauung*, the historian Eberhard Jäckel has demonstrated that Hitler did not possess a fully developed world view by 1919, when he was thirty.[7]

Hitler harbored standard socialist views well into 1919. Hitler's former immediate commander on the Western Front in World War I, Aide-de-Camp Hans Mend, asserted that his earlier underling had exclaimed towards the end of 1918 in Munich: "Thank God that the kings' crowns have fallen from the tree. Now we proletarians also have something to say."[8]

---

[5] Adolf Hitler, *Mein Kampf*, trans. Ralph Mannheim (Boston: Houghton Mifflin, 1943), 22.

[6] Brigitte Hamann, *Hitlers Wien: Lehrjahre eines Diktators* (Munich: Piper, 1996), 239–241, 499, 500.

[7] Hitler, *Mein Kampf*, 66; Eberhard Jäckel, *Hitlers Weltanschauung*, trans. Herbert Arnold (Middletown, CT: Wesleyan University Press, 1969), 117.

[8] "Protokoll aufgenommen am 22. Dezember 1939 mit Hans Mend, Reitlehrer und Verwalter auf Schloss Eltzholz Berg bei Starnberg a/See, ehemals Ulan im kgl. bayer. x. Ulanenregiment zugeteilt als Ordonnanzreiter im Oktober 1914 dem Inf. Rgt. 'List.' Seit Juni 1916 befördert zum Offizier – Stellvertreter und zugeteilt dem 4. bayer. Feldartillerieregiment, Munitionskolonne 143 (Tankabwehr). Bei der Truppe bekannt als der 'Schimmelreiter,'" BHSAM/AK, *Handschriftensammlung*, number 3231, 3.

Records suggest that Hitler served the socialist Bavarian government beginning in the middle of February 1919 as the *Vertrauensmann* (representative) of his military company in Traunstein outside of Munich. He transmitted propaganda from the socialist government to the soldiers in Traunstein's barracks. He was voted deputy battalion representative in April 1919, meaning that he was to ensure that the soldiers under his supervision remained loyal to the socialist Bavarian regime. Moreover, in subsequent years, Hitler earned scorn from the ranks of the National Socialist Party for not helping to overthrow the *Räterepublik* (Bavarian Soviet Republic) in May 1919.[9]

Hitler only began to develop a detailed anti-Bolshevik, anti-Semitic ideology beginning in the second half of 1919 through his collaboration with Eckart and Rosenberg, who served as his early mentors. Mend confirmed Hitler's rapid political lurch from the far left to the far right in postwar Munich. When he heard Hitler speak publicly at the beginning of 1920, he thought: "Adi has changed his colors, the red lad!"[10] In addition to borrowing anti-Bolshevik and anti-Semitic ideas from Eckart and Rosenberg, Hitler soon learned far right concepts that castigated "Jewish Bolshevism" from the Aufbau ideologues Scheubner-Richter and Vinberg as well.

Following World War I, White émigrés in general and Aufbau ideologues in particular used the Russian author Fedor Dostoevskii's right-wing views to further their political agendas. Aufbau's concentration on Dostoevskii's ideas formed part of what the German historian Otto-Ernst Schüddekopf has termed the spread of a "Dostoevskii myth" in postwar Germany.[11] To begin with, the Aufbau author Vinberg drew from Dostoevskii's views on the alleged Jewish peril, most notably as expressed in *Diary of a Writer*. In his 1922 work translated from Russian into German as *Der Kreuzesweg Russlands* (*Russia's Via Dolorosa*), Vinberg mentioned Dostoevskii first and foremost among those thinkers who had conceived the existence of a "powerful, organized, international, Jewish-Masonic power that endeavors to achieve world domination."[12] Vinberg cited a March 1877 passage from *Diary of a Writer*, but he altered it to lend it a more sinister aspect:

---

[9] Ian Kershaw, *Hitler 1889–1936: Hubris* (London: Penguin Press, 1998), 118, 120.

[10] Hans Mend, "Protokoll aufgenommen am 22. Dezember 1939," BHSAM/AK, *Handschriftensammlung*, number 3231, 4.

[11] Otto-Ernst Schüddekopf, *Linke Leute von rechts: Die nationalrevolutionären Minderheiten und der Kommunismus in der Weimarer Republik* (Stuttgart: W. Kohlhammer Verlag, 1960), 31.

[12] Fedor Vinberg, *Der Kreuzesweg Russlands: Teil I: Die Ursachen des Übels*, trans. K. von Jarmersted (Munich: R. Oldenbourg, 1922), 150, 153.

Their empire is drawing near, their entire empire! The triumph of the Jews is nearing, before which brotherly love, the truth, Christian sentiments, and the national pride of the European peoples will fade and recede. A heap of Jews will rise above humanity increasingly stronger and more powerful and will endeavor to make its mark on the entire world.

Dostoevskii had not written the last sentence about a "heap of Jews," but the gist of Vinberg's doctored citation conforms to what Dostoevskii did assert with regard to the Jews. Vinberg commented on his altered quote from Dostoevskii, "This prophecy of such a great authority on the human soul has been fulfilled. The entire world is now in the clutches of these Anti-Christs."[13] Vinberg granted Dostoevskii prophetic powers, particularly with regard to the "Jewish question."

Like his Aufbau colleague Vinberg, Rosenberg greatly respected Dosto-evskii. On the title page of his 1920 book, *Die Spur des Juden im Wandel der Zeiten* (*The Trail of the Jew through the Ages*), he quoted from Dostoevskii: "The Jewish idea is that of profiteering." Later in this work, he credited Dostoevskii with recognizing the basic Jewish principle of "exploiting all peoples."[14] In a February 1921 article in Eckart's newspaper *In Plain German*, Rosenberg argued that nationalist Russians needed to draw strength from the "old Slavic force." He asserted, "One already finds the prophecies for this [process] in Dostoevskii."[15] Rosenberg believed Dostoevskii's ideas to have a regenerative effect.

Rosenberg also praised Dostoevskii in his 1922 treatise, *Pest in Russland! Der Bolschewismus, seine Häupter, Handlanger und Opfer* (*Plague in Russia! Bolshevism, Its Heads, Henchmen, and Victims*), which admirably described the "essence and development of Jewish Bolshevism" according to the *Völkisch Observer*.[16] He labeled Dostoevskii "the greatest of all Russians." He argued that if one read Dostoevskii's *Diary of a Writer* carefully, then one could understand a great deal about the present horrible situation in the Soviet Union.[17] Like Vinberg, Rosenberg ascribed remarkable perceptive powers to one of Imperial Russia's most famous authors.

Aufbau propagandists disseminated Dostoevskii's assertions of a sinister Jewish world conspiracy to members of the German radical right, including

[13] Vinberg, *Der Kreuzesweg Russlands*, 25.
[14] Alfred Rosenberg, *Die Spur des Juden im Wandel der Zeiten* (Munich: Deutscher Volks-Verlag, 1920), 1, 81, 82.
[15] Rosenberg, "Das Verbrechen der Freimaurerei: Judentum, Jesuitismus, deutsches Christentum: VIII. Deutsches Christentum," *Auf gut deutsch: Wochenschrift für Ordnung und Recht*, February 28, 1921.
[16] "Die Pest in Russland," *Völkischer Beobachter*, July 5, 1922, 2.
[17] Rosenberg, *Pest in Russland! Der Bolschewismus, seine Häupter, Handlanger und Opfer* (Munich: Deutscher Volks-Verlag, 1922), 39.

National Socialists. Dostoevskii's influence on the early National Socialist movement manifested itself in a July 1921 edition of *Der Nationalsozialist* (*The National Socialist*), a replacement periodical for the temporarily outlawed *Völkisch Observer*. *The National Socialist* contained an article under the pseudonym "Alarich" titled, "Dostoevskii (Born 1821) and the Jewish Question." The essay quoted from Dostoevskii's *Diary of a Writer* from March 1877, with slight modifications:

What would happen if there were three million Russians and 80 million Jews in Russia instead of the other way around, what would the latter do with the Russians, how would they handle them? . . . Would they not simply make them into slaves? Or worse yet, would they not skin them completely? Would they not exterminate them entirely, not destroy them just as they had other peoples earlier in their ancient history?

The article in *The National Socialist* also cited the above-mentioned passage from Dostoevskii's March 1877 section of *Diary of a Writer*, which asserted of the Jews: "Their empire is approaching, their whole empire! The triumph of ideas is beginning before which feelings of philanthropy, thirst for the truth, Christian and national feelings, and even the racial pride of European peoples bow." The piece's commentary argued that the mystically inclined Russian author had expressed "timeless truths that have always held and will always hold as long as there are Jews."[18] National Socialists revered Dostoevskii's anti-Semitic ideas.

An unsigned essay in a January 1923 edition of the *Völkisch Observer*, "Dostoevskii as Politician and Prophet," quoted from a passage of Dostoevskii's that was first published in an anniversary edition of *Diary of a Writer* in 1906.[19] The article cited Dostoevskii's assertion: "When the entire wealth of Europe has been wasted, the bank of the Jew will remain. Then the Anti-Christ may come and anarchy rule." The commentary on Dostoevskii's warning asserted:

Anarchy already rules in Russia today . . . Russia ignored the admonitions of Dostoevskii and so the poet of yesterday will become the poet of the Russia of tomorrow, which with its return to the *völkisch* will have found its way home out of anarchy. For the rest of Europe, however, Dostoevskii is still the poet and admonisher for today, for perhaps already tomorrow "may the Anti-Christ come and anarchy rule."[20]

[18] Alarich, "Dostojewski (geb. 1821) und die Judenfrage," *Der Nationalsozialist*, July 14, 1921, 2, 3.
[19] Fedor Dostoevskii, *Tagebuch eines Schriftstellers*, trans. E. K. Rahsin (Munich: Piper, 1992), 641.
[20] "Dostojewski als Politiker und Prophet," *Völkischer Beobachter*, January 27, 1923, 3.

Such a detailed treatment of Dostoevskii's anti-Semitic warnings in the official National Socialist newspaper demonstrated considerable acceptance of the author's ideas among National Socialists.

Rosenberg owed a significant debt to Dostoevskii in forming his conception of the Jews as the manipulators of both capitalism and socialism/Bolshevism. Eckart, Vinberg, and Scheubner-Richter also treated the theme of a monstrous capitalist-Bolshevik embrace through the agency of the Jews. In a March 1921 article in the *Völkisch Observer*, Rosenberg credited Dostoevskii with recognizing "the continual growth of the Jewish stock exchange and the Jewish revolution." Rosenberg then asserted that now the "Jewish stock exchange has united with the Jewish Revolution."[21] Rosenberg stressed in an August 1921 edition of the *Völkisch Observer*, "It has come as the seer Dostoevskii prophesied 50 years ago: 'Now the times of great wars and great revolutions are coming. And the international Jewish bank will emerge victorious from them!'"[22]

Rosenberg argued that a capitalist–Bolshevik Jewish conspiracy existed on other occasions. In a March 1920 article in *In Plain German* that he wrote in collaboration with Eckart, Rosenberg argued that while the "most unscrupulous Jewish terror" in Russia "ruins the economy and industry; when all is said and done, it works for stock market speculators and big capitalists."[23] In his introduction to a work of verse and drawings that Eckart and his Baltic German assistant Kursell produced in 1921, *Totengräber Russlands* (*Russia's Gravediggers*), Rosenberg claimed: "The Bolsheviks were and are the envoys of the stock market Jews from all countries," and "it was Jewish money which paid for the machine of subversion." After the victory of "Jewish Bolshevism," the "Russian national assets" came under the control of "Jewish high finance and its satellites."[24]

Rosenberg also linked finance capitalism and Bolshevism with scheming Jews in two of his early major works. In his 1922 book *Plague in Russia!*, he asserted: "If one understands capitalism as the high-powered exploitation of the masses by a quite small minority, then there has never been a greater capitalist state in history than the Jewish Soviet government since the days of October 1917."[25] In his 1923 treatise *Die Protokolle der Weisen von Zion und die jüdische Weltpolitik* (*The Protocols of the Elders of Zion and Jewish World-Politics*), he labeled "Jewish high finance as the breeder of

[21] Rosenberg, "Schicksalswende in London!", *Völkischer Beobachter*, March 6, 1921, 2.
[22] Rosenberg, "Hochfinanz und Weltrevolution: Überblick," *Völkischer Beobachter*, August 4, 1921, 1.
[23] Dietrich Eckart/Rosenberg, "Zwischen den Schächern," *Auf gut deutsch*, March 5, 1920.
[24] Rosenberg, "Der jüdische Bolschewismus," *Völkischer Beobachter*, November 26, 1921, 1.
[25] Rosenberg, *Pest in Russland!*, 32.

Marxism, of terrorism," and he described the "world political cooperation of Jewish high finance with the most extreme Marxism." He further argued: "Nowadays the red and golden Internationals have openly become the Jewish National as they earlier secretly were."[26] Rosenberg thus claimed that whereas earlier, Jews had sought to control events from behind the scenes, they had now openly emerged as the driving force behind both finance capitalism and Bolshevism.

Rosenberg's views on the firm ties between both finance capitalism and Bolshevism through a worldwide Jewish conspiracy became official National Socialist ideology, as witnessed in Rosenberg's January 1923 essay, *Wesen, Grundsätze und Ziele der Nationalsozialistischen Deutschen Arbeiterpartei* (*Essence, Principles, and Objectives of the National Socialist German Worker's Party*).[27] Hitler thanked Rosenberg for crafting this "extension of the Party Program."[28] In his treatise, which was published in abbreviated form in a September 1923 edition of the *National Socialist*, Rosenberg examined the "greatest fraud of the 19th century, as it finally triumphed in Moscow in November 1917 and in Berlin in November 1918: the anticapitalist world revolution led by world capital." He asserted that "this enormous world fraud" had only been made possible by the fact that Jews led capitalism as well as Marxism.[29] Rosenberg's conception of a monstrous capitalist–Bolshevik embrace through the agency of world Jewry greatly influenced National Socialist ideology.

At the time of his close collaboration with Rosenberg in the publication of *In Plain German*, Hitler's mentor Eckart also argued that the Jews linked finance capitalism with Bolshevism. In a November 1920 essay, "'Jewry über alles'" ("'Jewry above Everything'"), Eckart maintained that both capitalism and Bolshevism represented means to the end of a Jewish world dictatorship. He wrote of a prevalent "error" that usually constituted a "conscious lie," namely that the Jews, given that they embodied capitalism to a certain degree, would never launch Bolshevism or even support it since it sought to destroy capital. He insisted: "As if the Jewish people, if it were one day to have unlimited power on earth, would not have everything under the sun, all gold and silver and the other riches of the world, everything but

---

[26] Rosenberg, *Die Protokolle der Weisen von Zion und die Jüdische Weltpolitik* (Munich: Deutscher Volks-Verlag, 1923), 45, 98, 101.

[27] Werner Maser, *Der Sturm auf die Republik: Frühgeschichte der NSDAP* (Stuttgart: Deutsche Verlags-Anstalt, 1973), 332.

[28] Hitler, speech on January 29, 1923, *Sämtliche Aufzeichnungen 1905–1924*, eds. Eberhard Jäckel and Axel Kuhn (Stuttgart: Deutsche Verlags-Anstalt, 1980), 824.

[29] Rosenberg, "Wesen, Grundsätze und Ziele der N.S.D.A.P.," *Der Nationalsozialist*, September 1, 1923, 1.

yet everything!"[30] Capitalism and Bolshevism for Eckart thus represented Jewish tools for achieving world domination.

In his work *Russia's Via Dolorosa*, the Aufbau ideologue Vinberg did not concern himself greatly with the alleged connections between high finance and Bolshevism through a worldwide Jewish conspiracy. He did, however, argue: "The Bolshevik movement as such in a certain sense is to be described as a purely Jewish one, and . . . certain Jewish banks are interested in it."[31] Vinberg tended to view matters from a religious standpoint and did not treat economic matters in detail, but he nevertheless propagated the basic White émigré thesis that Jewish capitalists had financed the Bolshevik revolution.

Vinberg's leader in Aufbau, Scheubner-Richter, upheld the idea of world Jewry's manipulation of both finance capitalism and allied Bolshevism. In a September 1922 essay in *Aufbau-Korrespondenz* (*Aufbau Correspondence*), Scheubner-Richter stressed that the worldwide victory of Bolshevism would entail the "enslavement of the German people through the Communist and golden-Jewish International."[32] He argued along similar lines in an article in a September 1923 edition of the *Völkisch Observer*, "Germany's Bolshevization." He maintained, "French chauvinism as the bailiff of international finance," like "Russian Bolshevism," in reality represented a "tool in the hands of the Jewish International."[33] He thus portrayed Germany as the victim of a worldwide conspiracy led by Jewish high finance that manifested itself in the twin threats of the French/Belgian occupation of the Ruhr Basin in the West and Bolshevik pressure from the East.

Hitler, who relied greatly upon Scheubner-Richter's advice regarding both domestic and foreign affairs, repeatedly treated the theme espoused by Aufbau White émigrés and Eckart that Jewish finance capitalism supported Bolshevism. In a June 1922 speech, Hitler blamed Jewish capital for the perils that faced Germany to the East and to the West. He employed a manner of reasoning similar to that of Scheubner-Richter in claiming: "Chinese henchmen in Moscow and black ones on the Rhine stand as cultural guardians of Jewish capitalism."[34] Hitler thus expressed a White émigré view of influential finance Jews hiring minions of color to perform their dirty work for them in both the Soviet Union and in the West.

---

[30] Eckart, "'Jewry über alles,'" *Auf gut deutsch*, November 26, 1920, 5.
[31] Vinberg, *Der Kreuzesweg Russlands*, 28.
[32] Max von Scheubner-Richter, "Der Katastrophe entgegen!", *Wirtschafts-politische Aufbau-Korrespondenz über Ostfragen und ihre Bedeutung für Deutschland*, September 6, 1922, 2.
[33] Scheubner-Richter, "Deutschlands Bolschewisierung," *Völkischer Beobachter*, September 21, 1923, 1.
[34] Hitler, speech on June 22, 1922, *Sämtliche Aufzeichnungen*, 645.

During his close political collaboration with Scheubner-Richter's Aufbau, Hitler often treated circumstances inside the Soviet Union to back his claim that Jewish finance capitalism lurked behind Bolshevism. In a September 1922 speech dealing with the Soviet Union's "New Economic Policy," he argued that private capitalism was "'temporarily'" being reinstated, but

the only capitalists are the Jews, and so the circle that Marxist theory aims at is complete: expropriation of private capitalism through socialization to state capitalism and back to private capitalism. In this process capital only changed big wigs and work methods changed. Only the Jew is proprietor and there is a 14-hour working day.

He warned, "A Jewification of the economy as in Russia is inevitably being carried out among us as well."[35] Hitler thus used perceived atrocious Soviet conditions as a model of things to come in Germany because of the insidious drive of Jewish capitalists for wealth and power.

Hitler emphasized during a January 1923 speech that the Marxist theory of class struggle was a swindle propagated by the Jews. He stressed that the National Socialist Party firmly believed that the gathering Bolshevik revolution in Germany "will not concern a struggle between the bourgeoisie and the proletariat, for, as in Russia, both will become the slaves of him who has seduced the one and led the other: the Jew. The NSDAP is rather of the conviction that this is about a racial struggle."[36] By 1923, Hitler had thoroughly internalized the Aufbau view that Jewish finance capitalists used Bolshevism to enslave European peoples, most notably Russians and Germans.

In his post-1923 writings, Hitler also labeled Bolshevism a pernicious outgrowth of Jewish capitalism. In *Mein Kampf*, he wrote of Bolshevism in "Russia" as a means "to give a gang of Jewish journalists and stock exchange bandits domination over a great people." In another section of his autobiography, he warned that the "Marxist shock troops of international stock exchange capital" sought to

break the back of the German national state for good and all . . . with friendly aid from outside. The armies of France must, therefore, besiege the German state structure until the *Reich*, inwardly exhausted, succumbs to the Bolshevistic shock troop of international Jewish world finance. And so the Jew today is the great agitator for the complete destruction of Germany.[37]

---

[35] Hitler, speech on September 28, 1922, *Sämtliche Aufzeichnungen*, 697.
[36] Hitler, speech on January 18, 1923, *Sämtliche Aufzeichnungen*, 796.
[37] Hitler, *Mein Kampf*, 376, 622, 623.

Hitler again linked capitalism and Bolshevism with the schemes of international Jewry in his unpublished 1928 sequel to *Mein Kampf* in which he primarily dealt with foreign policy matters. He asserted, "The national White Russia fought against the Jewish-speculative . . . international-capitalist Red Revolution." He further wrote of the current "Jewish-capitalist Bolshevik Russia."[38] Aufbau's views that the Jews used Bolshevism for the purposes of capitalist exploitation thus not only found expression in Hitler's early speeches, but in his later ideological works as well.

In addition to maintaining that Jewish financiers supported Bolshevism in order to achieve world rule, Aufbau ideologues and Eckart emphasized that the Bolshevik regime was an almost strictly Jewish undertaking. In *Aufbau Correspondence*, Scheubner-Richter asserted on one occasion that 80 percent of Soviet Commissars were Jews, while he later put the figure at 90 percent.[39] He also argued, "Today's 'Russian' Soviet government consists mainly of Jews."[40] In an April 1923 article, he emphasized that the "outrageous terror" in the former Russian Empire represented the "revenge of the Jews against the Russian people."[41]

Scheubner-Richter's Aufbau colleague Vinberg also treated the theme of the overwhelmingly Jewish nature of Bolshevism. In his work *Russia's Via Dolorosa*, he presented a historical schema in which over fifty years of "Jewish revolutionary agitation" in Imperial Russia had led to what others had termed the "Great All-Russian Revolution," but which deserved to be called the "Jewish Revolution." He further claimed that 545 leaders exercised dictatorial control over "Russia," of which 447 were Jews.[42]

Vinberg's ideological comrade in Aufbau, Rosenberg, who borrowed from Vinberg's ideas in his writings, consistently emphasized Bolshevism's Jewish nature.[43] He titled his first article for Eckart's *In Plain German*, "The Russian-Jewish Revolution." He claimed in his February 1919 essay that Jews in Russia had erected an "almost purely Jewish 'Russian' government" with Bolshevik leader Vladimir Lenin representing nothing but the "Russian

---

[38] Hitler, *Hitlers Zweites Buch: Ein Dokument aus dem Jahr 1928* (Stuttgart: Deutsche Verlags-Anstalt, 1961), 153, 154.

[39] Scheubner-Richter, "Judenverfolgungen in Sowjetrussland," *Aufbau-Korrespondenz*, October 25, 1922, 2; Scheubner-Richter, "Der Umfall des Patriarchen Tichon," *Aufbau-Korrespondenz*, July 27, 1923, 1.

[40] Scheubner-Richter, "Weltpolitische Umschau," *Aufbau-Korrespondenz*, July 13, 1923, 1.

[41] Scheubner-Richter, "Nansen verteidigt den Bolschewismus," *Aufbau-Korrespondenz*, April 19, 1923, 4.

[42] Vinberg, *Der Kreuzesweg Russlands*, 5, 20, 26.

[43] Johannes Baur, *Die russische Kolonie in München, 1900–1945: Deutsch–russische Beziehungen im 20. Jahrhundert* (Wiesbaden: Harrassowitz Verlag, 1998), 279; Walter Laqueur, *Russia and Germany: A Century of Conflict* (London: Weidenfeld and Nicolson, 1965), 116.

advertisement of the Jewish undertaking."[44] Rosenberg repeated his "Russian advertisement" charge regarding Lenin in his first book, *The Trail of the Jew through the Ages*. In this 1920 work, he also stressed that he had traveled in Russia from Petrograd in the north to the Crimea in the south in 1917 and 1918 and had noted that where Bolsheviks had gathered, "90 out of 100 of them were Jews."[45] In a March 1921 edition of *In Plain German*, he argued that approximately 90 percent of Soviet Commissars were Jews.[46] And he asserted in the *Völkisch Observer* in August 1921: "The names of all the Jewish executioners are available, of 550 governmental Commissars . . . 457 are Jews!"[47]

Rosenberg labeled Bolshevism a "Jewish dictatorship." He claimed in an April 1923 edition of the *Völkisch Observer* that "Bolshevism" represented a "purely Jewish dictatorship with the help of the scum of a people over the best of the nation."[48] Here he demonstrated his belief in the victim status of Russians at the hands of Jews. Rosenberg's assertions of Bolshevism's Jewish essence found widespread acceptance in Hitler's National Socialist Party. Writing in *In Plain German* in April 1921, Rosenberg credited the NSDAP alone among German political entities with expressing "the truth" about the "shameless Jewish dictatorship" over the peoples of the Soviet Union.[49]

Like Rosenberg, his assistant in *In Plain German*, Eckart viewed Bolshevism as a primarily Jewish phenomenon. In November 1919, he wrote in a manner similar to Rosenberg that "Jewish men of terror" truly led Bolshevism, with Lenin "only the one who has been put forward" as a front man.[50] He further asserted in February 1920 that of the total of 457 Soviet Commissars, 422 were Jews.[51] In a November 1920 article in *In Plain German*, Eckart cited an English source that placed the current number of Jewish Commissars at 446 out of 574.[52] Eckart continued to present Bolshevism as a Jewish menace after he began editing the *Völkisch Observer*

[44] Rosenberg, "Die russische-jüdische Revolution," *Auf gut deutsch*, February 21, 1919.

[45] Rosenberg, *Die Spur des Juden im Wandel der Zeiten*, 117.

[46] Rosenberg, "Hochverrat der deutschen Zionisten auf Grund ihrer eigenen Eingeständnisse erläutert, I," *Auf gut deutsch*, March 31, 1921.

[47] Rosenberg, "Der Pogrom am deutschen und am russischen Volke," *Völkischer Beobachter*, August 4, 1921, 3.

[48] Rosenberg, "Die jüdische Canaille: Stephan Grossmanns Verhöhnung des deutschen Volkes," *Völkischer Beobachter*, April 14, 1923, 1.

[49] Rosenberg, "Hochverrat der deutschen Zionisten auf Grund ihrer eigenen Eingeständnisse erläutert, II."

[50] Eckart, "Der Herr Rabbiner aus Bremen," *Auf gut deutsch*, November 11, 1919.

[51] Eckart, "Die Schlacht auf den Katalaunischen Feldern," *Auf gut deutsch*, February 20, 1920, 12.

[52] Eckart, "'Jewry über alles.'"

in August 1921 on Hitler's personal invitation.[53] Eckart asserted in an October 1921 edition of the National Socialist newspaper that the "true purpose of the Russian Revolution" represented the "murderous enslavement of an entire people by Jewry."[54]

Aufbau ideologues and their colleague Eckart consistently conceived overwhelming Jewish preponderance in Bolshevism, and they impressed this view forcefully upon Hitler. He claimed in an August 1920 speech that out of 478 Soviet delegates, 430 were Jews, "always the greatest enemies of the national Russian."[55] In the first article that he wrote for the *Völkisch Observer*, a January 1921 essay, "The *Völkisch* Idea and the Party," Hitler argued that out of a population of 150 million, there remained "perhaps only 600,000 who, not appalled at the hideousness of the Jewish blood dictatorship, do not damn this people and its diabolical infamies."[56] In Hitler's Aufbau-influenced view of Bolshevik Russia, a small Jewish minority oppressed millions through terror.

Hitler equated Bolshevism with Jewish rule in a March 1921 article in the *Völkisch Observer*, "Statesmen or National Criminals." He asserted: "Struggle against Bolshevism in Russia means the eradication of the Jews!" He argued, "The Russian worker will thoroughly solve the Jewish question" after recognizing the Jews as "devils" who had "promised heaven" but had created "hell." The "solution" that Hitler referred to did not mean the extermination of Jews along the lines of the *Endlösung* (Final Solution). He used imagery from the biblical Exodus to assert that the solving of the "Jewish question" in Russia would cause problems for Germany, for now "the great migration will begin. Russia today has become a desert. The Jew again longs for fleshpots. 'Joseph-Rathenau' Germany appears to them to be the Egypt of the future." While, he asserted, the Jews would not find a "Nile Delta," they would at least have a "Spree-Berlin."[57] At this point in his career, Hitler wanted to expel Jews from Germany, and he feared that more Jews would come to Germany when "Jewish Bolshevism" collapsed.

Hitler stressed the fundamentally Jewish nature of Bolshevism on other occasions. In April 1922, he asserted that "400 Soviet Commissars of Jewish nationality" lived lives of abundance, whereas 30 million Russians were reduced to eating "roots and grass" to prolong their lives for "a few weeks

[53] Eckart, "Vor dem Glockenschlag zwölf," *Völkischer Beobachter*, August 14, 1921, 1.
[54] Eckart, "Das 'siegreiche' Proletariat unter Standrecht," *Völkischer Beobachter*, October 26, 1921, 1.
[55] Hitler, speech on August 6, 1920, *Sämtliche Aufzeichnungen*, 172.
[56] Hitler, "Der völkische Gedanke und die Partei," *Völkischer Beobachter*, January 1, 1921, 1.
[57] Hitler, "Staatsmänner oder Nationalverbrecher," *Völkischer Beobachter*, March 15, 1921, 2.

or days."[58] In forming his concept of "Jewish Bolshevism," Hitler learned a great deal from Vinberg in particular. Aufbau leadership assigned Vinberg to hold detailed ideological discussions with Hitler by the fall of 1922 at the latest. As of October 1922, Vinberg had already held numerous lengthy personal discussions with Hitler.[59] Notes that Hitler made for a November 1922 speech demonstrated Vinberg's influence over his thinking on the "Jewish question." Hitler cited "Col[onel] Weinberg" [sic] that the Soviet Union represented a "Jewish state." He further jotted down, "Outcome: collapse à la Russia. Jewish dictatorship. Evidence (Weinberg) [sic]."[60]

Vinberg's colleagues Scheubner-Richter and Rosenberg in particular stressed that the "Jewish Bolshevik" dictatorship had killed millions of Russians through war, disease, starvation, and execution. In an October 1922 edition of *Aufbau Correspondence*, Scheubner-Richter estimated the costs of the "Bolshevik experiment" to the Russian people at approximately two million refugees and 35 million dead.[61] In an August 1921 *Völkisch Observer* article, "The Pogrom Against the German and the Russian Peoples," Rosenberg claimed of Russia: "A characteristic Jewish rule of terror was set up as world history had not yet seen . . . Over 30 million people have sunk away through murder, starvation, and cholera."[62] He revised his figures upwards in his 1923 *Protocols* work. He asserted, "Over 40 million Russians perished through the Jewish terror."[63] Hitler used the figure of 40 million Russian victims of starvation that the Jews had caused as early as an August 1921 speech.[64]

Scheubner-Richter and Rosenberg accused the "Jewish Bolshevik" regime of deliberately and systematically annihilating the nationalist Russian spiritual and intellectual leadership. Scheubner-Richter argued in an April 1922 *Aufbau Correspondence* article, "The Plunder of the Church": "Right at the beginning of its rule, Bolshevism began the methodical persecution of the Orthodox Church hand in hand with the general extermination of the Russian intelligentsia."[65] In a June 1923 article in *Aufbau Correspondence*, "The Third International at Work," he described the

[58] "Die 'Hetzer' der Wahrheit: Rede des Pg. Adolf Hitler in der Versammlung vom 12. April 1922 im Bürgerbräukeller zu München," *Völkischer Beobachter*, April 22, 1922, 7.

[59] DB report from November 11, 1922, RGVA (TsKhIDK), *fond* 7, *opis* 1, *delo* 386, reel 2, 160.

[60] Hitler, notes for a speech on November 2, 1922, *Sämtliche Aufzeichnungen*, 713, 716.

[61] Scheubner-Richter, "Judenverfolgungen in Sowjetrussland," 2.

[62] Rosenberg, "Der Pogrom am deutschen und am russischen Volke," 3.

[63] Rosenberg, *Die Protokolle der Weisen von Zion und die Jüdische Weltpolitik*, 81.

[64] Hitler, speech on August 19, 1921, *Sämtliche Aufzeichnungen*, 458.

[65] Scheubner-Richter, "Kirchenplünderung," *Aufbau-Korrespondenz*, April 14, 1922, 2.

Jewish scheme to establish the "rule of the international Jews." In Russia, this undertaking "began with the extermination of the Russian national intelligentsia."[66]

Like his Aufbau colleague Scheubner-Richter, Rosenberg accused "Jewish Bolsheviks" of annihilating nationalist Russians. In his above-mentioned August 1921 article in the *Völkisch Observer*, "The Pogrom against the German and the Russian Peoples," Rosenberg claimed: "A systematic destruction of the Russian national intelligentsia by the Jewish government began immediately after the Bolsheviks had triumphed."[67] In his 1922 work *Plague in Russia!* he asserted, "The Jewish conspirator took the place of the expelled or murdered leadership." Moreover, he argued, "Such a systematic eradication of the national Russian leadership would never ever have taken place if Russians had been at the head of the coup. It is well known that the true dictator of Soviet Russia is the Jew Lev Trotskii."[68] Here Rosenberg demonstrated pro-Russian and anti-Semitic views by ascribing terrible Soviet exterminations to sinister Jewish elements.

Rosenberg described horrific means that "Jewish Bolsheviks" allegedly used in their efforts to eliminate nationalist Russian spiritual and intellectual leaders. In his book *Plague in Russia!* he wrote of a sadistic type of torture widely attributed to "Jewish and Chinese" agents of the Chrezvychainaia Komissia po Borbe s Kontr-revolutsiei (Extraordinary Commission for the Struggle with Counter-revolution, usually referred to as the Cheka). This torment was euphemistically referred to as "pulling off gloves." In this gruesome process, Cheka agents supposedly dunked the victim's arms in boiling water, removed them, made circular cuts at the elbows, and stripped off the skin.[69]

Rosenberg's colleague Eckart emphasized the White émigré theme of the Jewish eradication of the nationalist Russian spiritual and intellectual leadership, often through horrific means. Eckart described the "pulling off gloves" form of torture in an April 1920 article, "That Which Kapp Wanted to Protect Us From." He attributed this atrocity to "Jewish Commissars" against "men, women, young girls, and even small children." Citing an English newspaper, he also depicted a method of torture whereby "Jewish Commissars" bound stone jars filled with live rats over the genitals of their prisoners and then used fire to force the vermin to gnaw their way into their

[66] Scheubner-Richter, "Die dritte Internationale an der Arbeit," *Aufbau-Korrespondenz*, June 7, 1923, 1.
[67] Rosenberg, "Der Pogrom am deutschen und am russischen Volke," 3.
[68] Rosenberg, *Pest in Russland!*, 23, 25.   [69] Rosenberg, *Pest in Russland!*, 78.

victims' flesh. Eckart further wrote of the "Jewish Commissars'" mission "to eradicate Christianity root and branch" through cruel methods.[70] Eckart's revulsion at sadistic "Jewish Bolshevik" means of destroying the Christian Russian leadership did not derive solely from White émigré sources, but White émigrés in general and Rosenberg in particular influenced Eckart's notions of "Jewish Bolshevism" as a hideous scourge of Christianity.

In a February 1920 edition of *In Plain German*, Eckart used the Zunder Document as evidence of the Jewish destruction of the nationalist Russian intelligentsia. It will be recalled that the Zunder Document was a spurious anti-Semitic propaganda piece from the Russian Civil War that purported to emanate from the Central Committee of the Israelite International League.[71] Eckart quoted the letter's assertion that allegedly came from Bolshevik Jews: "We must destroy the best and cleverest minds." He asserted, "Even if this document did not exist, it would be genuine, so precisely does it correspond to the Jewish way of thinking."[72] Eckart believed that Jewish thought called for the mass extermination of Gentiles.

Hitler learned from the assertions of Eckart, Scheubner-Richter, and Rosenberg that "Jewish Bolshevism" had virtually annihilated the nationalist Russian intelligentsia. In his notes for a December 1920 oration, he wrote: "The bloody Jew. The Russian mortuary. Slaughter of the intellectual leadership of a people. A people without brain-workers is lost (The Soviet X Dietrich E[c]kart X)."[73] In a July 1922 speech, Hitler claimed, "The Jew with his Revolution" sought his own "protection" through the "elimination of the evil national intelligentsia." He further stressed that "over 30 million people" in the Soviet Union had been "martyred, partly on the scaffold, partly through machine guns and similar means, partly in veritable slaughtering houses, and the rest through starvation in millions upon millions." In short: "An entire people is dying out there."[74] Hitler thus drew upon Eckartian and Aufbau thought in forming his view that the "Jewish Bolsheviks" decimated the Russian people and destroyed its intelligentsia.

In *Mein Kampf*, Hitler again treated the "Jewish Bolshevik" annihilation of the nationalist Russian intelligentsia. He drew upon Aufbau and

[70] Eckart, "Wovor uns Kapp behüten wollte," *Auf gut deutsch*, April 16, 1920.

[71] Norman Cohn, *Warrant for Genocide: The Myth of the Jewish World-Conspiracy and the "Protocols of the Elders of Zion"* (Chico, CA: Scholars Press, 1981), 119–121.

[72] Eckart, "Die Schlacht auf den Katalaunischen Feldern."

[73] Hitler, notes for a speech on December 8, 1920, *Sämtliche Aufzeichnungen*, 275.

[74] "Freistaat oder Sklaventum? Rede des Pg. Adolf Hitler in der Versammlung der national-sozialistischen Deutschen Arbeiterpartei vom 28. Juli 1922 im grossen Saale des Bürgerbräukellers in München," *Völkischer Beobachter*, August 16, 1922, 6.

Eckartian thought to describe a ruthless Jewish drive for world domination. With the stage set for the "last great revolution," Hitler argued:

The democratic people's Jew becomes the blood-Jew and tyrant over peoples. In a few years he tries to exterminate the national intelligentsia and by robbing the peoples of their natural intellectual leadership makes them ripe for the slave's lot of permanent subjugation.

He further asserted, "The most frightful example of this kind is offered by Russia, where [the Jew] killed or starved about thirty million people with positively fanatical savagery, in part amid inhuman tortures."[75] Hitler presented Russians as the greatest victims of international Jewry's insatiable drive to destroy nationalist intelligentsias in order to achieve world rule.

In his unpublished 1928 sequel to *Mein Kampf*, Hitler further dealt with the Aufbau/Eckartian theme of the "Jewish Bolshevik" annihilation of the former leading elements of Russian society in order to establish Jewish rule. He argued that the Imperial Russian ruling class had consisted "above all" of "very many Germans (Balts!)." The Aufbau members and Baltic Germans Scheubner-Richter and Rosenberg also believed this. Hitler argued, "Jewry exterminated the previous foreign upper strata with the help of Slavic racial instincts." In the conclusion of his work, he maintained: "The total victims of this Jewish struggle for hegemony in Russia amounted to 28–30 million dead for the Russian people" in "the most terrible crime against humanity of all times."[76] Hitler was outraged at what he regarded as the deliberate "Jewish Bolshevik" massacre of the best of the Russian people.

In addition to writing of horrible conditions in the Soviet Union, Vinberg, Scheubner-Richter, Rosenberg, and Eckart warned that "Jewish Bolshevism" threatened to overwhelm Germany. Rosenberg and Eckart stressed that "Jewish Bolsheviks" would eradicate the nationalist German intelligentsia after they had conquered Germany. In his work *Russia's Via Dolorosa*, Vinberg cautioned that "Jewish Bolshevism" threatened to engulf Germany. He asserted of the 1919 Spartacist uprising under the "Jewess Rosa Luxemburg," "The revolution in Germany developed according to the same Jewish directives as in Russia."[77] In a September 1923 article in *Aufbau Correspondence*, "Bolshevism Ready to Pounce!", Scheubner-Richter argued that "Jewish Bolshevism" with its atrocities was on the verge of spreading to Germany. He claimed: "The greatest danger that threatens Germany is

---

[75] Hitler, *Mein Kampf*, 326.   [76] Hitler, *Hitlers Zweites Buch*, 156, 158, 221.
[77] Vinberg, *Der Kreuzesweg Russlands*, 28.

not the black and white French, but Jewish Bolshevism."[78] Even at the time of the French/Belgian occupation of the Ruhr, Scheubner-Richter stressed the primacy of the "Jewish Bolshevik" peril.

Rosenberg feared the spread of the Bolshevik "plague" to Germany, for he firmly believed that the triumph of Bolshevism in Germany would bring with it the Jewish annihilation of the nationalist German intelligentsia. He stressed in a March 1921 edition of the *Völkisch Observer* that Jews threatened to carry out the "slaughter of the national leadership" in Germany followed by "bloody Jewish terror enforced with foreign troops as in Russia."[79] Here Rosenberg emphasized that the Jews sought to destroy the leading elements of a conquered people and then to use others to do their dirty work for them.

In the final installation of his essay printed in the *Völkisch Observer* in August 1921, "Anti-Semitism: An Economic, Political, National, Religious, and Moral Necessity," Rosenberg warned: "If things go on as of late, then the coming struggle will bring victory to Jewish Bolshevism and cost the best Germans their lives."[80] In his 1922 treatise, *Plague in Russia!*, Rosenberg cautioned, "The misery, starvation, and epidemic that already prevail in Russia are in store for the German people; it must prepare itself to hand down its national intelligentsia to eradication."[81] Rosenberg strongly believed that if "Jewish Bolsheviks" established their tyranny over Germany, then they would destroy the best of the German people just as they had allegedly eradicated the Russian nationalist intelligentsia.

In an article in a November 1920 edition of *In Plain German*, "'Jewry above Everything,'" Rosenberg's colleague Eckart argued that Jewish Bolsheviks threatened to conquer Germany as they had Russia. First he outlined the supposed Jewish campaign for world domination. To begin with, the "Jewish-contaminated press" had incited the peoples of the world to wage war. In the ensuing conflagration, Germany had defeated Imperial Russia so that "Jewish Bolshevism" could take root there. Jewish subversion in Germany had led to the "'Glorious Revolution' with almost nobody but Hebrews at the head." Eckart argued that there would soon arise "from the Neva to the Rhine, on the bloody ruins of the previous national traditions, a single Jewish empire, the most Christian-slaughtering dictatorship of the Jewish world savior Lenin and his Elias, Trotskii-Braunstein!"[82]

---

[78] Scheubner-Richter, "Der Bolschewismus sprungbereit!," *Aufbau-Korrespondenz*, September 29, 1923, 2.
[79] Rosenberg, "Schicksalswende in London!", 3.
[80] Rosenberg, "Antisemitismus: Eine wirtschaftliche, politische, nationale, religiöse und sittliche Notwendigkeit, (Schluss)," *Völkischer Beobachter*, August 21, 1921, 3.
[81] Rosenberg, *Pest in Russland!*, 93.   [82] Eckart, "'Jewry über alles,'" 2.

In an article in a May 1922 edition of the *Völkisch Observer*, "A New World War in Sight!", Eckart again warned of international Jewry's impending destruction of Germany. He lamented that a Jew, Germany's Foreign Minister Walther Rathenau (who was soon afterwards assassinated as part of a right-wing conspiracy in which Aufbau members participated), had officially recognized the Soviet Union. Eckart asserted that this act had "nothing to do with the German or the Russian peoples," but rather had been coordinated by "all the Jews of the world." He warned, "Israel stands directly in front of its ancient goal: just several months, and Jewish Bolshevism will have destroyed the German nationality, the only opposition that could pit itself against the 'people of God' on its path to (lawless) world rule."[83] Here Eckart portrayed the Germans as the last bulwark against Jewish efforts to eliminate the best of the Gentiles through bloody Bolshevism.

Drawing upon Eckartian and Aufbau thought, Hitler claimed that "Jewish Bolshevism" threatened to eliminate Germany's national, spiritual, and intellectual leadership. In the second essay that he wrote for the *Völkisch Observer*, "Is the Establishment of a *Völkisch* Newspaper that Seizes the Broad Masses a National Necessity?", which appeared in January 1921, he compared German conditions with those in Bolshevik Russia. He claimed that the Jews were inciting the masses for the "final blow against . . . what we call the state" in Germany, "like in Soviet Russia." With the destruction of the state, he meant the eradication of the nation's leading elements. He concluded his essay by stressing: "World history mercilessly takes revenge for neglected necessities. Look at Russia."[84] Hitler viewed the perceived Jewish annihilation of the leading Russian nationalists as a harbinger of what evils threatened to occur in Germany through the ruthless Jewish drive to power.

In one of his clearest anti-Bolshevik and anti-Semitic warnings, Hitler asserted in an April 1922 speech that Bolshevism under Jewish Commissars meant "bagging the intellectual head of the nation, that is, bringing it to the scaffold." He emphasized: "As in Russia, exactly so with us." He then asked where National Socialists could look for assistance. He asserted, "The left . . . cannot help," whereas "the right would like to help," but it could not do so since it had "still not grasped that it is not necessary to be an enemy of the Jew to be dragged to the scaffold by him one day in accordance with the Russian model." The right had failed to

---

[83] Eckart, "Ein neuer Weltkrieg in Sicht!", *Völkischer Beobachter*, May 17, 1922, 1.

[84] Hitler, "Ist die Errichtung einer die breiten Massen erfassenden Völkischen Zeitung eine nationale Notwendigkeit?" *Völkischer Beobachter*, January 30, 1921, 1, 3.

understand that all that was necessary to be executed was "to have a head and not to be a Jew."[85] Hitler believed that his movement alone, which fused certain nationalist and socialist ideas, could ward off the threatened "Jewish Bolshevik" annihilation of the nationalist German intelligentsia.

In the conclusion of his unpublished 1928 sequel to *Mein Kampf*, Hitler went beyond his warnings that "Jewish Bolsheviks" threatened to eradicate nationalist Germans. He asserted that the Jews by their very nature worked to destroy the national intelligentsias of all peoples through Bolshevism in order to achieve world rule. He asserted of "the Jew,"

His ultimate goal is denationalization, the muddled half-breeding of the other peoples, the lowering of the racial level of the most superior, as well as the domination of this racial mush through the extermination of the *völkisch* intelligentsias and their replacement by the members of his own people. The result of the Jewish world struggle will hence always be bloody Bolshevization, which is in reality the destruction of the peoples' own intellectual upper strata so that he himself is able to rise to become the master of humanity.[86]

In this telling passage, Hitler combined *völkisch* German and anti-Bolshevik, anti-Semitic White émigré beliefs. He expressed *völkisch* thought by warning of imperiled racial purity through the agency of the Jews. By labeling what he regarded as the deliberate Jewish "half-breeding" of other peoples along with the elimination of their leading elements as "Bolshevization," he also demonstrated the considerable degree to which events in the Soviet Union as interpreted by Aufbau White émigrés and Eckart had captured and held his imagination. Hitler offered a meta-historical narrative of "the Jew" as the agent of "bloody Bolshevization," which sought to destroy the "*völkisch* intelligentsias" of all peoples in order to enable Jewish world domination.

In the early 1920s, Hitler's colleagues Eckart and the Aufbau ideologues Scheubner-Richter, Vinberg, and Rosenberg clearly regarded the Jews as a mortal threat, but they did not publicly propose exterminating Jews along the lines of the National Socialist policy that became known as the Final Solution. As noted in Chapter Three, Eckart favored incarcerating leading Jews in Germany.[87] In an early article in *In Plain German*, he also suggested expelling the Jews from Germany. He queried, "If we were rid of them, would we not at least have the advantage over earlier times of not having to see, hear, or smell them any more?"[88] In another early article in *In Plain*

---

[85] "Die 'Hetzer' der Warheit," 7.   [86] Hitler, *Hitlers Zweites Buch*, 221.

[87] Eckart's questioning at the AGM on July 10, 1920, RGVA (TsKhIDK), *fond* 567, *opis* 1, *delo* 2496, 17.

[88] Eckart, "Der Baccalaureus," *Auf gut deutsch*, October 23, 1919, 10.

German, Eckart sympathized with expelling the Jews from Germany when he made a play on words regarding a German town that had no Jews: "Incidentally, no Jews in Lorch? Hark!" (Übrigens – keine Juden in Lorch? Horch!).[89]

Despite all his warnings against "Jewish Bolshevism," Scheubner-Richter did not propose sweeping anti-Semitic measures in the pages of *Aufbau Correspondence* or the *Völkisch Observer*. Scheubner-Richter's colleague Vinberg made some vague anti-Semitic threats in his 1922 work, *Russia's Via Dolorosa*. He warned the Jews, "You are dancing on a volcano! . . . The peoples who have been deceived by you will get their bitter revenge against you and pay you back for your crimes!" In another passage, he asserted: "The end of Jewish-Masonic rule is approaching! A new Russia will arise and ruthlessly smash its enemies down."[90] Vinberg did not specify precisely what he meant by this, but he clearly had menacing intent.

Vinberg's Aufbau colleague Rosenberg wished to implement severe restrictions against the Jews. He recommended measures similar to those that the far right Union of the Russian People had advocated in 1906 or that the *völkisch* leader Heinrich Class had proposed in his 1912 work, *If I Were the Kaiser*. In the above-mentioned August 1921 article in the *Völkisch Observer*, "The Pogrom against the German and the Russian Peoples," Rosenberg called for the "complete removal of the Jews from all posts, offices, public agencies, leading economic authorities, and cultural institutions." He warned: "If this does not take place, then the pogrom against the German people will follow that against the Russian one."[91]

Rosenberg made similar anti-Semitic demands in the final installation of his essay, "Anti-Semitism: An Economic, Political, National, Religious, and Moral Necessity," which appeared in the August 21, 1921 edition of the *Völkisch Observer*. He demanded, "Out with the Jews from all parties." He further advocated "the proper assessment of all Eastern Jews, the strictest supervision of the indigenous ones, the closing of Zionism that pursues English–Jewish policy, the confiscation of its monies and the expulsion of its members to their English saints or to the Promised Land." He cautioned: "If this does not take place, then none of the generations still living today has the prospect of ever again living in the German fatherland."[92]

Eckart and Aufbau ideologues did not propose physically exterminating the Jews in the early 1920s, and they lacked the power to carry out a

---

[89] Eckart, "Trotz alledem!", *Auf gut deutsch*, July 11, 1919, 11.
[90] Vinberg, *Der Kreuzesweg Russlands*, 112, 222.
[91] Rosenberg, "Der Pogrom am deutschen und am russischen Volke," 3.
[92] Rosenberg, "Antisemitismus, (Schluss)," 3.

large-scale slaughter of Jews at the time in any case. Rosenberg did, however, learn from what he regarded as the typical "Jewish Bolshevik" methods of extermination. He helped to form the chilling concept that Hitler's National Socialist state later put into practice during World War II, namely that eliminating a nation's intelligentsia rendered the people as a whole easy to dominate.

While castigating what he regarded as the bloody "Jewish Bolshevik" extermination of the Russian national intelligentsia, Rosenberg also found a certain method to this madness. (We have already seen in the previous chapter that Rosenberg's Aufbau superior Scheubner-Richter learned from Bolshevik methods of subversion followed by strict centralization and militarization.) Rosenberg noted in his 1922 work, *Plague in Russia!*, "If one robs a people of its intellectual blossom, then it is, as a people, actually no longer in existence. Then only the masses remain, which, if one knows their instincts, are usable for anything, at least for a while."[93] In his 1923 *Protocols* book, he emphasized that "Jewry" could establish a dictatorship over a people "only with the assistance of the directionless masses who have been robbed of their national intelligentsia," as had been the case in Bolshevik Russia.[94] While he loathed "Jewish Bolsheviks," Rosenberg nonetheless learned from the ruthless methods of the eradication of political foes that he attributed to them.

APOCALYPTIC ANTI-JUDEO-BOLSHEVISM

In addition to regarding Bolshevism as an extremely dangerous, concrete political threat, White émigré Aufbau ideologues depicted the far right crusade against threatened "Jewish Bolshevik" chaos in religiously inspired apocalyptic terms. They warned of a terrible nationalist struggle against Bolshevism similar to the battle between Christ and Anti-Christ dealt with in the biblical Book of Revelation. They cast the anti-Bolshevik fight in terms of Aryan, most notably German and Russian, versus Jew. Eckart and his pupil Hitler drew from the apocalyptic dimension of anti-Bolshevik, anti-Semitic White émigré Aufbau thought.

Of the leading Aufbau ideological trio of Scheubner-Richter, Rosenberg, and Vinberg, the last possessed the most pronounced religious outlook. Vinberg, who was described as an "extremely religious" man, tended to view

---

[93] Rosenberg, *Pest in Russland!*, 23.
[94] Rosenberg, *Die Protokolle der Weisen von Zion und die Jüdische Weltpolitik*, 112.

events from a theological standpoint.[95] He regarded the National Socialists as upholders of Christianity. In a May 1923 letter, he praised the *Völkisch Observer* as a "courageous newspaper that so openly supports the spiritual traditions of Christian Germany."[96] Vinberg cast his support of Grand Prince Kirill Romanov for the Tsarist throne in religious terms as well. He wrote in the pro-Kirill *Vestnik russkago monarkhicheskago obedineniia v Bavarii* (*Bulletin of the Russian Monarchical Union in Bavaria*) that he edited: "We are still in satanic darkness, surrounded by ant-Christian forces." He exhorted White émigrés to further the "great cause of Russia's salvation."[97]

Like the mystically inclined Imperial Russian author Sergei Nilus, who had played a crucial role in popularizing *The Protocols of the Elders of Zion*, Vinberg viewed Jews as a satanic and apocalyptic force. In his work *Russia's Via Dolorosa*, he had the "Zionist wise men" declare: "You should finally recognize that our way is that of evil, the way of proud, all-conquering, ruthless Satanism." In another passage, he asserted of "the Jews," "The entire world is now in the clutches of these Anti-Christs." Vinberg expressed a mystical vision of triumph over these "Anti-Christs." He described a dream of his in which a "holy, wonderful ray . . . penetrates this infinite darkness that shrouds our tormented homeland and leaves it trembling before the inevitable reckoning of the Day of Judgment." Here Vinberg referred to the positive aspect of the Book of Revelation, namely the prospect of ultimate salvation for the just, which is often overlooked in light of Revelation's gripping description of chaos and destruction.

Vinberg referred to Revelation in another section of *Russia's Via Dolorosa*. After warning "you master Jews" in Russia, "We do not like your government at all," he stressed:

The time will never come in which we will be one with you. Pick up our holy *Book of Revelation* and read in it what Saint John says. Then you will understand that we are faithful Christians and that we will never bow before your triumph . . . We will certainly be destroyed in the struggle with you, as you are still just too strong, but not those who will come after us. In the end you too will be destroyed, for we already feel the victory of our swords and firmly believe that the truth cannot be desecrated by falsehood forever. The light must finally penetrate the darkness and triumph over evil.[98]

---

[95] Josefine Trausenecker's testimony included in a PDM report to the BSMI from March 30, 1922, BHSAM, BSMI 22, number 71624, fiche 4, 14.

[96] Vinberg, "Der wackere Zentralverein," *Völkischer Beobachter*, May 9, 1923, 3.

[97] Vinberg, editorial, *Vestnik russkago monarkhicheskago obedineniia v Bavarii*, April 7, 1923, 2, 3, GARF.

[98] Vinberg, *Der Kreuzesweg Russlands*, 2, 18, 25, 116.

Vinberg thus held out the prospect of eventual Christian victory over the satanic Jewish Anti-Christs who directed Bolshevism.

Aufbau's leader Scheubner-Richter did not exhibit a mystical sense of religiosity to the extent that Vinberg did. He did, however, consistently treat the Bolshevik persecution of Orthodox Christian leaders in his newspaper articles, and he demonstrated a sound sense of broad Russian religious sentiments inside Soviet borders. In a July 1923 edition of *Aufbau Correspondence*, he noted that ever more sects had formed in the Soviet Union "in which religious fanaticism is paired with political and religious anti-Semitism." These sects believed that the "'Anti-Christ' had climbed down to the earth and had seized possession of the holy Kremlin, and . . . all crop failures and all other afflictions came to the Russian people since it continued to tolerate the rule of the Anti-Christ in the holy Kremlin."[99] While he did not personally share these views literally, Scheubner-Richter nonetheless presented them in a sympathetic light.

Scheubner-Richter used apocalyptic imagery in his calls to arms, as in an article for the *Völkisch Observer* in September 1923, "Germany's Bolshevization." He stressed that "*völkisch* Germany" knew that it had to fight against the "Jewish International" to decide the "fate of Europe, yes, perhaps the fate of the entire world." This struggle would determine whether "national culture, *völkisch* individuality, and Christianity" would persevere or whether they would be "melted together in an international mush."[100] Here Scheubner-Richter portrayed nationalist Germans as the protectors of order and light against approaching "Jewish Bolshevik" chaos and darkness.

Scheubner-Richter's colleague Rosenberg increasingly opposed Christian Churches as institutions, but he nonetheless favored certain self-sacrificing elements of Christianity in the vein of the *völkisch* thinkers Richard Wagner and Houston Stewart Chamberlain.[101] Rosenberg ended his first book, *The Trail of the Jew through the Ages*, by calling for the dawning of the "day of Christian-Germanic thinking." He also demanded apocalyptically: "The Christian spirit and the filthy Jewish spirit must be separated; the Bible is to be split up with a sharp cut as Christ and Anti-Christ."[102] Here he presented a dichotomy between the redeeming Germanic spirit and the sinister Jewish essence.

---

[99] Scheubner-Richter, "Der Umfall des Patriarchen Tichon," 2.

[100] Scheubner-Richter, "Deutschlands Bolschewisierung," 1.

[101] Robert Cecil, *The Myth of the Master Race: Alfred Rosenberg and Nazi Ideology* (London: B. T. Batsford Ltd., 1972), 82.

[102] Rosenberg, *Die Spur des Juden im Wandel der Zeiten*, 162, 163.

Rosenberg treated "Jewish Bolshevism" with the language of a biblical scourge. In his book *Plague in Russia!*, for instance, he asserted, "A frenzy, an indescribably cynical sadism, an insanity" was "raging in the East." Faced with this menace, the possible outcomes for Europe were either that "the West sinks in bloody smoke," or "a purposeful minority of German men alter course with ruthless determination."[103] In his 1923 *Protocols* work, Rosenberg asserted that Russia offered an "example of the most monumental sort of . . . Jewish world destruction."[104] Rosenberg thus attributed a sinister and apocalyptic influence on world affairs to the Jews.

Rosenberg's colleague and Hitler's mentor, Eckart, used apocalyptic language when discussing the Jewish peril, which he specifically related to conditions in the Soviet Union. Eckart used the Book of Revelation in treating the menace of "Jewish world rule" as begun in Russia. In a March 1919 article in *In Plain German*, Eckart used the Book of Revelation as a warning of impending Jewish destruction. He emphasized:

All in all it is about Jewish world rule. It began in Russia, now it is our turn. They cry out, "Dictatorship of the proletariat," but what is meant is the "dictatorship over the proletariat," better said, over all non-Jews . . . How does it go in the Apocalypse, reworked by me? Seven-headed from the pool / Has the beast climbed up / And the old dragon gave him / Strength to vanquish simple-mindedness / Gave him tongues to all peoples / So that he speaks great things / And with cunning blasphemies / Traps his victims twice.[105]

In a February 1920 article in *In Plain German*, Eckart stressed that once again "the Russian chaos" threatened Christendom, this time driven by "Israel's vengeful spirit." He quoted Revelation 6:8, "And I looked, and behold, a pale horse & his name that sate on him was Death, and hell followed with him: and power was given unto them, over the fourth part of the earth to kill with sword, & with hunger, and with death, and with the beastes of the earth.'" Eckart applied this biblical prophecy to the current political situation. He asserted, "With the beasts of the earth. With the bestialized masses of the Russian people . . . over mountains of corpses."[106] Eckart lamented Jewry's destructive role in Russia, which he tied in with apocalyptic notions.

Finally, Eckart warned of "Jewish Bolshevism" apocalyptically in a May 1922 article in the *Völkisch Observer*. He claimed that "national Russia" stood

---

[103] Rosenberg, *Pest in Russland!*, 74.
[104] Rosenberg, *Die Protokolle der Weisen von Zion und die Jüdische Weltpolitik*, 41.
[105] Eckart, "Das Karnickel," *Auf gut deutsch*, March 28, 1919.
[106] Eckart, "Die Schlacht auf den Katalaunischen Feldern."

ready to send the "murderous riff raff" of Jewish Bolsheviks and their "bestial following . . . into hell." Therefore the "pan-Jew is moving heaven and earth" to bring about the "apocalyptic break-in of Jewish Bolshevism . . . into the long-since tottering European cultural world!"[107] Eckart regarded "Jewish Bolshevism" as a demonic apocalyptic force that threatened to destroy all of Europe.

Influenced by Eckart, Rosenberg, Scheubner-Richter, and Vinberg, Hitler used the horrible state of affairs in the Soviet Union as the primary example of what he regarded as the Jewish proclivity for apocalyptic devastation. In a July 1922 speech, he asserted, "The Jew" destroyed only to "collapse himself with the destruction." He named the Soviet Union as the best example of this calamitous process. He maintained, "The Jew . . . must extend each and every thing internationally. How long? Until the entire world lies in ruins and drags him himself down into the ruins. Today this has been virtually, nay completely, achieved in Russia." In Hitler's mind, the horrendous conditions in the Soviet Union demonstrated the ultimately fatal consequences of the irredeemably materialist and world-destroying Jewish essence.

In this speech, Hitler asserted that Bavaria had an anti-Bolshevik "mission" against the Jewish "scourge of God" whereby it could "perhaps hinder this conflagration of the East from spreading further in Europe so that the Jewish world scourge finally will be checked and the deliverance of European culture in the face of this Asiatic horde will come again."[108] In his political views, Hitler espoused Aufbau and Eckartian notions of "Jewry" as an apocalyptic force that threatened to cause the catastrophic downfall of Germany and the rest of Europe. He pledged to fight against the "Jewish would scourge" with all of his strength.

In *Mein Kampf*, Hitler expressed his apocalyptic belief that the Jews threatened to destroy the world through the spread of Bolshevism, and he promised to fight against Jewry. He maintained: "If, with the help of his Marxist creed, the Jew is victorious over the other peoples of the world, his crown will be the funeral wreath of humanity and this planet will, as it did thousands of years ago, move through the ether devoid of men." He asserted, "Hence today I believe that I am acting in accordance with the will of the Almighty Creator: by defending myself against the Jew, I am fighting for the work of the Lord."[109] Hitler adopted Aufbau and Eckartian conceptions of "Jewish Bolshevism" as an apocalyptic force that threatened

---

[107] Eckart, "Das bayerische Orakel von Genua," *Völkischer Beobachter*, May 24, 1922, 1.
[108] "Freistaat oder Sklaventum?" 6, 8.   [109] Hitler, *Mein Kampf*, 65.

to ruin Germany and even the entire world, and he promised to struggle against this dark menace.

CONCLUSION

In the early years of the Weimar Republic, the leading Aufbau ideological trio of Max von Scheubner-Richter, Fedor Vinberg, and Alfred Rosenberg, acting in conjunction with the prominent *völkisch* theorist Dietrich Eckart, played a fundamental role in shaping National Socialist ideology. In warning against the horrors of "Jewish Bolshevism," these "four writers of the apocalypse" expressed a particularly virulent form of White émigré conspiratorial and apocalyptic anti-Semitic thought that radicalized early National Socialist beliefs. Hitler learned a great deal from the conspiratorial-apocalyptic anti-Semitic views of Scheubner-Richter, Vinberg, Rosenberg, and Eckart, as he had not been an anti-Semite and had considered himself a socialist well into 1919.

Drawing inspiration from the anti-Semitic ideas of the Imperial Russian author Fedor Dostoevskii, the four writers of the apocalypse argued that a vast Jewish world conspiracy, which manipulated both predatory finance capitalism and bloodthirsty Bolshevism, threatened to ruin Germany and even the world. The four colleagues maintained that Bolshevism was an almost strictly Jewish phenomenon. They stressed that "Jewish Bolshevism" had killed millions upon millions of Russians through war, disease, starvation, and misrule and, what was worse, had systematically eliminated the Russian nationalist intelligentsia. "Jewish Bolsheviks" threatened to destroy the best Germans in the near future as well.

While the ideological quartet clearly viewed international Jewry that controlled finance capitalism and Bolshevism as a mortal danger to Germany, they did not propose physically exterminating Jews, and at least one of them, Rosenberg, learned from "Jewish Bolshevik" atrocities. Eckart variously favored imprisoning leading Jews in Germany and expelling all Jews from Germany. Scheubner-Richter did not advocate large-scale anti-Semitic measures in either *Aufbau Correspondence* or the *Völkisch Observer*. Vinberg made some imprecise threats against Jewry. Rosenberg proposed removing Jews from all leading public positions. While he despised Bolshevism, Rosenberg nonetheless perceived a certain logic in what he regarded as the "Jewish Bolshevik" method of physically exterminating political enemies.

The Aufbau and Eckartian warnings of "Jewish Bolshevism" as the most menacing manifestation of an international Jewish finance conspiracy that sought to achieve world domination, but inevitably had to lead to world destruction, imparted an apocalyptic anti-Bolshevik and anti-Semitic missionary spirit and drive to Hitler's National Socialist movement. Although Aufbau ceased to act as a powerful political force in 1923 and Eckart died that same year, as we shall see, Aufbau left a considerable anti-Bolshevik, anti-Semitic ideological legacy to Hitler after 1923, and it also provided a substantial political, financial, and military heritage to the National Socialist Party.

CHAPTER 9

Aufbau's legacy to National Socialism

While Aufbau clearly played a formative role in shaping early anti-Bolshevik, anti-Semitic National Socialist ideology, the historian Walter Laqueur has minimized the heritage that Aufbau left to National Socialism after 1923. In his work *Russia and Germany*, Laqueur asserts that National Socialism did not need White émigré support after it had become a mass movement in the course of the 1920s.[1] While National Socialist–White émigré collaboration did decrease markedly in the aftermath of the failed Hitler/Ludendorff Putsch of November 1923, Aufbau nonetheless bequeathed a powerful political, financial, military, and ideological legacy to National Socialism.

Aufbau's legacy to National Socialism took several forms. The death of First Lieutenant Max von Scheubner-Richter, Aufbau's *de facto* leader and Hitler's closest political advisor, in the Hitler/Ludendorff Putsch served as an example of heroic sacrifice for the National Socialist cause. White émigrés continued to raise significant funds for the NSDAP after 1923. In the vein of Aufbau, Hitler continued to use White émigrés, especially Ukrainian nationalists, to destabilize Soviet rule after the failure of the Hitler/Ludendorff Putsch. Hitler's preoccupation with winning the Ukraine for Germany along the lines of Aufbau policy led him to divert powerful armed forces away from Moscow in 1941, thereby diminishing German chances of victory in World War II.

Early anti-Bolshevik and anti-Semitic National Socialist ideology, which relied greatly on Aufbau thought, found pronounced expression in the Third Reich's final years. In addition to his wish to gain *Lebensraum* (living space) in the East, Hitler's intense anti-Bolshevism that he had developed during his period of collaboration with Aufbau led him to launch a hazardous military crusade against the Soviet Union. Aufbau views of the

---

[1] Walter Laqueur, *Russia and Germany: A Century of Conflict* (London: Weidenfeld and Nicolson, 1965), 53.

"Jewish Bolshevik" peril, which had greatly influenced National Socialist ideology in the early 1920s, helped to motivate the National Socialist attempt to annihilate European Jewry in what was euphemistically termed the Final Solution.

Former Aufbau members served the post-1923 National Socialist cause. Alfred Rosenberg's Baltic German colleague Arno Schickedanz, Aufbau's former deputy director, acted as the number two man in the *Aussenpolitisches Amt* (Foreign Policy Office) of the NSDAP. The former 1919 Latvian Intervention commander Colonel Pavel Bermondt-Avalov and his associate General Konstantin Sakharov played leading roles in a Russian émigré National Socialist organization known for its initials ROND. Beginning in 1936, Aufbau's former vice president, General Vladimir Biskupskii, directed the Russische Vertrauensstelle (Russian Trust Authority) that oversaw White émigrés in Germany within the framework of the NSDAP. The former head of Aufbau's Ukrainian section, the Cossack leader Colonel Ivan Poltavets-Ostranitsa, worked closely with Hitler and Rosenberg to strengthen a Ukrainian National Socialist movement that helped Germany in its conflicts with Poland and the Soviet Union.

After Scheubner-Richter's death, Rosenberg served as the linchpin connecting Hitler to key White émigrés and their views. He shaped National Socialist ideology and policy in a variety of official capacities. He edited the National Socialist newspaper the *Völkischer Beobachter* (*Völkisch Observer*), led the Foreign Policy Office of the NSDAP, acted as the Representative of the Führer for the Supervision of the Entire Intellectual and Ideological Political Instruction and Education of the NSDAP, assisted Hitler as the Representative of the Führer for the Central Treating of Questions of the East European Area, and ultimately served as the State Minister for the Occupied Eastern Territories during World War II. In this last post, he coordinated White émigré operations to organize pro-National Socialist Soviet citizens for the German war effort, and he helped to implement the atrocities of the Final Solution.

THE MEMORY OF SCHEUBNER-RICHTER

The most intense period of National Socialist–White émigré collaboration ended with the disastrous November 8/9, 1923 Hitler/Ludendorff Putsch in which Aufbau's guiding figure and Hitler's closest advisor, Scheubner-Richter, was killed. Yet Scheubner-Richter's memory was preserved in the National Socialist Party. Hitler honored his fallen comrade by giving his widow Mathilde the task of creating the National Socialist Party Archives in August 1926. In this endeavor, Mathilde collaborated with Heinrich Himmler, who went on to become the leader of the SS.[2] Hitler spoke respectfully of Mathilde in January 1942 when he reminisced about Scheubner-Richter's "sacrifice" for the National Socialist cause. He enthused: "What dignity his wife displayed!"[3]

After he came to power in January 1933, Hitler regularly commemorated the events of November 8/9, 1923, in which Scheubner-Richter had participated, with great pomp and reverence as a heroic undertaking that had inspired nationalist resurgence. He placed a laurel wreath at the memorial to his fallen comrades, most notably Scheubner-Richter, with the inscription, "And you have triumphed after all!"[4] He spoke annually along the lines of his November 1935 oration commemorating the 1923 Putsch:

This brave action was not in vain. For in the end the great national movement came out of it . . . While our enemies believed to have destroyed us, in reality, the seeds of the movement were flung over all of Germany at a stroke . . . And for us [these martyrs] are not dead. These temples are no tombs, but an eternal sentry. Here they stand for Germany and keep watch for our people. Here they lie as faithful witnesses of our movement.[5]

In National Socialist ideology, which emphasized the theme of heroic death, Scheubner-Richter assumed a place of honor.

Scheubner-Richter's Aufbau activities eventually helped to pave the way for friendly relations between Hitler's Germany and Hungary. Soon after Hitler became the German Chancellor in January 1933, the right-wing Hungarian Minister-President Gyula Gömbös ordered his ambassador in Berlin to visit the Führer as soon as possible: "On my behalf, pass my best regards and wishes . . . Recall that ten years ago, on the basis of our common principles and ideology, we were in contact via Mr. Scheubner-Richter . . . Tell Hitler my firm belief that the two countries have to cooperate in foreign and domestic policy."[6] Scheubner-Richter, Hitler's "irreplaceable" advisor, proved to have been a good National Socialist representative.

[2] Interview with Mathilde Scheubner-Richter on April 3, 1936, NSDAPHA, BAB, NS 26, number 1263, 4.

[3] Adolf Hitler, *Hitler's Table Talk 1941–44: His Private Conversations*, trans. Norman Cameron and R. H. Stevens, 2nd edn. (London: Weidenfeld and Nicolson, 1973), 173.

[4] Hitler, *Hitler: Reden und Proklamationen 1932–1945*, vol. 1, ed. Max Domarus (Munich: Süddeutscher Verlag, 1965), 222.

[5] Hitler, speech on November 8, 1935, *Hitler: Reden und Proklamationen*, vol. I, 552, 554.

[6] Ivan Berend, *Decades of Crisis: Central and Eastern Europe before World War II* (Berkeley: University of California Press, 1998), 310.

Scheubner-Richter's former indispensable assistant in Aufbau, General Vladimir Biskupskii, continued to play the leading role in the circle around the Tsarist throne claimants Kirill and Viktoria Romanov after the failure of the Hitler/Ludendorff Putsch. Biskupskii officially served as the minister of war in Kirill's exile government.[7] He developed into the leading White émigré personality in Europe.[8] In a December 1924 interview with the State Commissioner for the Supervision of Public Order, Biskupskii described himself as Kirill's representative in Germany. He stressed that he sought to win as many White émigrés as possible for Kirill's cause, and he propagated German–Russian rapprochement in the vein of the nineteenth-century German Chancellor Otto von Bismarck. Biskupskii claimed that as soon as the Weimar Republic stopped supporting the Soviet regime, Bolshevism would collapse.[9]

As of the late 1920s, Biskupskii collaborated with conspiratorial pro-Kirill monarchists headquartered in Moscow itself who sought to overthrow the Bolsheviks and to institute an alliance between nationalist Russian and German states. With the assistance of Major Josef Bischoff, the former commander of the Iron Division in the 1919 Latvian Intervention who currently operated in the vicinity of Vienna, Biskupskii supplied Russian nationalists inside the Soviet Union with significant amounts of weapons purchased outside of Germany.[10]

Biskupskii's patrons Kirill and Viktoria suffered financial ruin in the aftermath of the November 1923 Hitler/Ludendorff Putsch. Along with other considerable funds that the couple had placed at Aufbau's disposal, the 500,000 gold marks that Kirill and Viktoria had lent General Erich von Ludendorff to further the "German-Russian national cause" had disappeared when Hitler and Ludendorff's undertaking had collapsed.[11] Nonetheless, Biskupskii channeled considerable funds to aid Hitler's rise to power in the early 1930s.[12] He likely received much of this money from

[7] RKÜöO report from November 20, 1925, RGVA (TsKhIDK), *fond* 772, *opis* 1, *delo* 100, 5.
[8] PDM report to the BSMÄ from January 31, 1929 in possession of the RKÜöO, RGVA (TsKhIDK), *fond* 772, *opis* 3, *delo* 81a, 68.
[9] RKÜöO report from December 12, 1924, RGVA (TsKhIDK), *fond* 772, *opis* 3, *delo* 81a, 61.
[10] PDM report to the BSMÄ from January 31, 1929 in possession of the RKÜöO, RGVA (TsKhIDK), *fond* 772, *opis* 3, *delo* 81a, 69, 70.
[11] Letter from Vladimir Biskupskii to Arno Schickedanz from October 21, 1939, APA, BAB, NS 43, number 35, 13; Biskupskii, subpoena from March 11, 1930, BAB, APA, NS 43, number 35, 129.
[12] DB report from October 12, 1936, RGVA (TsKhIDK), *fond* 7, *opis* 1, *delo* 386, reel 1, 30.

Kirill and, more importantly, from Viktoria, with whom he maintained a rather indiscreet affair.[13]

The sources of Kirill and Viktoria's post-1923 funding are not entirely clear. It is known that Colonel Boris Brazol, a former Aufbau member who had aided Scheubner-Richter by writing anti-Semitic literature, the president of the Russian Monarchical Club in New York, and the White émigré contact man with Henry Ford, the wealthy anti-Semitic American industrialist and politician, managed to gather large sums of money for Kirill in 1924 when Viktoria visited America.[14] Brazol likely continued to act as a conduit between Ford and Kirill in the 1930s who transferred money from the former to the latter.

Hitler's National Socialist regime granted Brazol organizational prerogatives on German soil. In the summer of 1938, Brazol, who was by this time an American citizen, helped to organize a clandestine anti-Comintern congress in Germany with the approval of Hitler's secret police, the Gestapo, and Himmler's SS. The assembly included representatives from America, Canada, France, England, and Switzerland. Himmler himself took an interest in Brazol in August 1938, and he commissioned a certain Müller of the SS to write a report on the White émigré's earlier activities.[15]

Besides Biskupskii and Brazol, other White émigrés who had belonged to Aufbau and who supported the National Socialist movement continued to back Kirill's claim to the Tsarist throne after 1923, most notably Aufbau's last leader, the Baltic German Otto von Kursell, and Biskupskii's comrade General Konstantin Sakharov. Kursell, the National Socialist whose greatest fame came when he was commissioned to draw portraits of Hitler, maintained good relations with Kirill and visited him frequently in the years following the Hitler/Ludendorff Putsch.[16] Sakharov, who corresponded regularly with Hitler during the latter's imprisonment for his November 1923 putsch attempt, coordinated relations between Kirill's supporters in Germany and abroad, including in the Soviet Union.[17]

The former 1919 Latvian Intervention commander Colonel Bermondt-Avalov, who, like Sakharov, had supported Kirill's bid for the Tsarist throne and had collaborated with Aufbau, led two National Socialist Russian

---

[13] RKÜöO report from July 1927, RGVA (TsKhIDK), *fond* 772, *opis* 1, *delo* 91, 51.

[14] DGBer report to the AA from December 27, 1924, PAAA, 83584, 177.

[15] Letters from Müller to Himmler from July 12 and August 29, 1938, RGVA (TsKhIDK), *fond* 500, *opis* 1, *delo* 677, 1, 3.

[16] RKÜöO report from May 7, 1925, RGVA (TsKhIDK), *fond* 772, *opis* 4, *delo* 52, 145.

[17] SG report from March 11, 1924, RGVA (TKhIDK), *fond* 1, *opis* 18, *delo* 2381, 2.

émigré organizations in the early 1930s. In the course of 1932, he directed the formation of the Russkoe Osvoboditelnoe Natsionalnoe Dvizhenie (Russian National Liberation Movement, better known for its initials ROND).[18] Soon after he came to power in January 1933, Hitler, who knew Bermondt-Avalov personally, granted him the right to lead ROND along National Socialist lines.[19] Hitler also ordered the creation of a political science school within ROND. The Kirill supporter and former Aufbau member General Sakharov led the institution's military section.[20]

ROND, a militaristic organization, enjoyed a great degree of sympathy among the German population.[21] The White émigré association possessed paramilitary groups patterned on the NSDAP's Sturmabteilung (Storm Section, SA). ROND used the SA's Horst Wessel Song as its hymn. ROND members also attacked political opponents and Jews along the lines of the SA. The official uniform of the White émigré organization displayed a pronounced National Socialist character. ROND dress included a black shirt with a green and white swastika.[22]

ROND only existed for a short time. The largely autonomous German Foreign Office opposed pro-Kirill activities in Germany and pressured Hitler to ban ROND.[23] Hitler dissolved ROND in October 1933.[24] ROND was reconstituted as the Deutsch–Russische Standarte (German–Russian Standard) with Bermondt–Avalov in the leading role.[25] The German–Russian Standard had approximately 6,000 members.[26] Former citizens of the Russian Empire, whether ethnic Russians or not, could join the organization, with the explicit exception of Jews and Freemasons. "Aryans" from other countries could also be granted membership. Members absolutely had to exhibit a "National Socialist *Weltanschauung*."[27] Bermondt-Avalov damaged the Standard's cause when he was arrested for embezzling 50,000

[18] DB report from May 22, 1936, RGVA (TsKhIDK), *fond* 7, *opis* 4, *delo* 168, reel 1, 2.

[19] Report from Friedrich Möllenhoff to the APA from June 26, 1934, RGVA (TsKhIDK), *fond* 519, *opis* 3, *delo* 11b, 69; "The Liquidation of the Nansen Office and the Problem of Political Refugees," IIA report from January 23, 1938, RGVA (TsKhIDK), *fond* 284, *opis* 1, *delo* 69, 8.

[20] DB report from July 24, 1933, RGVA (TsKhIDK), *fond* 7, *opis* 1, *delo* 386, reel 1, 72.

[21] AA report from September 28, 1933, PAAA, 31666, 37.

[22] "The Liquidation of the Nansen Office," IIA report from January 23, 1938, RGVA (TsKhIDK), *fond* 284, *opis* 1, *delo* 69, 8.

[23] AA report from February 15, 1934, PAAA, 31667, E667445.

[24] SG report to the Interior Ministry from December 13, 1933, RGVA (TsKhIDK), *fond* 1, *opis* 27, *delo* 12541, 101.

[25] DB translation of a report from a White émigré source from December 6, 1938, RGVA (TsKhIDK), *fond* 7, *opis* 1, *delo* 299, reel 1, 73.

[26] SN report to the DB from June 2, 1934, RGVA (TsKhIDK), *fond* 7, *opis* 1, *delo* 922, reel 3, 248.

[27] Memorandum from Pavel Bermondt-Avalov's Partei Russischer 'Oswoboshdenzy' included in a Gestapo report from July 6, 1934, RGVA (TsKhIDK), *fond* 1323, *opis* 2, *delo* 171, 335, 336.

marks in August 1934, imprisoned for three months, and then expelled from Germany. He resurfaced in Rome, where he sought to lead a group of White émigré fascists under Benito Mussolini's Fascist regime, but with little success.[28]

Bermondt-Avalov's former collaborator/rival in the 1919 Latvian Intervention, General Biskupskii, experienced difficulties with the National Socialist leadership in the early 1930s before he attained a position of influence in the Third Reich in 1936. The NSDAP's Eastern expert Rosenberg in particular maintained a reserved attitude towards Biskupskii despite all of the general's former financial and political assistance to the National Socialist cause. Rosenberg and Biskupskii had a bit of a falling out. Correspondence from the early 1930s indicates that while he had actively worked to establish an autonomous Ukraine in the context of Aufbau in the early 1920s, Biskupskii now opposed Rosenberg's increasingly aggressive plans to smash the Soviet Union and to replace it with several weak states without a uniting Tsar.[29]

Biskupskii wrote Rosenberg in December 1931 and warned him against advocating a policy of allying Germany with England against Russia. He called such a strategy "the greatest aberration." The White émigré general stressed that he had nothing against Rosenberg personally, but it was "painful" for him to see such views in the party whose "entire ethos and ideology" accorded with his own. He stressed that he and the NSDAP had shared the "same understanding and the same sympathy up until the year 1923," but now the Party seemed to be "among the most bitter enemies of Russia" with its idea of the "carving up of Russia." Biskupskii ended his letter by emphasizing that while he opposed Rosenberg politically, he had always had "sympathy" with him personally and treasured "the best memories of our earlier common work."[30]

Rosenberg was polite in his reply to Biskupskii, but he nevertheless emphasized his differences of opinion with the general. He stressed: "I certainly have gotten to know many splendid people in Russia so that I think back to them and to much in Russian life with only the greatest sympathy." He noted, however, that the chances that an internal revolt would overthrow Bolshevism appeared slim to none. He stressed that "Bolshevized Russia"

[28] SN report from June 1935 included in an SN report to the DB from July 3, 1935, RGVA (TsKhIDK), *fond* 7, *opis* 1, *delo* 922, reel 3, 238.
[29] Letter from Biskupskii to Alfred Rosenberg from December 22, 1931, APA, BAB, NS 43, number 35, 182 ob.
[30] Letter from Biskupskii to Rosenberg from December 22, 1931, APA, BAB, NS 43, number 35, 182, 182 ob.

could only be defeated through an "at least economically-politically united coalition" of powers. Moreover, he argued that Germany could not direct its foreign policy in accordance with the "hopes and wishes of national Russiandom, for the Russian Empire as a political power that national Russiandom longs for does not exist, and no one can say today if it will arise again."

In his reply to Biskupskii, Rosenberg further stressed that the White émigré general's ideas did not address "Germany's necessities of life with regard to the question of space." Rosenberg accused Biskupskii of "marked naivety" in thinking that Germany should deal with its "population surplus" simply by putting its "capable engineers and inventors" at the disposal of the "coming Russia."[31] Here Rosenberg clearly informed Biskupskii that the German need for *Lebensraum* (living space) in the East overruled the wishes of the White émigrés whom Biskupskii represented. This correspondence reflects Rosenberg's sense of acceptance in Germany as an ethnic (Baltic) German, whereas Biskupskii, with his Russian (more properly Ukrainian) roots, remained more of an outsider.

After Hitler came to power in January 1933, Biskupskii vainly sought to gain more influence in Eastern matters. On March 31, 1933, Hitler named Rosenberg the leader of the Aussenpolitisches Amt (Foreign Policy Office) of the NSDAP with the former Aufbau deputy director Arno Schickedanz as his chief of staff. Hitler used the Foreign Policy Office to circumvent the German Foreign Office, which he viewed as a "society of conspirators" directed against National Socialism.[32] Sensing opportunity, Biskupskii congratulated Rosenberg on his appointment. He then suggested that as a "basic principle," Rosenberg's bureau should "receive some similarity in its structure with the organization of the III International, with a plan of work for the long term." He noted that the Foreign Policy Office would likely receive a Russian Section soon, and he proposed himself for a leading role in this department. Along the lines of his earlier Aufbau endeavors, he wished to organize this Russian Section as a "strictly conspiratorial cell."[33]

Biskupskii suffered hardship during the first year of Hitler's Germany. Rosenberg did not respond to his repeated offers to lead a Russian Section of the NSDAP Foreign Policy Office. Rosenberg's colleague Schickedanz sought to spare the pride of Biskupskii, his former chief in Aufbau.[34] Worse

---

[31] Letter from Rosenberg to Biskupskii from December 30, 1931, BAB, NS 43, number 35, 183, 184.

[32] Robert Cecil, *The Myth of the Master Race: Alfred Rosenberg and Nazi Ideology* (London: B. T. Batsford Ltd., 1972), 173, 174.

[33] Letter from Biskupskii to Rosenberg from April 6, 1933, KR, BAB, NS 43, number 35, 179, 179 ob.

[34] Letters from Biskupskii to Arno Schickedanz from May 5 and 31, 1933, APA, BAB, NS 43, number 35, 113, 120.

for Biskupskii, the Gestapo, briefly imprisoned him in October 1933 as part of its efforts to curtail the legitimist movement behind Kirill. After his release, Gestapo authorities told the White émigré leader that they would contact him if they needed his assistance, but that he and the pro-Kirill movement he represented should lay low for the time being. Biskupskii then advised Kirill to suspend his political activities until a more favorable climate developed in Germany.[35]

Biskupskii finally achieved recognition from the National Socialist government in May 1936, when he was named the head of the newly created Russische Vertrauensstelle (Russian Trust Authority).[36] Biskupskii won out over General Sakharov, who was also considered to be a suitable leader for the pro-National Socialist White émigré community in Germany.[37] Biskupskii's Russian Trust Authority was to unite all White émigrés on German soil and to alleviate internecine power struggles.[38] Biskupskii's organization incorporated the remnants of Bermondt-Avalov's German-Russian Standard and oversaw the approximately 125,000 White émigrés living in Germany.[39]

Hitler personally named all of the personnel for Biskupskii's agency, including the women employed as secretaries. He insisted that Lieutenant Sergei Taboritskii serve as the Russian Trust Authority's deputy director. Taboritskii was one of the former Aufbau members who had attempted to assassinate the Constitutional Democratic leader Pavel Miliukov in March 1922. Taboritskii had joined the National Socialist cause openly in 1927 upon his release from prison.[40] Soon after Hitler's ascension to power, Taboritskii had been rumored to possess a paid position within NSDAP Headquarters in Munich.[41] Taboritskii increasingly overshadowed Biskupskii in the Russian Trust Authority.[42] Lieutenant Piotr Shabelskii-Bork, Taboritskii's accomplice in the attempted assassination of Miliukov and the White émigré who had brought *The Protocols of the Elders of Zion* from the Ukraine to Germany, also assisted Biskupskii's organization.[43] He

[35] Letter from Piotr Shabelskii-Bork to Heinrich Lammers from November 4, 1933, forwarded to the AA, PAAA, 31667, E667442.
[36] DB report from May 22, 1936, RGVA (TsKhIDK), *fond* 7, *opis* 4, *delo* 168, reel 1, 1.
[37] DGR report to the AA from April 24, 1936, PAAA, 31668, 255.
[38] Gestapo report from July 7, 1936, BAB, 58, number 270, fiche 1, 37.
[39] DB report from April 23, 1940, RGVA (TsKhIDK), *fond* 7, *opis* 1, *delo* 404, reel 2, 109; SN report to the DB from November 6, 1936, RGVA (TsKhIDK), *fond* 7, *opis* 1, *delo* 386, reel 1, 26.
[40] DB reports from March 1930 and October 12, 1936, RGVA (TsKhIDK), *fond* 7, *opis* 1, *delo* 390, reel 8, 602; *delo* 386, reel 1, 30.
[41] DB report from June 19, 1933, RGVA (TsKhIDK), *fond* 7, *opis* 1, *delo* 386, reel 1, 83.
[42] DB report from December 15, 1938, RGVA (TsKhIDK), *fond* 7, *opis* 1, *delo* 954, reel 7, 578.
[43] DB report from April 23, 1940, RGVA (TsKhIDK), *fond* 7, *opis* 1, *delo* 404, reel 2, 109.

regarded the Russian Trust Authority as a means of opposing "world Jewry, Freemasonry, and Communism."[44]

In his capacity of leader of the Russian Trust Authority, Biskupskii officially served under the somewhat hostile NSDAP Eastern specialist, Rosenberg, but he had supporters in high places.[45] The Gestapo, though it had once imprisoned him, had helped Biskupskii to become the head of the Russian Trust Authority in the first place.[46] In return, Biskupskii sent intelligence reports to the Gestapo.[47] Biskupskii also enjoyed the patronage of Propaganda Minister Josef Goebbels.[48] In April 1938, Goebbels ordered Biskupskii to establish a course in Berlin to train police units composed of Germans, Russians, and Ukrainians for eventual service in the Ukraine.[49]

In the tradition of Aufbau, Biskupskii's Russian Trust Authority improved Kirill's standing in Germany. Biskupskii's longstanding personal relationships with Hitler, Rosenberg, and other National Socialist leaders in particular helped the pro-Kirill movement to expand its German base.[50] The White émigré community in Germany under Biskupskii's leadership generally hoped that Hitler's armed forces would attack the Soviet Union, topple the Bolsheviks, and place Kirill atop a new Russian monarchy. Since Biskupskii remained a convinced supporter of Kirill, French intelligence viewed his placement at the head of the Russian émigré community in Germany as evidence that Hitler wished to install Kirill as the leader of a nationalist Russian state after the overthrow of Bolshevism.[51] After Kirill died in October 1938, the White émigré community in Germany under Biskupskii's direction generally supported Kirill's son Vladimir as the future head of a nationalist Russia.[52]

While Biskupskii ultimately attained a position of authority over White émigré matters in the Third Reich, Hitler and Rosenberg paid far more attention to the former leader of Aufbau's Ukrainian section, Colonel Ivan Poltavets-Ostranitsa. In his work *Russia and Germany*, the historian Walter

---

[44] Letter from Shabelskii-Bork to Biskupskii from June 20, 1935 in possession of the Gestapo, RGVA (TsKhIDK), *fond* 501, *opis* 3, *delo* 496a, 6.

[45] SN report to the DB from July 23, 1936, RGVA (TsKhIDK), *fond* 7, *opis* 1, *delo* 386, reel 1, 52.

[46] Seppo Kuusisto, *Alfred Rosenberg in der nationalsozialistischen Aussenpolitik 1933–1939*, trans. Christian Krötzl (Helsinki: Finska Historiska Samfundet, 1984), 137.

[47] APA report from December 1, 1938, BAB, NS 43, number 35, 68.

[48] Kuusisto, *Alfred Rosenberg in der nationalsozialistischen Aussenpolitik*, 137.

[49] SN report to the DB from April 4, 1938, RGVA (TsKhIDK), *fond* 7, *opis* 1, *delo* 954, reel 1, 7.

[50] DB report from May 22, 1936, RGVA (TsKhIDK), *fond* 7, *opis* 4, *delo* 168, reel 1, 2.

[51] SN report from August 5, 1936 included in an SN report to the DB from August 7, 1936, RGVA (TsKhIDK), *fond* 7, *opis* 1, *delo* 386, reel 1, 35.

[52] Biskupskii's report included in a May 16, 1939 letter from Schickedanz to Lammers, BAB, NS 43, number 35, 2.

Laqueur noted that National Socialist Eastern policy continued to support Ukrainian separatists after 1923.[53] Biskupskii resented the attention that Hitler and Rosenberg gave Poltavets-Ostranitsa.[54] Unlike Biskupskii, Poltavets-Ostranitsa maintained very close relations with both Hitler and Rosenberg after 1923. From Munich, he continued to lead his National Ukrainian Cossack Organization, which collaborated with Hitler's National Socialist Party. The secret police of the Weimar Republic described the Organization as the "national Ukrainian *völkisch* movement."[55] Poltavets-Ostranitsa used a Ukrainian coat of arms and a swastika as the symbol of his union.[56] The National Ukrainian Cossack Organization received subsidies from the NSDAP, and the *Völkisch Observer* printed propaganda on its behalf.[57]

Rosenberg had high hopes for fruitful collaboration with Poltavets-Ostranitsa, who assumed the title of Ukrainian Hetman, or leader, in 1926. Rosenberg desired assistance from an autonomous, allied Ukraine along the lines that Poltavets-Ostranitsa advocated. In 1927, Rosenberg wrote a book, *Der Zukunftsweg einer deutschen Aussenpolitik* (*The Future Path of a German Foreign Policy*). This work aroused the special interest of the Sztab Glówny Oddzial drugi (Main Headquarters Second Section), the primary Polish intelligence agency, for its assertion that "an alliance between Kiev and Berlin and the creation of a common border" served as a "*völkisch* and state necessity for future German policy."[58]

In his foreign policy work, Rosenberg further stressed the need to use ethnic separatism in the Soviet Union, particularly in the Ukraine and the Caucasus, to overthrow Bolshevism and to limit the power of the subsequent Russian state. He emphasized the Ukraine's importance as a valuable source of raw materials as well as a market for German industrial goods. He thereby presented views that he had adopted during his time of activity in Aufbau in tandem with Poltavets-Ostranitsa in the early 1920s.[59]

Soon after Hitler became the Chancellor of Germany on January 30, 1933, Poltavets-Ostranitsa wrote him a congratulatory letter. He assured Hitler: "The Ukrainian Cossacks congratulate you and your movement on your achieved victory." He noted that the Ukrainian Cossacks under

---

[53] Laqueur, *Russia and Germany*, 112.
[54] Letter from Biskupskii to Schickedanz from April 20, 1933, KR, BAB, NS 43, number 35, 112.
[55] RKÜöO report from May 28, 1925, RGVA (TsKhIDK), *fond* 772, *opis* 4, *delo* 52, 204.
[56] DB report from January 19, 1925, RGVA (TsKhIDK), *fond* 7, *opis* 1, *delo* 953, reel 1, 48.
[57] SGOD report from 1929, RGVA (TKhIDK), *fond* 308, *opis* 7, *delo* 265, 4.
[58] SGOD report from December 22, 1928, RGVA (TsKhIDK), *fond* 308, *opis* 7, *delo* 265, 8.
[59] Cecil, *The Myth of the Master Race*, 163; Kuusisto, *Alfred Rosenberg in der nationalsozialistischen Aussenpolitik*, 109.

his leadership had collaborated with nationalist German circles since the Bolshevik Revolution. He further emphasized that National Socialists had long known that

Germany's freedom and space in the East are bound together with the freedom of the Ukraine and the Caucasus as the factors that alone are in a position to weaken the Russian pan-Slavic and pan-Communist danger for Europe, since they strive for a true alliance and friendship with national strength against Russia, against Poland, and against France. I have also adopted this idea, which Your Excellency has written on your standards, with Ukrainian Cossacks in the Ukraine and in the emigration, and I am firmly determined to go with [you] hand in hand, foot by foot, step by step through all difficulties, in complete belief in your victory.

Then Poltavets-Ostranitsa made an even stronger plea for increased collaboration between the Ukrainian Cossacks he represented and Hitler's Germany. He emphasized, "We hope not only for your help, but also for your patronage, just as Hetman Ivan Masepa hoped for from the King of Sweden Karl XII in the year 1709." Poltavets-Ostranitsa further noted that he had included a memorandum that presumably dealt with detailed plans for closer military, political, and economic cooperation between Hitler's government and Ukrainian Cossacks. Poltavets-Ostranitsa closed his letter with the rousing words: "*Heil* Hitler, and your standard from the Rhine to the Caucasus!"[60] Poltavets-Ostranitsa thus wished for National Socialism to spread far to the East.

Poltavets-Ostranitsa considerably influenced the early National Socialist regime, which sought to use his Ukrainian independence movement to undermine the Soviet Union.[61] Polish intelligence in May 1933 attributed great influence to Poltavets-Ostranitsa in the new Hitler government.[62] In the summer of 1933, the French military intelligence agency the Second Section reported that National Socialist leadership wished to establish a Ukrainian satellite state that would replace the overseas colonies that Germany had lost as a result of World War I.[63] Rosenberg planned the creation of a marginally independent pro-German Ukraine composed of territory currently part of the Soviet Union and Poland. He granted Poltavets-Ostranitsa considerable powers to organize Ukrainian émigrés who worked towards this goal. Hitler personally invited the Ukrainian

---

[60] Letter from Ivan Poltavets-Ostranitsa to Hitler from February 10, 1933, KR, BAB, NS 8, number 100, 55–57.
[61] SN report o the DB from December 16, 1933, RGVA (TsKhIDK), *fond* 7, *opis* 1, *delo* 953, reel 1, 34.
[62] SGOD report from May 15, 1933, RGVA (TsKhIDK), *fond* 308, *opis* 7, *delo* 265, 33.
[63] DB report from August 11, 1933, RGVA (TsKhIDK), *fond* 7, *opis* 1, *delo* 954, reel 5, 357.

Cossack leader to relocate from Munich to Berlin.[64] Poltavets-Ostranitsa acted as the NSDAP's expert on Ukrainian matters. He periodically provided reports on Ukrainian issues to Rosenberg's Foreign Policy Office.[65]

Rosenberg intensified his support of Poltavets-Ostranitsa's Ukrainian independence movement in the spring and summer of 1934. In April 1934, Poltavets-Ostranitsa sent a representative of his National Ukrainian Cossack Organization to the Japanese Embassy in Berlin with the permission of Rosenberg's Foreign Policy Office. This envoy presented a plan of action in case of a war against the Soviet Union that called for primarily Ukrainian Cossacks within the USSR to support a Japanese attack.[66] Rosenberg gave the welcoming address at a conference of Ukrainian émigrés held in Berlin in the summer of 1934 that dealt with the military training of Ukrainian exiles for use in a war against the Soviet Union. Representatives of Hermann Göring's Luftwaffe (Air Force) along with leading Army officers attended. The military training of Ukrainian émigrés subsequently took place in Berlin, in Hungary, and in the Balkans.[67]

A letter Poltavets-Ostranitsa wrote Hitler in May 1935 indicates close military coordination between the National Socialist regime and the National Ukrainian Cossack Union. Poltavets-Ostranitsa offered the armed support of his Cossacks now that Hitler had reinstated conscription and had begun building a large standing army in defiance of the Treaty of Versailles. Poltavets-Ostranitsa stressed: "The Ukrainian Cossacks have fought in conjunction with the NSDAP against the enemies of the National Socialist *Weltanschauung.*" He pledged, "If Germany should be attacked from one side or another," then "the Ukrainian Cossacks are ready to fight immediately in the ranks of the German army. I hereby place all able-bodied members of the Ukrainian Cossacks fit for action in Germany and abroad at the disposal of Your Excellency."[68] Poltavets-Ostranitsa regarded national Ukrainian interests as concurrent with those of Hitler's Germany.

Poltavets-Ostranitsa experienced serious difficulties soon after he had written Hitler to promise the armed support of his Ukrainian Cossacks. Largely because of his reputation as a swindler, he could not raise large numbers of followers in Germany and in the Ukraine.[69] He further damaged his cause in late 1935 when he was discovered to have forged a letter

[64] SG report to the DB from June 27, 1933, RGVA (TsKhIDK), *fond* 7, *opis* 1, *delo* 922, reel 4, 318, 319.
[65] DB report from June 19, 1933, RGVA (TsKhIDK), *fond* 7, *opis* 1, *delo* 386, reel 1, 85.
[66] SGOD report from November 1935, RGVA (TsKhIDK), *fond* 453, *opis* 1, *delo* 53, 4.
[67] "The Liquidation of the Nansen Office," IIA report from January 23, 1938, RGVA (TsKhIDK), *fond* 284, *opis* 1, *delo* 69, 9.
[68] Letter from Poltavets-Ostranitsa to Hitler from May 23, 1935, PAAA, 31668, 56, 57.
[69] SG report to the DB from June 27, 1933, RGVA (TsKhIDK), *fond* 7, *opis* 1, *delo* 922, reel 4, 319.

from Rosenberg and to have passed information to Soviet agents.[70] Rosenberg's Foreign Policy Office stopped financing him, and he was even briefly imprisoned in a concentration camp.[71] Poltavets-Ostranitsa suddenly found himself to be a pariah.

Poltavets-Ostranitsa was rehabilitated beginning in 1936. The NSDAP member and former Aufbau leader for a short period, Otto von Kursell, wrote Schickedanz of the Foreign Policy Office on Poltavets-Ostranitsa's behalf. Schickedanz responded that he would ensure that the Ukrainian Cossack again received financial assistance.[72] Polish intelligence from 1937 reported that Rosenberg again strongly backed Poltavets-Ostranitsa.[73] The Ukrainian Cossack leader continued to work for the National Socialist Party, as witnessed by his name in NSDAP payroll records from 1937 and 1938.[74] French intelligence noted in December 1938 that Rosenberg, in collaboration with Poltavets-Ostranitsa, had been charged with aiding the Ukrainian independence movement based in the Ukraine that distributed anti-Bolshevik propaganda and carried out terrorist acts.[75] While he had damaged his reputation through his deceit, Poltavets-Ostranitsa continued to play a significant role in prewar National Socialist foreign policy.

Hitler's shocking turn toward Josef Stalin's Soviet Union in 1939 placed White émigrés in Germany such as Poltavets-Ostranitsa in a very difficult situation. The conclusion of the German–Soviet Non-Aggression Pact, commonly known as the Hitler–Stalin Pact, on August 23, 1939 stunned Germany's White émigré community. The influence of Rosenberg and Schickedanz's Foreign Policy Office had declined significantly in 1939. Hitler had left Rosenberg and Schickedanz out of the loop with regard to his arrangements to divide Poland between Germany and the Soviet Union.[76] The German–Soviet partition of Poland beginning in September 1939, which initiated World War II, occurred in a manner similar to what the Aufbau Generals Erich von Ludendorff and Vladimir Biskupskii had

[70] Letter from Harald Siewert to Reinhard Heydrich from November 22, 1935 in possession of the APA, RGVA (TsKhIDK), *fond* 1358, *opis* 2, *delo* 642, 122.
[71] Kuusisto, *Alfred Rosenberg in der nationalsozialistischen Aussenpolitik*, 133; SGOD report from November 1935, RGVA (TsKhIDK), *fond* 453, *opis* 1, *delo* 53, 4.
[72] Letter from Schickedanz to Otto von Kursell from April 29, 1936, RGVA (TsKhIDK), *fond* 519, *opis* 4, *delo* 26, 320.
[73] SGOD report from January 20, 1937, RGVA (TsKhIDK), *fond* 308, *opis* 3, *delo* 405, 4.
[74] APA memorandum from December 7, 1937, RGVA (TsKhIDK), *fond* 519, *opis* 4, *delo* 26, 170; Schickedanz, APA memorandum from December 5, 1938, RGVA (TsKhIDK), *fond* 519, *opis* 3, *delo* 39, 345.
[75] DB reports from December 6 and 15, 1938, RGVA (TsKhIDK), *fond* 7, *opis* 1, *delo* 299, reel 1, 81; *delo* 954, reel 7, 577.
[76] Cecil, *The Myth of the Master Race*, 178, 181.

envisioned in 1923, with the significant difference that Aufbau had wished to divide Poland between National Socialist German and Russian states.[77]

With the National Socialist–Bolshevik alliance, Rosenberg, who had consistently upheld a vehement anti-Bolshevik *Weltanschauung*, found himself in an uncomfortable position. For a period of time, he was forbidden to hold public speeches, and some of his books, notably *Plague in Russia!*, were banned.[78] Soon after the signing of the Hitler–Stalin Pact, Rosenberg wrote in his diary: "I have the feeling as if this Moscow-Pact will one day take revenge on National Socialism . . . How can we still speak of Europe's deliverance and structuring when we must ask Europe's destroyers for help?"[79] He detested National Socialist Germany's collaboration with the Soviet Union despite its expediency.[80]

When Biskupskii, the head of the Russian Trust Authority, learned of the Hitler–Stalin Pact, he rushed to three different German ministries to gain an overview of the situation. He was assured that the new treaty would not affect the position of White émigrés in Germany. He further received the pledge that the agreement he had concluded with Ludendorff in 1923 still remained in effect. These assurances helped to mollify him.

In conversations with another White émigré, Biskupskii noted that Soviet leaders were following an imperialist, nationalist foreign policy, with little trace of Communism. He emphasized that he had long predicted a nationalist evolution in the Soviet Union. Biskupskii stressed that the internal situation in the Soviet Union was such that the Germans should find it relatively easy to place a "people's monarchy" in charge in place of Bolshevik leadership. He hoped to play a leading role in this Russian monarchical system, which would represent a Russian form of National Socialism.[81]

While Biskupskii sought to regard the Hitler–Stalin Pact in a positive light, the National Socialist–Soviet alliance shocked the White émigré community in Germany that he represented. White émigrés in Germany generally believed that the treaty meant the end of Germany's support of the Russian monarchical cause.[82] A Reichssicherheitshauptamt (State Security Main Office, RSHA) decree from October 25, 1939 curtailed White

77 Translation of Biskupskii's September 7, 1939 comments, APA, BAB, NS 43, number 35, 48.
78 Translated article from *Göteburgs Handels- och Sjöfarts-Tidning*, Nr. 237 included in a *Sonderbeilage zum SD-Pressebericht* Nr. 39, October 13, 1939, RGVA (TsKhIDK), *fond* 500, *opis* 3, *delo* 129, reel 3, 369.
79 Rosenberg, entry in *Das Politische Tagebuch Alfred Rosenbergs* (Göttingen, Seraphim, 1956), cited from Hitler, *Hitlers Tischgespräche im Führerhauptquartier 1941–1942*, 2nd edn. (Stuttgart: Seewald Verlag, 1965), 344.
80 DB report from October 25, 1941, RGVA (TsKhIDK), *fond* 7, *opis* 1, *delo* 404, reel 1, 11.
81 Translation of Biskupskii's September 7, 1939 comments, BAB, NS 43, number 35, 48.
82 APA report [1940], BAB, NS 43, number 35, 7.

émigré freedoms. While the RSHA did not outlaw existing White émigré organizations and newspapers, "Russian, Ukrainian, Cossack, and Caucasian" émigré organizations in Germany were to limit their activities. For instance, White émigré groups could not propagate anti-Soviet propaganda, they could not hold open meetings, and they could not advertise for new members.[83] National Socialist–White émigré collaboration reached a low point during National Socialist Germany's brief partnership with the Soviet Union.

The cooperation between Hitler and Stalin that so discomfited Germany's White émigré community did not last long. Hitler soon returned to his intense anti-Bolshevik roots, which he had largely developed during his close interaction with Aufbau in the early 1920s. Even while German armed forces were still engaged in the French Campaign in June 1940, Hitler expressed his intention "to take action against this menace of the Soviet Union the moment our military position makes it at all possible." He issued the first directive for the invasion of the Soviet Union in August 1940 under the telling name Aufbau Ost (Reconstruction East). In titling his planned Soviet campaign Aufbau Ost, Hitler demonstrated the lasting impression that Aufbau's warnings against "Jewish Bolshevism" had made on his thinking.[84]

Rosenberg in particular had vehemently urged Hitler to invade the Soviet Union, and he collaborated closely with Hitler in determining Eastern occupation policies.[85] Rosenberg had a two-hour conference with Hitler on April 2, 1941 concerning the upcoming administration of conquered Soviet territories. In his notes, Rosenberg wrote of this meeting:

I discussed the racial and historical situation in the Baltic Sea provinces, the Ukraine and its battle against Moscow, the necessary economic link with the Caucasus, etc. The Führer then developed in detail the projected move to the East . . . The Führer asked me about the likely response of the Russian, soldierly and humanly, under great pressure, about the present Jewish situation in the Soviet Union and other matters.

Hitler ended the conference by stressing: "Rosenberg, your great hour has arrived now."[86]

---

[83] RSHA decree from October 25, 1939, BAB, 58, number 1031, fiche 1, 25, 25 ob.

[84] Alan Clark, *Barbarossa: The Russian-German Conflict, 1941–45* (London: Weidenfeld and Nicolson, 1995), 24.

[85] DB report from October 25, 1941, RGVA (TsKhIDK), *fond* 7, *opis* 1, *delo* 404, reel 1, 11.

[86] Fritz Nova, *Alfred Rosenberg: Nazi Theorist of the Holocaust* (New York: Hippocrene Books, 1986), xviii.

Rosenberg gained greater influence over Hitler's Eastern planning in the course of April 1941. Early in the month, he submitted a detailed memorandum to Hitler outlining the planned administration of former Soviet territories. In accordance with basic Aufbau policy, the most economically important Soviet regions, the Ukraine, the Don area, and the Caucasus, were to be combined into a Black Sea Confederation that would oppose Great Russian expansion. The Baltic States were to be united. The Great Russian region was slated for the harshest treatment. On April 20, 1941, his birthday, Hitler appointed Rosenberg to serve as the Beauftragter des Führers für die zentrale Bearbeitung der Fragen des osteuropäischen Raumes (Representative of the Führer for the Central Treating of Questions of the East European Area).[87] In his new post, Rosenberg greatly influenced Hitler's plans for ruling former Soviet areas.

The German Wehrmacht (Armed Forces) attacked the Soviet Union on June 22, 1941, beginning Hitler's anti-Bolshevik crusade that was known as Operation Barbarossa. Army Group Center, which contained 1.6 million of the 2.5 million German soldiers on the Eastern Front, captured approximately 330,000 prisoners and 3,332 tanks by July 3, 1941.[88] Advance units of the powerful army group traversed the Dnepr River, the last important natural barrier before Moscow, on July 11, 1941. Army Group Center captured another 309,110 prisoners and destroyed or seized 3,205 tanks in the Smolensk pocket, only 200 miles from Moscow, by August 5.[89] According to the military historian Albert Seaton, if Hitler had ordered Army Group Center to advance on Moscow in August, then "nothing could have saved the Soviet capital."[90]

On August 18, 1941, the Chief of the Army High Command General Colonel Walter Brauchitsch and his Chief of Staff General Franz Halder urged Hitler to order an immediate offensive against Moscow.[91] Hitler refused. He asserted: "The most important objective to be achieved before the onset of winter is not the capture of Moscow but the seizure of the Crimea and of the coal-mining region on the Donets [in the Ukraine],

[87] Cecil, *The Myth of the Master Race*, 192, 193; Kuusisto, *Alfred Rosenberg in der nationalsozialistischen Aussenpolitik*, 16.
[88] Bryan Fugate, *Operation Barbarossa: Strategy and Tactics on the Eastern Front, 1941* (Novato, CA: Presidio Press, 1984), 95; Klaus Reinhardt, *Moscow – The Turning Point: The Failure of Hitler's Strategy in the Winter of 1941–42*, trans. Karl B. Keenan (Providence, RI: Berg, 1992), 24.
[89] R. H. S. Stolfi, *Hitler's Panzers East: World War Two Reinterpreted* (Norman, OK: University of Oklahoma Press, 1991), 119; Albert Seaton, *The Russo-German War 1941–45* (London: C. Tinling, 1971), 129, 130; Seaton, *The Battle for Moscow: 1941–42* (New York: Stein and Day, 1971), 168.
[90] Seaton, *The Battle for Moscow: 1941–42*, 168.
[91] Seaton, *The Russo-German War*, 143.

and the cutting off of Russian oil-supplies from the Caucasus."[92] Hitler accordingly sent powerful elements of Army Group Center south into the Ukraine.[93] Hitler's emphasis on winning the Ukraine for Germany in the tradition of Aufbau, while leading to short-term gains, helped to bring about the ultimate military defeat of the Third Reich.

Hitler's drive southwards into the Ukraine, where the local population welcomed German troops as in 1918, led to a short-term stunning tactical victory and a long-term strategic disaster.[94] The Wehrmacht captured 665,000 prisoners and 884 tanks in a pocket around Kiev, but the battle lasted until the end of September 1941. Army Group Center thus could not launch its offensive against Moscow until October 2, 1941. The Soviet High Command had been amazed when Army Group Center had not advanced against Moscow in August 1941. Fully aware of Moscow's key strategic, military, economic, and political importance, the Soviet High Command had used the two months that Hitler had afforded it on the Central Front to rest its troops, to build new defensive lines, and to bring up substantial reinforcements. On December 6, 1941, the Red Army launched a massive counter-attack in front of Moscow with over 100 divisions. Soviet forces hurled Army Group Center's exhausted, freezing, and dispirited troops far away from the Soviet capital. After the German attack on Moscow collapsed, Operation Barbarossa failed as well. Hitler's Third Reich never recovered from this military setback.[95]

While German armed forces still occupied Eastern territories, Rosenberg attained a high position of authority in administering conquered Soviet areas. He initially could not implement his ideas of treating Ukrainians and other Eastern peoples leniently, but he gained a belated measure of success in late 1944 when the National Socialist regime began using the captured General A. A. Vlassov's Russian Liberation Army against the Red Army. Hitler secretly named Rosenberg the Reichsminister für die besetzten Ostgebiete (State Minister for the Occupied Eastern Territories) on July 17, 1941. The public announcement of Rosenberg's appointment to this post came on November 18, 1941.[96] In accordance with Aufbau's principles, Rosenberg did not group conquered peoples of the Soviet Union together as Russians. Instead, his State Ministry possessed subdivisions,

---

[92] Hitler, *Hitler's War Directives 1939–1945*, ed. and trans. H. R. Trevor-Roper (London: Sidgwick and Jackson, 1964), 95.

[93] Seaton, *The Russo-German War*, 143, 145.   [94] Cecil, *The Myth of the Master Race*, 193.

[95] Seaton, *The Russo-German War*, 129, 145, 146; Reinhardt, *Moscow – The Turning Point*, 60, 71, 421; Fugate, *Operation Barbarossa*, 294.

[96] Cecil, *The Myth of the Master Race*, 196.

most notably the Reichskommissariat Ostland (State Commissionership East Land), composed of the formerly independent Lithuanian, Latvian, and Estonian states with most of Belarus as well, and the Reichskommissariat Ukraine (State Commissionership Ukraine).[97]

Rosenberg advocated treating peripheral nationalities in conquered Soviet territories moderately, but he had difficulties putting his policies into practice. Rosenberg and his colleague Schickedanz (the latter of whom would have served as the State Commissioner of the Caucasus had the German drive to capture the region not failed in the aftermath of the disastrous 1942–1943 defeat at Stalingrad) did not possess the influence that they desired. Hitler tended to favor those who advocated a severe approach to peripheral Eastern groupings. Rosenberg and Schickedanz had to watch disapprovingly as their ideas of close collaboration with Ukrainians and a relatively lenient attitude towards other Eastern peoples frequently lost out to brutal policies against what were sometimes referred to as "subhumans."[98]

Rosenberg's May 19, 1943 meeting with Hitler demonstrated his inability to implement a moderate course of cooperation with Ukrainians. Rosenberg complained of the insubordination and brutal policies of his nominal subordinate, the Reichskommissar Ukraine (State Commissioner Ukraine) Erich Koch. Hitler defended Koch's ruthless actions. He stressed that the difficult circumstances of the time necessitated a merciless occupation of the Ukraine to extract economic resources and labor.[99] Rosenberg was not allowed to turn the Ukraine into a quasi-autonomous protectorate under moderate occupation policies as he desired. In general, Rosenberg increasingly lost power-political struggles as World War II progressed.[100] Largely because of the spectacle of his being "buffeted about hopelessly in the struggle for power in the Party" in the last years of the Third Reich, as the historian Alan Bullock has worded it, scholars have unjustly underestimated Rosenberg's overall importance to National Socialism.[101]

Rosenberg saw his ideas of making greater use of captured soldiers from the Soviet Union partially vindicated in late 1944. Rosenberg had supported

---

[97] Karlheinz Rüdiger, "Reichsminister für die besetzten Ostgebiete Alfred Rosenberg," [November 1941], KR, BAB, NS 8, number 8, 2.

[98] Cecil, *The Myth of the Master Race*, 193, 204; Kuusisto, *Alfred Rosenberg in der nazionalsozialistischen Aussenpolitik*, 111; Max Hildebert Boehm, "Baltische Einflüsse auf die Anfänge des Nationalsozialismus," *Jahrbuch des baltischen Deutschtums*, 1967, 68.

[99] Copy of a Martin Bormann report in possession of RSHA from June 10, 1943, BAB, 58, number 1005, fiche 1, 10–12 ob.

[100] Christine Pajouh, "Die Ostpolitik Rosenbergs 1941–1944," *Deutschbalten, Weimarer Republik und Drittes Reich*, ed. Michael Garleff (Cologne: Böhlau Verlag, 2001), 167.

[101] Alan Bullock, *Hitler: A Study in Tyranny* (New York: Harper and Row, 1962), 80.

using the forces of the captured Red Army General Vlassov, who despised
Bolshevism, against the Soviets. In a May 1943 newspaper interview, Vlassov
had lamented that his Russian Liberation Army existed virtually only on
paper. He had regretted that his plans to create a powerful anti-Bolshevik
army from captured Red Army soldiers had not been heeded, but he had
stressed that sooner or later National Socialist leadership would recognize
the need for such a force.[102] The hour of Vlassov's Russian Liberation Army
came late in 1944, when the Wehrmacht, Propaganda Minister Goebbels,
and finally the SS partially adopted Rosenberg's thesis of the necessity of
making extensive use of the populations of the Soviet Union to overthrow
Bolshevik rule. When Reichsführer SS (State Leader SS) Himmler finally
backed General Vlassov's Russian Liberation Army in October 1944, however, the tide had long since irrevocably turned against the Germans on the
Eastern Front.[103]

During Germany's battle against the Soviet Union, Rosenberg's chargé
Colonel Ivan Poltavets-Ostranitsa supported National Socialism in an advisory capacity.[104] In March 1942, the Ukrainian Cossack leader held personal
talks with Field Marshall Wilhelm Keitel relating to matters on the Eastern
Front. He proposed that Caucasian and Turkestani forces be given official
standards with great pomp and ceremony in the near future. Keitel agreed
with his suggestion.[105] Moreover, on April 15, 1942, Hitler gave Poltavets-
Ostranitsa a victory by granting Cossacks a special status and allowing them
to perform combat duty for the National Socialist cause.[106]

As fortunes turned increasingly against the Wehrmacht on the Eastern
Front, Poltavets-Ostranitsa continued to support the German war effort
steadfastly. In a February 1943 letter to Rosenberg, he noted the exemplary service that Cossacks had already given the Wehrmacht. He urged
his former Aufbau comrade to make greater use of this "warlike people,"
which could be mobilized into a fighting force of over one and half million
soldiers for the "liberation of the Eastern territories from Bolshevism."[107]
In April 1943, Poltavets-Ostranitsa submitted an essay to Rosenberg's State
Ministry in which he outlined the postwar Cossack state he envisioned.

[102] Vladimir Despotuli's report of his conversation with A. A. Vlassov on May 24, 1943, RGVA
(TsKhIDK), *fond* 1128, *opis* 1, *delo* 1, 27.
[103] Cecil, *The Myth of the Master Race*, 198.
[104] DB report from October 25, 1941, RGVA (TsKhIDK), *fond* 7, *opis* 1, *delo* 404, reel 1, 11.
[105] Letter from Poltavets-Ostranitsa to Rosenberg from February 3, 1943, RGVA (TsKhIDK), RMbO,
fond 1358, *opis* 3, *delo* 53, 3, 4.
[106] RMbO report from January 10, 1943, BAB, 6, number 157, fiche 1, page 6.
[107] Letter from Poltavets-Ostranitsa to Rosenberg from February 3, 1943, RGVA (TsKhIDK), RMbO,
fond 1358, *opis* 3, *delo* 53, 1.

The official languages of this entity were to be German, Ukrainian, and Russian. Hitler himself would regulate the borders of the Cossack nation, which was to stretch roughly from what had been Eastern Poland to the Ural Mountains.[108] As he had in his time of work in Aufbau, Poltavets-Ostranitsa sought to unite the interests of Cossacks with those of National Socialists.

Poltavets-Ostranitsa witnessed the Third Reich recognize the exemplary Cossack service for the National Socialist cause. On November 10, 1943, Rosenberg and Field Marshall Keitel made a proclamation to the Cossacks in which they praised Cossack courage in the fight against Bolshevism. Their declaration stressed: "The German Army has found honest and loyal allies in the Cossacks." The Cossacks who fought on Germany's side in the war were to be granted special privileges in the Third Reich and were to receive an autonomous Cossack state after the end of hostilities on the Eastern Front.[109] The Wehrmacht, far from advancing, however, retreated from this time onwards. Poltavets-Ostranitsa ultimately ended his service for the Third Reich in the Rasse und Siedlungshauptamt – SS (SS Race and Settlement Main Office) based in Prague during the final stages of the war.[110]

"THE STRUGGLE BETWEEN CHAOS AND FORM"

As a final sinister legacy to National Socialism, Aufbau ideology with its conspiratorial and apocalyptic views of the "Jewish Bolshevik" world menace helped to spur the National Socialist enslavement and annihilation of European Jewry. In particular, the former Aufbau member Rosenberg disseminated intense anti-Semitic notions that inspired German hatred of Jews. Rosenberg acted as the leading anti-Semitic ideologue in the NSDAP after Hitler himself. He edited the National Socialist periodical the *Völkisch Observer*. In 1934, Hitler recognized Rosenberg's substantial contributions to the National Socialist *Weltanschauung* by appointing him the Representative of the Führer for the Supervision of the Entire Intellectual and Ideological Political Instruction and Education of the NSDAP.

---

[108] RMbO memorandum on Poltavets-Ostranitsa's essay from April 16, 1943, BAB, 6, number 157, fiche 2, page 43 ob.

[109] Memorandum from Cossack leaders to the RMbO from April 10, 1944, BAB, 6, number 158, fiche 1, page 1.

[110] Check receipt from the RuSHA-SS/VP sent to Poltavets-Ostranitsa on April 8, 1945, RGVA (TsKhIDK), *fond* 1372, *opis* 3, *delo* 35, 32.

In addition to propagating vitriolic anti-Semitic views himself, Rosenberg fostered the anti-Semitic careers of men who had either belonged to or been associated with Aufbau, most notably his Rubonia Fraternity comrade Schickedanz, Gregor Schwartz-Bostunich, and General Sakharov. Schickedanz, who had served as Aufbau's Deputy Director and Vice President Biskupskii's secretary, proved his anti-Semitic credentials though his 1927 work, *Das Judentum: Eine Gegenrasse* (*Jewry: a Counter Race*). Rosenberg invited Schickedanz to serve as the Berlin representative of the *Völkisch Observer* in February 1930.[111]

As for Schwartz-Bostunich, who had worked for Aufbau and the NSDAP under Scheubner-Richter's guidance, Rosenberg asked him to write for the *Völkisch Observer* in 1925.[112] Schwartz-Bostunich also provided the ideological basis for the National Socialist leader Julius Streicher's notorious anti-Semitic publication, *Der Stürmer* (*The Stormer*).[113] Hitler called upon Schwartz-Bostunich to hold an important speech along with Streicher in March 1926. The White émigré's anti-Semitic views increasingly received attention among National Socialist leadership.[114]

Rosenberg's chargé Schwartz-Bostunich supported the National Socialist Party ideologically in the 1930s as well. In the early part of the decade before Hitler's ascension to power, he gave speeches on behalf of the NSDAP with titles such as "The Frenzy of Bolshevism" and "Jewish World Rule." He won over many Communists to the National Socialist cause.[115] After Hitler became the German Chancellor in January 1933, Schwartz-Bostunich presented anti-Semitic and anti-Masonic reports to the State Security Main Office (RSHA).[116] He also rose in Himmler's SS. He achieved the rank of SS Obersturmbannführer in January 1937 before retiring from active duty.[117]

The former Aufbau member General Sakharov received support for his anti-Bolshevik, anti-Semitic views from Rosenberg's Foreign Policy Office of the NSDAP. Rosenberg's agency concluded that Sakharov's 1937 brochure, *Judas Herrschaft im Wanken! Antisemitische Front in der*

[111] Kuusisto, *Alfred Rosenberg in der nationalsozialistischen Aussenpolitik*, 45.

[112] Gregor Schwartz-Bostunich, *SS-Personalakten*, SS-OStubaf., IZG, Fa 74, 1; Michael Hagemeister, "Das Leben des Gregor Schwartz-Bostunich, Teil 2," *Russische Emigration in Deutschland 1918 bis 1941: Leben im europäischen Bürgerkrieg*, ed. Karl Schlögel (Berlin: Akademie Verlag, 1995), 212.

[113] Laqueur, *Russia and Germany*, 122.

[114] Schwartz-Bostunich, *SS-Personalakten*, SS-OStubaf., IZG, Fa 74, 1.

[115] Letter from Schwartz-Bostunich to Rosenberg from January 8, 1933, KR, BAB, NS 8, number 100, 141.

[116] RSHA report from March 14, 1934, BAB, 58, number 7560, 7.

[117] *Dienstaltersliste der Schutzstaffel der NSDAP* (SS-Obersturmbannführer und SS- Sturmbannführer): *Stand vom 1. Oktober 1944* (Berlin: Reichsdruckerei, 1944), RGVA (TKhIDK), *fond* 1372, *opis* 5, *delo* 89, 6; State Treasurer Franz Xaver Schwartz's report to Rosenberg from May 5, 1943, KR, BAB, NS 8, number 207, 29.

Sowjetunion (Judas' Rule Tottering!: Anti-Semitic Front in the Soviet Union), presented a "very interesting" picture of "Jewish rule in Bolshevism" and admirably analyzed "the signs of a future Jewish pogrom in Russia as the world has never seen before." Rosenberg's Foreign Policy Office concluded that Sakharov's work was "perfectly suitable to convince simple-minded people of the role of Jewry in Bolshevism."[118] Sakharov advanced a thesis that Aufbau had disseminated as one of its key ideological points, namely that Bolshevism represented a primarily Jewish undertaking.

Of all former Aufbau members, Rosenberg made the most important ideological contributions to the NSDAP in the post-Hitler/Ludendorff Putsch period. He proved second only to Hitler himself in formulating National Socialist ideology. As the editor of the *Völkisch Observer*, he collaborated closely with Hitler on ideological matters. Rosenberg also served as the first National Socialist to present Party views at a large international conference abroad. At the Volta Congress in Rome in November 1932, he asserted that the challenge of the age was to create and to consolidate a "people's socialism . . . against the capitalist plutocrats as well as against Jewish Bolshevism."[119] Here Rosenberg referred to his notion that the Jews manipulated both finance capitalism and Bolshevism.

Rosenberg received official status as Hitler's greatest ideological assistant in the Third Reich. In 1934, Hitler named him the Beauftragter des Führers für die Überwachung der gesamten geistigen und weltanschaulichen Schulung und Erziehung der NSDAP (Representative of the Führer for the Supervision of the Entire Intellectual and Ideological Political Instruction and Education of the NSDAP). In this post, Rosenberg greatly influenced cultural, church, and school affairs. Moreover, he played an important role in shaping SS courses.[120] Hitler demonstrated his appreciation for Rosenberg's ideological contributions to National Socialism at the *Reichsparteitag* (State Party Day) in 1937. He granted Rosenberg the National Prize for Art and Science as the first living German for his contributions to the National Socialist *Weltanschauung*.[121]

It is worth noting that, as important as Rosenberg proved to the ideological development of National Socialism, Hitler did not always agree with his ideas. For instance, Hitler critiqued Rosenberg's 1930 *magnum opus*,

[118] APA/AO report from October 21, 1937, RGVA (TKhIDK), *fond* 1358, *opis* 2, *delo* 643, 124.
[119] [Alfred Rosenberg], "Der Kampf zwischen Chaos und Gestalt: Zur Ernennung des Reichsleiters Alfred Rosenberg zum Reichsminister für die besetzten Ostgebiete," a draft used to create an official press release [November 1941], KR, BAB, NS 8, number 8, 19, 20.
[120] Boehm, "Baltische Einflüsse," 67; Nova, *Alfred Rosenberg*, 237.
[121] "Der Kämpfer Alfred Rosenberg: Zur Ernennung des Reichsleiters zum Reichsminister für die besetzten Gebiete," *Parteipresse-Sonderdienst*, Nr. 368, November 17, 1941, KR, BAB, NS 8, number 8, 7.

Der Mythus des 20. Jahrhunderts: Eine Wertung der seelisch-geistigen Gestaltenkämpfe unserer Zeit (*The Myth of the Twentieth Century: An Evaluation of the Spiritual-Intellectual Formation Struggles of Our Time*), which castigated the Christian Churches and advocated a religious German "blood" myth.[122] In an April 1942 conversation, Hitler argued that the title of Rosenberg's work gave a false impression. As a National Socialist, one should not stress the myth of the twentieth century, but should instead juxtapose the belief and knowledge of the twentieth century against the myth of the nineteenth century.[123] Despite Hitler's criticism, Rosenberg's *Myth* reached a distribution of roughly one million copies, second only to Hitler's *Mein Kampf* in the Third Reich.[124]

While they did not always see eye to eye ideologically, Hitler clearly agreed with Rosenberg's views of the dire threat posed by "Jewish Bolshevism." As we have seen, while he had belonged to Aufbau, Rosenberg had warned of a conspiratorial Jewish alliance between finance capitalism and Bolshevism. Hitler had espoused this idea since his period of close collaboration with Aufbau in the early 1920s. He demonstrated his belief in world Jewry as the driving force behind international finance capitalism and Bolshevism in his infamous speech before the Reichstag, by then a ceremonial parliament, on January 30, 1939. Hitler stressed: "If international finance Jewry in and outside Europe should succeed in plunging peoples into a world war again, then the result will not be the Bolshevization of the earth and with it the victory of Jewry, but the destruction of the Jewish race in Europe."[125]

In a May 30, 1942 speech that Hitler gave to a group of newly promoted officers, he demonstrated an apocalyptic anti-Semitism that Aufbau ideologues including Rosenberg had helped to instill in him. Hitler stressed the dangers that the Soviet Union, the "giant in the East," presented. There the "international Jew" as the "driving element" had long threatened Germany, for the "international Jew" had decided: "The time had come to erect its thousand-year empire with the help of another world that had been done out of its national intelligentsia."[126] Hitler used apocalyptic anti-Semitism in the vein of Aufbau thought in general and Rosenberg's views in particular to justify his ruthless war in the East.

Hitler ordered the mass murder of Jews as a means of destroying the "Jewish Bolshevik" menace, and Rosenberg aided him in this mission. As

---

[122] Cecil, *The Myth of the Master Race*, 82, 93.
[123] Hitler, conversation on April 11, 1942, *Hitlers Tischgespräche*, 269.
[124] Nova, *Alfred Rosenberg*, 8.
[125] Hitler, speech on January 30, 1939, *Reden und Proklamationen*, vol. 2, 1058.
[126] Hitler, secret speech on May 30, 1942, *Hitlers Tischgespräche*, 497.

an early measure of what became an ever-larger genocide, Hitler issued the notorious Commissar Decree on June 6, 1941. This directive commanded State Leader SS Himmler's special forces, the Einsatztruppen (Task Troops), to execute all captured Red Army political commissars, many of whom were Jewish, in the imminent war against the Soviet Union.[127] The Historian Christopher Browning believes that Hitler decided to exterminate civilian Jews in the Soviet Union in mid-July 1941.[128] If Browning is correct, then Hitler's resolution to implement this decisive phase of what became known as the Final Solution coincided with his appointment of Rosenberg as the State Minister for the Occupied Eastern Territories.

Rosenberg viewed his genocidal anti-Semitic actions in the occupied East as retaliation for the depredations of "Jewish Bolshevism." The November 18, 1941 press release dealing with Rosenberg's public assumption of the State Minister post stressed that the White émigré had entered politics since "he wanted to protect the German people from the same fate that he had lived through in Moscow."[129] A composition that Rosenberg himself most likely wrote in preparation for the November press release, "The Struggle Between Chaos and Form: On the Appointment of State Leader Alfred Rosenberg to State Minister for the Occupied Eastern Territories," stressed his service in incorporating the "struggle against Jewish Bolshevism" into the "*Weltanschauung* struggle of the movement." The most belligerent section of this essay, which referred to the large-scale destruction of Jews, did not appear in the official press release:

Bolshevism is in essence the form of the Jewish world revolution, the enormously calculated "messianic" attempt to take revenge on the eternally foreign character of the Europeans and not just the Europeans. And destiny has decided against Jewry. The victorious battles of the German struggle for liberation have created a new basis for Europe. The German advance in the Bolshevik East will lead to the complete elimination of Jewish-Bolshevik rule in this area. That which Jewry once planned against Germany and all peoples of Europe, that must it itself suffer today, and responsibility before the history of European culture demands that we do not carry out this fateful separation with sentimentality and weakness, but with clear, rational awareness and firm determination.[130]

State Minister for the Occupied Eastern Territories Rosenberg facilitated the mass slaughter of Jews behind the Eastern Front. In August 1941, he

[127] Fugate, *Operation Barbarossa*, 43, 44.

[128] Christopher Browning, *Nazi Policy, Jewish Workers, German Killers* (Cambridge: Cambridge University Press, 2000), 27.

[129] "Der Kämpfer Alfred Rosenberg," *Parteipresse-Sonderdienst, Nr. 368*, November 17, 1941, KR, BAB, NS 8, number 8, 7, 8.

[130] [Rosenberg], "Der Kampf zwischen Chaos und Gestalt," [November 1941], KR, BAB, NS 8, number 8, 16, 18, 19.

issued a decree specifying who was to be considered a Jew in the East, thereby providing guidelines for Germans and their auxiliaries to follow in deciding whom they would single out for slave labor or extermination.[131] Rosenberg supported the creation of the anti-Semitic *Deutsche Ukraine-Zeitung* (*German Ukraine-Newspaper*) in January 1942. In an appeal in the paper's first edition, he hinted at the German-led mass murder of Jews in the Ukraine. He noted that Germany had taken over control of the Ukraine in order to assure that "Bolshevik conditions" and the "rule of Jewry" would never return.[132] Rosenberg found numerous anti-Semitic collaborators in the Ukraine. Many Ukrainian auxiliary police units slaughtered Jews under German occupation.[133]

In his 1923 work, *The Protocols of the Elders of Zion and Jewish World-Politics*, Rosenberg had asserted of the "Jewish Bolshevik" regime: "The terror that has sent waves upon waves of blood across the broad Russian plains from the Gulf of Finland to the mountains of the Caucasus . . . is not a Russian flare up, but a methodical massacre of a great people."[134] Beginning in the summer of 1941, Rosenberg possessed authority over roughly this same region. He worked in the framework of the Final Solution to facilitate another "methodical massacre" in order to eradicate what he perceived as the "Jewish Bolshevik" world menace. The postwar Nuremberg Tribunal stressed that, among his other crimes, Rosenberg had "helped to formulate the policies of . . . extermination of Jews," and the court sentenced him to death by hanging.[135]

CONCLUSION

Aufbau bequeathed a substantial financial, political, military, and ideological legacy to National Socialism from 1924 to 1945. Hitler's NSDAP received considerable financial assistance from White émigré circles after 1923. Hitler used the tragic death of his most important early advisor, Aufbau's guiding figure Max von Scheubner-Richter, as an example of selfless sacrifice for the good of National Socialism. Alfred Rosenberg and

[131] Rosenberg, RMbO decree from August 1941, BAB, 6, number 74, fiche 1, 32, 33.
[132] "Deutsche Ukraine-Zeitung erschienen: Aufrufe Rosenbergs und Kochs an die Ukrainer," *Krakauer Zeitung,* January 25, 1942, 4.
[133] Christopher Browning, "Ordinary Germans or Ordinary Men? A Reply to the Critics," *The Holocaust and History: The Known, the Unknown, the Disputed, and the Reexamined,* eds. Michael Berenbaum and Abraham J. Peck (Bloomington: Indiana University Press, 1998), 257.
[134] Rosenberg, *Die Protokolle der Weisen von Zion und die Jüdische Weltpolitik* (Munich: Deutscher Volks-Verlag, 1923), 43.
[135] Nova, *Alfred Rosenberg,* 219.

his former Aufbau colleagues Deputy Director Arno Schickedanz and Vice President General Vladimir Biskupskii held leading positions in the Third Reich. Both before and after the 1941 German invasion of the Soviet Union, Hitler used White émigrés, notably Ukrainian Cossacks behind Colonel Ivan Poltavets-Ostranitsa, to undermine the Soviet Union. Hitler upheld Aufbau's emphasis on winning the Ukraine for Germany. He gave the region precedence over Moscow in 1941. He thereby undermined German prospects for victory in World War II.

Conspiratorial and apocalyptic Aufbau thought continued to influence anti-Bolshevik, anti-Semitic National Socialist views after 1923, primarily through the agency of Rosenberg. The fundamental Aufbau conception of a monstrous Jewish alliance between predatory finance capitalism and murderous Bolshevism, notably as interpreted by Rosenberg, significantly influenced the National Socialist *Weltanschauung* long after the Hitler/Ludendorff Putsch of 1923. Although he entered into a brief tactical alliance with the Soviet Union, Hitler's dread of the "Jewish Bolshevik" peril, which he had internalized during his years of cooperation with Aufbau, came to the fore in 1941. In that fateful year, Hitler sought to eradicate "Jewish Bolshevism" by launching a risky military crusade against the Soviet Union and inaugurating the mass murder of European Jews. As the State Minister for the Occupied Eastern Territories, Rosenberg aided Hitler in both of these quintessentially National Socialist endeavors.

Conclusion

Historians should discard the notion of a linear German *Sonderweg* (special path) that led directly to Adolf Hitler's Third Reich. The American scholar Daniel Goldhagen in particular presents an overly simplistic version of the *Sonderweg* thesis in his book *Hitler's Willing Executioners.* He asserts, "The Holocaust was a *sui generis* event that has a historically specific explanation," notably "enabling conditions created by the long-incubating, pervasive, virulent, racist, eliminationist antisemitism of German culture."[1] Instead of focusing solely on alleged German peculiarities in the vein of Goldhagen, historians should understand the genesis and development of National Socialism in the context of cross-cultural interaction between defeated groups from World War I and the Bolshevik Revolution: alienated *völkisch* (nationalist/racist) Germans and vengeful White émigrés. While the National Socialist movement largely developed in a *völkisch* framework, many White émigrés made crucial political, military, financial, and ideological contributions to National Socialism.

Hitler's National Socialist movement would not have arisen in the form it did without the twin upheavals of World War I and the Bolshevik Revolution. Far right movements in both the German and Russian Empires, while stronger in the latter than in the former, proved politically weak. Imperial German culture did develop coherent *völkisch* views with redemptive overtones. In particular, the philosopher Arthur Schopenhauer, the composer Richard Wagner, and the author Houston Stewart Chamberlain urged the German people to transcend the shallow materialism that they associated with the Jews and to attain redemption by negating the will to live. Despite this detailed philosophy, no *völkisch* movement with mass appeal developed before the disastrous outcome of World War I. Neither Heinrich Class' Pan-German League, Ludwig Müller von Hausen's Association against

---

[1] Daniel Goldhagen, *Hitler's Willing Executioners: Ordinary Germans and the Holocaust* (New York: Alfred A. Knopf, 1996), 419.

the Presumption of Jewry, nor Wolfgang Kapp's German Fatherland Party gained broad popular support. Kapp and Class also failed to replace the Kaiser with a military dictatorship under the *völkisch* General Erich von Ludendorff in 1917.

In the Russian Empire, far rightists achieved greater political success than their *völkisch* German counterparts, but they soon declined in importance. Beginning in the revolutionary year 1905, the Black Hundred movement, which drew from the apocalyptic ideas of the authors Fedor Dostoevskii and Vladimir Solovev, gained a mass following. Led by the Union of the Russian People, Black Hundred organizations disseminated anti-Western, anti-socialist, and anti-Semitic views to a relatively wide audience. Imperial Russian conservative revolutionaries cast their political struggle in apocalyptic terms by associating the Jews with the Anti-Christ. They proposed drastic restrictions against the Jews in order to protect what they regarded as the imperiled Tsar, altar, and people. Yet while radical rightists in the Russian Empire succeeded politically much more than *völkisch* Germans, the Black Hundred movement soon fragmented, and Imperial Russian far rightists could not thwart the Bolshevik seizure of power in October 1917.

With the collapse of Imperial Russia that Black Hundred forces had been unable to hinder, German troops were able to advance deep into former Imperial Russian territories. The German occupation of the Ukraine beginning late in World War I engendered large-scale cooperation between right-wing German and Russian or Ukrainian officers. This interaction in turn fostered further anti-Bolshevik and anti-Semitic collaboration between rightist Germans, including National Socialists, and Whites/White émigrés in both Germany and abroad. The German Ukrainian Intervention furthered the pro-nationalist German careers of leading White officers who went on to serve the National Socialist cause, including General Vladimir Biskupskii, Colonel Ivan Poltavets-Ostranitsa, Colonel Pavel Bermondt-Avalov, Lieutenant Sergei Taboritskii, Colonel Fedor Vinberg, and Lieutenant Piotr Shabelskii-Bork.

German forces retreating from the Ukraine in the winter of 1918/1919 brought thousands of sympathetic White officers with them, including Shabelskii-Bork, who carried the incendiary anti-Semitic forgery *The Protocols of the Elders of Zion* with him to Berlin. After receiving them from Shabelskii-Bork, the *völkisch* publicist Hausen had the *Protocols* translated into German, and then he published them with commentary. The *Protocols'* monstrous depiction of a ruthless Jewish drive for world domination through the means of both insatiable finance capitalism and bloody revolutionary upheaval greatly influenced many *völkisch* Germans and White émigrés, including Hitler's early mentors, the *völkisch* publicist Dietrich Eckart and his White émigré assistant Alfred Rosenberg. The *Protocols* also significantly affected Hitler's own anti-Semitic *Weltanschauung* (world view), particularly through their assertion that the Jews used starvation as a means to destroy nationalist resistance. The *Protocols* provided Hitler with a sharp weapon against what he perceived as the menace of international Jewry.

In addition to leading to the transfer of the *Protocols* from the Ukraine to Germany, the German occupation of the Ukraine in 1918 set a precedent for further German–White military collaboration, most notably as witnessed in the 1919 Latvian Intervention. In this campaign, a combined force of German Freikorps (volunteer corps) and White units fought under Colonel Bermondt-Avalov, a White officer who had served in the Ukraine under German occupation. Bermondt-Avalov sought to work "hand in hand with Germany" to topple the Bolshevik regime. After some initial successes, the Latvian Intervention failed militarily, largely because of increasing opposition from the Entente (Britain and France) and the primarily socialist German government. The operation nonetheless strengthened the solidarity between right-wing Germans and Whites, who viewed themselves as trapped by Bolshevik expansion from the East, Entente pressure from the West, and the betrayal of the Weimar German government in the middle.

As well as serving as a German/White anti-Bolshevik crusade abroad, the Latvian Intervention tied into the first right-wing attempt to overthrow the Weimar Republic, the Kapp Putsch of March 1920. Many *völkisch* Germans and White émigrés, including veterans of the Latvian Intervention, participated in this coup. Leading *völkisch* Germans other than Kapp who supported this unsuccessful undertaking included General Ludendorff, his advisor Colonel Karl Bauer, Captain Hermann Ehrhardt, who led the troops that occupied Berlin and sent the German government fleeing, and even Hitler and Eckart. Notable White émigré participants in the doomed putsch included the Baltic German Max von Scheubner-Richter, who had helped to plan the Imperial German advance into the Baltic region in World War I, Biskupskii, Bermondt-Avalov, Vinberg, Shabelskii-Bork, and Taboritskii.

After the Kapp Putsch collapsed in Berlin, leading *völkisch* Germans and White émigrés regrouped in Bavaria, where the Kapp Putsch had succeeded. Former rightist German and White émigré Kapp Putsch conspirators and their wealthy Bavarian backers soon established economic and military relations with General Piotr Vrangel's Southern Russian Armed Forces, which were situated on the Crimean Peninsula in the Ukraine. Scheubner-Richter led a dangerous mission to the Crimea to stipulate the terms of the cooperation between his far right German and White émigré backers in Bavaria and Vrangel's regime. Scheubner-Richter held fruitful negotiations with Vrangel that led to large-scale collaboration between the right-wing Germans and White émigrés he represented and Vrangel's government. This alliance soon crumbled, however, because of the Red Army's stunningly rapid victory over Vrangel's forces.

This brief German/White émigré/White connection nonetheless spurred the creation of the Munich-based Aufbau Vereinigung (Reconstruction Organization), a conspiratorial anti-Entente, anti-Weimar Republic, anti-Bolshevik, and anti-Semitic association of *völkisch* Germans, including National Socialists, and White émigrés. First Secretary Scheubner-Richter and Vice President Biskupskii *de facto* led Aufbau. Hitler collaborated closely with Aufbau from 1920 to 1923. At least four White émigré Aufbau members also belonged to the National Socialist Party: Scheubner-Richter, Deputy Director Arno Schickedanz, who had fought in the Latvian Intervention, and two close collaborators with Hitler's mentor Eckart, Otto von Kursell and Rosenberg. Other White émigré Aufbau members who did not belong to the National Socialist Party but who nonetheless supported it included Biskupskii, Poltavets-Ostranitsa, Vinberg, Shabelskii-Bork, and Taboritskii. Max Amann, a German, acted both as Aufbau's second secretary and as the secretary of the National Socialist Party. Scheubner-Richter also introduced Hitler to General Ludendorff in the framework of Aufbau, thereby setting in motion a political alliance that culminated in the calamitous November 1923 Hitler/Ludendorff Putsch.

After its consolidation as an influential *völkisch* German–White émigré alliance in the first half of 1921, Aufbau tried and failed to unite all White émigrés in Germany and beyond. Aufbau organized the May–June 1921 Monarchical Congress at Bad Reichenhall (in Bavaria), which lent White émigrés worldwide the appearance of unity. Aufbau nonetheless could not unify all European White émigrés behind the Tsarist candidate Grand Prince Kirill Romanov for a pro-National Socialist crusade against the Bolsheviks, which would establish nationalist Russian, Ukrainian, and Baltic successor states.

Aufbau fought bitterly against the pro-French Supreme Monarchical Council under the former leader of a faction of the Union of the Russian People, Nikolai Markov II. The Council backed Grand Prince Nikolai Nikolaevich Romanov, who lived in Paris and maintained close relations with the French government, for Tsar. The Supreme Monarchical Council counted on French military assistance to reconstruct Imperial Russia in its former borders. In its acrimonious struggle against the Council, Aufbau went so far as to envision a risky tactical alliance with the Red Army. Internecine struggle among White émigrés in Germany aided the still unstable Soviet regime.

Hitler's rising National Socialist Party supported Aufbau in its struggle against Markov II's pro-French Supreme Monarchical Council. Hitler allied himself with Kirill Romanov's candidacy for the Tsarist throne in return for Kirill's considerable financial support of the National Socialist movement through Aufbau as an intermediary. Aufbau proved a valuable source of funding for the early National Socialist Party in general. The conspiratorial organization helped to finance Hitler's National Socialists by providing money from wealthy Aufbau members or allies including Kirill and by channeling funds from the prominent anti-Semitic American industrialist and politician Henry Ford.

While Aufbau could not unite all White émigrés in Europe behind Kirill, it did convince Hitler that nationalist Germans and Russians should ally against Bolshevism, the Entente, the Weimar Republic, and Jewry. The Aufbau ideologues Scheubner-Richter, Vinberg, and Rosenberg maintained that the Jews had pitted Imperial Germany and the Russian Empire against each other although the two nations had possessed complementary interests. The Jews had done this, the Aufbau colleagues argued, to set the stage for their own tyrannical world rule. While he later enacted brutal policies towards the Russians in World War II, in his early political career, Hitler adopted Aufbau's pro-Russian standpoint by repeatedly urging nationalist Germans and Russians to overcome their recent Jew-instigated hostilities by combining their forces against international Jewry, which manifested itself most horrifyingly in "Jewish Bolshevism."

In addition to calling for a nationalist German–Russian alliance, Aufbau acted as a terrorist organization. The Aufbau colleagues Biskupskii and Bauer placed a death contract on Aleksandr Kerenskii, the former head of the 1917 Provisional Government in Russia. The Aufbau members Shabelskii-Bork and Taboritskii, most likely under the urging of their superior Vinberg, attempted to murder the Russian Constitutional Democratic leader Pavel Miliukov, but they accidentally killed another prominent Constitutional Democrat, Vladimir Nabokov, instead. At least three Aufbau members with ties to the NSDAP, Biskupskii, Ludendorff, and Ludendorff's advisor Bauer, colluded in the most shocking assassination of the Weimar Republic, that of Germany's Foreign Minister Walther Rathenau. In these last two crimes, Aufbau members collaborated with Captain Ehrhardt's Organization C, a conspiratorial far right association based in Munich that engaged in terrorism, coordinated anti-Weimar

Republic and anti-Bolshevik military preparations, and maintained close ties with the National Socialist Party.

As well as supporting Aufbau's terrorist activities, Hitler's National Socialists collaborated with Aufbau to overthrow the Soviet Union through subversion and military interventions. Aufbau's military schemes to topple the Soviet Union became those of the National Socialist movement, as Aufbau's *de facto* leader Scheubner-Richter served as Hitler's foreign policy advisor and one of his closest counselors in general. Aufbau directed anti-Bolshevik subversion in the Soviet Union and planned broad military advances into the Ukraine, the Baltic region, and the Great Russian heartland in order to crush Bolshevism and to establish National Socialist Russian, Ukrainian, and Baltic states. Hitler approved of Aufbau's Eastern strategy, as he had not yet developed his idea of Germany's need to gain *Lebensraum* (living space) in the East. He especially wished to wrest the agriculturally and industrially valuable Ukraine from Soviet control through collaboration with the Ukrainian Cossack leader Poltavets-Ostranitsa, who led Aufbau's Ukrainian section.

In addition to scheming with National Socialists to overthrow the Soviet Union, Aufbau helped to guide National Socialist efforts to topple the Weimar Republic through the means of paramilitary force. Hitler's closest advisor Scheubner-Richter played a key role in the preparations for a right-wing putsch against the Weimar Republic that was to be launched from Bavaria under the leadership of Hitler and Ludendorff. Scheubner-Richter developed a militant plan of action that borrowed from the Bolshevik model. While he hated "Jewish Bolshevism," he nonetheless admired the "energy" of the (Jewish) Soviet Commissar for War Lev Trotskii. Scheubner-Richter also esteemed the Bolshevik example where, as he believed, a few determined men had changed world history, and he attributed the effective tactics of subversion followed by ruthless centralization and militarization to Trotskii. While he never worded it that clearly, in effect, Scheubner-Richter wished to play Trotskii to Hitler's Lenin by leading a national revolutionary force to reconstitute Germany through violent means.

In late 1922 and 1923, Scheubner-Richter collaborated with Hitler and General Ludendorff to lead various paramilitary groupings that finally coalesced into the Kampfbund (Combat League), which displayed increasing militancy towards the Weimar Republic. National Socialist and Aufbau anti-Weimar Republic cooperation climaxed in the disastrous Hitler/ Ludendorff Putsch of November 1923, which Scheubner-Richter had goaded Hitler to launch. Scheubner-Richter marched at Hitler's side during this doomed undertaking until he was shot fatally in the heart. The collapse of the Hitler/Ludendorff Putsch caused a low point in National Socialist–White émigré collaboration, but Hitler nonetheless placed two Aufbau members in charge of the NSDAP during his imprisonment: Rosenberg and Amann.

While Aufbau failed to place Hitler and Ludendorff in charge in Germany, it greatly influenced National Socialist ideology. Early anti-Bolshevik and anti-Semitic National Socialist thought developed largely as a post-World War I mixture of *völkisch*-redemptive German and conspiratorial-apocalyptic White émigré views. National Socialist ideology combined *völkisch* notions of Germanic racial and spiritual superiority with apocalyptic White émigré ideas of threatened world ruin at the hands of insidious international Jewish conspirators. Hitler only began to crystallize his anti-Bolshevik, anti-Semitic *Weltanschauung* in late 1919, when he started learning from his early mentors Eckart and Rosenberg. He soon became acquainted with the anti-Bolshevik and anti-Semitic beliefs of Scheubner-Richter and Vinberg as well. The Aufbau White émigrés Scheubner-Richter, Vinberg, and Rosenberg, along with their *völkisch* colleague Eckart, influenced National Socialist ideology as the "four writers of the apocalypse," who warned of ever-expanding "Jewish Bolshevik" destruction.

The four writers of the apocalypse argued along the lines of Dostoevskii that international Jewry manipulated both rapacious finance capitalism in the West and bloodthirsty Bolshevism in the East. They stressed that "Jewish Bolshevism" had killed many millions of Russians through misrule and enforced starvation. The ideological quartet emphasized that worse than this, "Jewish Bolsheviks" had systematically annihilated the nationalist Russian intelligentsia. The four writers of the apocalypse maintained that "Jewish Bolsheviks" threatened to spread this terrifying process of extermination to Germany and beyond. While Rosenberg vilified what he perceived as the quintessential Bolshevik practice of eradicating political enemies, he nonetheless appreciated the efficacy of this method. Eckart, Scheubner-Richter, Vinberg, and Rosenberg adopted an apocalyptic standpoint in their arguments by asserting that "Jewish Bolshevism" threatened to ruin Germany, Europe, and even the entire world. Hitler assumed the apocalyptic stance of his four ideological colleagues by pledging to fight the alleged Jewish drive to destroy the world through the spread of Bolshevism.

Aufbau thought significantly influenced early National Socialist ideology, and Aufbau bequeathed a powerful legacy to National Socialism after 1923 as well. Scheubner-Richter's death in the Hitler/Ludendorff Putsch served as an example of heroic sacrifice for the National Socialist cause. Biskupskii continued to channel funds to the NSDAP after 1923, and he led White émigrés in the Third Reich as the head of the Russian Trust Authority. Rosenberg held high posts in the Third Reich, such as leader of the National Socialist Foreign Policy Office along with his colleague Schickedanz and State Minister for the Occupied Eastern Territories. Hitler and Rosenberg worked to detach the Ukraine from the Soviet Union in collaboration with Poltavets-Ostranitsa. During World War II, Hitler's desire to gain the Ukraine for Germany in the tradition of Aufbau led him to divert strong formations of the German Army southwards away from Moscow in 1941, thereby granting the Red Army a valuable respite.

Moreover, Aufbau's early warnings of the "Jewish Bolshevik" peril radicalized later National Socialist anti-Bolshevism and anti-Semitism. After a period of compromise while attaining power and then consolidating their rule, Hitler's National Socialists returned to their original intense anti-Bolshevik and anti-Semitic roots, which Aufbau had greatly influenced, by invading the Soviet Union and exterminating millions of Jews in the Final Solution. As the State Minister for the Occupied Eastern Territories, Rosenberg aided Hitler in both of these quintessentially National Socialist undertakings. To a considerable degree, apocalyptic White émigré conceptions of the "Jewish Bolshevik" menace found their expression in heinous National Socialist deeds.

When given the opportunity under the cover of World War II, the National Socialist regime sought to destroy European Jewry, and it came dangerously close to succeeding. The most striking feature of the Final Solution proved its rationalized irrationality. Great numbers of Germans and their auxiliaries from Eastern and Western Europe devoted large amounts of scarce resources to slaughtering millions of Jews at the same time that a total war was raging which was to end either in glorious victory or abject defeat. National Socialists placed a high priority on exterminating Jews when military interests dictated using as many of them as possible for slave labor. This skewed policy indicated the considerable degree to which Hitler had internalized the apocalyptic White émigré standpoint that the Jews threatened to ruin Germany and the rest of the world as they had Russia.

Historians have generally overlooked the fundamental political, financial, military, and ideological contributions that White émigrés made to National Socialism. This book has partially redressed this historiographical weakness, but scholars should conduct much more research on National Socialist–White émigré collaboration, especially in newly accessible Eastern European archives. When we examine the roots of National Socialism, we find alienated *völkisch* Germans collaborating with vengeful White émigrés. In locating the pivotal hinge of the turbulent twentieth century, historians need to focus on the broad stretch of territory between the Rhine and Volga Rivers. War and revolution there created large numbers of rancorous White émigrés, several of whom played crucial roles in the making of National Socialism with its virulent anti-Bolshevik and anti-Semitic ideology. Hitler's National Socialists in turn committed grave crimes in the name of combating "Jewish Bolshevism," and these National Socialist atrocities undermined Western ideals of historical progress.

Bibliography

PERSONAL INTERVIEW

Hass, Julia (Otto von Kursell's daughter). Personal interview, January 21, 2003.

UNPUBLISHED ARCHIVAL MATERIALS

BAB: BUNDESARCHIV (FEDERAL ARCHIVES IN BERLIN)

Alldeutscher Verband (Pan-German League). 8048, number 117.

APA: Aussenpolitisches Amt (Foreign Policy Office, specifically for the NSDAP). NS 43, number 35.

Baltenverband (Baltic League). 8012, numbers 2, 4, 7, 9, 11.

Baltischer Vertrauensrat (Baltic Trust Council). 8054, number 2.

Gestapo: Geheime Staatspolizei (Secret State Police). 58, number 270.

Jaenicke, Franz. "Lebenslauf." Luckenwalde, July 1, 1923. RKÜöO. 1507, number 329.

"Der Kämpfer Alfred Rosenberg: Zur Ernennung des Reichsleiters zum Reichsminister für die besetzten Gebiete." *Parteipresse-Sonderdienst*, Nr. 368, November 17, 1941. KR. NS 8, number 8.

KR: Kanzlei Rosenberg (Rosenberg Chancellery). NS 8, numbers 8, 20, 100, 207.

Kursell, Otto von. "Die Linie im Leben Max von Scheubner-Richters." *Dr. Ing. M. E. von Scheubner-Richter gefallen am 9. November 1923*. Munich: Müller und Sohn, November 1923. NSDAPHA. NS 26, number 1263, 4.

—. "Die Trauerfeierlichkeiten: Einäschung auf dem Münchner Ostfriedhof am 17. November 10 Uhr früh." *Dr. Ing. M. E. von Scheubner-Richter gefallen am 9. November 1923*. Munich: Müller und Sohn, November 1923. NSDAPHA. NS 26, number 1263, 3.

Nemirovich-Danchenko, Georgii. "Ein schöner Tod." *Dr. Ing. M. E. von Scheubner-Richter gefallen am 9. November 1923*. Munich: Müller und Sohn, November 1923. NSDAPHA. NS 26, number 1263, 4.

NSDAPHA: NSDAP Hauptarchiv (NSDAP Main Archives). NS 26, numbers 1259, 1263.

"Reichszentrale für Heimatdienst." RKÜöO. 1507, number 23.

RK: Reichskanzlei (State Chancellery). 43, number 2448/4.

RKÜöO: Reichskommissar für die Überwachung der öffentlichen Ordnung (State Commissioner for the Supervision of Public Order). 134, numbers 66, 68, 69, 76, 78, 170, 173; 1507, numbers 23, 208, 211, 214, 325, 327, 329, 339, 343–345, 388, 440–442, 557, 558, 568.

RMbO: Reichsministerium für die besetzten Ostgebiete (State Ministry for the Occupied Eastern Territories). 6, numbers 74, 157, 158.

RMI: Reichsministerium des Innern (State Ministry of the Interior). 1501, number 14139.

[Rosenberg, Alfred.] "Der Kampf zwischen Chaos und Gestalt: Zur Ernennung des Reichsleiters Alfred Rosenberg zum Reichsminister für die besetzten Ostgebiete." [November 1941.] KR, NS 8, number 8, 14–20.

—. Memoirs. KR, NS 8, number 20.

RSHA: Reichssicherheitshauptamt (State Security Main Office). 58, numbers 1005, 1031, 7560.

Rüdiger, Karlheinz. "Reichsminister für die besetzten Ostgebiete Alfred Rosenberg." KR, [November 1941], NS 8, number 8, 2–5.

Scheubner-Richter, Mathilde von. Interview on April 3, 1936. NSDAPHA. NS 26, number 1263, 4–7.

Stahlhelm (Steel Helmet). 72, number 261.

Taube, Georg. "Der Esten Krieg." [1920.] 8025, number 15.

Weber, Friedrich. "An die Herren Landes- und Kreisleiter!" September 26, 1923. RKÜöO. 1507, number 343, 314.

BAK: BUNDESARCHIV KOBLENZ (FEDERAL ARCHIVES IN KOBLENZ)

Class, Heinrich. Essay fragment. 1936. *Kleine Erwerbung* 499.

—. *Wider den Strom*, vol. II. *Kleine Erwerbung* 499.

Kapp, Wolfgang. "An das deutsche Volk!" [March 1920.] *Nachlass* 309, number 7.

—. Correspondence. *Nachlass* 309, numbers 7, 20.

—. "Zur Vorgeschichte des März-Unternehmens." 1922. *Nachlass* 309, number 7.

BA/MF: BUNDESARCHIV, MILITÄRARCHIV FREIBURG
(FEDERAL ARCHIVES, MILITARY ARCHIVES IN FREIBURG)

"Die Ereignisse im Baltikum vom Herbst 1918 bis Ende 1919." January 1920. RWM, *Nachlass* 247, number 91.

Goltz, Rüdiger von der. "Erste Versuche." *Nachlass* 714, number 14.

—. Personal papers. *Nachlass* 714, number 1.

Groener, Wilhelm. Correspondence, military reports, and personal papers. *Nachlass* 46, numbers 172, 173.

Hoffmann, Max. Correspondence. *Nachlass* 37, number 2.

Pabst, Waldemar. "Auszug aus meinem Lebenslauf." 1954. *Nachlass* 620, number 1.

—. "Das Kapp-Unternehmen." 1952. *Nachlass* 620, number 3.

—. "Nachkriegserlebnisse als 1a und Stabschef der Garde-Kav.- (Schü) Division." *Nachlass* 620, number 2.

BHSAM: BAYERISCHES HAUPTSTAATSARCHIV MÜNCHEN
(BAVARIAN STATE ARCHIVES IN MUNICH)

BSMÄ: Bayerisches Staatsministerium des Äussern (Bavarian Foreign Ministry).
33, number 97676; 36, numbers 103009, 103456, 103472, 103476/1, 103476/2.
BSMI: Bayerisches Staatsministerium des Innern (Bavarian Interior Ministry). 22,
numbers 71525, 71624, 71625, 73675, 73685, 73694; 25, numbers 81592, 81594.
Ehrhardt, Hermann. *Deutschlands Zukunft: Aufgaben und Ziele.* Munich: J. F.
Lehmanns Verlag, 1921. *Sammlung Personen,* number 3678.
"Verpflichtung." 22, number 73675, fiche 4, 89.

BHSAM/AK: BAYERISCHES HAUPTSTAATSARCHIV MÜNCHEN,
ABTEILUNG KRIEGSARCHIV (BAVARIAN STATE ARCHIVES IN
MUNICH, MILITARY ARCHIVES DEPARTMENT)

Endres, Theodor. "Aufzeichnungen über den Hitlerputsch 1923." 1945. *Handschriftensammlung,* number 925.
Mend, Hans. "Protokoll aufgenommen am 22. Dezember 1939 mit Hans Mend,
Reitlehrer und Verwalter auf Schloss Eltzholz Berg bei Starnberg a/See, ehemals Ulan im kgl. bayer. x. Ulanenregiment zugeteilt als Ordonnanzreiter
im Oktober 1914 dem Inf. Rgt. 'List.' Seit Juni 1916 befördert zum Offizier-
Stellvertreter und zugeteilt dem 4. bayer. Feldartillerieregiment, Munitionskolonne 143 (Tankabwehr). Bei der Truppe bekannt als der 'Schimmelreiter.'"
Handschriftensammlung, number 3231.

BSAM: BAYERISCHES STAATSARCHIV MÜNCHEN
(BAVARIAN REGIONAL ARCHIVES IN MUNICH)

"An die Münchener Bevölkerung!" PDM, Number 6711, 5.
PDM: Polizeidirektion München (Munich Police Headquarters). Numbers 6697,
6698, 6707–6709, 6711, 6803.

GARF: GOSUDARSTVENNYI ARKHIV ROSSIISKOI FEDERATSII
(STATE ARCHIVES OF THE RUSSIAN FEDERATION, MOSCOW)

ATsVO: Administretivnyi Tsentr vnepartinnogo obedineniia (Administrative
Center of the Non-Party Association, a Russian émigré organization in
Prague). *Fond* 5893, *opis* 1, *dela* 39, 46, 47, 70, 201.
Lampe, Aleksandr. *Dnevnik* (Diary). *Fond* 5853, *opis* 1, *dela* 3, 7–11, 13.
ROVS: Russkii obshii-voinskii soiuz (Russian Universal Military Union). *Fond*
5826, *opis* 1, *delo* 123.
Soiuz russkago naroda (Union of the Russian People). *Fond* 116, *opis* 1, *dela* 1, 6,
807.
Vsevelikoe Voisko Donskoe (Great Don Host). *Fond* 1261, *opis* 1, *delo* 40.

GSAPKB: GEHEIMES STAATSARCHIV PREUSSISCHER
KULTURBESITZ (SECRET STATE ARCHIVES OF PRUSSIAN
CULTURAL PROPERTY, BERLIN)

JM: Justizministerium (Department of Justice). *Repositur* 84a, number 14953.

Kapp, Wolfgang. Correspondence, personal papers, collected materials. *Repositur* 92, numbers 455, 460, 792, 801, 815, 839, 840/1.

Kühn, Erich. "Werbung für Mitarbeit." Munich: J. F. Lehmanns Verlag, June 1916. *Repositur* 92, number 792.

LGPO: Landesgrenzpolizei Ost (National Border Police East). *Repositur* 77, title 1809, number 9; title 1810, numbers 1, 2, 4, 6; title 1813, numbers 2, 6, 8.

Schwarze, Elisabeth. "Einleitung." *Nachlass Wolfgang Kapp.* 1997.

Shabelskii-Bork, Piotr. Correspondence. *Repositur* 84a, number 14953.

—. "Über Mein Leben." March 1926. *Repositur* 84a, number 14953, 91–110.

SKöO: Staatskommissar für öffentliche Ordnung (State Commissioner for Public Order). *Repositur* 77, title 1812, number 25.

Wagener. "Bericht über die augenblickliche Lage in Mitau." Berlin, September 8, 1919. *Repositur* 92, number 815.

IZG: INSTITUT FÜR ZEITGESCHICHTE (INSTITUTE FOR
MODERN HISTORY, MUNICH)

Hering, Johann. Interview on August 29, 1951. ZS 67.

Interrogation of Ambassador Herbert von Dirksen from October 1945, The National Archives, Records of the Department of State, Special Interrogation Mission to Germany, 1945–46. Number 679, roll 1.

Reicheneder, Walburga. Interview on January 11, 1952. ZS 119.

Rosenberg, Alfred. "Meine erste Begegnung mit dem Führer." The National Archives, Records of the Reich Ministry for the Occupied Eastern Territories, 1941–45. Number 454, roll 63.

Rossbach, Gerhard. Interview on December 13, 1951. ZS 128.

Schickedanz, Arno. [May] 1919 report to Max von Scheubner-Richter. ZS 2368.

Schwartz-Bostunich, Gregor. *SS-Personalakten, SS-OStubaf.* Fa 74.

Skoropadskii, Pavel. *Erinnerungen von Pavlo Skoropadsky aufgeschrieben in Berlin in der Zeit von Januar bis Mai 1918.* Trans. Helene Ott-Skoropadskii. Berlin, 1918. Ms 584.

Weiss. Correspondence. Fa 88.

PAAA: POLITISCHES ARCHIV DES AUSWÄRTIGEN AMTES
(POLITICAL ARCHIVES OF THE FOREIGN OFFICE, BERLIN)

AA: Auswärtiges Amt (Foreign Office). Numbers 31490, 31665–31668, 83377, 83379, 83578–83582, 83584.

RGASPI: ROSSIISKII GOSUDARSTVENNYI ARKHIV
SOTSIALNO-POLITICHESKOI ISTORII (RUSSIAN STATE ARCHIVES
OF SOCIO-POLITICAL HISTORY, MOSCOW)

Dzerzhinskii, Feliks. Papers. *Fond 76, opis 3, delo 400.*
KI: Komintern (Communist International). *Fond 495, opis 33, delo 306.*

RGVA: ROSSIISKII GOSUDARSTVENNYI VOENNYI ARKHIV
(RUSSIAN STATE MILITARY ARCHIVES, MOSCOW)

Bermondt-Avalov, Pavel. Military papers. *Fond 40147, opis 1, delo 18.*
OKL: O. K. London (military organization). Military reports. *Fond 40147, opis 1, delo 48.*

RGVA (TSKHIDK): FORMER TSENTR KHRANENIIA
ISTORIKO-DOKUMENTALNYCH KOLLEKTSII (CENTER FOR THE
PRESERVATION OF HISTORICAL-DOCUMENTARY COLLECTIONS,
NOW PART OF RGVA, MOSCOW)

AGM: Amtsgericht München (Munich District Court). *Fond 567, opis 1, delo 2496.*
APA: Aussenpolitisches Amt (Foreign Policy Office, specifically for the National Socialist Party). *Fond 519, opis 3, dela 11b, 39; opis 4, delo 26; fond 1358, opis 2, dela 642, 643.*
Bermondt-Avalov, Pavel. Correspondence. *Fond 603, opis 2, delo 30.*
—. "Das Erbe der Revolution und des Bolschewismus." RKÜöO. *Fond 772, opis 3, dela 71, 22–30.*
DB: Deuxième Bureau (Second Section, French intelligence; the originals of these files are now back in Paris). *Fond 7, opis 1, dela 299, 386, 390, 404, 876, 878, 922, 953, 954, 1255; opis 2, delo 2575; opis 4, delo 168; fond 198, opis 9, delo 4474; opis 17, delo 203.*
Despotuli, Vladimir. Personal papers. *Fond 1128, opis 1, delo 1.*
Dienstaltersliste der Schutzstaffel der NSDAP (SS-Obersturmbannführer und SS-Sturmbannführer): Stand vom 1. Oktober 1944. Berlin: Reichsdruckerei, 1944. *Fond 1372, opis 5, delo 89.*
Foch, Ferdinand. Military reports (the original file is now back in Paris). *Fond 198, opis 17, delo 406.*
Gestapo: Geheime Staatspolizei (Secret State Police). *Fond 500, opis 1, delo 677; fond 501, opis 3, delo 496a; fond 1323, opis 2, delo 171.*
Hausen, Ludwig Müller von. Correspondence, personal papers, collected materials. *Fond 577, opis 1, dela 1, 2, 6, 27, 213, 218, 219, 221, 479, 541, 844, 853; opis 2, dela 9, 10, 130, 131.*
Horbaniuk. *"Zur ukrainischen Führerfrage."* 1926. RKÜöO. *Fond 772, opis 1, delo 105b.*
IIA: International Information Agency, Paris. *Fond 284, opis 1, delo 69.*
"The Liquidation of the Nansen Office and the Problem of Political Refugees." January 23, 1938. IIA. *Fond 284, opis 1, delo 69.*

MMFP: Mission Militaire Française en Pologne (French Military Mission in Poland; the originals of these files are now back in Paris). *Fond* 198, *opis* 2, *delo* 1031; *fond* 1703, *opis* 1, *dela* 350, 440.

Müller-Leibnitz. "II. Der Feldzug im Baltikum 1919." [1937?] *Fond* 1255, *opis* 2, *delo* 48.

—. "V. Der Rückmarsch der 10. Armee im Winter 1918/19." [1937?] *Fond* 1424, *opis* 1, *delo* 13.

Nicolai, Walther. *Tagebuch* (Diary). *Fond* 1414, *opis* 1, *dela* 15, 16, 18–22.

PKAH: Privatkanzlei Adolf Hitler (Adolf Hitler Private Office). *Fond* 1355, *opis* 1, *delo* 3.

Poltavets-Ostranitsa, Ivan. *Curriculum vitae.* 1926. RKÜöO. *Fond* 772, *opis* 1, *delo* 105b.

QB: Quatrième Bureau (Fourth Section; the originals of these files are now back in Paris). *Fond* 198, *opis* 17, *delo* 484.

RKÜöO: Reichskommissar für die Überwachung der öffentlichen Ordnung (State Commissioner for the Supervision of Public Order). *Fond* 772, *opis* 1, *dela* 91, 96, 100, 101, 105b, 108; *opis* 2, *dela* 129b, 179, 189; *opis* 3, *dela* 71, 81a, 539, 781, 927; *opis* 4, *dela* 13, 52.

RMbO: Reichsministerium für die besetzten Ostgebiete (State Ministry for the Occupied Eastern Territories). *Fond* 1358, *opis* 3, *delo* 53.

RSHA: Reichssicherheitshauptamt (State Security Main Office). *Fond* 500, *opis* 1, *dela* 452, 504.

RuSHA-SS: Rasse und Siedlungshauptamt-SS (SS Race and Settlement Main Office) *Fond* 1372, *opis* 3, *delo* 35.

Scheubner-Richter, Max von. "Abriss des Lebens- und Bildungsganges von Dr. Max Erwin von Scheubner-Richter." April 1923. *Fond* 1414, *opis* 1, *delo* 21.

SG: Sûreté Générale (General Security; the originals of these files are now back in Paris). *Fond* 1, *opis* 14, *delo* 3242; *opis* 18, *delo* 2381; *opis* 27, *dela* 12518, 12523, 12541.

SGOD: Sztab Główny Oddział drugi (Main Headquarters Second Section, Polish intelligence). *Fond* 308, *opis* 3, *delo* 405; *opis* 7, *delo* 265; *fond* 453, *opis* 1, *delo* 53.

"Tagebuchauszug von General der Infanterie a. D. Hasse." December 2, 1919. *Fond* 1255, *opis* 2, *delo* 42.

NEWSPAPERS

AUFBAU: ZEITSCHRIFT FÜR WIRTSCHAFTS-POLITISCHE FRAGEN OST-EUROPAS

"Auszug aus den Satzungen." Number 2/3, August 1921. RKÜöO. BAB, 43/I, number 131, 498.

"Der I. Kongress zum wirtschaftlichen Wiederaufbau Russlands in Reichenhall: Erster Tag, 29. Mai 1921." Number 2/3, August 1921, 5. RKÜöO. BAB, 43/I, number 131, 503.

"Der I. Kongress zum wirtschaftlichen Wiederaufbau Russlands in Reichenhall: Sechster Tag, 3. Juni 1921." Number 2/3, August 1921, 14. RKÜöO. BAB, 43/I, number 131, 514.

Nemirovich-Danchenko, Georgii. "Der wirtschaftliche Aufbau Russlands." Number 2/3, August 1921, 2. RKÜöO. BAB, 43/I, number 131, 500.

Scheubner-Richter, Max von. "Der russische Wiederaufbaukongress in Bad Reichenhall: Ein Rückblick und Ausblick von Dr. M. E. von Scheubner-Richter." Number 2/3, August 1921, 1, 2. RKÜöO. BAB, 43/I, number 131, 499, 500.

AUF GUT DEUTSCH: WOCHENSCHRIFT FÜR ORDNUNG UND RECHT

Eckart, Dietrich. "Der Baccalaureus." October 23, 1919.

—. "Das ist der Jude! Laienpredigt über Juden- und Christentum von Dietrich Eckart." [August/September], 1920.

—. "Das fressende Feuer." August 22, 1919.

—. "Der Herr Rabbiner aus Bremen." November 11, 1919.

—. "In letzter Stunde." March 15, 1921.

—. "'Jewry über alles.'" November 26, 1920.

—. "Das Judentum in und ausser uns: Grundsätzliche Betrachtungen von Dietrich Eckart: I." January 10, 1919.

—. "Das Judentum in und ausser uns: Grundsätzliche Betrachtungen von Dietrich Eckart: IV." January 31, 1919.

—. "Kapp." April 16, 1920.

—. "Das Karnickel." March 28, 1919.

—. "Die Midgardschlange." December 30, 1919.

—. "Die Schlacht auf den Katalaunischen Feldern." February 20, 1920.

—. "Tagebuch." October 10, 1919.

—. "Theorie und Praxis." September 12, 1919.

—. "Trotz alledem!" July 11, 1919.

—. "Wovor uns Kapp behüten wollte." April 16, 1920.

—. /Alfred Rosenberg. "Zwischen den Schächern." March 5, 1920.

Rosenberg, Alfred. "Hochverrat der deutschen Zionisten auf Grund ihrer eigenen Eingeständnisse erläutert, I." March 31, 1921.

—. "Hochverrat der deutschen Zionisten auf Grund ihrer eigenen Eingeständnisse erläutert, II." April 20, 1921.

—. "Russe und Deutscher." April 4, 1919.

—. "Die russische-jüdische Revolution." February 21, 1919.

—. "Russische Stimmen." March 28, 1919.

—. "Das Verbrechen der Freimaurerei: Judentum, Jesuitismus, deutsches Christentum. IV. Freimaurerei und Judentum." January 15, 1921.

—. "Das Verbrechen der Freimaurerei: Judentum, Jesuitismus, deutsches Christentum: VIII. Deutsches Christentum." February 28, 1921.

BLAGOVEST: ZHURNAL RUSSKOI MONARKHICHESKOI NARODNO-GOSUDARSTVENNOI MYSLI

Ismailov, Nikolai. "Chudesnyi son." December 1919, 2, 3. GARF.
Purishkevich, Vladimir. "Bez zabrala." December 1919, 1–2. GARF.

BAYERISCHER KURIER

"Ausnahmezustand im Reich und in Bayern. Eine deutliche Absage." October 4, 1923. BSAM, PDM, number 6708, 151.

CHASOVOI

"Sionskie Protokoly." January 23, 1919, 1. GARF.

DEUTSCHES ABENDBLATT

Bermondt-Avalov, Pavel. "Offener Brief an die Engländer." May 8, 1921. RKÜöO. RGVA (TsKhIDK), *fond* 772, *opis* 3, *delo* 71, 11–15.

GÖTEBURGS HANDELS- OCH SJÖFARTS-TIDNING

Translated article on Rosenberg. Nr. 237. *Sonderbeilage zum SD-Pressebericht Nr. 39*, October 13, 1939. RSHA. RGVA (TsKhIDK), *fond* 500, *opis* 3, *delo* 129, reel 3, 369.

HAMBURGER ILLUSTRIERTE

Frank, Wolfgang. "Professor Otto v. Kursell: Wie ich den Führer zeichnete." March 6, 1934. BHSAM, *Sammlung Personen*, number 7440, 12.

KRAKAUER ZEITUNG

"Deutsche Ukraine-Zeitung erschienen: Aufrufe Rosenbergs und Kochs an die Ukrainer." January 25, 1942, 4.

NARODNYI TRIBUN: ORGAN PURISHKEVICHA

Edition of October 24, 1917.
Purishkevich, Vladimir. Editorial. September 5, 1917, 1.
Vinberg, Fedor. "Kontrasty." October 22, 1917, 2.
—. "Voesposobnost." October 19, 1917, 2, 3.

DER NATIONALSOZIALIST

Alarich. "Dostojewskii (geb. 1821) und die Judenfrage." July 14, 1921, 2, 3.
Rosenberg, Alfred. "Wesen, Grundsätze und Ziele der N.S.D.A.P." September 1, 1923, 1.

PRIZYV

"Liubopytnyi Dokument." February 6, 1920. RGVA (TsKhIDK), *fond* 577, *opis* 1, *delo* 541, 2.

RUSSKOE ZNAMIA

Chernyi, Andrei. "'Mirnoe' zavoevanie Rossii." July 19, 1907, 1, 2.
"Istoriia ubiistva Iuschinskago." August 9, 1913, 1.
Purishkevich, Vladimir. "Izbiratelnaia programma Soiuza Russkago Naroda, Russkomu Narodu." September 19, 1906, 2–3.
Soiuznik, U. "Russkim detiam." July 7, 1911, 2.

SVOBODA I PORIADOK

Bork, Aleksandr. Editorial. December 1, 1913, 1.

VESTNIK RUSSKAGO MONARKHICHESKAGO
OBEDINENIIA V BAVARII

Vinberg, Fedor. Editorial. April 7, 1923, 2, 3. GARF.

THULE-BOTE

Sebottendorff, Rudolf von. "Aus der Geschichte der Thule Gesellschaft." Gilbhart (October) 31, 1933. BSAM. SAM, number 7716, 9, 1, 2.
—. "Die Thule Gesellschaft." Gilbhart (October) 31. BSAM, SAM, number 7716, 10, 2, 3.

VÖLKISCHER BEOBACHTER

"Adolf Hitlers Ehrentag." April 22/23, 1923, 1.
"Das Attentat in Berlin." April 1, 1922, 2.
"Aufstand in der Ukraine." March 14, 1923, 3.
Chamberlain, Houston Stewart. "Gott will es! Betrachtung über den gegenwärtigen Zustand Deutschlands." November 9, 1923, 1.
"Deutsche Maifeier." May 3, 1923, 1, 2.
"Dietrich Eckart." March 23, 1923, 5.
"Dostojewski als Politiker und Prophet." January 27, 1923, 3, 4.
Eckart, Dietrich. "Das bayerische Orakel von Genua." May 24, 1922, 1.
—. "Ein neuer Weltkrieg in Sicht!" May 17, 1922, 1.
—. "Das 'siegreiche' Proletariat unter Standrecht." October 26, 1921, 1.
—. "Vor dem Glockenschlag zwölf." August 14, 1921, 1.
"Erneuerung." May 4, 1923, 4.
"Freistaat oder Sklaventum? Rede des Pg. Adolf Hitler in der Versammlung der national-sozialistischen Deutschen Arbeiterpartei vom 28. Juli 1922 im grossen Saale des Bürgerbräukellers in München." August 16, 1922, 5–8.

"Die Geheimnisse der Weisen von Zion." April 22, 1920, 1.

"Die Geheimnisse der Weisen von Zion." June 27, 1920, 2.

"Die 'Hetzer' der Wahrheit: Rede des Pg. Adolf Hitler in der Versammlung vom 12. April 1922 im Bürgerbräukeller zu München." April 22, 1922, 5–8.

Hitler, Adolf. "Ist die Errichtung einer die breiten Massen erfassenden Völkischen Zeitung eine nationale Notwendigkeit?" January 27, 30, 1921, 1–3.

——. "Staatsmänner oder Nationalverbrecher." March 15, 1921, 1, 2.

——. "Die Urschuldigen am Weltkriege: Weltjude und Weltbörse." April 15/16, 1923, 1.

——. "Der völkische Gedanke und die Partei." January 1, 1921, 1, 2.

"Ein jüdisches Geheimdokument." February 25, 1920, 1.

"Die Kosaken und Grossfürst Kyrill." September 20, 1922, 4.

National Socialist Party leadership. "Grundsätzliches Programm der national-sozialistischen Deutschen Arbeiterpartei." July 19, 1922, 1.

"Die Pest in Russland." July 5, 1922, 2.

"Positiver Antisemitismus." November 4, 1922, 1.

"Die Protokolle der Weisen von Zion und die jüdische Weltpolitik." August 21, 1923, 3.

Rodionov, Ivan. "Opfer des Wahnsinns." October 2–November 9, 1923.

Rosenberg, Alfred. "Antisemitismus: Eine wirtschaftliche, politische, nationale, religiöse und sittliche Notwendigkeit, (Schluss)." August 21, 1921, 3.

——. "Hochfinanz und Weltrevolution: Überblick." August 4, 1921, 1.

——. "Der jüdische Bolschewismus." November 26, 1921, 1, 2.

——. "Die jüdische Canaille: Stephan Grossmanns Verhöhnung des deutschen Volkes." April 14, 1923, 1.

——. "Nationalsozialismus im Weltkampf." April 7, 1923, 2, 3.

——. "Der Pogrom am deutschen und am russischen Volke." August 4, 1921, 3.

——. "Schicksalswende in London!" March 6, 1921, 2, 3.

——. "Von Brest-Litowsk nach Versailles." May 8, 1921, 5.

Scheubner-Richter, Max von. "Deutschlands Bolschewisierung." September 21, 1923, 1.

——. "Die Rote Armee." March 21–23, 1923.

"Die Ukraine und Russland." August 29, 1923, 3.

"Vaterländische Feier." November 8, 1922, 4.

Vinberg, Fedor. "Der wackere Zentralverein." May 9, 1923, 3.

"Wer waren die Mörder des Zaren?" September 9, 1920, 2.

WIENER MORGENZEITUNG

"Ein Mörderkongress in Budapest." July 1, 1922. AA. PAAA, 83580, 32.

WIRTSCHAFTS-POLITISCHE AUFBAU-KORRESPONDENZ ÜBER OSTFRAGEN UND IHRE BEDEUTUNG FÜR DEUTSCHLAND

"Aus der russisch-monarchistischen Bewegung." July 20, 1923, 2.

"In der Krim bei Wrangel." April 19, 1923, 4.

Kartsov, Iurii. "Existiert die Schuldfrage überhaupt?" October 4, 1922, 3.

Nemirovich-Danchenko, Georgii. "Russland und Deutschland: Gedanken eines russischen Emigranten." May 24, 1923, 1–3.

Romanov, Kirill. "An das russiche Volk!" Included in Max von Scheubner-Richter, "Zwei bedeutsame Deklarationen." August 16, 1922, 1–4.

"Die 'Russische Tribüne' über die Regierungsformen in Russland." August 25, 1923, 3, 4.

Scheubner-Richter, Max von. "Allgemeine Wirtschaft und Politik." October 11, 1922, 3.

—. "Bittere Betrachtungen." April 19, 1923, 1, 2.

—. "Dem Bolschewismus entgegen." September 9, 1921, 1.

—. "Der Bolschewismus sprungbereit!" September 29, 1923, 1, 2.

—. "Deutsche Wirtschaftspolitik." October 13, 1921, 1, 2.

—. "Die dritte Internationale an der Arbeit." June 7, 1923, 1, 2.

—. "Die Faszisten als Herren in Italien." November 1, 1922, 1, 2.

—. "Fürst Lwow, der Expremier – als Defraudant." October 27, 1921, 4.

—. "Im Eilmarsch zum Abgrund!" July 26, 1922, 1–4.

—. "Interventionsabsichten gegen Sowjetrussland." June 14, 1923, 1, 2.

—. "Judenverfolgungen in Sowjetrussland." October 25, 1922, 2.

—. "Der Katastrophe entgegen!" September 6, 1922, 1, 2.

—. "Kirchenplünderung." April 14, 1922, 2.

—. "Klarheit." January 17, 1923, 1–2.

—. "Miljukow in Berlin." March 31, 1922, 1.

—. "Nansen verteidigt den Bolschewismus." April 19, 1923, 3, 4.

—. "Die Rote Armee: Was wir von Sowjetrussland lernen können!" March 22, 1923, 1–3.

—. "Rückblicke und Parallelen." July 19, 1922, 1–4.

—. "Russische Terroristen." April 14, 1922, 1.

—. "Russland und England." May 17, 1923, 1, 2.

—. "Der Umfall des Patriarchen Tichon." July 27, 1923, 1, 2.

—. "Was wir von unseren Feinden lernen können!" January 14, 1922, 1, 2.

—. "Weltpolitische Umschau." July 13, 1923, 1, 2.

—. "Worum es sich handelt." September 17, 1921, 1, 2.

—. "Zum fünften Jahrestag der Revolution." November 9, 1923, 1, 2.

—. "Zwei bedeutsame Deklarationen." August 16, 1922, 1–4.

"Ukraine und Nationalsozialismus." May 17, 1923, 3, 4.

PUBLISHED PRIMARY WORKS

Bermondt-Avalov, Pavel. *Im Kampf gegen den Bolschewismus: Erinnerungen von General Fürst Awaloff, Oberbefehlshaber der Deutsch-Russischen Westarmee im Baltikum.* Hamburg: Von J. J. Augustin, 1925.

Chamberlain, Houston Stewart. *Foundations of the Nineteenth Century*, vols. I and II. Trans. John Lees. New York: Howard Fertig, 1968.

—. *Richard Wagner.* Trans. G. Ainslie Hight. Philadelphia: J. B. Lippincott Co., 1900.

Class, Heinrich. *Wider den Strom: Vom Werden und Wachsen der nationalen Opposition im alten Reich*, vol. I. Leipzig: Koehler, 1932.

Dostoevskii, Fedor. *Dnevnik pisatelia. Polnoe sobranie sochinenii F. M. Dostoevskago*, vols. X and XI. Saint Petersburg: A. F. Marks, 1895.

—. *Tagebuch eines Schriftstellers*. Trans. E. K. Rahsin. Munich: Piper, 1992.

Einhart [Class]. *Deutsche Geschichte*, second edn. Leipzig: Dietrich'schen Verlagsbuchhandlung, 1909.

Frymann, Daniel [Class]. *Wenn ich der Kaiser wär' – Politische Wahrheiten und Notwendigkeiten*, fifth edn. Leipzig: Dietrich'schen Verlagsbuchhandlung, 1914.

Goltz, Rüdiger von der. *Meine Sendung in Finnland und im Baltikum*. Leipzig: Koehler, 1920.

—. *Die Schuld*. Greifswald: L. Bamberg, 1921.

Hitler, Adolf. *Hitler: Reden und Proklamationen 1932–1945*, vols. I and II. Ed. Max Domarus. Munich: Süddeutscher Verlag, 1965.

—. *Hitler's Table Talk 1941–44: His Private Conversations*. Trans. Norman Cameron and R. H. Stevens, second edn. London: Weidenfeld and Nicolson, 1973.

—. *Hitlers Tischgespräche im Führerhauptquartier 1941–1942*, second edn. Stuttgart: Seewald Verlag, 1965.

—. *Hitler's War Directives 1939–1945*. Ed. and trans. H. R. Trevor-Roper. London: Sidgwick and Jackson, 1964.

—. *Hitlers Zweites Buch: Ein Dokument aus dem Jahr 1928*. Stuttgart: Deutsche Verlags-Anstalt, 1961.

—. *Mein Kampf*. Trans. Ralph Mannheim. Boston: Houghton Mifflin, 1943.

—. *Sämtliche Aufzeichnungen 1905–1924*. Eds. Eberhard Jäckel and Axel Kuhn. Stuttgart: Deutsche Verlags-Anstalt, 1980.

Kursell, Otto. "Dr. Ing. Max Erwin von Scheubner-Richter zum Gedächtnis." Ed. Henrik Fischer. Munich, 1969.

Nemirovich-Danchenko, Georgii. *V Krymu pri Vrangele: Fakty i itogi*. Berlin: Oldenburg, 1922.

Rosenberg, Alfred. *Pest in Russland! Der Bolschewismus, seine Häupter, Handlanger und Opfer*. Munich: Deutscher Volks-Verlag, 1922.

—. *Das Politische Tagebuch Alfred Rosenbergs*. Göttingen: Seraphim, 1956. Cited in Hitler, *Hitlers Tischgespräche im Führerhauptquartier 1941–1942*, second edn. Stuttgart: Seewald Verlag, 1965.

—. *Die Protokolle der Weisen von Zion und die Jüdische Weltpolitik*. Munich: Deutscher Volks-Verlag, 1923.

—. *Die Spur des Juden im Wandel der Zeiten*. Munich: Deutscher Volks-Verlag, 1920.

Schopenhauer, Arthur. *The World as Will and Idea*, vols. I and III. Trans. R. B. Haldane and J. Kemp. London: Kegan Paul, Trench, Trübner and Co., 1909.

Spisok chlenov Russkogo Sobraniia s prilozheniem istoricheskogo ocherky sobraniia. Saint Petersburg: Tip. Spb. Gradonachalstva, 1906.

Trotsky, Leon. *My Life: The Rise and Fall of a Dictator*. London: Thornton Butterworth, 1930.

Vinberg, Fedor. *Der Kreuzesweg Russlands: Teil I: Die Ursachen des Übels*. Trans. K. von Jarmersted. Munich: R. Oldenbourg, 1922.

Wagner, Richard. "Appendix to 'Judaism in Music.'" *Richard Wagner's Prose Works*, vol. III. Trans. William Ashton Ellis. London: Routledge and Kegan Paul Ltd., 1894.

—. "Erkenne dich selbst." *Gesammelte Schriften und Dichtungen*, vol. X. Leipzig: C. F. W. Siegel, 1907.

—. *Götterdämmerung*. *Gesammelte Schriften und Dichtungen*, vol. III. Leipzig: C. F. W. Siegel, 1907.

—. "Heldenthum und Christenthum." *Gesammelte Schriften und Dichtungen*, vol. X. Leipzig: C. F. W. Siegel, 1907.

—. "Das Judenthum in der Musik." *Gesammelte Schriften und Dichtungen*, vol. V. Leipzig: C. F. W. Siegel, 1907.

—. "Religion und Kunst." *Gesammelte Schriften und Dichtungen*, vol. X. Leipzig: C. F. W. Siegel, 1907.

—. *Das Rheingold*. *Gesammelte Schriften und Dichtungen*, vol. III. Leipzig: C. F. W. Siegel, 1907.

—. *Siegfried*. *Gesammelte Schriften und Dichtungen*, vol. III. Leipzig: C. F. W. Siegel, 1907.

—. "Über Staat und Religion." *Gesammelte Schriften und Dichtungen*, vol. VIII. Leipzig: C. F. W. Siegel, 1907.

—. *Die Walküre*. *Gesammelte Schriften und Dichtungen*, vol. III. Leipzig: C. F. W. Siegel, 1907.

—. "Was nützt diese Erkenntniss?" *Gesammelte Schriften und Dichtungen*, vol. X. Leipzig: C. F. W. Siegel, 1907.

SECONDARY SOURCES

Aly, Götz and Susanne Heim. *Das Zentrale Staatsarchiv in Moskau ("Sonderarchiv")*. Düsseldorf: Hans-Böckler-Stiftung, 1992.

Arendt, Hannah. *The Origins of Totalitarianism*. New York: Harcourt Brace Jovanovich, 1979.

Ascher, Abraham. *The Revolution of 1905: Russia in Disarray*. Stanford: Stanford University Press, 1988.

Baldwin, Peter. *Reworking the Past: Hitler, the Holocaust, and the Historians' Debate*. Boston: Beacon Press, 1990.

Baur, Johannes. "Russische Emigranten und die bayerische Öffentlichkeit." *Bayern und Osteuropa: Aus der Geschichte der Beziehungen Bayerns, Frankens und Schwabens mit Russland, der Ukraine, und Weissrussland*. Ed. Hermann Beyer-Thoma. Wiesbaden: Harrassowitz Verlag, 2000, 461–478.

—. *Die russische Kolonie in München 1900–1945: Deutsch–russische Beziehungen im 20. Jahrhundert*. Wiesbaden: Harrassowitz Verlag, 1998.

Berend, Ivan. *Decades of Crisis: Central and Eastern Europe before World War II.* Berkeley: University of California Press, 1998.

Blackbourn, David. *Marpingen: Apparitions of the Virgin Mary in a Nineteenth-Century German Village.* New York: Vintage Books, 1993.

Boehm, Max Hildebert. "Baltische Einflüsse auf die Anfänge des Nationalsozialismus." *Jahrbuch des baltischen Deutschtums,* 1967, 56–69.

—. *Das eigenständige Volk in der Krise der Gegenwart.* Vienna: Wilhelm Braumüller, 1971.

Bracher, Karl Dietrich. *The German Dictatorship: The Origins, Structure, and Effects of National Socialism.* Trans. Jean Steinberg. New York: Holt, Rinehart and Winston, 1970.

Browning, Christopher. *Nazi Policy, Jewish Workers, German Killers.* Cambridge: Cambridge University Press, 2000.

—. "Ordinary Germans or Ordinary Men? A Reply to the Critics." *The Holocaust and History: The Known, the Unknown, the Disputed, and the Reexamined.* Eds. Michael Berenbaum und Abraham J. Peck. Bloomington: Indiana University Press, 1998, 252–265.

Brüggemann, Karsten. "Max Erwin von Scheubner-Richter (1884–1923) – der 'Führer der Führers'?" *Deutschbalten, Weimarer Republik und Drittes Reich.* Ed. Michael Garleff. Cologne: Böhlau Verlag, 2001, 119–145.

Bullock, Alan. *Hitler: A Study in Tyranny.* New York: Harper and Row, 1962.

Burleigh, Michael and Wolfgang Wippermann. *The Racial State: Germany 1933–1945.* Cambridge: Cambridge University Press, 1991.

Cecil, Robert. *The Myth of the Master Race: Alfred Rosenberg and Nazi Ideology.* London: B. T. Batsford Ltd., 1972.

Clark, Alan. *Barbarossa: The Russian-German Conflict, 1941–45.* London: Weidenfeld and Nicolson, 1995.

Cohn, Norman. *Warrant for Genocide: The Myth of the Jewish World-Conspiracy and the "Protocols of the Elders of Zion."* Chico, CA: Scholars Press, 1981.

Cord, William O. *The Teutonic Mythology of Richard Wagner's "The Ring of the Nibelungen".* Queenston, Ont.: Edwin Mellen Press, 1991.

Crozier, Brian. *The Rise and Fall of the Soviet Empire.* Rocklin, CA: Prima Publishing, 1999.

Dawatz, W. *Fünf Sturmjahre mit General Wrangel.* Trans. Georg von Leuchtenberg. Berlin: Verlag für Kulturpolitik, 1927.

Engelmann, Ralph. *Dietrich Eckart and the Genesis of Nazism,* diss. Washington University. Ann Arbor: University Microfilms, 1971.

Erger, Johannes. *Der Kapp-Lüttwitz-Putsch: Ein Beitrag zur deutschen Innenpolitik 1919/20.* Düsseldorf: Droste Verlag, 1967.

Fest, Joachim C. *Hitler.* Trans. Richard and Clara Winston. New York: Harcourt Brace Jovanovich, 1974.

Field, Geoffrey G. *Evangelist of Race: The Germanic Vision of Houston Stewart Chamberlain.* New York: Columbia University Press, 1981.

Franz-Willing, Georg. *Ursprung der Hitlerbewegung 1919–1922.* Preussisch Oldendorf: K. W. Schütz KG, 1974.

Friedländer, Saul. "Hitler und Wagner." *Richard Wagner im Dritten Reich: Ein Schloss Elmau-Symposium.* Eds. Friedländer and Jörn Rüsen. Munich: Verlag C. H. Beck, 2000, 165–178.

—. *Nazi Germany and the Jews: Volume I: The Years of Persecution, 1933–1939.* New York: HarperCollins, 1997.

Fugate, Brian. *Operation Barbarossa: Strategy and Tactics on the Eastern Front, 1941.* Novato, CA: Presidio Press, 1984.

Ganelin, Rafael. "Beloe dvizhenie i 'Protokoly sionskikh mudretsov.'" *Natsionalnaia pravaia prezhde i teper: Istoriko-sotsiologicheskie ocherki, chast 1: Rossiia i russkoe zarubezhe.* Saint Petersburg: Institut Sotsiologii rossiiskoi akademii nauk, 1992, 124–129.

—. "Chernosotennye organizatsii, politicheskaia politsiia i gosudarstvennaia vlast v tsarskoi Rossii." *Natsionalnaia pravaia prezhde i teper: Istoriko-sotsiologicheskie ocherki, chast 1: Rossiia i russkoe zarubezhe.* Saint Petersburg: Institut Sotsiologii rossiiskoi akademii nauk, 1992, 73–111.

—. "Rossiiskoe chernosotenstvo i germanskii natsional-sotsializm." *Natsionalnaia pravaia prezhde i teper: Istoriko-sotsiologicheskie ocherki, chast 1: Rossiia i russkoe zarubezhe.* Saint Petersburg: Institut Sotsiologii rossiiskoi akademii nauk, 1992, 130–151.

Goldhagen, Daniel. *Hitler's Willing Executioners: Ordinary Germans and the Holocaust.* New York: Alfred A. Knopf, 1996.

Goltz, Eduard Freiherr von der. *Kriegsgedächtnisbuch des Geschlechts der Grafen und Freiherrn von der Goltz.* Potsdam: Stiftungsverlag, 1919.

Gregor-Dellin, Martin. *Richard Wagner: His Life, His Work, His Century.* New York: Harcourt Brace Jovanovich, 1983.

Grimsted, Patricia Kennedy. *Archives of Russia Five Years After: "Purveyors of Sensations" or "Shadows Cast to the Past"?* Amsterdam: International Institute of Social History, 1997.

—. "Displaced Archives and the Restitution Problems on the Eastern Front in the Aftermath of the Second World War." *Contemporary European History,* vol. 6, March 1997, 45–64.

—. *Trophies of War and Empire: The Archival Heritage of Ukraine, World War II, and the International Politics of Restitution.* Cambridge: Harvard University Press, 2001.

Hagemeister, Michael. "Die 'Protokolle der Weisen von Zion' und der Basler Zionistenkongress von 1897." *Der Traum von Israel: Die Ursprünge des modernen Zionismus.* Ed. Heiko Haumann. Weinheim: Beltz Athenäum Verlag, 1998, 250–273.

—. "Das Leben des Gregor Schwartz-Bostunich, Teil 2." *Russische Emigration in Deutschland 1918 bis 1941: Leben im europäischen Bürgerkrieg.* Ed. Karl Schlögel. Berlin: Akademie, 1995.

—. "Der Mythos der 'Protokolle der Weisen von Zion.'" *Verschwörungstheorien: Anthropologische Konstanten – historische Varianten.* Eds. Ute Caumanns and Matthias Niendorf. Osnabrück: Fibre Verlag, 2001, 89–102.

—. "Sergej Nilus und die 'Protokolle der Weisen von Zion.'" *Jahrbuch für Antisemitismusforschung der Technischen Universität Berlin*. Ed. Wolfgang Benz. Frankfurt am Main: Campus Verlag, 1996, 127–147.

—. "Vladimir Solov'ëv: Reconciler and Polemicist." *Eastern Christian Studies 2: Selected Papers of the International Vladimir Solov'ëv Conference held at the University of Nijmegen, the Netherlands, in September 1998*. Leuven: Peeters, 2000, 287–296.

Hamann, Brigitte. *Hitlers Wien: Lehrjahre eines Diktators*. Munich: Piper, 1996.

Hannaford, Ivan. *Race: The History of an Idea in the West*. Washington, DC: The Woodrow Wilson Center Press, 1996.

Havill, Adrian. *The Spy Who Stayed out in the Cold: The Secret Life of FBI Double Agent Robert Hanssen*. New York: St. Martin's Press, 2001.

Heiden, Konrad. *Der Führer: Hitler's Rise to Power*. Trans. Ralph Mannheim. Boston: Houghton Mifflin, 1944.

Helb, Woldemar. *Album Rubonorum, 1875–1972*, fourth edn. Neustadt an der Aisch: Verlag Degener & Co., 1972.

The Hitler Trial: Before the People's Court in Munich, vol. I. Trans. H. Francis Freniere. Eds. Lucie Karcic and Philip Fandek. Arlington: University Publications of America, 1976.

Hosking, Geoffrey. *Russia: People and Empire 1552–1917*. Cambridge: Harvard University Press, 1997.

Jäckel, Eberhard. *Hitlers Weltanschauung*. Trans. Herbert Arnold. Middletown, CT: Wesleyan University Press, 1969.

Joffe, Joseph. "Goldhagen in Germany." *The New York Review of Books*, November 28, 1996, 18–21.

Kershaw, Ian. *Hitler 1889–1936: Hubris*. London: Penguin Press, 1998.

Klatt, Rudolf. *Ostpreussen unter dem Reichskommissariat 1919/1920*. Heidelberg: Quelle & Meyer, 1958.

Kuusisto, Seppo. *Alfred Rosenberg in der nationalsozialistischen Aussenpolitik 1933–1939*. Trans. Christian Krötzl. Helsinki: Finska Historiska Samfundet, 1984.

Laqueur, Walter. *Russia and Germany: A Century of Conflict*. London: Weidenfeld and Nicolson, 1965.

Leverkühn, Paul. *Posten auf ewiger Wache: Aus dem abenteurreichen Leben des Max von Scheubner-Richter*. Essen: Essener Verlagsanstalt, 1938.

Maier, Charles. *The Unmasterable Past: History, Holocaust, and German National Identity*. Cambridge: Harvard University Press, 1988.

Maser, Werner. *Der Sturm auf die Republik: Frühgeschichte der NSDAP*. Stuttgart: Deutsche Verlags-Anstalt, 1973.

Medrzecki, Wlodzimierz. "Bayerische Truppenteile in der Ukraine im Jahr 1918." *Bayern und Osteuropa: Aus der Geschichte der Beziehungen Bayerns, Frankens und Schwabens mit Russland, der Ukraine, und Weissrussland*. Ed. Hermann Beyer-Thoma. Wiesbaden: Harrassowitz Verlag, 2000, 441–460.

Mosse, George. *The Crisis of German Ideology: Intellectual Origins of the Third Reich*. New York: Howard Fertig, 1964.

—. *German Jews Beyond Judaism*. Bloomington. Indiana University Press, 1985.

Nolte, Ernst. *Der europäische Bürgerkrieg 1917–1945: Nationalsozialismus und Bolschewismus.* Frankfurt am Main: Propyläen Verlag, 1987.

Nova, Fritz. *Alfred Rosenberg: Nazi Theorist of the Holocaust.* New York: Hippocrene Books, 1986.

Pajouh, Christine. "Die Ostpolitik Rosenbergs 1941–1944." *Deutschbalten, Weimarer Republik und Drittes Reich.* Ed. Michael Garleff. Cologne: Böhlau Verlag, 2001, 167–195.

Plewnia, Margarete. *Auf dem Weg zu Hitler: Der "völkische" Publizist Dietrich Eckart.* Bremen: Schünemann Universitätsverlag, 1970.

Pool, James and Suzanne. *Hitlers Wegbereiter zur Macht.* Trans. Hans Thomas. New York: The Dial Press, 1978.

Pulzer, Peter. *The Rise of Political Anti-Semitism in Germany & Austria.* Cambridge: Harvard University Press, 1988.

Quellen zur Geschichte der UdSSR und der deutsch–sowjetischen Beziehungen 1917–1945. Potsdam: Zentrales Staatsarchiv, 1984.

Raskin, D. I. "Ideologiia russkogo pravogo radikalizma v kontse XIX nachale XX vv." *Natsionalnaia pravaia prezhde i teper: Istoriko-sotsiologicheskie ocherki, chast 1: Rossiia i russkoe zarubezhe.* Saint Petersburg: Institut Sotsiologii rossiiskoi akademii nauk, 1992, 5–47.

Reinhardt, Klaus. *Moscow – The Turning Point: The Failure of Hitler's Strategy in the Winter of 1941–42.* Trans. Karl B. Keenan. Providence, RI: Berg, 1992.

Rogger, Hans and Eugen Weber. *The European Right: A Historical Profile.* Berkeley: University of California Press, 1965.

Rogger, Hans. *Russia in the Age of Modernization and Revolution 1881–1917.* New York: Longman, 1983.

Rollin, Henri. *L'Apocalypse de notre temps: Les dessous de la propagande allemande d'après des documents inédits.* Paris: Gallimard, 1939.

Rose, Detlev. *Die Thule Gesellschaft: Legende – Mythos – Wirklichkeit.* Tübingen: Grabert-Verlag, 1994.

Russische Emigration in Deutschland 1918 bis 1941: Leben im europäischen Bürgerkrieg. Ed. Karl Schlögel. Berlin: Akademie, 1995.

Sabrow, Martin. *Der Rathenaumord: Rekonstruktion einer Verschwörung gegen die Republik von Weimar.* Munich: Oldenbourg, 1994.

Schlögel, Karl, Katharina Kucher, Bernhard Suchy, and Gregor Thum. *Chronik russischen Lebens in Deutschland 1918–1941.* Berlin: Akademie Verlag, 1999.

Schlögel, Karl. *Der grosse Exodus: Die Russische Emigration und ihre Zentren 1917 bis 1941.* Munich: C. H. Beck, 1994.

—. "Russische Emigration in Deutschland 1918–1941: Fragen und Thesen." *Russische Emigration in Deutschland 1918 bis 1941: Leben im europäischen Bürgerkrieg.* Ed. Karl Schlögel. Berlin: Akademie, 1995.

Schüddekopf, Otto-Ernst. *Linke Leute von rechts: Die nationalrevolutionären Minderheiten und der Kommunismus in der Weimarer Republik.* Stuttgart: W. Kohlhammer Verlag, 1960.

Schüler, Winfried. *Der Bayreuther Kreis von seiner Entstehung bis zum Ausgang der Wilhelminischen Ära.* Münster: Verlag Aschendorff, 1971.

Seaton, Albert. *The Battle for Moscow: 1941–42.* New York: Stein and Day, 1971.

—. *The Russo-German War 1941–45.* London: C. Tinling, 1971.

Skarenkov, L. K. "Eine Chronik der russischen Emigration in Deutschland: Die Materialien des General Aleksej A. von Lampe." *Russische Emigration in Deutschland 1918 bis 1941: Leben im europäischen Bürgerkrieg.* Ed. Karl Schlögel. Berlin: Akademie, 1995.

Smolin, A. V. *Beloe dvizhenie na Severo-Zapade Rossii 1918–1920.* Saint Petersburg: Dmitrii Bulanin, 1999.

Stepanov, S. A. *Chernaia Sotnia v Rossii 1905–1914.* Moscow: Izdatelstvo Vsesoiuznogo zaochnogo politekhnicheskogo instituta, 1992.

Stolfi, R. H. S. *Hitler's Panzers East: World War Two Reinterpreted.* Norman, OK: University of Oklahoma Press, 1991.

Theweleit, Klaus. *Male Fantasies,* vols. I and II. Trans. Erica Carter and Chris Turner. Minneapolis: University of Minnesota Press, 1989.

Thoss, Bruno. *Der Ludendorff-Kreis 1919–1923: München als Zentrum der mitteleuropäischen Gegenrevolution zwischen Revolution und Hitler-Putsch.* Munich: Stadtarchiv München, 1978.

Vetter, Matthias. "Die Russische Emigration und ihre 'Judenfrage.'" *Russische Emigration in Deutschland 1918 bis 1941: Leben im europäischen Bürgerkrieg.* Ed. Karl Schlögel. Berlin: Akademie, 1995.

Volker, Ullrich. "Hitlers willige Mordgesellen: Ein Buch provoziert einen neuen Historikerstreit: Waren die Deutschen doch alle schuldig?" *Ein Volk von Mördern? Die Dokumentation zur Goldhagen-Kontroverse um die Rolle der Deutschen im Holocaust.* Ed. Julius Schoeps. Hamburg: Hoffmann und Campe, 1996, 89–92.

"Wandering Jew." *The Jewish Encyclopedia.* 1916.

Webb, James. *The Occult Establishment.* La Salle, IL: Open Court, 1976.

Weiner, Marc A. *Richard Wagner and the Anti-Semitic Imagination.* Lincoln: University of Nebraska Press, 1995.

Williams, Robert. *Culture in Exile: Russian Émigrés in Germany, 1881–1941.* Ithaca: Cornell University Press, 1972.

Zelinsky, Hartmut. *Sieg oder Untergang: Sieg und Untergang. Kaiser Wilhelm II., die Werk-Idee Richard Wagners und der "Weltkampf."* Munich: Keyser, 1990.

Index

NEW STUDIES IN EUROPEAN HISTORY

Books in the series

People and Politics in France, 1848–1870
ROGER PRICE

Nobles and Nation in Central Europe
WILLIAM D. GODSEY, JR.

Technology and the Culture of Modernity in Britain and Germany, 1890–1945
BERNHARD RIEGER